Chain of Blame

Chain of Blame

*How Wall Street
Caused the Mortgage
and Credit Crisis*

Paul Muolo
Mathew Padilla

WILEY

John Wiley & Sons, Inc.

Published by John Wiley & Sons, Inc., Hoboken, New Jersey.
Published simultaneously in Canada.

For general information on our other products and services or for technical support, please contact our Customer Care Department within the United States at (800) 762-2974, outside the United States at (317) 572-3993 or fax (317) 572-4002.

Wiley also publishes its books in a variety of electronic formats. Some content that appears in print may not be available in electronic books. For more information about Wiley products, visit our web site at www.wiley.com.

Library of Congress Cataloging-in-Publication Data:

Muolo, Paul.
    Chain of blame : how Wall Street caused the mortgage and credit crisis / Paul Muolo, Mathew Padilla.
        p.   cm.
    Includes bibliographical references and index.
    ISBN 978-0-470-55465-4 (paper)
        1. Mortgages—United States.   2. Mortgage loans—United States.   3. Financial crises—United States.   4. Stock exchanges—United States.   I. Padilla, Mathew.   II. Title.
    HG5095M86   2008
    332.7'20973—dc22   2008021463

Printed in the United States of America

10   9   8   7   6   5   4   3   2   1

Contents

Introduction

Financial Ashes

And you may ask yourself, "Well ... how did I get here?"
—The Talking Heads

On Wednesday morning, April 22, 2009, David Kellermann, the acting chief financial officer of Freddie Mac—a $750 billion mortgage giant chartered by the federal government—was found hanging from the neck on a piece of exercise equipment in the basement of his Vienna, Virginia, home. Throughout the early morning, reports of his apparent suicide were broadcast on CNBC, the nation's premier business channel. A year earlier, the suicide of the CFO of a large mortgage company might've made headlines in the business section of the *New York Times* (especially for a government-chartered mortgage company), but on CNBC the death of Kellermann was treated like an O. J. Simpson–like event. Not only was a camera crew from the General Electric–owned network parked in front of the house Kellermann shared with his wife and young daughter, but local TV crews and wire service reporters blanketed the suburban neighborhood of well-coiffed lawns and 4,000-square-foot homes in the Hunter Mills Estates subdivision in suburban Virginia. It was a perfect spring morning, until now.

Eight months earlier, during the waning days of the Bush White House, Freddie Mac and a sister company, Fannie Mae, and had been taken over by Uncle Sam and declared insolvent. The general public and business press had been caught off guard. The world knew the two were losing money, but a government takeover had been shot down by their chief regulator, James Lockhart, a few months earlier. "These two aren't going to fail," Lockhart told a trade press reporter.

Outside of Washington, D.C., Fannie and Freddie, or "FanFred," as they were known inside the Capital Beltway, were hardly household names—unless of course you happened to work in the residential mortgages or write about them for a living. Fannie and Freddie weren't just any old mortgage companies. Together they owned or guaranteed about 60 percent of all the home mortgages in the United States.

At the time of Kellermann's death, the two mortgage investing giants were wards of the government. In early September 2008 Lockhart of the Federal Housing Finance Agency had suddenly reversed course and pulled the switch, having the government seize control of Fannie and Freddie. The first thing he did was fire their CEOs—Daniel Mudd of Fannie Mae, the son of famed broadcaster Roger Mudd, and Richard Syron, a lifelong regulator and banker from Boston who had been at the helm of Freddie Mac for four years.

In the fall, Kellermann had been named acting CFO of Freddie. A 16-year veteran of Freddie, he was known inside the company as an affable family man who doted on his young daughter. Over the previous five years, Freddie Mac had cleaned house of an army of top executives and support staff who had played roles in a $5 billion accounting scandal where the publicly traded company had actually understated earnings by that amount, saving the money for a rainy day when it might need some extra earnings. The company's previous CEO, Leland Brendsel, a former university professor, for the past decade had marketed the firm to Wall Street analysts as "Steady Freddie," a company that never missed an earnings projection. But now Freddie and Fannie were bleeding red ink at the expense of taxpayers. Together the two had received $100 billion from the Treasury to keep their net worth positions (the difference between the value of their assets and their liabilities) above zero. The seeds of their demise had been sown beginning in 2004 by investing $400 billion of their assets in risky mortgages and bonds that went by the names of subprime and alt-A. Traditionally, most of their business entailed buying only prime or good "A" credit quality loans. The two had veered off course from their conservative underwriting roots of buying only the most pristine of mortgages.

But as wards of the government, they were being used by the new White House under Barack Obama to continue their government mission of buying mortgages from lenders to provide liquidity to the housing market—that is, banks, savings and loans, credit unions, and a dying breed of nonbank lenders. Fannie and Freddie were back to acquiring only prime loans, but they continued to post huge losses from their $400 billion foray into nonprime land. As Armando Falcon, their former regulator, put it: "I don't think they'll ever be profitable again."

Then came the Kellermann suicide. He was 41 years old. That morning the press, CNBC front and center, seemed to be salivating for a clue that the acting CFO had somehow been involved in financial skulduggery at Freddie Mac. But by day's end there was no such revelation. A few years earlier the company had been the subject of a criminal investigation by the Federal Bureau of Investigation into its $5 billion accounting scandal, but no charges were ever filed. In the days that followed, according to interviews with Freddie Mac employees and regulators, Kellermann had come under increasing stress at the company as its finances worsened. He'd been working late and had lost weight. To clear the air and set the record straight, Freddie's interim CEO, John Koskinen, issued a statement calling Kellermann a man of "great talents," someone who had risen from a starter job as financial analyst and dedicated 16 years of his life to the company. He and other employees at the government-sponsored enterprise (GSE) had seen their retirement accounts, which consisted of Freddie Mac stock, reduced to a pile of ashes. As far as its stock was concerned, the company was near worthless, its future in doubt.

Kellermann was not involved in any financial scandal regarding his employer. It appeared that the stress of the situation had been too much for him. If the TV media had gone off the deep end, intimating that perhaps his death was somehow related to Freddie Mac's financial decline, maybe they couldn't be blamed. In the summer of 2009 the nation was mired in a financial downturn that had been dubbed the Great Recession. By the fall of 2009 the national unemployment rate was climbing to

10 percent. A broader jobless reading that tracked part-time workers who wanted full-time work pegged the jobless rate at 16.5 percent.

During the preceding months President Obama had the U.S. Treasury prop up General Motors (GM) and Chrysler—once beacons of the nation's industrial strength—with billions of dollars of taxpayer money. (GM even owned a subprime mortgage company, as did CNBC's parent, General Electric.) The two automakers eventually succumbed to bankruptcy, leaving the impression that the newly elected Democrat had more or less socialized the U.S. auto industry. But back in the fall, then President Bush had shepherded a $700 billion bailout of the nation's banking system and Wall Street through Congress. Bush, the nation's first president with a master's degree in business administration and an avowed laissez-faire capitalist, had partially socialized U.S. financial institutions by forcing them to allow the government to buy preferred stock in them. Talk show hosts on radio and cable blathered on: Who was a bigger socialist—Bush or Obama?

Meanwhile, the nation was wallowing in debt; Americans were losing their homes in record numbers; jobs were disappearing; the stock market had crashed, losing 40 percent of its value over 18 months; and a New York financier named Bernie Madoff was on his way to prison for 150 years for running a $50 billion Ponzi scheme that had nothing at all to do with the nation's mortgage crisis. The housing market looked like a bit of a Ponzi scheme itself. In coastal states—California in particular—home values were falling at rate of 20 percent or more a year after rising as much most of the decade. At the center of the housing crisis was Angelo Mozilo, a once well-respected and admired mortgage banker, who almost overnight had become one of the poster children of the crisis. He was once an icon in the mortgage industry, a man most executives wanted to emulate. He had set the tone—if Angelo was doing something, then the rest would follow.

★   ★   ★

I first met Mozilo, the co-founder and CEO of Countrywide Home Loans, 22 years ago. It's hard to put an exact date on it, though I do remember the first time he came to my Washington office on G Street two blocks from the White House. He was dressed in a dark gray suit, and was wearing a white shirt with a blue collar and a red tie. It was the kind of shirt that investment bankers wore when they appeared on CNBC to discuss the vicissitudes of the stock market. Later on I would learn that Angelo was none too fond of investment bankers, though he did like the shirts they wore. (He also was a big fan of CNBC.)

During his visit to my office he had a PR flack (as we journalists like to call them) at his side, but the PR man (who has since gone down the road) was there strictly as a formality. You might say he was corporate bling. He was there because every CEO, of course, had his own PR man. Angelo, by this time, was already at the epicenter of the mortgage industry in the United States. He needed a PR man like he needed an extra brain. Back then no one spoke for Angelo Mozilo. When he talked no one interrupted him to help clarify or shape his message. The CEO of a firm that would one day become the nation's largest residential lender knew exactly what he wanted to say before he said it.

One reason Angelo came to trust me as a reporter had to do with a book I co-wrote about the savings and loan (S&L) crisis of the late 1980s and early 1990s, *Inside Job: The Looting of America's Savings and Loans*. He had read the book, admiring its detail and its financial morality tale—a story about so-called honest businesspeople who took advantage of newly passed laws that allowed them to loot federally chartered S&Ls (thrifts). He was genuinely appalled by the audacity of both legitimate businessmen (real estate developers mostly) and con artists who were allowed to own S&Ls and treat them like their own personal piggy banks. The S&L crisis led to the indictment of hundreds of men (and a handful of women). Dozens went to prison. Others walked.

Angelo lobbied me on one point, and he said it almost every time we talked about the S&L crisis—that the criminality inherent in the thrift mess could never happen in the world of residential mortgage banking, where loans were securitized into bonds and sold every day by the billions. (The huge thrift losses were caused by commercial real estate boondoggles and junk bond investments.) "The capital markets are the regulator in our business," I recalled him saying. "Wall Street would snuff it out." He wasn't crazy about the Street, but he believed that because Wall Street firms were the gatekeepers between the lenders (and hence the homeowners) and the institutional investors, it was in their best interests to keep everything clean, to promote honesty and integrity.

He had made this argument before subprime lending began to boom in 2003. He believed it down to his toes—that Wall Street (despite his contempt for it) would keep the housing market honest because the Street controlled the mortgage bond business, where most of the money for home lending came. It was in the Street's best interests. I wasn't so sure. I became even less sure when the losses (the nice word being write-downs) at banks and Wall Street firms topped $300 billion in the spring of 2008. To me and my co-author, Mathew Padilla, something had gone awry. A million or so people had lost their homes to foreclosure. Two or three million would follow in their path by the end of the decade. It wasn't just housing and mortgages that were ailing. It seemed as though the nation was getting hit from all different directions: rising energy and commodities prices, falling home values, banks pulling credit lines of all sorts including commercial and student loans. The mortgage virus had spread, infecting the entire body, and had caught fire overseas. It was as though the U.S. economy, which had burned so brightly during the Bush years, was a mirage. Angelo had been deadly wrong. The capital markets— Wall Street—had failed us. This is the story of how it happened.

PAUL MUOLO
December 2009

Cast of Characters

Descriptions include only information that is relevant to the stories in this book.

The Central Cast

Roland Arnall: founder of Ameriquest Mortgage, Long Beach Mortgage, and other subprime lenders; chairman, Ameriquest Capital Corporation.

Eric Billings: co-founder, chairman, and chief executive of investment banker Friedman Billings Ramsey (FBR).

Michael Blum: managing director in charge of global asset-based finance at Merrill Lynch.

Ralph Cioffi: founder and senior portfolio manager of Bear Stearns' two subprime hedge funds.

Robert Cole: co-founder and CEO of New Century Financial Corporation.

Bill Dallas: First Franklin founder and chief executive. Dallas also started Ownit Mortgage Solutions, which Merrill Lynch owned part of.

Patrick Flood: president and chief executive of HomeBanc Mortgage.

Ed Gotschall: co-founder of New Century Financial Corporation.

Steven Holder: co-founder of New Century Financial Corporation.

Stanford Kurland: president of Countrywide Financial and later on CEO and partial owner of PennyMac, a mortgage vulture fund.

David Loeb: co-founder of Countrywide; Angelo Mozilo's onetime boss and partner.

Brad Morrice: co-founder, president, and CEO of New Century Financial Corporation.

Angelo Mozilo: co-founder, chairman, and chief executive officer of Countrywide Financial.

Stanley O'Neal: Merrill Lynch CEO.

Lewis Ranieri: co-inventor of the mortgage-backed security (MBS); former vice chairman of Salomon Brothers.

Jim Rokakis: treasurer of Cuyahoga County, Ohio.

Warren Spector: co-president of Bear Stearns; supervisor in charge of Bear Stearns Asset Management (BSAM).

The Supporting Players

Adam Bass: outside counsel to Ameriquest who eventually joined the company and became vice chairman of Ameriquest Capital Corporation; nephew to Roland Arnall.

Betsy Bayer: first vice president of compliance at Countrywide.

Ben Bernanke: Federal Reserve chairman, Bush and Obama administrations.

Kenneth Bruce: Merrill Lynch stock analyst who covered Countrywide.

Warren Buffett: unofficial advisor to Mozilo.

James Cayne: CEO of Bear Stearns.

"Carl Chamberlain": contract underwriter for the PCI Group/ Clayton Holdings.

Craig Cole: Long Beach Mortgage executive who worked for Roland Arnall.

Peter Samuel Cugno: management trainee at Beneficial Finance.

George Davies: loan trader at Merrill Lynch.

Timothy Geithner: Treasury secretary (Obama administration).

Alan Greenspan: Federal Reserve chairman (Bush administration).

Joy Jenise Jackson: director and manager of Metropolitan Money Store, a foreclosure "rescue" company.

Russell and Becky Jedinak: The husband–and–wife team that managed Guardian Savings and later on Quality Mortgage.

James Johnson: chairman and CEO of Fannie Mae; friend of Angelo Mozilo.

Gary Judis: chief executive officer of Aames Financial.

Kirk Langs: executive in charge of retail mortgage lending at Ameriquest.

Wayne Lee: executive in charge of wholesale/broker mortgage lending at Argent Mortgage, an affiliate company and arm of Ameriquest.

Jack Mayesh: chief executive of Long Beach Financial Corporation/Long Beach Mortgage, a wholesale mortgage lender.

Mike McMahon: Sandler O'Neill stock analyst who covered Countrywide. He also was a warehouse lending executive at First Interstate, which lent money to subprime lenders.

Henry Paulson: Treasury secretary in the Bush administration; also the former head of Goldman Sachs.

Dan Phillips: founder and chief executive officer of First Plus Financial, a high-LTV lender.

Charles Prince: chief executive of Citigroup; former general counsel, Commercial Credit.

Jonas Roth: Countrywide executive in charge of the firm's early trading desk.

David Sambol: president and chief operating officer of Countrywide who replaced Stan Kurland.

Rick Simon: press spokesman for Countrywide.

Rock Tonkel: senior executive and president of Friedman Billings Ramsey (FBR).

Chain of Blame

Chapter 1

Angelo Speaks, the Worldwide Contagion Begins

*The mortgage business is the only business I know where you earn a
ton of money in one year and give it all back during the next three.*
— FRANK HATTEMER, A DISCIPLE OF LEWIS RANIERI

The earnings conference call between the chief executive officer
and the Wall Street community is a delicate kabuki where bad
news is often couched in somber tones and fuzzy adjectives to
soften the blow. But don't tell that to Angelo Mozilo—the Bronx-born,
perpetually tanned CEO and co-founder of Countrywide Financial
Corporation, America's largest home mortgage lender.

On July 24, 2007, the 68-year-old Mozilo and eight of his senior
lieutenants at the publicly traded Countrywide, a company that a few
months earlier had been worth $25 billion on paper, marched down
the carpet from the corporate suite to a 30-foot conference table in the
boardroom, where the top equities analysts from Bear Stearns, Merrill
Lynch, Morgan Stanley—Wall Street's elite—and others were waiting

on the telephone to hear what he had to say about the housing and mortgage markets.

To many on the other end of the line Mozilo was more than just the co-founder of an almost 40-year-old company, one he had built from scratch after starting out his career as a 14-year-old runner delivering documents and bank checks around Manhattan, Brooklyn, and Queens, hopping buses and subways to keep the costs down for the midtown lender he worked for. In the summer of 2007, Mozilo *was* the market, and had been for years. He didn't just sit in on board meetings. He actually closed loans for the company, working with homeowners to gauge the business, what the customer wanted. "To keep my fingers in it, still," he would say. He also would personally handle certain "FOA" or "Friends of Angelo" loans where discounts and fee reductions were given to friends, family members, business acquaintances, and politicians.[1]

Mozilo didn't want to lose touch with what the business of home lending was all about. He never wanted to forget his roots. A product of public schools and colleges, he was a second-generation Italian-American who not only looked like clothing designer Ralph Lauren but dressed like him as well. He wore tailored suits, handmade shirts, gold cuff links. His hair was gray but not one hair was out of place, never. No matter where he spoke, whether it was on the trading floor at Lehman Brothers or to the Horatio Alger Association, which had inducted him into its Hall of Fame in 2003, chances are he would be the best-dressed guy in the room. With his tight skin and perfect teeth, he looked like a male model, a 68-year-old male model, one who had come out of retirement for one last photo shoot for the fall fashion issue of the Sunday *New York Times Magazine*.

---

[1] Among many mortgage lenders it was not an unusual practice to waive fees and waive certain loan underwriting guidelines if they had personal or business ties to the CEO or other senior executives. "Friends of Angelo" loans were given out to politicians such as Senator Chris Dodd, a Democrat from Connecticut, as well as journalists, including at least one nationally syndicated columnist, and the host of a PBS show and her husband. This information was provided to the authors by the man managing the program for Countrywide. He did not want to be quoted by name. At one point he hoped to write a book about his experiences at Countrywide but later dropped the idea. Depending on the year, Dodd was either the chairman of the powerful Senate Banking Committee or ranking minority member of the same panel.

In private he had a penchant for bashing competitors, peppering his nonpublic comments with four-letter words. He rarely forgot his enemies. "He's not one to forget when someone hurts him," said a friend of 20 years. Among his brethren in the home lending industry, he acknowledged few peers. He admired Richard Kovacevich of Wells Fargo because Dick, as he called him, knew how to cross-sell—that is, offer other products to the mortgage customer. But Kovacevich was about it. About a mortgage executive at a large West Coast thrift, Mozilo had this to say: "He's fucking incompetent. I wouldn't even let him manage one of my branches. Utterly pathetic."

As for those on Wall Street, if he had his way he'd throw them into a burning pit and apply more gasoline. He needed them but wouldn't hide his disdain for them. Mozilo once told a reporter from the *New York Times*: "I run into these guys on Wall Street all the time who think they're something special because they went to Ivy League schools." He had never forgotten how back in 1969, when he was starting Countrywide, the Street had turned him down for loans to grubstake his career. "No one gave us a chance," he had said. He wasn't the type of person to forget it, either—but he learned to live with it. And the irony of it all was that early in his career while doing office chores for a small mortgage company, Mozilo had once aspired to be a trader working the floor of the New York Stock Exchange (NYSE).

His dream of working at the NYSE was now buried in the past, in the haze of the late 1950s. As a young man growing up in New York, he grew to believe—whether or not it was true—that if you were Jewish or Italian and worked on Wall Street, you were assigned to what he called the "bowels" of a company like, say, Merrill Lynch. The backroom or basement, those weren't places where he wanted to be—well, at least not for very long.

Angelo, as everyone called him, had as much patience with Wall Street firms as a pit bull would with a newborn kitten. But, as Mozilo knew, he didn't always get to play the pit bull role. He had a reputation for having somewhat of a chip on his shoulder—especially in regard to the Street— but also that he was someone who knew the mortgage industry better than anyone else. Mozilo had left the Bronx long before, but he would admit from time to time that the Bronx hadn't necessarily left him. After all, he had created a model company, one that made mortgages not by using deposits but by borrowing money from others—banks and, yes, eventually Wall Street. (In time he would relent and buy his own bank, but only because Countrywide had grown too large for its own bankers.) Here was a man who over the course of 40 years had taken a tiny company from obscurity to the top of the heap in making home mortgages to Americans, past the gargantuans of banking—past Kovacevich's Wells Fargo, past Citigroup, past JPMorgan Chase, past BankAmerica, past them all. In the summer of 2007 it looked as though he had won the game, but the game—home lending—suddenly turned treacherous.

Those who knew him said Mozilo ate and slept mortgages. There was never any question about his love for the business. When he went to bed most nights, and when he woke up in the morning, mortgages were foremost in his mind. He had made Countrywide the biggest and the best in the business, and his goal was to keep it that way. He would brag to reporters of the company's corporate culture, one in which employees who wanted to find themselves in the executive suite would work weekends and late nights. "If not, they don't last too long here," he told a reporter.

To some, Countrywide was his bride. Not that he wasn't a family man. He had been married to the same woman for 50 years. He was the father of five children and had nine grandkids. His sons Chris, Eric, Mark, and David were managers at Countrywide, and his daughter Lisa was an executive in human resources (HR), while her husband, Casey Fitzpatrick, executed loan trades with Wall Street. Angelo's brother Ralph worked there for a while, as did his cousin Ray Malzo, who had followed him from New York to California and helped him get the company off the ground in the 1970s. Malzo left after a few years, taking his Countrywide stock and investing it in a Harley-Davidson dealership. Mozilo saw his cousin's departure from the company as a betrayal, said a mutual friend. "Angelo would complain that Ray just didn't have the right vision for Countrywide," said the friend.

To those who knew him well, the idea that Mozilo would retire was ridiculous. Sure, he had promised to slow down and pick a successor by the end of 2006, but December 31 came and went and, well, there was no successor. Not that he hadn't tried—supposedly. There was Stanford Kurland, an accountant by training who had risen through the ranks at Countrywide and was ensconced as its president and chief operating officer, the number-two banana at its Southern California headquarters in suburban Calabasas. Stan and Angelo were said to be somewhat close. During conference calls Mozilo would sometimes let Kurland take the reins, explaining the company's financials to analysts.

In the fall of 2006 Countrywide's public relations department began gearing up for a media campaign to send Kurland on the road to greet Wall Street equities analysts and the press. A public relations woman for Countrywide bragged how she'd convinced him to shed a few pounds and buy better suits. She'd coached him on how to deal with the press. "He's really well spoken now," she said. (The intimation was that as an accountant he once had the social skills of a turtle, which was far from acceptable for someone who would be succeeding the über-polished Mozilo.)

The idea was to introduce Kurland as the "new" Angelo. There was a problem, though: There was no such thing as a "new" Angelo. There was only the original. As that day grew closer, it became clear to Mozilo that Kurland envisioned Mozilo's future role as a docile chairman only. Kurland believed that Mozilo would only show up for board meetings, bang the gavel, and spend his newly found leisure time attending his grandkids' soccer games and playing golf at the local country club with his close friends Howard Levine, a commercial mortgage banker, and James Johnson, the former head of Fannie Mae. Angelo loved his grandkids, but he wasn't about to spend almost all of his spare time with them.

Stan's vision was not Angelo's vision. "He was fucking crazy if he thought that I wasn't going to have anything to do with the company after I retired," Mozilo told a friend. And that was that. In short order, Kurland resigned from Countrywide in October. A press release issued by the company said Stan had left to pursue "other career interests." Translation: Mozilo kicked him out of the company, pushed him overboard headfirst, and never looked back. Countrywide was his baby, his creation. If some accountant thought Angelo was going to sit on the sidelines, well, he had another thing coming. At least that's what Mozilo confided to some.

So, here he was on July 24—earnings day—nine months later still very much in charge, very much at the helm. Wall Street analysts like Morgan Stanley's Ken Posner and Paul Miller from Friedman Billings Ramsey, and dozens of others (the press as well), were waiting to hear what Angelo had to say. On July 24, Countrywide was scheduled to report its second quarter results. In the normal course of business the second quarter conference call would be a routine affair, but on this particular day, at this particular point in time, all was not well in the mortgage and housing industries.

Loan delinquencies were rising to 20-year highs. Subprime borrowers (those with bad credit) were defaulting on their payments as never before. Since 2002, subprime had been the hottest lending niche in the business, accounting for 20 percent of new mortgages written in the United States. Over the previous five years, home lenders had originated an eye-popping $2.6 trillion in mortgages to people with bad credit, and delinquencies had been just fine. But not anymore. Home sales were falling to five-year lows—and even worse, home prices were starting to slip. Anyone who worked in mortgages or housing knew this: Home prices never fall. They're not supposed to. It just doesn't happen. Well, not since the Great Depression, that is.

Mortgage lenders were beginning to close their doors at a rate that hadn't been seen since the nation's savings and loan (S&L) crisis of the late 1980s. But administration officials from the Bush White House, including Treasury Secretary Henry Paulson, were explaining away the nation's housing woes and the emerging subprime crisis as something that was "contained"—that it wouldn't "affect America's healthy economy," in Paulson's words. It wouldn't spread to the global markets. And Paulson was a smart guy. Handpicked by President George W. Bush the year before, he had been the chairman of Goldman Sachs, the bluest of Wall Street's blue bloods. He was an Ivy Leaguer, a man who knew what the hell he was talking about.

Yet, cracks were starting to show—not just in the mortgage market but on Wall Street, Paulson's home turf. Several months earlier, two hedge funds that had been created by Bear Stearns, a firm whose history was built on risk analysis—that is, knowing a good investment from a bad one—had begun to lose money. There was talk on the Street and in the financial press that the Bear Stearns hedge funds—once valued at $40 billion—might even collapse. And what exactly had these funds invested in? Answer: mortgage bonds that had been created from subprime loans. It wasn't just mortgage bonds that the hedge funds had bought into, but a relatively new type of bond called a collateralized debt obligation (CDO). A CDO was a security created from other securities. The Bear Stearns hedge funds also were making side bets on other subprime bonds by purchasing hundreds of insurance policies called credit default swaps (CDSs). American International Group, New York, one of the largest insurance companies in the world, was in the process of writing up to $40 billion in credit default swap policies. Grouped together, these investments—these CDSs—were called derivatives, which meant they were derived from loans or bonds that Bear Stearns didn't necessarily own. The bets being made by senior managing director Ralph Cioffi, who was in charge of the hedge funds, boiled down to this: Bear Stearns was bullish on the future of housing, and subprime in particular.

But Bear Stearns wasn't the only investment banking firm playing the subprime game. The biggest names on Wall Street—Citigroup, Lehman Brothers, Merrill Lynch, and Swiss investment banker Credit Suisse—were all doing the same thing. They were buying billions of dollars' worth of subprime mortgages from nonbank lenders, securitizing them, and then resecuritizing them into CDOs, selling some of them overseas. Almost every mortgage they put into a bond was a loan made to a borrower who either had bad credit or was considered a stated-income risk. Stated-income mortgages worked like this: The borrowers stated their income and the lenders believed them. It was a wildly popular product and for obvious reasons: Borrowers got what they wanted even though they had to pay a slightly higher interest rate for it. Wall Street loved any type of loan that was paying a higher rate than the conventional or "A" paper rate of good credit quality mortgages sold to Fannie Mae and Freddie Mac, two congressionally chartered mortgage giants whose mission in life was to buy such loans.

A higher-yielding mortgage meant that a Wall Street firm like Bear Stearns could create a higher-yielding bond to sell to an investor. Every time a bond salesman at Bear (or any other firm) sells a bond, he takes a fraction of the deal for himself. On a $50 million bond, the commission might be an eighth of a point, which works out to $62,500. Bond commissions are not openly publicized and can vary greatly depending on what type of bond is being sold. But one equation rings true—the higher the yield on the bond, the higher the bond sale commission. Subprime mortgages were the highest-yielding loans around that were backed by something tangible: a house. Right smack in the middle of Wall Street's thirst for yield were Angelo Mozilo and Countrywide. Even though Mozilo hadn't started out as a subprime mortgage banker, he was now number one in that business as well. Countrywide wrote more subprime loans than anyone else. That's what Angelo had designed Countrywide to do: enter a market and dominate it. That's what a man who eats, sleeps, and lives mortgages does. "Our goal is to be number one in all the markets," he would say.

As doubts began to mount about the ability of subprime borrowers to keep paying on mortgages backed by homes that were now worth less, Countrywide became part of the story, whether Mozilo liked it or not. As he prepared his comments that July morning, he realized that moving Countrywide into subprime lending was, perhaps, the worst business decision he had ever made in his life. Up until now he had a reputation as a man who had spent his life putting people in homes— minorities and immigrants as well as the middle class, people like his father, who had been a butcher. All that was about to change.

As the microphone opened up on the third floor, Angelo and his top executives at the company laid out the second quarter results: earnings down by one-third to $400 million. On the surface, that may not have seemed so bad. After all, if Angelo and the equity analysts who followed his every move knew anything, they knew that residential lending was a cyclical business, one where profits boomed for a few years and then flattened out, only to revive once again. But then came the conference call Q&A— where analysts got their chance to grill the CEO. Before their microphones were opened up, Angelo, ever the proud father of Countrywide, reminded the experts who followed his company that Countrywide's team was "best in class," that they would weather the storm.

He added that even though the housing market was tanking—and the business of lending on homes right along with it—Countrywide was in a "position to capitalize" on the market's wreckage, that as other lenders failed, Countrywide would pick up market share, meaning his company would get a bigger piece of the pie, something equities analysts loved to hear. Gaining market share was what it was all about— not just in mortgages but in any business. In the mortgage business, the bigger machine you operated, the more money you made. Angelo's creation had a 15 percent market share, which meant that 15 out of every 100 loans closed in the United States belonged to Countrywide. It was an impressive number. But Angelo wanted 20 percent. That's just the kind of guy he was.

Countrywide, even though it, too, was having trouble that quarter, would make lemonade out of lemons. It was a message that Mozilo had been stressing for the past nine months. Everyone in the business—as well as the analysts who followed his company for their rich clients—had heard the Mozilo mantra. "We're well positioned to capitalize" on the industry's problems, he repeated. As other lenders failed, Countrywide would only grow stronger, feeding on the carcasses of others, raiding their demoralized employees and offering them jobs. To Angelo, it was a beautiful way to do business. He and Countrywide would grow stronger as everyone else grew weaker.

But then a question came from Paul Miller, an analyst at Friedman Billings Ramsey, an investment banking firm based in northern Virginia, a firm that, ironically, owned a failing subprime lender of its own. "Angelo, when do you see things improving out there?" asked Miller.

The Countrywide CEO, known for his bluntness above all else, reminded them that "no one" had seen the housing and mortgage downturn coming. "Bear Stearns, Merrill Lynch, S&P's [Standard & Poor's]. No one," Angelo said. There he was, bashing Wall Street again. But Angelo, as he would admit later, hadn't seen it coming, either. He knew it was going to be bad, but he didn't think it would be quite this bad.

Angelo was asked another question or two and then was pressed again about when housing prices and sales might finally come out of their swoon. He shot back quickly. "I'd say 2009," he said. "It takes a long time to turn a battleship around. That's what this is—a huge battleship. We need to slow it down, stop it, and then turn it around: 2009."

Some analysts were wondering: 2009? That was two years away. Sitting at their desks on the other end of the phone, watching blinking computer screens, that wasn't the kind of reassuring talk that equities analysts wanted to hear. An analyst asked a question of another Countrywide executive, and then Mozilo butted in at the end of the executive's answer.

If anything, he wanted to make sure that these folks on Wall Street fully understood the situation. He wasn't about to whitewash it. He wasn't a put-on-your-best-face kind of guy. His ability to cut through the malaise of the situation (or as he would call it, "the bullshit") was what endeared him to analysts, certain competitors, and definitely members of the media. Mozilo told the audience on the other end of the line without hesitation, "We are experiencing a huge price depression, one we have not seen before—not since the Great Depression."

The Great Depression? Analysts didn't want to hear that, either. Mentioning the "D" word in relation to anything financial was akin to saying the world was about to end. The next day, Countrywide's stock skidded 11 percent. On paper, investors lost millions. Some analysts believed it would have skidded even more if the investment banking community hadn't swallowed, hook, line, and sinker, Mozilo's boast that even though the mortgage and housing markets looked bleak, Countrywide would capitalize on all the carnage by gaining market share. Market share was his mantra.

Still, Mozilo's remark about the Great Depression savaged the stock market. The Dow Jones Industrial Average plunged 226 points. It was the worst decline in four months, which in the scheme of things may not have seemed that bad, but the New York Stock Exchange had indeed set a record that day: 4.16 billion shares of stock changed hands, a sign that investors were heading for the exits big-time. They were nervous. Had Angelo's comments wiped out billions of dollars in stock value? It looked that way. "The 'Great Depression' comment he made was just irresponsible," said an investment banker who served on industry panels with Angelo. "He started it."

In the weeks ahead, the stock market would recover by a hundred points here and there and slip by just as much and then some. Within a month the Dow would drop by a thousand points.[2] While the Dow sank, Mozilo cashed in stock options, unloading thousands of shares in Countrywide. Over the previous year he had cashed in stock options and sold $140 million worth of company stock. People noticed. And when it was pointed out by columnists and short sellers, he bristled. In an interview with the trade newspaper *National Mortgage News*, he boasted, "I started this company with my own money. I have created $25 billion in value for shareholders. It's been one of the best-performing stocks on the NYSE. I gave them 98 percent and took 2 percent. And they [the shareholders] didn't have to do the work. I did it for them."

A few days after the Countrywide conference call, the two Bear Stearns hedge funds that had invested in subprime CDOs and credit

---

[2] By March 2008 the Dow Jones Industrial Average had lost 2,200 points.

default swaps collapsed for good. The funds were now worth just 10 percent of their peak value, if that. Warren Spector, the Bear Stearns co-president who had ultimate responsibility for the funds, had been canned within days of Mozilo's "Great Depression" comment. Spector, a 20-year veteran of Bear Stearns who had shepherded the firm's foray into residential mortgages two decades earlier, was considered by many on the Street as something of an analytical genius who had rarely made a bad call in mortgages. Not anymore.

Meanwhile, in Atlanta, a residential lender called HomeBanc Mortgage, a midsize nonbank a fraction of Countrywide's size, was struggling to stay afloat. HomeBanc, which once had been part of a savings and loan, was managed by a handful of executives who a few years earlier had worked at a Countrywide competitor called HomeSide Lending. Headquartered in Jacksonville, Florida, HomeSide had been a target of Mozilo's in the trade press. The Countrywide chairman and CEO had bashed HomeSide because instead of making mortgage loans directly to consumers through retail branches, the company bought already-originated loans from other firms. Mozilo strongly believed that the practice of buying newly originated loans from other lenders would eventually bankrupt the company, because the profit margins on such a strategy were so thin. (Ironically, Mozilo was doing the same thing, but he still used retail branches and loan brokers to gather mortgages.) In time, he would be proved right. HomeSide collapsed two years after being bought by an Australian bank. "They didn't know what the fuck they were doing," he said of HomeSide's management. The Australian bank, National Bank of Australia, lost $2 billion on HomeSide. It left America with its tail between its legs, Mozilo bragged.

HomeBanc, though, was a direct lender to consumers through its retail storefront branches. And it wasn't a subprime lender, either. In the summer of 2007 it was struggling to survive because all the bad news in the subprime sector had caused its bankers to rethink the strategy of lending money to HomeBanc. HomeBanc was a nonbank that employed 450 loan officers, many of whom had no prior experience in the mortgage business, which is sort of like running a soccer team by hiring baseball players, hoping you can teach them the game. (Loan officers work with the public, selling them different mortgage products.)

HomeBanc CEO Patrick Flood (unlike his next in command, Kevin Race) was not a former employee of HomeSide. Flood was a born-again Christian who made prospective employees take what he called a "values test" before he would hire and then train them to make loans to the public. HomeBanc had 22 branches, and each one had a Christian chaplain on call. Its human resources director was Ike Reighard, a close friend of Flood's who had once held bible studies at HomeBanc. Reighard, the founder of a megachurch in suburban Atlanta, had once told Flood, "God has prepared me all of my life for this job."

The Reverend had no professional HR experience, but that didn't matter to Flood. He felt that a pastor who could counsel churchgoers about divorce, kid problems, and money woes would make a fine HR chief. "Our 450 loan officers may've had no prior experience," he would later explain, "but we had the best service out there." Maybe so, but by August Flood was no longer at the company, the board forcing him to resign in January because HomeBanc's loan originations were sinking right along with its stock price. (Like Countrywide, HomeBanc was publicly traded on the NYSE.)

By early August, after Mozilo had already painted his bleak picture of the business, HomeBanc's stock had drifted down to 60 cents from a onetime high of $10. Its shareholders were not happy. HomeBanc's bankers pulled the plug. On Friday afternoon, August 10, Kevin Race, Flood's successor, gathered some of his staff in a conference room at the lender's headquarters, giving them the bad news. "We're shutting down," he said.

The strange thing about HomeBanc's failure is that when it filed its bankruptcy court papers a few days later, it listed liabilities (what it owed) of $4.9 billion and assets of $5.1 billion, which meant that even though no bankers (JPMorgan Chase, Bear Stearns, and several foreign banks) would lend it any money, it actually had a net worth of $200 million—not bad for a failed company. Had Mozilo's comments played a role in its death?

It was hard to pin HomeBanc's failure on Angelo. He had no control over what the money center banks did in regard to his competitors. (Both HomeBanc and Countrywide were top lenders in Georgia.) After all, HomeBanc wasn't a subprime lender. But by this time subprime lenders were failing every week—at a rate of 10 a month, at least. When HomeBanc ascended into mortgage heaven, guess who stepped in to purchase five of its highest-performing storefront branches in Georgia? Mozilo and Countrywide. He once again was making good on his promise to prosper from the mortgage industry's meltdown. As others died, he would get stronger: his mantra.

One of his favorite ploys was to find out which loan officers at open (as well as failed) lending shops were the highest performers. A high performer was a loan officer who had a kick-ass client list of potential customers, someone who could work a network of prospects, bringing them in as loan customers. Selling a mortgage to a consumer (whether for buying a new house or for refinancing one) was just like selling a car or washing machine or expensive stereo. Mozilo knew that gangbuster loan officers—men and women who worshipped the movie *Glengarry Glen Ross* and the phrase "ABC" or "always be closing"—whether they worked directly with home buyers or gathered loans through mortgage brokers, were worth their weight in gold. Those were the people he wanted to hire. He would personally interview some of them himself.

A marketing officer at Impac Mortgage in Southern California, a Countrywide competitor, tells a story of just how aggressive Mozilo and Countrywide could be in their recruiting of loan officers. "There was a news story in the local paper that we were having trouble, which caused some of our employees to get nervous. The afternoon the story appeared about us, a car pulls into our parking lot with a big cardboard advertisement on the roof. The ad said something like 'If you're worried about your job, call this number.' At first, a few of us laughed. But then we started getting concerned. After a half hour the car was still there in the parking lot. We were getting annoyed. Someone from the company went down there and told that car to get the hell out of our parking lot. We called the phone number—it was a phone number at Countrywide."

When Countrywide agreed to buy the five branches from the now-dead HomeBanc, employees who worked at those branches were elated to have jobs and be working for Countrywide—the nation's largest lender of home mortgages, a Fortune 500 company that employed 60,000. Countrywide had a bank affiliate. It had depositors, little old ladies from Pasadena with certificates of deposit and savings accounts. It didn't need to depend solely on Wall Street and money center banks to keep its business going. Countrywide was rock solid. Angelo Mozilo was the poster child of mortgage lending in the United States. He was a frequent guest on CNBC, the business channel, and friends with one of its chief anchors, Maria Bartiromo. He—and Countrywide—would be around forever.

At least, that's what the ex-HomeBanc workers thought.

★   ★   ★

On Wednesday, August 15, Jim Israel, an advertising salesman for *National Mortgage News*, the largest industry trade publication that covered mortgages, was driving down a four-lane street in Pasadena, California, a city where Countrywide was once headquartered. In years past Israel had sold advertisements in *National Mortgage News* to Countrywide, but he wasn't having much luck this year. As for Pasadena, the story goes, back in 1997 Mozilo had requested financial assistance from the city. "He wanted the city to help us develop space for Countrywide," said Rick Simon, a public relations executive at the lender. "They turned us down." In 1997 Countrywide employed 10,000 across the United States, 1,000 of them in Pasadena. Angered by Pasadena's reluctance to help him, Mozilo bought the old Lockheed Martin headquarters 34 miles west in Calabasas, at the foot of the Santa Monica Mountains. In short order Angelo gave Pasadena's mayor the Bronx cheer.

Even though Countrywide had bolted Pasadena for the more business-friendly confines of Calabasas, the company still maintained back offices and even a bank branch there. A few weeks earlier, Israel had tried to arrange a sales meeting with Countrywide's marketing department but was rebuffed. "They told me, don't even bother coming by," he said. Driving down the street that afternoon, Israel saw a crowd of about 40 people milling around outside Countrywide's Pasadena branch. "I kept looking at those people, thinking it was a protest or something," said Israel. "As I kept driving I looked in my rearview mirror. I didn't know what it was."

It would not be uncommon for a protest to be held outside a Countrywide branch—or the branch of any other large home lender for that matter. By the summer of 2007 home foreclosures were rising to their highest level in 15 years. Public interest groups like ACORN[3]

---

[3] ACORN, a consumer activist group, stands for Association of Community Organizations for Reform Now.

routinely staged protests outside the headquarters and branches of large lenders like Countrywide, trying to convince them to go easy on late payers. But what Israel witnessed that afternoon wasn't a protest against a big, bad mortgage lender. As he later remembered, it didn't seem as though any of those 40 people milling around outside the branch were holding a protest sign.

The next day Israel picked up the *Los Angeles Times* and found out what the fuss was all about. Countrywide's Pasadena branch—and branches throughout Southern California—had been the subject of a good old-fashioned run on the bank where panicked depositors, fearful that they might lose their life savings, lined up to yank all their money out. The nation hadn't witnessed any bank runs since the S&L crisis two decades earlier, and before that, the Great Depression. (It seemed as though Mozilo's "Great Depression" comment was coming back to haunt him again.)

The newspaper reported that those pulling out cash included a Los Angeles Kings hockey player and a middle-aged banker named Bill Ashmore. Ashmore was a top executive at Impac Mortgage—the same company that Countrywide had tried to raid for employees. Like every other mortgage lender in the land, Impac had seen its stock price ravaged over the past year. It was now trading at just over a dollar, compared to a yearly high of $12. Impac's specialty was "alt-A" lending, a loan product best described as not quite subprime, but not quite prime, either. Impac, like HomeBanc, was a nonbank. It, too, borrowed money from Wall Street. It didn't use deposits. Depending on which analyst you talked to, it looked as though Impac was on the gurney as well.

Ashmore worked in nearby Irvine. That morning, at the behest of his wife, he drove his Porsche Cayenne to Countrywide's Laguna Niguel office. Scott Reckard, a reporter from the *Los Angeles Times*, was staking out the parking lot, hoping to talk to nervous depositors pulling their life savings from the branch. (Countrywide's newspaper and radio ads targeted senior citizens. Pasadena and the surrounding towns had more than their fair share of well-to-do seniors.) Reckard approached Ashmore, not knowing who he was—the president of a Countrywide competitor, an ailing one at that. (Reckard would later say that running into Ashmore "was one of those serendipitous things that occur maybe once a decade. I drove to the nearest Countrywide office, saw that there were a dozen people inside waiting to get their dough, approached the first guy who left, and it turned out to be Ashmore.")

Ashmore was a little like Mozilo in that if you asked him the right question he could be a chatty fellow. He told the reporter that he had just cashed in a $500,000 certificate of deposit, transferring it over to an account at Bank of America, the third largest bank in the United States, one that was considered a pillar of financial stability. "It's because of the fear of bankruptcy," Ashmore said as he approached his Porsche. "It's got my wife totally freaked out. I just don't want to deal with it. I don't care about losing 90 days' interest. I don't care if it's FDIC insured." (The FDIC, or Federal Deposit Insurance Corporation, a government agency, insured each account up to $100,000.)

The strange thing was that Countrywide wasn't bankrupt, not even close—at least that's what Mozilo believed. There was no logical reason for the run on its branches. Mozilo was none too pleased that the *Los Angeles Times* had published the physical locations of Countrywide's Southern California branches. (The adjectives he used to describe the newspaper started with the letter *f*.) Countrywide Financial Corporation, the parent company, owned a savings and loan that boasted $60 billion in deposits. Sixty billion in deposits went a long way—but not when you were originating $400 billion a year in home mortgages, which Countrywide was on track to do in 2007. So, like HomeBanc and Impac, Countrywide borrowed from Wall Street firms and the money center banks. It had $190 billion in loans it could draw upon.

The reason for the run: Before the stock market opened Wednesday morning—before Countrywide was besieged by nervous customers like Ashmore—an equities analyst at Merrill Lynch named Kenneth Bruce wrote a critical research report on the company, suggesting that if enough "financial pressure" was placed on Countrywide, it might have to file for bankruptcy protection. Two weeks earlier, Bruce, who was in his late 40s, had told Merrill Lynch's institutional and retail clients to buy Countrywide shares. Now he was calling it a "sell." Bruce wasn't just any old equities analyst. He had worked at Countrywide for five years, under Angelo's new successor-in-waiting, David Sambol, Countrywide's president.

In two weeks' time, Bruce had abruptly changed his opinion about Countrywide. Word of the "sell" rating and the mention of bankruptcy roiled the markets, sending Countrywide's shares into a nosedive. Six months earlier its shares were at $40. After the Bruce missive, its shares were at $19 and sinking fast. Mozilo was furious. Investors in Countrywide's stock had seen billions of dollars in value disappear—*poof*. When Bruce worked at Countrywide, Angelo never met him. "I have no idea who he was," he later said. (He also had a few choice words for Bruce, none of which were printable in a family newspaper.)

"I don't know what his motivation was," Mozilo said a few days later. "He had just confirmed us as a 'buy' two weeks earlier. It was like yelling 'fire' in a crowded theater. He put my 60,000 employees at risk. He panicked our senior citizen depositors. And the thing is that he doesn't know what the fuck he's talking about. He doesn't even have his facts right."

The facts, as Mozilo saw them, were that Countrywide, even though it had stopped making most types of subprime loans, was liquid, meaning enough banks were willing to lend Countrywide money despite Bruce's disparaging comments. Countrywide had $190 billion in loans available to it. However, Bruce didn't see it that way. Bruce said that yes, banks and Wall Street had agreed to lend Countrywide such a large sum, but those deals could be terminated at any time, and at a moment's notice.

Bruce had another connection to Countrywide that Mozilo didn't realize. Ten years earlier he was an intern at the investment banking firm of Sandler O'Neill working under Mike McMahon, a stock analyst who closely covered Countrywide and was on friendly terms with Mozilo. "Ken worked for me for two months," said McMahon. "I told him he was too smart to be doing this kind of work. Eventually, he moved on." (Further adding to the web of connections was the fact—never published—that Mozilo earlier in the year had been talking to Sandler O'Neill's senior managing principal, Jimmy Dunne, about merging the investment banker with Countrywide.) Bruce went from Sandler O'Neill to Countrywide's capital markets group to Merrill Lynch, whose CEO, Stanley O'Neal, was a golfing buddy of Mozilo's. (After Bruce's comments wreaked havoc on Countrywide's stock, Mozilo, still steamed, told one friend, "Next time I see Stan I'm going to punch him in the nose." He was half kidding, said the friend.)

It wasn't so much that Bruce had told Merrill Lynch's institutional and retail customers to dump the stock, but that he was suggesting that the nation's largest mortgage lender and servicer, the House of Angelo—one that was closing in on a market share approaching 20 percent—could go belly-up. Just how bad were things in the mortgage market? The subprime sector, where 20 percent of home borrowers got their loans, had just about seized up. Wall Street firms were still buying mortgages from subprime lenders but at greatly reduced prices and volumes. The phrase *credit crunch* was starting to be used liberally by financial commentators on television. Home buyers with good credit could still get mortgages, but home prices were falling and defaults were rising.

All summer President Bush's Treasury secretary, Henry Paulson, no matter where he traveled, had been making the same speech—that the problems in the U.S. mortgage business, the subprime market in particular, had not sparked what was being called a "worldwide contagion." No one was listening, though. Stocks were now tumbling in Asia, Europe, and Latin America. Bruce's bankruptcy call on Countrywide had capped off a week of horrific news. Rumors were starting to spread that subprime CDOs sold by Wall Street firms such as Merrill Lynch and Morgan Stanley were causing losses overseas at banks in Europe and Australia.

To some, though, Angelo was getting his comeuppance. To some, Mozilo's July 24 comments about the housing market being in the worst shape since the Great Depression had started the ball rolling. But this ball was no longer small. It had grown into a boulder and then a landslide, rolling downhill toward Mozilo and the 60,000 employees who worked at his Calabasas-based baby, Countrywide. "Angelo's mouth finally got him in trouble," said Lew Sichelman, a nationally syndicated housing columnist who had covered the company for 30 years.

Even President Bush was being asked about the mortgage crisis at press conferences. (Mortgages weren't typically topic A during presidential Q&As.) Bush kept repeating what he had always believed—that the U.S. economy was strong, that there would be no government bailout of mortgage lenders. But the President's words didn't convince Jim Cramer, a former hedge fund manager who runs a stock picking show on CNBC. On the Friday before Bruce's "sell" rating, Cramer—who on his show *Mad Money* often referred to Mozilo as a "good friend" and implored CNBC's viewers to buy Countrywide's shares—was describing the stock market meltdown, the worldwide contagion, as "Armageddon." Not only was he using the word "Armageddon," but he was shouting it out at the top of lungs, jumping up and down on the set like a child having a temper tantrum. "This is Armageddon," Cramer repeated to his viewers. Reporter Erin Burnett looked at Cramer as though he had lost his mind.

Back in Calabasas, Mozilo couldn't have agreed more with Cramer's assessment. Thanks to one word uttered by Merrill Lynch's Ken Bruce (bankruptcy), Countrywide was now facing financial Armageddon—even though it had earned almost $2 billion the year before. On the Wednesday that Bruce made his bankruptcy utterance, the Countrywide founder had been scheduled to appear on CNBC at 4 P.M. Eastern time. He was a no-show. Countrywide's stock continued to trade downward like a rock thrown off an airplane. Instead of talking to Maria Bartiromo, the CNBC anchor, Angelo was working the telephones, trying to get his lenders, his bankers, to calm down.

He tried to convince them that despite what that "moron" (his words to a friend) Bruce had said, Countrywide was going to be okay. It had earned $2 billion just the year before. But it didn't really matter what Angelo thought. When he called around to calm Countrywide's bankers, to plead with them to continue lending money to his company—so Countrywide could continue funding the American dream of home ownership for millions of Americans—he got the cold shoulder. Wall Street hadn't forgotten that chip on his shoulder. Their collective answer to him: Drop dead.

"They said, 'We have our own problems,'" Mozilo explained. "These were guys I had been banking with for 40 years." For the first time in a long time, when Angelo spoke no one was listening, at least not the way he wanted them to.

Over the next few days, ashen-faced Countrywide executives worked around the clock at the Calabasas headquarters. Betsy Bayer, who worked in the compliance department, remembered that "you could see the stress on their faces. They were working monster hours. I think some people were caught up in denial or they looked like a deer caught in the headlights."

In Manhattan at the corporate offices of JPMorgan Chase something else was afoot. Jamie Dimon, the chairman and CEO of the bank/investment bank, was trying to convene a meeting of Country-wide's five largest commercial paper lenders, including Citigroup and Bank of America (BoA). As commercial paper lenders, these firms had lent and committed some of the $190 billion that Angelo spoke of. Dimon, according to one of his advisors, was concerned that each of the five was wasting valuable time trying to negotiate individually with Countrywide. "Jamie was not comfortable with Countrywide's chances of survival," said the advisor.[4] It looked as though Bruce was not alone in his belief that Countrywide could go under. (McMahon from Sandler would later describe Bruce's call on Countrywide as a "gutsy pick," one that perhap's had some truth to it.)

As Countrywide's stock continued on a downward trajectory, Mozilo worked the telephones and convinced an old friend, Ken Lewis, the president and CEO of Bank of America, to invest $2 billion of its money in a special class of preferred stock that was convertible to common stock and paid a 7.25 percent dividend. Under a deal that Mozilo personally negotiated, BoA got the shares for $18 a pop, giving the bank a 16 percent stake in the nation's largest lender and servicer of home mortgages. The investment by BoA was enough to calm Dimon's fears. It wasn't exactly luck on Angelo's part. Over the previous two years he and Lewis had talked informally about BoA buying Countrywide in its entirety. At one point the talks turned serious and BoA even began conducting due diligence, sending a team of analysts to scour Countrywide's books. Angelo got cold feet and backed out. The company was coming off its two most profitable years ever, and it appeared the good times wouldn't end.

Five years earlier, according to *National Mortgage News*, Country-wide had almost struck a deal to become a private label lender and servicer for BoA. Under Mozilo's plan, BoA could get rid of its entire mortgage department, and Countrywide, for a fee, would service and originate all of BoA's home mortgages. (The story got little attention from the news dailies that covered Countrywide.) Angelo had person-ally courted BoA's Ken Lewis about the idea. The move could have saved the Charlotte, North Carolina–based bank hundreds of millions

---

[4] The advisor, an investment banker, spoke under the condition his name not be used.

of dollars a year. Angelo at one point thought he was close on the private label agreement, but Lewis eventually balked, fearful that he would be putting the bank's mortgage customers in the hands of a company that might try marketing credit cards and home equity loans—the latter being a huge and profitable business for the Charlotte bank.

Bank of America's $2 billion investment in Countrywide wasn't the first time in its history that BoA had bailed out Mozilo. Back in 1970 when Countrywide was a struggling young company, BoA had purchased a Florida bank that had a $75,000 outstanding loan to Countrywide. One of the first things BoA did when it bought the Florida bank was to call in the loan. "I told them I had three kids, a wife, and no money," said Mozilo. BoA could close him down and lose the loan or let him continue operating with the chance that eventually the loan would be paid in full. They bit. Mozilo got his loan extended.

Some 37 years later, BoA had saved the day once more. When the investment was announced publicly, Countrywide's shares spiked upward to $24.50. The bank was now sitting on a paper gain of $700 million, and Ken Lewis looked like a financial Einstein—all for listening to an old friend named Angelo who needed some money. But in the months ahead the good times would not last, and BoA's masterstroke would soon look like a financial disaster. By January 2008 Countrywide's shares were down to $8, which meant BoA and Lewis were sitting on a loss of well over $1 billion. Mozilo and Lewis had a lot of explaining to do to their respective shareholders.

Chapter 2

The Repo Man Meets the Bald Granny

A Short History of Subprime

In the summer of 2007, Angelo Mozilo's bluntness about the sorry state of the mortgage and housing markets caught many in the industry by surprise, especially Merrill Lynch & Company and its CEO, Stanley O'Neal, who five short months earlier had spent $1.3 billion to buy First Franklin Financial Corporation of San Jose, the fourth largest originator of subprime loans in the land. The seller was National City Corporation of Cleveland, a commercial bank that eight years earlier had bought First Franklin (a nonbank) from Bill Dallas, a 25-year veteran of the mortgage industry whose best quality, according to some, was revving up his sales force of account executives (AEs) to gather subprime mortgages from thousands of loan brokers from coast to coast.

"Bill is really a guy who can rally the troops to sell things," said one competitor who went head-to-head with Dallas. "He can make them move. He knows how to make it rain—but when he does, he doesn't have an umbrella and galoshes." Dallas, he said, had a penchant—for better or worse—for overpaying the AEs who gathered residential mortgages from independent loan brokers. Among his professional accomplishments, Dallas listed a joint venture with Rupert Murdoch's Fox television network to own and manage the Fox Sports Grill, a small chain of upscale restaurants that catered to consumers who liked to eat casual food and watch sporting events on big-screen TVs. Another career highlight was the fact that he was the trustee for teenage entertainers Mary-Kate and Ashley Olsen and the chairman of Dualstar Entertainment Group, a holding company that controlled the twins' assets. What wasn't listed on his resume was the fact that he knew Angelo Mozilo and happened to live in the same Agoura Hills neighborhood. Mozilo's Countrywide competed against First Franklin.

Mozilo's opinion of First Franklin? True to form, he didn't pull any punches here, either: "In my opinion, Bill was operating a flawed company. It was flawed operationally, structurally, and culturally." Did he have anything nice to say about Dallas? "Bill impressed a lot of people. He's a salesman. He's a neighbor of mine."

Even though he didn't have much in the way of warm things to say about the First Franklin co-founder,[1] one thing could be said of Bill Dallas—when he sold the subprime lender to National City he made a killing on the sale: $325 million, doubling the money he and his venture capital backers, CIVC Partners of Chicago, had put into the company. After that, he did what any sensible subprime executive would have done: He took the money, signed a noncompete clause, and sat out of the business, serving only as chairman emeritus of First Franklin and concentrating on his other investments. (A chairman emeritus shows up for board meetings six times a year, bangs a gavel, and collects a salary, often having absolutely nothing to do with the day-to-day operations of a company.)

Meanwhile, National City was handing off First Franklin to Merrill Lynch, a name synonymous with the retail stock brokerage trade. Merrill, by this time, was one of the last of Wall Street's investment banking giants that didn't own a subprime origination company. By purchasing First Franklin it was making a costly bet that the business—which was starting to fray because of rising delinquencies and concerns about flatlining home values—would be just fine over the long haul. O'Neal and the Merrill executives who ran the mortgage group were betting

---

[1] First Franklin was founded by Bill Dallas and family members in the 1980s. About a decade later, Fred Baldwin, a veteran subprime executive, merged his company, Trillium Mortgage, into First Franklin. Some in the mortgage industry credited Baldwin as a co-founder of First Franklin as well.

that the early signs of trouble in subprime and housing were temporary and that the market would snap back.

Mozilo and Merrill's Stan O'Neal were friends. Merrill Lynch was one of a handful of investment banks that helped raise capital (in the form of stock and bonds) for Countrywide over the years. The two served together on the Business Council, a voluntary group of executives that held court with elected officials, including the president of the United States. Even though they were somewhat close, O'Neal never tipped his hand to Mozilo regarding his intentions to buy First Franklin. "Here they were getting under our kimono," said Mozilo. "I later asked Stan about it. He said, 'It's part of our plan.'"

Mozilo knew what that plan was. Merrill Lynch increasingly had become one of the hungriest buyers of subprime loans on Wall Street. But it had to pay other lenders for the product—that is, the loans. It planned to keep doing that, but figured it could really ramp up its loan purchases—which ultimately would wind up in mortgage bonds that it could sell worldwide—if it owned its own lending operation, First Franklin. That was all well and good with the top executives at National City. When the deal finally went down in February of 2007 and the bank had the $1.3 billion wired into its cash account, some of its executives were dancing in the aisles at the bank's headquarters in Cleveland, according to George Ostendorf, an investment banker from Chicago who had a friend at National City.[2] "They were giving each other the high fives," said Ostendorf.

---

[2] National City sold the risk-inherent First Franklin to Merrill Lynch for $1.3 billion. The price—almost $1 billion more than what National City had paid back in 1999 for the subprime lender—was for First Franklin and two affiliates. Despite the sale (and the celebrating in the corporate suite), the bank would not escape entirely unscathed from the mortgage crisis. In the fourth quarter of 2007, National City posted a $333 million loss, tied in part to delinquencies and write-downs on alt-A mortgages and second-lien home equity loans held on its books. In time, it also would stop funding mortgages through loan brokers and close its wholesale channel where such loans were produced. In the first quarter of 2008 it lost $171 million and was forced to raise $7 billion in equity from outside investors. By the fall of 2008 it was in danger of failing and by year-end it was sold to PNC Financial Services of Pittsburgh, a bank that absolutely loathed most aspects of the residential mortgage business. One of PNC's first moves as the new owner of National City was to shut down its warehouse lending group, which lent money to nonbank mortgage firms.

When Peter Samuel Cugno of California read that Merrill Lynch was buying First Franklin, he just scratched his head. As the CEO of his own Southern California mortgage company, he had dealt with Merrill in the late 1980s when the investment bank operated what was called a trading desk out of its office in Philadelphia. Cugno's company, Financial Services Funding Group (FSFG), would originate a subprime loan and sell it to Merrill's desk for a negotiated price, and then Merrill would resell it (flip it, so to speak) to an institutional buyer for an even higher price. "As long as Merrill stayed in the game as a middleman, I thought they'd be okay," he said.

Cugno was a bit like Mozilo in some ways. Born a few years apart, both were Italian-Americans who loved the Southern California climate, talked a tough game of business, and knew their respective niches in the home lending industry. But that's where the similarities ended. Mozilo had spent almost his entire career lending money to Americans with good credit, whereas Cugno had spent his entire career lending to Californians with bad credit. "A" paper lending was a huge business. The origination of home mortgages to people with bad credit—at least until 2002—was a small pond, but it was a business Cugno loved, despite some of its personal pitfalls. Cugno, as his friends might tell you, was a little rough around the edges when it came to his personal appearance. He was Oscar Madison to Mozilo's Felix Unger.

In 2002 the U.S. housing market began to recover from the terrorist attacks of 9/11. Interest rates were low, and a national housing recovery—thanks to a succession of rate cuts by the Federal Reserve under Alan Greenspan—was well under way. Wall Street firms like Bear Stearns, Credit Suisse, Deutsche Bank, and Lehman Brothers began doing something that Cugno could not quite comprehend: They were buying billions of dollars' worth of subprime loans from nonbank mortgage lending firms. The activity made Cugno think of the 1960s, of his early days as a management trainee at Beneficial Finance, one of the granddaddies of the subprime movement. He wondered, why was Wall Street buying subprime loans? "Back when I was a 20-year-old snot-nosed amateur at Beneficial, all Wall Street meant to me was a bunch of guys who were stockbrokers," he said.

When he was a young man, Cugno wasn't all that keen on stockbrokers. The way he saw it, he was a frat boy who liked going to parties and chasing women. Wall Street, to him, meant Ivy Leaguers with white shoes and a handful of finance degrees. He loathed such people. (He and Mozilo saw eye-to-eye on that issue.) Now, 40 years later, investment bankers from New York were buying subprime loans—a lot of subprime loans. When he saw what the Street was doing in the early 2000s he got a sick feeling in his stomach, and it wasn't just the cancer he was suffering from. "That was the beginning of the end as I remember it—when they started to see the potential for them to get hip-deep in this biz and suck out some serious money," he said. "But their mistake was that to do that, they needed to no longer be someone who put others together—like the trading desk operation—but to saddle up, own the lender, and take on some serious risk."

* * *

As a management trainee for Beneficial Finance in the 1960s, Cugno knew what risk was all about. He lived it. When Cugno started out his career in the subprime mortgage business, he was what some people called a "repo man." In street terms (not Wall Street terms, that is), a repo man was someone who took back items from deadbeat borrowers. He was someone who repossessed items—by any means necessary (usually legal).[3] Back then the word *subprime* didn't exist, and the last thing in the world a white-shoe investment banking firm like Merrill Lynch (or Bear Stearns or any other firm headquartered on the island of Manhattan) wanted was to be in the business of repossessing people's cars, stereo equipment, or homes for that matter.

As a management trainee for Beneficial, a company founded in 1914 in Elizabeth, New Jersey (a sister city to Newark), young Cugno's job was to originate small personal loans to office workers and blue-collar wage slaves living in the San Fernando Valley in Southern California. After the loan was made, he would service the debt (collect the monthly payments), and in the event the loan became late, cure the

---

[3] In the consumer finance business, the word *repo* pertained to repossession or the taking back of property (a car for instance) that collateralized a personal loan. By the 1980s the word *repo* (on Wall Street, at least) was jargon for "repurchase agreement," whereby a lender pledged loans to an investment banking firm or a commercial bank in exchange for a loan totaling tens or hundreds of millions of dollars.

note, that is, make the borrower make a payment. If borrowers were late, Cugno would call them on the telephone after a couple of friendly letters failed to do the job. "You owe us a lot of money," he would tell them. "I will find out where you work." And that's just what he did. He would wake up at four in the morning and follow them to their place of employment. "I would go to their desk and I would say, 'I'm from Beneficial. I'm here for the payment. I don't care if your kid is sick.'"

He was a repo man for items both big and small—pianos and furniture, too. Taking back indoor merchandise could be tricky. "That stuff was in the house," he said. "Sometimes I was afraid of getting shot, so I tried not to go through the window. I tried not to do anything illegal." His goal, as always, was to go into a house by invitation. The first order of business was to call the borrowers and let them know that Beneficial was on its way to take back the furniture. Luckily for him, most delinquent borrowers knew the jig was up and cooperated. (By the time he left Beneficial in 1979 he could boast that he'd never been shot by a customer.)

Cars—he repossessed those, too. It was another four in the morning, better-to-do-it-in-the-pitch-darkness type of job. He would go the deadbeat's house. If he saw his asset sitting in the driveway, he would call the tow truck, show the driver his certificate of title to the automobile, and that was that. The car got hoisted up on the tow chain, and Beneficial's collateral would be wheeled down the street in the gentle stillness of a Southern California morning, before the milkman arrived and the (former) owner realized that he'd be taking the bus to work that morning—that is, if he had a job.

In the early 1960s that's what Beneficial Finance was all about. It was a publicly traded company that made small-balance consumer loans to millions of Americans. It wasn't a bank that took deposits (savings and checking accounts) from the public. That was the point. When it was founded in 1914 its business model was that it lent money to consumers who *couldn't* get loans from banks. Back then the loans were used to buy durable goods such as appliances and furniture. The borrowers would then pay back Beneficial in installments. Beneficial's first office allowed consumers to borrow up to $300. By 1924 the lender boasted 80 offices and was making $13 million in loans a year. Its average loan size back then? A whopping $100. In 2007 the average size of a subprime mortgage was $180,000, according to Source Media, the publisher of *American Banker*, *National Mortgage News*, and other trade periodicals.

During the Great Depression, banks didn't exactly endear themselves to the American public by foreclosing on thousands upon thousands of homes—not to mention wide swaths of farmland. After the bank failures of the early 1930s, President Franklin Delano Roosevelt signed into law the Federal Deposit Insurance Corporation, which helped the banking industry financially but didn't totally alleviate its public image problem of being the bad guy that took away people's homes and personal property. Banks weren't to be trusted. In the years leading up to World War II, Beneficial thrived by paying close attention to a middle-class customer base that still viewed banks (and even savings and loans) with suspicion. Beneficial—which had little in the way of competition from other upstart consumer finance firms—beat the banks in the business of making personal loans by having its salespeople offer customers "personalized service, getting to know the names and ages of customers' children and taking other steps that made customers feel more comfortable than if they were applying for a loan at a bank." So said the *International Directory of Company Histories*.

By the mid-1960s when Cugno joined as a management trainee fresh out of the Army, Beneficial had 1,200 retail consumer finance offices in the United States and Canada. Its origination volume was less than $900 million, its average loan size just $370. It was peanuts in the scheme of things. Cugno knew it and Beneficial knew it. All that changed just about the time Cugno started his career in subprime (even though it wasn't called subprime then). "Beneficial," he said, "wanted to make larger loans and more money." And that meant one thing and one thing only: It needed to get into the business of lending money to its base—to Americans who were strapped for cash and who, for one reason or another, avoided their neighborhood bank or S&L. Beneficial needed to begin originating loans secured by residential real estate—a borrower's home.

And that's exactly what it did. But there were two very important distinctions between what Beneficial began doing in the 1960s and what banks and savings and loans (thrifts) had been doing for decades. Beneficial and its management trainees, Peter Cugno among them, originated second liens or "second deeds of trust." Oftentimes the first lien was held in a portfolio by a bank or thrift. Back then there was no active secondary market where banks and S&Ls could sell their mortgages. They held on to them. The other distinction? Second mortgages were made to Americans with, well, less than perfect credit. After all, if they had good credit they wouldn't need to take out another mortgage on top of their already existing first mortgage, or so the thinking went.

In the 1960s most banks and savings and loans didn't make second mortgages. It just wasn't done, because the business of making a second (but smaller) mortgage on top of a first was considered risky. And that's where the Cugnos and the Beneficial Finances of the world came in: risk. Beneficial, as any business would, expected to be compensated for its risk—in the form of charging the consumer a higher interest rate on these second deeds of trust. If the going rate for a first lien was 9 percent, Beneficial would charge a rate five or six percentage points higher for the second—14 percent, 15 percent. In short order, an industry was born. Beneficial Finance, a publicly traded company whose forte for 45 years had been making small $100 loans, was now making loans of $1,000 or more. The collateral: a house. (By the time Cugno parted ways with Beneficial, its average loan size was $17,000.)

When Beneficial made the decision to enter the residential loan arena, that meant different chores for Cugno and his fellow management trainees. Cugno admits that the term *management trainee* was just parlance for learning how to be a loan officer. "It took two years," he said. "Soup to nuts. You make the loan and you're the debt collector." As a loan officer, he did everything from taking the borrower's application to servicing the loan (making sure the payments were made on time) and then foreclosing on the mortgage if that's what needed to be done. Unlike subprime lenders of the modern era, Beneficial's loan officers were a bit more cautious as to who they lent money to.

When a loan application came in to Cugno's branch, the first thing he would do was pull a credit report from one of the three national credit reporting repositories—Experian, TransUnion, or TRW. "The cost of pulling a credit report was $1.25 per lookup, per customer," he said. "The principal issue for us was the credit history of the borrower." Other issues were how much the house was worth and how much equity there was. If a customer didn't have equity in the home, Beneficial wouldn't make a second mortgage on the property.

Lenders like Beneficial were comfortable only if the mortgage they held on a house had an acceptable loan-to-value (LTV) ratio. If a house in Orange County was worth $100,000 and the home buyer had a mortgage of $80,000 on it after having made a $20,000 down payment, that meant the mortgage had an LTV of 80 percent. (Key to the process was obtaining an independent appraisal from a company that had no ties to Beneficial.) In the second lien consumer finance niche that Beneficial trailblazed in the 1960s, the company would not extend credit to a homeowner if the first and second mortgages (combined) would have an LTV above 80 percent. Beneficial did not originate first mortgages for Californians and other consumers who were looking to buy a new or existing home. Its specialty was making second mortgages (second deeds of trust) to customers who had owned their house for years and had seen their abode rise in value—so much so that Beneficial and loan officers like Cugno would grant them another loan. "I made the loan, underwrote it, and Beneficial kept it in its portfolio," he said.

In short order, Cugno had graduated from making loans on cars and furniture to originating mortgages backed by homes. He did so because that's what Beneficial wanted to do—make larger loans, make more money. It also meant that repossessing or foreclosing on a house could be a trickier proposition for Beneficial and its management trainees. "If a home loan went bad, that meant I had to eat shit," he said. "That was my account, and I had to get all that fucking money back for my boss or it was my job." ("Hard money" lending was one term used to describe the type of loans Cugno was making.)

When a home went into foreclosure, he would play by the rules. If Beneficial was the only lender, that simplified matters. Beneficial would foreclose and gain title to the property. "But it could get ugly sometimes," Cugno admitted. The next step was to get the foreclosed-upon mortgage customer out of the house. "We'd gain title and the customer would still be in the house, not wanting to move. You would have to show up with the marshal, who would have his shotgun with him. He would be standing there with his bullhorn, in the street. He'd have his dogs," recalled Cugno.

"If the marshal had to, he'd kick in the door, guns drawn, dogs barking," Cugno said. "You might have the bald granny in there, the kids, the grandkids. We'd put all their stuff on the sidewalk. Then we'd board up the windows with nails and hammers." The final item on the to-do list? The Beneficial management trainee would then hire a company to put a chain-link fence around the house. "It was something trainees did all the time, all over the country," he said.

Foreclosing on his customers was not a task that Cugno relished, but he accepted it as part of the job. As he neared retirement, he began to regret the repos he had performed in his youth. "It makes me sad to think I did stuff like that," he said, "but I was young then and thought differently. But repos? That's what you do when you're young. It was part of the job."

If loan officers had to embarrass the customers into paying by visiting them at the office in front of their supervisor, that's what they did. "You would try to get the boss's money back any way you could," he said. Whatever Cugno and his fellow loan officers were doing seemed to work for Beneficial. By the time he left the company in 1979, the firm's losses on residential loans were a scant 1 percent. This was on $4 billion in residential second liens that the company held on its books. By the mid-1970s Beneficial was earning record profits of $100 million a year through all sorts of interest rate cycles.

These were the roots of a business that Wall Street, in the new century, was so hungry to get into.

★   ★   ★

Beneficial's success was lost somewhat on Angelo Mozilo. In the early to mid-1970s he and his partner, David Loeb, were busy managing a very young mortgage banking company called Countrywide Credit Industries, which went public on the New York Stock Exchange in 1969, raising $450,000. (They were hoping for $3 million.) The two men, who had met while working for a home lending company that Loeb owned part of, launched the first version of Countrywide on Loeb's kitchen table in his apartment at 99th Street and Park Avenue in Manhattan. To hear Mozilo tell it, the owners of Loeb's previous company had itchy fingers—they couldn't keep their hands off of the lender's escrow accounts, which legally belonged not to the company but to the customers who had borrowed money from it. "They wanted to play games with the cash accounts, so I quit," said Mozilo.

Six months after selling its stock to the public, Countrywide's shares were trading for less than $1 apiece. Mozilo and Loeb were struggling to keep the company afloat. "There were periods when we had no capital at all," remembered Mozilo. The housing market in the New York area wasn't exactly on fire. Countrywide, it might be said, was risk averse; when it made mortgages it wasn't taking any chances. Countrywide was not a bank or savings and loan. In its early years it was a nondepository (nonbank) mortgage company that lent money to consumers not by using deposits (it didn't have any) but borrowing money from larger money center banks. (These lines of credit to Countrywide were called "warehouse" loans.) Its lenders included Bank of America (a company Ken Lewis would later lead) and Chase Manhattan Bank of New York (which would later become JPMorgan Chase, Jamie Dimon's company).

Under Mozilo and Loeb, Countrywide originated only first lien mortgages that were insured by two government agencies: the Federal Housing Administration (FHA) and the Veterans Administration (VA). If a mortgage went into foreclosure, the government—not Countrywide—would take the hit. That may seem like an easy way to make a living, but it wasn't. As a nondepository mortgage banker, Countrywide had a ton of competition, namely 6,000 S&Ls that had a lock on the business of originating first mortgages. Savings and loans could either keep the mortgages on their books or sell them off to two government-chartered investing companies—the Federal Home Loan Mortgage Corporation, also known as Freddie Mac, or the Federal National Mortgage Association (Fannie Mae).

At the time (though this would change), Countrywide didn't have access (the ability) to sell its mortgages to Fannie Mae and Freddie Mac. To keep the company afloat, Loeb remained in New York while Mozilo left his wife and kids back east, at least for a little while, and moved to Los Angeles to open branches for Countrywide. There was one central reason for being in Southern California in the 1970s. The housing market was hot. "We have to be in California, because that's where 25 percent of the business is," Mozilo told Loeb.

While in California opening retail branches, Mozilo wasn't paying any attention to Beneficial. Mortgage banking companies that borrowed money from big banks to make residential loans to mom-and-pop Americans didn't fund second liens. This left the second deed of trust industry wide open for Beneficial to snatch up. Even though Mozilo wasn't paying any attention to Beneficial, that didn't mean other businesspeople weren't watching and following in its footsteps.

By the early 1970s, other consumer finance companies had sprung up to originate second liens. The term *subprime* still had not reared its head in the mortgage industry or the rest of the world at large. If a second lien lender like Beneficial was funding a mortgage, it was called "nonconforming," which meant it didn't conform to conventional "A" paper standards set by government-sponsored Fannie Mae and Freddie Mac. The term *subprime* did not become widely used until the early 1990s. And even then, the phrases *B&C lending* and *hard money lending* that preceded *subprime* were used to distinguish these second liens from "A" paper loans eligible for sale by lenders to Fannie and Freddie. As Cugno knew, "A" paper firms like Mozilo's Countrywide "did not want to know us. We were lepers, scum of the earth. That's how we were viewed."

Lepers or not, soon enough other consumer finance companies had begun to come out of the woodwork to originate second liens. Another phrase to describe what these consumer finance firms were doing was "home equity" lending, which meant a borrower could get a loan as long as he or she had spare cash (equity) locked up in the value of the house. In the early 1970s, on the East Coast a consumer finance company called The Money Store (TMS) was beginning to gain traction. Founded by New Jersey businessman Alan Turtletaub, The Money Store began to advertise heavily on television and radio. Its TV commercials, shown often during Yankees games and on the independent station WPIX, featured Yankee Hall of Famer Phil Rizzuto. Rizzuto, as every Yankee (and Met) fan knew, was also the team's play-by-play commentator who spent half the game regaling listeners about his glory days with the Bronx Bombers of the 1940s and 1950s and saying hello to his old neighbors on 188th Street.

As a shortstop, Rizzuto's nickname was the Scooter, and he was the kind of pitchman who gave viewers the warm fuzzies. You trusted the Scooter. After all, how could you not trust a Yankee all-star who played alongside giants of the game like Joe DiMaggio and Mickey

Mantle, a man who made sliding catches and diving throws? In a Money Store commercial that ran frequently in the 1970s, Rizzuto, hair graying, his eyes beaming through an oversized pair of aviator glasses, stood in front of a retail store window, The Money Store name emblazoned in big black letters, the Scooter telling viewers, "If you need money." An 800 number would be superimposed on the bottom of the screen. It worked.

The Money Store, under Alan Turtletaub and his oldest son, Marc, began to expand east to west, branching out in the hottest market of all: California. Mozilo and his partner Loeb weren't the only ones who realized that California accounted for one-quarter of the U.S. home loan market. The Money Store found enough success in the Golden State that Marc Turtletaub opened a second ("dual") headquarters in West Sacramento, just outside the state capital. It leased a 400,000-square-foot gold ziggurat-shaped office building on the Sacramento River. In time, the younger Turtletaub, like many lending CEOs, would become a generous donor to federally elected officials. He was also a friend of Bill Clinton and, like other FOBs (friends of Bill), got to sleep in the Lincoln bedroom.

The Money Store and Beneficial were far from being the only consumer finance companies with loan officers (management trainees) pounding the pavement in search of credit-impaired customers who needed to borrow against the value of their homes. As the 1980s wore on, companies like Associates First Capital Corporation of Dallas,[4] Household Finance of Illinois, and United Companies in Louisiana (among other firms) were making second lien home equity loans as well as personal loans, issuing credit cards, offering lease financing, and selling other products that were a little bit too scary for the banking industry.

Banks and S&Ls that offered deposit and checking accounts to the public were at somewhat of a competitive disadvantage to consumer finance companies, because they were subject to a usury law that capped how much interest they could charge for loans. The whole point of being a hard money lender was that you took on risk and

---

[4] After Beneficial, Associates was the second oldest consumer finance company in the United States. Associates would eventually be sold to Citigroup.

expected to be compensated for that risk, whether it was five, six, or seven points above the "A" paper loan rate. And there was yet one more advantage to being a consumer finance company: There were no pesky federal regulators in Washington to deal with.

Depending on where they were located, consumer finance companies also might be subject to usury laws, but Beneficial, Cugno's employer, found a way around them. "If you worked for Beneficial," said Cugno, "you got a 'personal property broker license,' which was exempt from state laws," which meant usury laws. Consumer finance companies and all their management trainees or loan officers would get state licenses. And there was yet one more advantage to being a consumer finance company, especially one that was making loans (second liens) secured by a house. Congress passed the Tax Reform Act of 1986—signed into law by President Reagan—which eliminated the ability of consumers to deduct interest payments on credit cards, auto loans, and all types of personal loans. Worried about a growing budget deficit, the politicians were hoping that by eliminating the tax deduction, this newfound money would feed the federal coffers.

At first, it looked like the law might spell trouble for Beneficial, Associates, The Money Store, and the rest of the consumer finance industry. If consumers could no longer deduct the interest payments on their cars, credit cards, or personal loans, they might stop spending, which ultimately might hurt the consumer finance industry. Instead, it shifted borrowing—to some degree—away from personal loans to an asset class where Americans could still deduct the interest payments: the home.

★   ★   ★

Before he began a second career as a stock analyst covering the world's largest mortgage lender (Countrywide) for Sandler O'Neill in the investment bank's West Coast office, Mike McMahon was a warehouse lending executive. As a warehouse official for First Interstate Bank in Los Angeles, McMahon's job was not to lend on warehouses (as the layman might think) but to find nondepository mortgage banking firms (like Countrywide) and extend large multimillion-dollar loans to them so these nonbanks could in turn make mortgage loans to Joe and

Mary Sixpack. (Remember, nonbanks or nondepositories didn't have savings accounts that they could pool together to make mortgages.)

McMahon's father was a Realtor, and from dinner table conversations he learned the basics of the housing finance system of the pre-1980s era. When someone bought a house they typically made a down payment of 20 percent. If they couldn't come up with a down payment that large, sometimes they'd borrow the money from a consumer finance company. Besides being in the business of making second liens (loans) for paying off credit cards, medical bills, and car loans (all these categories fell under the rubric of "debt consolidation"), some consumer finance companies were beginning to get involved in helping their customers buy homes. One of those firms was Aames Financial, a consumer finance company, managed and partly owned by a former actor named Gary Judis.

Judis, according to the *Los Angeles Business Journal*, was the son of a "business minded" mother and jeweler who taught him how to play piano. At age 20 he was part of a repertory company that included actors Richard Chamberlain, Sally Kellerman, and Leonard Nimoy. He had bit roles in the television series *Doctor Kildare* and a theatrical movie called *Zebra in the Kitchen*, which wasn't exactly Academy Award material. Judis did a short stint in the Air Force, and after his discharge he found himself driving his Thunderbird down Wilshire Boulevard from Beverly Hills to downtown Los Angeles. As he motored by the palm trees and wide streets, he sized up the buildings.

"I realized that all the big buildings were owned by banks, life insurance companies, and S&Ls," he later told the *Business Journal*. "They were the wealthiest corporate entities in the world." It appealed to Judis. Acting was fine, but even though he was handsome with the face of a cherub, he wasn't leading man material. He saw those tall buildings and said, "I had to be the captain of something."

He gave up acting and started a small mortgage firm called Capital Home Loan, which he later merged with an existing consumer finance company called Aames Financial. Those early years weren't always easy sledding. At one point Aames was on the verge of bankruptcy. Judis gathered up all his corporate papers and made it over to his attorney's office at Slate & Leoni on Wilshire Boulevard. According to one version of the story—which he told to a fellow mortgage banker—he was sitting in the waiting room, hoping to see his attorney, when an old lending client and friend came walking down the hallway. "What are you doing here?" asked the friend.

"I don't think I can make a go of it anymore," Judis said.

"How much do you need?" the man asked.

"About a million dollars," said Judis.

"Let's get out of here. I'll lend it to you." The man was Berry Gordy, the music producer and founder of Motown Records.

When Gordy was a struggling young music producer, Judis had lent money to him to buy a house in Los Angeles. (The mortgage industry has a long history of not exactly being color blind when it comes to making home loans to minorities, African-Americans in particular. Redlining, the practice of not making mortgages in certain zip codes, was a common practice up until the 1970s, and some say longer. When it came to making mortgages to minorities, Aames was among the more liberal.)

Under Judis' stewardship, Aames recovered. He was one the first mortgage executives to aggressively advertise on television and radio. (Countrywide was another.) Even though he had hung up his acting spurs, he used his talents—good looks and a booming voice—to star in Aames' commercials. He hired topflight agencies like Chiat/Day to produce the commercials. By the late 1980s, Aames was originating $80 million in loans, a very respectable volume. At this time subprime lending was still mostly second-lien based, representing less than 5 percent of all mortgages originated in the nation. But even though volumes were small, profits (and profit margins) were high.

With the S&L industry beginning to fail, Aames and other subprime firms were beginning to get more attention from large regional banks that were looking to expand their business lending units. Consumer finance companies fit the bill. Enter Mike McMahon of First Interstate. McMahon was an avid reader of the trade press. One article he saw sparked his interest in Aames: that Wall Street firms might soon start securitizing second deeds of trust (home equity loans) that were being originated by consumer finance companies. Being based in Los Angeles, McMahon was familiar with Aames and Judis from the commercials he saw on television. He started doing some research.

Large commercial banks, to some degree, were already lending money to consumer finance giants like Beneficial, Household, and

Associates, but the smaller firms such as Aames weren't as fortunate—at least not yet. Aames, McMahon discovered, was making second deeds of trust to credit-impaired consumers at 14 percent. These home equity loans averaged $15,000 or so. Where did Aames get the money to lend out to the consumer? From "doctors and dentists," McMahon discovered.

Rich professionals who were looking to put their extra cash to work were the backbone of the subprime industry in the 1960s, 1970s, and early 1980s. "Aames would make a loan at 14 percent, clip the coupon, keep 1 percent for themselves, and pass on the 13 percent to the end investor," said McMahon. (Presumably the principal amount of the loan would be repaid, so Aames was keeping 1 percent as its monthly fee. The rest went to the investor.) One day while visiting Aames' chief financial officer, McMahon saw him signing a stack of checks. He asked the CFO what he was doing. The reply: signing checks for Aames' investors, the doctors and dentists. Judis, who played Dr. Vincent on the TV show *Dr. Kildare*, was using doctors to fund Aames' operation. TV had taught him well: Doctors had tons of discretionary income and weren't exactly content to put their hard-earned money into low-yielding certificates of deposit.

McMahon saw an opportunity. He would replace all those individual checks that Aames had initially received from its investors (the doctors and dentists) with one big check from First Interstate. First Interstate had already been making warehouse loans to other mortgage banking firms. This would be one of its first subprime clients. But McMahon never got to make his pitch to Judis. Right before he was ready to pounce, the Los Angeles office of Prudential Securities, a midsize Wall Street firm, swooped in and offered Aames what was then considered a stunning amount of credit: a $90 million warehouse line. "I was only going to offer Judis $10 million," said McMahon. (Years later, telling the story, McMahon couldn't remember the executive's name at Prudential, just that "he was a chubby German guy who once took me to lunch at Spago.")

Prudential wasn't just lending money to Aames and making a profit on it. The Wall Street firm had cut a deal with Judis to buy all the second liens it was funding. Prudential began pooling the loans and securitizing them into mortgage bonds. A decade earlier, a bond trader from Salomon Brothers named Lewis Ranieri had pioneered the securitization of mortgages, but that product involved only the purchase of "A" credit quality loans, not subprime mortgages or second liens. Prudential saw dollar signs for two reasons: First, the loans Aames was originating carried much higher yields, five or six percentage points higher than "A" credit quality; and second, it could bypass Fannie Mae and its sibling company, Freddie Mac, entirely. Prudential took Ranieri's idea and ran with it—focusing on a whole new type of loan: subprime seconds.

If Aames had originated a $10,000 second lien, Prudential would offer "105" for it, which meant it paid five points (5 percent) or $10,500 for it. Aames would still retain a fee to service the loans it sold to Prudential. The Wall Street firm paid those five points because after figuring out all those years of interest payments, five points was a bargain. Subprime loans did not refinance very often for one very good reason: Lending money to people with bad credit was a risky proposition, and there wasn't much in the way of competition.

Aames was still a retail lender, which meant it only made loans directly to consumers through its storefront branches—most of which were in California. Thanks to the money Prudential was lending, it began to grow rapidly, increasing its branch network to other states. Its loan volume took off. Word began to spread about the Aames-Prudential alliance, and soon new mortgage banking firms were springing up to copy what the consumer finance companies like Aames, Associates First Capital Corporation, Beneficial, and the other old-line firms were doing.

Instead of using the money of private investors like dentists and doctors, these lenders could turn to Wall Street. Dan Phillips of Dallas, Texas, a former loan officer at Beneficial who went through the same management trainee program that Cugno cut his teeth on (he, too, started out as a repo man), came up with a slightly different wrinkle on the second lien subprime formula. He created a company called First Plus Financial that would lend borrowers up to 125 percent of the value of their homes.

To some lending professionals it sounded like an insane concept—lending up to 25 percent more than a house was worth? Phillips was hardly crazy, though. He didn't lend to homeowners with bad credit;

instead he lent to people with good credit, ones who had high FICO[5] scores (a credit rating that acts as a report card grading the borrower's ability to pay personal debts). First Plus didn't make first liens, only seconds, and charged 12 percent and 13 percent at a time when "A" paper lenders were charging about 8 percent. If a consumer had a house worth $100,000 with a $90,000 mortgage on it (meaning it had an LTV of 90 percent), Phillips was willing to lend another $35,000. However, the LTVs rarely got as high as 125 percent. "It was usually about 110 percent to 112 percent," said Barry Tennenholtz, who served as the company's treasurer. Asked about the high interest rates on the second liens, Tennenholtz said First Plus's customers didn't mind paying it. "It was still cheaper than using a credit card."

Thanks to Prudential opening the subprime door for Wall Street, First Plus found willing lenders in New York at the investment banking houses of Bear Stearns & Company and Deutsche Bank. Loan originations took off, and by 1996 First Plus was a publicly traded company. The lead underwriter on its initial public offering (IPO) was Bear Stearns. Phillips became close with a managing director at Bear Stearns named Warren Spector who worked on the fixed income side of the firm. Fixed income meant bonds. Even though Spector wasn't directly involved with the mortgages that First Plus was securitizing through Bear, he (according to Phillips) was directly involved in negotiating the lender's warehouse lines. "Any problems that I had with warehouse or ABS,[6] I would call Warren and he would take care of it," Phillips said.

Spector, who was rising rapidly in the hierarchy at Bear Stearns, never flew to Dallas to spend time with the First Plus management team. But Phillips frequently traveled to New York. The two men

---

[5] Developed by Fair Isaac & Company, a FICO score is a numerical grade based on a consumer's past history of paying bills. (The higher the score, the better.) Fair Isaac, which began developing scoring models in the late 1950s, has never fully disclosed what exactly goes into its computations, but the scores are based on credit reports developed by the three national credit reporting repositories: Experian, TransUnion, and Equifax. The use of FICO scores to judge a borrower's credit did not become a standard practice in the residential mortgage industry until the 1990s.

[6] ABS stands for asset-backed security, a bond backed by subprime loans. The term ABS is used to distinguish subprime bonds from conventional mortgage-backed securities (MBSs) backed by "A" paper credit quality loans bought by Fannie Mae and Freddie Mac.

golfed together and played poker—sometimes with Miami Dolphins quarterback Dan Marino, who was the lender's version of Phil Rizzuto except for being younger and better looking. (Marino also didn't dress in checked pants and striped suit jackets.)

It appeared for a while that First Plus was a cash machine, blowing away earnings expectations. It was borrowing money from Wall Street at 6 percent and lending it out at 12 percent. Its stock hit $62 a share in 1997 and then began to creep down in early 1998. During the first half of 1997, First Plus earned $68 million while originating just $2 billion in loans. By comparison, Norwest Mortgage of Minneapolis,[7] a bank-owned mortgage company, earned $69 million on $23 billion in originations. (During that same period Mozilo's Countrywide earned $66 million on loan originations of $18 billion.) It appeared that by originating just a fraction of what Norwest and Countrywide were doing, First Plus was a virtual money machine. (And there is nothing Wall Street likes more than being associated with money machines.) Phillips bragged to stock analysts that his company was so good that he wouldn't sell out, not even at $100 a share. All that changed in the summer of 1998.

One afternoon Phillips called Paul Muolo, a reporter he knew at *National Mortgage News*, and posed a blunt question: "What the hell is going on out there? The bond market has gone wacky." A few days later the answer came. Russia had devalued its currency, the ruble, placing a moratorium on all its international debt payments. This event, quickly dubbed "the Russian debt crisis," caused Wall Street firms— Bear Stearns, Deutsche Bank, Lehman Brothers, and others—to rethink all their bond sales activities, including their business loans to nonbank subprime lenders that were selling their mortgages into securities.

With Prudential's relationship with Aames paving the way, several Wall Street firms had rushed into the subprime market mid-decade, taking nondepository mortgage companies (old and new alike) public. Firms like Bear Stearns and Lehman Brothers managed the IPOs for them, bought and securitized their subprime mortgages, and lent them money through warehouse lines of credit. Companies that went public or

---

[7] Norwest later merged with Wells Fargo Bank, the resulting institution taking the Wells Fargo name.

raised new equity during this first subprime bull market included Aames, Amresco Residential Credit, Cityscape Financial, ContiMortgage (owned in part by a grain company), Delta Funding, IMC Mortgage, The Money Store, and a handful of others. Subprime, a tiny business that had started with repo men like Peter Cugno, was now big business.

But throughout 1998 the share prices of all these newly minted public firms began to crumble. It wasn't because the loans they were making to credit-impaired borrowers were going delinquent at an astronomical rate. That wasn't the case at all. Three short years earlier, stock analysts at the very same Wall Street firms that were financing these subprime upstarts were giving the new breed of subprime non-banks "buy" ratings.

In 1998 the term *hedge fund* was somewhat new. A hedge fund was a private investment company that didn't have to disclose anything to the public, because its shares were privately held. Hedge funds didn't issue bonds (usually). However, they invested in bonds. Many were managed by former investment bankers at the big boys: Salomon Brothers, Merrill Lynch, Lehman Brothers, and Bear Stearns. When nonbanks like The Money Store and First Plus securitized subprime loans in the mid-1990s, they would carve up the cash flow on the underlying mortgages into different bond classes or tranches. The senior or least risky bonds would be sold by Wall Street firms to their best clients, including the hedge funds. The "B" pieces often would be kept by the nonbank lender. On a $100 subprime bond, $90 million in senior bonds would be sold, with $10 million being kept by the lender. Gain-on-sale (GOS) accounting rules allowed the lender to book all the future cash flows on the risky bonds the lender retained. The reason they were risky? The lender kept the piece where all the interest payments were. If the loans wound up being prepaid earlier because consumers refinanced, the lender potentially could be in a world of hurt.

How much (in dollars) these future cash flows would be worth and how long the "B" piece would last were open to interpretation. And since the lender was allowed to book earnings on money it hadn't actually collected, it was one big guessing game—openly encouraged by the Wall Street underwriters and warehouse lenders that were financing its operations: firms like Bear Stearns.

As long as First Plus, The Money Store, and the others conservatively valued the "B" pieces they kept, everything would be fine—in theory. But that's not what happened. The assumptions made by First Plus (and many other publicly traded lenders) during this era were overly optimistic. The biggest mistake many of these firms made was that the subprime mortgages they had securitized would stick around for years longer than they had forecasted. Mike McMahon, the stock analyst, saw the problem coming. "They were way too optimistic on the life of the loans," he said. "Everyone was guessing with limited historical data." Historical data? As far as securitization went, subprime mortgages had no history. "Everyone was guessing," said McMahon. "These weren't Fannie, Freddie, and FHA loans where there's 40 years of past data to look at on how they'd perform."

When the Russian debt crisis began to unfold, hedge funds stopped buying the least risky bonds. That was trouble enough. With no hedge funds buying the good subprime bonds, that meant there would be no place to put subprime loans. (Banks and S&Ls weren't about to own them, at least not back then.) Complicating matters was the collapse of Long-Term Capital Management (LTCM), a huge private hedge fund operated by John Meriwether, a former star bond trader at Salomon Brothers. Under Meriwether, LTCM was speculating in international bond markets and had bet the wrong way on Russian debt—just as that nation was devaluing the ruble. LTCM's biggest problem: It had borrowed $125 billion from commercial banks and investment banking firms. It had lost so much money that the Federal Reserve Bank of New York stepped in and orchestrated a rescue plan for LTCM.[8]

Between the Russian debt crisis and the collapse of LTCM, some Wall Street firms grew skittish and began cutting back on how much money they would lend to subprime nonbanks. But something else was afoot: Many subprime loans funded the previous two years began prepaying (refinancing) much faster than The Money Store and First Plus ever anticipated. (And yes, delinquencies were starting to creep up a bit.) All the gain-on-sale (GOS) assumptions that had been made by

---

[8] The rescue plan was unprecedented. The Fed had never before stepped in to rescue a nondepository, but, worried about all the bank loans extended to Meriwether's firm, the Fed felt compelled to act.

these public firms turned out to be wrong—very wrong. The earnings they had booked through GOS never materialized. Short sellers (investors who make money by betting that a stock will go down in value) began targeting the subprime sector. In April 1998 First Plus's shares traded as high as $50. By early 1999 they would be worthless. In 10 months' time the share price for Cityscape Mortgage went from $32 to zero. Others followed in their tracks, slipping into bankruptcy as their assumptions about how long their mortgages would stick around evaporated.

This first subprime crisis got little attention in the general media, including the *New York Times* and the *Wall Street Journal*, which were busy covering the Russian debt crisis and meltdown of LTCM. When a hedge fund managed by a former Salomon Brothers star bond trader like Meriwether blows up, it's sexy news. (Meriwether was also a friend of mortgage-backed security inventor Lew Ranieri.) The subprime industry of the 1990s was still relatively small, accounting for just under 10 percent of all mortgages funded in the United States.

But investors in First Plus and two dozen other public subprime firms lost hundreds of millions of dollars. One after another, the nonbank subprime lenders fell like outdoor Christmas ornaments being swept off the tree in high winds. Subprime executives like Dan Phillips were stunned. An industry that looked highly profitable 12 months earlier had been just about wiped off the map. Phillips was finished in the business. He appealed to Warren Spector, his friend at Bear Stearns, for help, but to no avail. "Warren was there when you needed him," said Phillips, "but there was nothing he could do." First Plus filed for bankruptcy, and its assets were sold. The buyer: Angelo Mozilo's Countrywide.

Phillips and his competitors were sunk by their assumptions on prepayments—plus a new unwillingness on Wall Street to lend them money. (Again, subprime delinquencies were not all that bad during this era.) Historically, subprime loans never refinanced very quickly. The average 30-year "A" paper loan that Fannie Mae bought from lenders had an actual life span of seven to eight years. (Homeowners rarely keep the same loan for 30 years because of personal relocations, opportunities to refinance, and other such reasons.)

Subprime loans were supposed to last even longer, because, historically, homeowners with bad credit had a harder time getting a new loan. But all that changed with the rise of this new class of sub-prime firms in the 1990s. Beneficial Finance, Household Finance, and Associates First Capital—all the old-line consumer finance/subprime lenders—had for the most part stuck to a simple strategy of only originating loans on a retail basis through their branches. All three also held on to their loans. They didn't securitize them, so there were no fancy gain-on-sale rules to worry about.

First Plus, Cityscape, ContiMortgage, and others were not retail storefront lenders. They relied heavily on a whole new breed of freelance mortgage officers called loan brokers. Brokers were not full-time or even part-time employees of First Plus. Instead, they worked for themselves, bringing loan packages to Dan Phillips' doorstep. It was then up to Phillips and his crew to approve the mortgage. If the loan looked good, First Plus would pay the broker a fee, usually one or two points of the loan amount (the fees could vary).

The use of loan brokers had started in the 1980s, pioneered by, among other people, Angelo Mozilo of Countrywide. As the subprime industry began to spiral down in 1998–1999, Countrywide was just then sticking its toe in the water. It had avoided the sector entirely. When it began funding what were called "A–" loans (the highest quality of the subprime spectrum that includes A– to D), Countrywide didn't use brokers. It made subprime loans only through its retail loan branches. When executives at First Plus and elsewhere began seeing their loans refinance years earlier than expected, they pointed the finger in one direction: loan brokers. They discovered that because brokers worked on a commission basis only, they would take customers they had brought to The Money Store and refinance them six months later over at Cityscape Financial or ContiMortgage, or anywhere else for that matter. "The broker has a 'little black book' of customers," said Mike McMahon. "He makes a point on every loan. If he makes a point on every loan, he will refinance that customer again and again and again."

Chapter 3

The Death of the Bailey Building and Loan, the Rise of Millionaire Loan Brokers and Countrywide

To use loan brokers or not to use loan brokers—it was a Shakespearian dilemma that Angelo Mozilo was having with his partner David Loeb in the early 1980s. Born 14 years apart in New York City, the two men were business partners as well as close friends. During their early days running Countrywide out of Loeb's kitchen on Park Avenue in Manhattan, they'd go to the opera together with their families, including Loeb's parents. Mozilo once described his friend as "sort of introverted—he had an accounting degree," but when it came to discussing the company's business strategy with Mozilo he was anything but. The reason the two men were having this debate in the first place had its roots in a watershed event in the history of housing finance—and the American economy—called the savings and loan crisis.

In 1984 Countrywide Credit Industries was still a nondepository mortgage banking firm that relied on warehouse lines of credit from large commercial banks. (It was about 15 years away from buying a federally insured bank.) Like most mortgage bankers of that time, Mozilo's shop offered only two main loan products: government-insured Federal Housing Administration (FHA) and Veterans Administration (VA) loans, and conventional "A" paper mortgages that could be sold to Fannie Mae, the government-chartered mortgage investing giant headquartered in Washington, D.C.

Up until 1970 Fannie Mae could only purchase FHA/VA loans from lenders, but Congress—in a attempt to help a money-losing Fannie Mae—amended its government charter, allowing it to buy other types of loans, in particular good credit quality "A" loans as long as these mortgages had 20 percent down payments on them or private mortgage insurance that covered early losses. In the 1970s Countrywide was headquartered on Wilshire Boulevard in Pasadena, a suburb of Los Angeles. Right across the street from Mozilo's suite was the California regional office of Fannie Mae. As savings and loans (S&Ls) began to fail in record numbers, Countrywide found itself with more business than ever before, which pleased Mozilo and Loeb no end. Countrywide sold its non-government-insured "A" credit quality loans to Fannie Mae and then later on to Freddie Mac as well.[1]

Something, though, had to be done about all the dead S&Ls that were piling up. In 1982 President Ronald Reagan stepped through the French doors of the White House Oval Office into the sunlight of an autumn morning, strolled to the podium, made a short speech, and signed a bill called the Garn–St Germain Depository Institutions Act of 1982. It was the second year of Reagan's presidency. The former California governor told an audience of S&L executives, bankers,

---

[1] Freddie Mac was chartered by Congress in 1970 to buy mortgages from S&Ls exclusively. Fannie Mae was originally set up to purchase only government-insured—Federal Housing Administration and Veterans Administration—mortgages. Eventually nonbank mortgage lenders sued to gain access to Freddie Mac and won. In time nonbanks like Countrywide began selling their conventional mortgages to both these government-chartered enterprises.

members of Congress, staffers, and journalists that the bill—which bore the names of Republican Senator Jake Garn of Utah and Democratic Congressman Fernand St Germain of Rhode Island—would cut S&Ls loose from the girdle of old-fashioned regulation. One of Reagan's campaign platforms was deregulation, to get government off the backs of businesses to help the struggling economy create new jobs. When Reagan took office in 1981, mortgage rates were in nosebleed territory: 14 percent. (And this was for home buyers with good credit.) A year later rates would be even higher—16 percent.

For well over 50 years S&Ls—which in some quarters were called building and loans (B&Ls)—financed most homes purchased by Americans. For decades the system worked flawlessly. And because it worked so flawlessly, it appeared that Loeb and Mozilo's Countrywide was destined to be a bit player. The American lifestyle was centered around the single-family home, funded by S&Ls that made 30-year fixed-rate loans. S&Ls pooled together the deposits of their customers and lent the money out in the form of mortgages. Nonbank mortgage firms like Mozilo's Countrywide were hemmed in, more or less, to making FHA/VA mortgages while the S&Ls dominated the market for loans to Americans with good credit. At best, FHA/VA represented 15 percent to 20 percent of the entire mortgage business, relegating Countrywide and other nonbank mortgage firms to second-class citizen status. There Mozilo and Loeb lived at the back of the bus, eking out a decent living in government-backed loans.[2]

Besides being a small part of the housing finance business, FHA/VA mortgages always had higher delinquencies than the "A" paper first mortgages that S&Ls made. But the delinquencies on FHA/VA loans didn't keep mortgage executives like Mozilo up at night for one very good reason—they were insured by the government. If a mortgage went south, Uncle Sam would step in and make the mortgage firm that serviced these loans whole again. It was a nice little business— but it was a *little* business. In the 1990s when FHA and VA delinquencies began to soar into the stratosphere, mortgage executives jokingly

---

[2] Again, this second-class citizen status ended in 1970 when Fannie Mae was allowed to buy non-government-insured "A" paper loans.

began to refer to FHA/VA as "the government's subprime program." Subprime loans, historically, went bad at a higher rate than "A" paper loans and at about the same rate as FHA/VA loans.

It's a cliché, but owning a home became sacred like Mom, Chevrolets, and apple pie. It's hard to pin down exactly when the phrase "the American dream of home ownership" became part of the political and housing lexicon, but by the 1980s any mortgage executives trying to curry favor with Congress would always use the phrase when addressing their business concerns, which might include too much regulation for them (so they believed), or too little regulation of their competitors. It helped if those executives' companies donated money to the campaigns of members of Congress and senators who sat on committees with oversight authority over their business. Donations gave them access, an ability to be heard in Congress. Lobbying was a cost of doing business, and any lender that didn't lobby in Washington probably didn't do as well as those that did.

Industry trade groups comprised of companies and their executives who made their living off of either housing or mortgages created an informal political alliance to beat down any type of legislation that might harm their bottom line (whether or not it was good for consumers). The alliance included, first and foremost, the National Association of Home Builders (whose members made their livings from home building); the National Association of Realtors (new and existing home sales); Fannie Mae and Freddie Mac (two government-chartered mortgage investing giants that purchased mortgages from mortgage bankers, S&Ls, and commercial banks); and the Mortgage Bankers Association. All of these trade groups had permanent management staffs but each year elected an annual president who became the face of that industry, traveling the nation making rah-rah speeches, meeting politicians, and getting their photographs in the newspaper. Being the annual president of a housing or mortgage trade group meant being the chief public relations (PR) person for spreading the good news about the American dream of home ownership.

Depending on the issue, two other trade groups might join this alliance: the National Association of Mortgage Brokers (catering to nonbank, nonfunding intermediaries) and the National Home Equity Mortgage Association, which was a more PR-friendly way of saying, "We represent subprime lenders." The message of these groups—all based in the nation's capital—was clear and went something like this: "Don't pass any bills that will hurt our bottom line and ability to grow. If you hurt us you will hurt the home buyer. You don't want to do that. Don't mess with housing and mortgages. It's like spitting on your mother or that Chevrolet sitting in the driveway." If Congress and the White House didn't go along, they'd wind up looking like communists. What was there not to like? As long as the political donations kept flowing into their campaigns, it seemed like a perfect symbiotic relationship between the private sector (housing and mortgages) and the elected officials who governed them.

The building and loan as an institution was immortalized in the Frank Capra classic *It's a Wonderful Life*. Jimmy Stewart starred as George Bailey, the head of a neighborhood thrift called the Bailey Building and Loan. When panic set in during the Great Depression and depositors commenced a run on the Bailey B&L, George tried to calm the fears of his Bedford Falls, New York, customers, explaining that he didn't have all of their money right there in the branch—their deposits were invested in each other's homes.[3] As the Depression lingered, Congress in 1934 established the Federal Savings and Loan Insurance Corporation,[4] which insured deposits up to $5,000—an enormous sum of money in those days. After the Depression ended, the S&L industry enjoyed what might be called its golden days of being a so-called 3-6-3 business: Thrifts paid 3 percent for deposits, lent it out in the form of 6 percent 30-year loans, and drove to the golf course at 3:00 in the afternoon for a quick game of 18 holes and a cocktail afterward.

The S&L industry—12,000 institutions strong in 1920—hit the skids in the 1970s for two reasons: By law S&Ls were capped at paying just 5.5 percent for deposits, and inflation by 1979 was running at 13.3 percent per year. Because they could pay only that much to

---

[3] Under the original building and loan model, all those tiny deposit accounts would be pooled. Once a critical mass was achieved, the cash was used to finance the construction of a house. When the home's construction was completed, the builder would be paid off and the end loan wound up at the B&L. Homes were built one at a time, not in huge tracts.

[4] The FSLIC, as it was known, eventually went bankrupt during the S&L crisis, its obligations taken over by the Federal Deposit Insurance Corporation (FDIC), the deposit insurer for commercial and community banks.

their depositors, those once-loyal customers turned in their passbook accounts, trading them for money market accounts offered by investment banking/brokerage firms like Merrill Lynch. Over a few years $250 billion in deposits had walked out the doors of the nation's S&Ls. By 1980, 85 percent of savings and loans were losing money. Factor in the higher mortgage rates of the late Carter/early Reagan years, and it was an ugly stew.

And that's not all. S&Ls held on to many of the mortgages they originated. This was a time when Americans didn't move and refinance their loans so often. Two years before the Garn–St Germain Act, Congress passed a law freeing S&Ls from having to cap their deposits and money market accounts at 5.5 percent. The removal of the rate cap solved one problem but created another: All those little old ladies, waving their passbook accounts, returned to their neighborhood Bailey Building and Loan, depositing their savings but at a new, much higher interest rate. The S&L executives were happy because they were getting their lost deposits back, which they could presumably lend out at more than they were paying the little old ladies. The difference between the interest rate that the S&L was paying each year for deposits and receiving from its mortgages was its gross profit before expenses were deducted.

In a perfect world, if an S&L was paying 7 percent for its deposits but lending all that money out at 10 percent, it was making 3 percent or 300 basis points. (One percent equals 100 basis points.) But in the S&L industry nothing was perfect. Because S&Ls held on to most of their mortgages, keeping them in their portfolios, they were now lending money out at, say, 14 percent, but they had existing mortgages that they had funded years earlier yielding 6 percent or less. This created a huge mismatch between their cost of funds and existing mortgages, making an already precarious situation all the more treacherous. When Reagan signed the Garn–St Germain[5] bill, he said the legislation would create more housing, more jobs, and growth for the economy. "All in all," he proclaimed, "I think we've hit the jackpot."

---

[5] Garn was chairman of the Senate Banking Committee, St Germain his counterpart on the House Banking Committee. Both received large political donations from industry executives and trade groups for which they had oversight responsibility.

The bill, which applied only to S&Ls that were incorporated using a federal charter, allowed these insured depositories to invest 40 percent of their assets in nonresidential real estate. This was a huge change for an industry that had done one thing and one thing only for 150 years—have all of its deposits in home mortgages. It also allowed S&Ls to have just one shareholder,[6] and in a move that attracted real estate developers of all stripes, it permitted an entrepreneur to purchase an S&L and capitalize it using noncash assets such as land. The developers noticed. They began buying thrifts or starting them from scratch (de novo). And there was one last ingredient that led to the S&L mess: State legislatures saw their power (and donations from real estate and financial service businesses) begin to decline because the federal S&L charter had been liberalized. (Why give money to state pols when the power rested with the feds?) Some states decided to best the Garn–St Germain Act by offering owners of state-chartered S&Ls even greater investment powers. That's where California assemblyman Pat Nolan came in.

Two things were golden in California: its hills and its housing market, a market that was financed by S&Ls. A Republican from Glendale, Nolan[7] was an associate of a number of S&L executives. He sponsored the Nolan Act, which became state law in early 1983, a few months after Reagan signed the bipartisan Garn–St Germain bill. The Nolan Act made Garn–St Germain look conservative by comparison. To motivate entrepreneurs to open new (or buy existing) California-chartered S&Ls, the law allowed virtually anyone to own a thrift, attract as many deposits as they could, and invest 100 percent of those deposits not just in real estate (commercial or residential) but in an asset class called "direct investments." What was a direct investment? Answer: anything you wanted. Really.

The Nolan Act ignited a rush by real estate developers to open new S&Ls—from south of San Diego up north to small nook-and-cranny

---

[6] Previously, the rule mandated that there be a minimum of 400 shareholders with no one owning more than 25 percent.

[7] In 1988 Nolan, who had become California Assembly minority leader, resigned his position amid reports that he and other state legislators had been targeted by an FBI sting operation investigating influence peddling and political corruption. Nolan denied all wrongdoing.

towns scattered around Santa Rosa in the Napa Valley. The only thing the state required—besides a valid application—was that the person or persons owning the new thrift have a minimum net worth of $2 million (and land counted). "Can you imagine?" later remarked Edwin Gray, chairman of the Federal Home Loan Bank Board (FHLBB), the nation's federal S&L regulator. "Any business, any entrepreneur [in California] could get a charter and could run whatever operation he wanted on the credit of the U.S. government. Imagine that. You could choose any business you wanted to be in. Just incredible."

Gray, a former PR man for Reagan when he was governor of California, was stuck with the job of overseeing a whole new breed of S&L operator.[8] He had one major disadvantage—a lack of bank examiners. The philosophy of the Reagan administration was that deregulation meant fewer regulators and examiners, so their num- bers were cut. At the same time, many states trimmed their examina- tion staffs as well. This new generation of S&L operator—particularly in California—had nothing in common with George Bailey. Few of them would make home mortgage lending their mission. After Garn– St Germain and the Nolan Act, it wasn't long before a whole new round of S&L failures rippled across the United States like a trail of fallen dominoes. The autopsy of each looked much the same as the others: A developer buys or starts a savings and loan and begins financ- ing commercial projects that he has a stake in, usually paying himself huge development fees and not worrying much about the financial viability of the deal.

In time, the S&L crisis—thanks to federal and then state dereg- ulation—would cost the American taxpayers $150 billion, and that didn't even include the interest costs on the government borrowing that much money. Wall Street had a role in the crisis as well. When deregulation came along, Merrill Lynch saw a business opportu- nity and jumped on it. S&Ls accepted two types of deposits, retail accounts from their neighborhood customers (the little old ladies

---

[8] Gray inherited the job in May 1983 from Richard Pratt, a college professor from Utah and a crony of Senator Garn's. After leaving the FHLBB, Pratt would become a top executive at Merrill Lynch. His tasks included, among other things, convincing S&Ls to securitize residential mortgages through Merrill.

with their passbook accounts) and so-called brokered deposits, where a large investment banking house would bundle together accounts of \$100,000[9] and shop this money nationwide to fast growing S&Ls that were in search of funds they could use to finance their commercial real estate projects. Merrill was among the largest of all deposit brokers working the phones on Wall Street. When the FHLBB's Gray tried to rein in rogue S&L operators he felt were abusing deregulation, he clashed repeatedly with Reagan's Treasury secretary, Donald Regan. Who was Don Regan? Answer: the former head of Merrill Lynch. One thing he had claimed credit for was creating a market for brokered deposits.

Charles Keating was a big fan of brokered deposits. Not only would Keating's Lincoln Savings use federally insured (brokered) deposits to finance luxury hotels and housing developments in the scrub-brush desert of outer Phoenix at the foot of Camelback Mountain, but he would put these developments (direct investments under the Nolan Act) on the books of the S&L, assigning a value multiple times their true worth. (Lincoln Savings was based in Southern California, ACC in Phoenix where Keating lived.) In the late 1980s Keating and Lincoln became the public face of the S&L crisis, thanks partly to large donations the press-shy Arizonan gave to five U.S. senators, including Republican John McCain. Prodded by Keating, the five senators lobbied and pressured the FHLBB's Gray and his senior examiners in California to go easy on Keating, portraying the developer/S&L operator as a misunderstood businessman who had saved a failing savings and loan, Lincoln.[10] Gray's examiners informed the five senators that Keating, in their belief, was a crook who was about to become the subject of a criminal investigation by the Federal Bureau of Investigation for accounting fraud and booking profits that weren't there. In April 1989 federal examiners working for the Federal Savings and Loan Insurance Corporation seized control of the S&L. Lincoln's failure alone would cost the government \$4 billion. A year later Keating was

---

[9] In 1980, Congress, in a late-night session, increased the federal insurance on deposits to \$100,000 from \$40,000.

[10] By the time Keating took control of Lincoln Savings in 1984, the S&L, which had been losing money, was profitable again.

convicted on state charges of defrauding Lincoln's customers by trying
to pass off retail-sized junk bonds as insured deposits.

★   ★   ★

If anyone in the mortgage industry thought Mozilo and Loeb weren't
watching the meltdown of the S&L industry, wondering what it meant
for Countrywide, they were mistaken. Mozilo was an avid reader of the
trade press and the *Wall Street Journal*, and was an FNN junkie. (FNN,
available only on cable TV, stood for Financial News Network. In 1991
NBC bought FNN, renaming it CNBC and later branding the station
"America's Business Network." Maria Bartiromo, a favorite anchor of
Mozilo's, joined CNBC in 1993.) Mozilo would rise at four in the morning, drive to his office in Pasadena, don his sweats, and work out while
watching FNN. Then he hit the phones, selling loans, deciding where to
open Countrywide's next office, or figuring out how to get more capital
into his company. He was aggressive in his pursuits, or as Loeb once said,
Mozilo "was a performer in a business where there are few performers."

In the mid-1980s Mozilo and Countrywide were no longer being
entirely ignored by the titans on Wall Street. The chief reason had to do
with the creation of a new financial instrument called the mortgage-
backed security (MBS). At Salomon Brothers, Lew Ranieri, who had
worked his way up from the mailroom to the trading desk, had pioneered
a security, a bond that was backed by the monthly payments homeowners made on their residences. Ranieri, a product of the rough-and-tumble
neighborhood of Brownsville in Brooklyn, took those cash flows and had
Salomon carve them up into (generally) four tranches. Each tranche was
a slice of the larger bond and carried a different yield and risk. Ranieri
felt comfortable with the collateral for these bonds because the loans (the
collateral) backing them were conventional loans eligible for purchase by
Fannie Mae and Freddie Mac. "These types of loans had a 30-, 40-, 50-
year history," he would say. "You could figure out how they would perform based on decades of history." In other words, conventional home
mortgages made to consumers with good credit were not risky assets.

During the early days of the MBS revolution (1980 to 1983)
Salomon Brothers, along with another pioneer in MBSs, First Boston,
had the mortgage securities market to itself. Larry Fink, the head

of mortgage trading at First Boston, took Ranieri's MBS idea and perfected it by creating an instrument that was more predictable—the collateralized mortgage obligation (CMO)—by setting up a trust, a legal entity that guaranteed payments to bondholders. (The original MBS that Salomon came up with didn't have this.) It wasn't long before other Wall Street houses noticed what Ranieri and Fink were up to, and began competing against them. All this played into Mozilo and Loeb's fortunes. Investment bankers, seeing that S&Ls were falling into a black hole, began paying more attention to nondepository mortgage banking firms like Countrywide. Why? Because they—not the S&Ls—were now the ones dominating the business of originating home mortgages to the nation's consumers.

Mozilo, that chip firmly planted on his shoulder, left the task of listening to Wall Street's pitches to Loeb. "He would go out to ball games with them," said Mozilo. "He loved that stuff. He was our trader." While Mozilo spent his time in California finding ways to originate more loans than his competitors, Loeb went out to dinner with investment bankers in New York. "At this point the Street was fighting over them," said one Countrywide executive. "Chuck Ramsey from Bear Stearns had this limo with horns on the grill. In his suit jacket he'd have a couple of beers. He'd pick up David and they'd go out to the best restaurants in town."

When Countrywide went public in 1969 it had hoped to raise $3 million in seed money, but, as Mozilo told it, the initial public offering (IPO) market "hit a hole." Countrywide raised just $450,000. Until S&Ls started failing en masse, it didn't have any luck with the Merrill Lynches of the world. In 1981 (the year before S&L deregulation) Countrywide raised $3 million more. In 1983, its prospects looking up, Bear Stearns came in and sold $11 million in convertible preferred stock for Countrywide. It was good to be a nonbank mortgage lender that didn't take deposits like the Bailey Building and Loan did.

And then there were those failing S&Ls. When a savings and loan collapsed, all its employees, including the mortgage loan officers, lost their jobs. With dozens of S&Ls closing every week, loan officers steeped in the knowledge of how to correctly originate and underwrite a residential mortgage began walking the streets, looking for work. "They had no place to go," said Mozilo. "I saw an opportunity."

Loan officers working in Countrywide's retail branches had their marching orders: produce or consider a career elsewhere. (It was part of Countrywide's corporate culture to be "AC," always closing.) It was stressed to them from on high (Mozilo) that they should milk leads from Realtors to find customers. Realtors were at the point of sale where the rubber met the road, where the customer made the decision to sign a contract to buy a house. It was something Mozilo had spotted early on in his career after he had graduated from messenger boy darting around Manhattan to a young loan officer: At the Realtor's office was where the chain reaction of housing began. After a husband and wife signed a sales contract to buy a house, the man and woman would turn to each other and say, "Now we need to get a loan."

"I had Realtors as customers already," Mozilo said. If he could use independent, newly laid off loan officers who had years, in some cases decades, of experience to be freelancers for Countrywide, he could really ramp up the company's origination volume. "In the late 1980s the S&Ls were letting some terrific people go," said Mozilo. He told Loeb, "They have ties to Realtors, too. There is a whole new business developing out there, and we need to be in it. But we don't have a mechanism for it."

Loeb didn't like the idea one bit. He had grave concerns about using these independent loan agents and was worried that they would wind up competing against Countrywide's retail branches. "Don't do it," he warned Mozilo. The publicly traded Countrywide was now, after more than a decade, beginning to be taken seriously by Wall Street. Independent loan agents working for Countrywide? The idea was to pay these agents, these loan brokers, one point if they brought Countrywide a loan it could fund. On a $100,000 loan (remember that this is 1980s prices in California) that would be a $1,000 commission.

When Mozilo figured how much it cost the company to maintain a retail branch, pay the staff (including its own loan officers), pay their health and insurance benefits, and pay utilities, and factored in the cost of advertising and marketing to the public, giving the broker a point was a pretty good deal for Countrywide. If the independent loan broker (a former loan officer for a now-defunct S&L) didn't produce, then he (it was mostly a male-dominated field then) didn't get paid. It would cost Countrywide nothing. Mozilo liked that equation. Loeb feared that because the broker had "no skin the game" (the broker could not be forced to buy back a bad loan he facilitated), there could be major loan quality issues.

Loeb stood firm against using brokers. "They're crooks," he told his younger friend. But Mozilo insisted that Countrywide open up a wholesale division using loan brokers to sell its mortgage products. Loeb had one last thought on brokers, telling Mozilo: "I think it's going to be a big mistake."

★ ★ ★

The movement away from retail loan officers working as salaried employees for S&Ls, community banks, and mortgage bankers to an industry dominated—beginning in the 1990s—by loan brokers didn't start with the implosion of the savings and loan industry. But the demise of neighborhood thrifts ignited what's called "the broker move-ment"—the rise of independent sales agents working as commission-only freelancers for Countrywide, Chase Home Finance, Wells Fargo, Washington Mutual, and dozens of other mortgage giants. Depending on whose version of history you subscribe to, loan brokers were in existence as far back as the 1940s. David Gold, a loan broker from Florida, remembered that his father started his own brokerage firm in Fort Lauderdale in 1955. Five years later Florida launched one of the first trade organizations to represent loan brokers. Where did these Florida brokers come from? They used to work at S&Ls, com-munity banks, or even at consumer finance companies like Beneficial, Household Finance, TransAmerica, and others. Just how much experi-ence did a loan officer or broker need in this era? In Peter Cugno's opinion, the basic requirements were these: "You had to be a high school graduate. You had to be clever, mature, and have an upbeat personality."

In the 1970s and early 1980s as more Americans graduated from college, the requirements to become a loan officer increased to include not only a college degree but preferably a major in business admin-istration or finance. Newbies, as they were sometimes called, would start on smaller-balance mortgages or assist an experienced loan officer before they could go it alone. It was a craft that had to be learned, an apprenticeship, like being a bricklayer, plumber, or electrician. Angelo Mozilo did not invent loan brokers. He just liked them, or at least what they could do for him: help Countrywide take its loan originations to a whole new level. "The loans were coming to us," said Mozilo. In his mind you never turned down something that good. It was business. Countrywide's retail office could sort through the loan applications, underwrite some, and reject the ones that didn't meet its standards.

Loan brokers were around prior to the S&L carnage days, but were hardly a force in the business. They were a speck in the eye of a much larger industry. Few mortgage professionals noticed them, because their ranks were so small. But lending executives who recalled the early days of brokers remembered one distinct thing about them: Many brokers (again, pre-S&L) did not specialize in easy "A" credit quality mortgages that could be safely originated and then placed on the books of an S&L. They originated hard-to-place loans, ones that had something wrong with them, making them ineligible for sale to Fannie Mae and Freddie Mac. Loan brokers specialized in subprime mortgages where they could earn two or three points per deal.

In 1984 Countrywide officially launched its wholesale division where it would originate mortgages brought to the company by brokers. It was what Mozilo called a "slow build," but he was determined to see it through. Even though Loeb had lost the battle, Mozilo recognized his friend's concerns and agreed to proceed cautiously in the new venture. As S&Ls continued to fail, more former loan officers went into business for themselves, working out of their homes. A movement was born. Wholesale lending began to pick up at Countrywide. Mozilo instituted an incentive program for brokers. "We offered them volume discounts," he said.

The loans that brokers brought to Mozilo's shop were either eligible for sale to Fannie Mae or Freddie Mac or insured by the FHA or VA. Countrywide was still a nonbank, relying on warehouse lines of credit. As soon as it funded a loan it would pledge the mortgage into a security, which would be sold through Wall Street. "We turned those loans over as quickly as possible," said Mozilo. Countrywide didn't have a balance sheet to keep loans on. The only thing it retained was the servicing rights. On a 7.25 percent loan, for example, Countrywide would keep 0.25 percent (25 basis points) of that yield and pass the rest of the monthly payment on to whichever party owned the loan or end bond.

As Countrywide began to increase its reliance on brokers, other companies that originated mortgages began to take notice. Some had even started using brokers before Mozilo, blazing the trail to some degree. One of those early innovators was the husband-and-wife team of Russell and Rebecca Jedinak of Huntington Beach, 40 miles down the California coast from Los Angeles. The Jedinaks were part of the rush of real estate developers who had heard about the Nolan Act and realized that owning an S&L was like a gift from heaven. They named their thrift Guardian Savings and Loan.

Russ and Becky, as they were known throughout the California lending community, worked different ends of the business. Russ was the developer who found plots of land to build on, the idea man who cut the deals, while Becky, a Realtor by training, handled the book-keeping on the back end. Greg Bowcott, who did business with them, described the pair like this: "Russ was classic frat boy: teeth, grins, and handshakes. After that you ended up talking to Becky, who was very attractive but with all the warmth of a porcupine."

Prior to getting into real estate, Russ was a pharmaceutical sales-man for American Home Products, the maker of Robitussin and Advil. By the time he turned 23 he was already a national sales manager. Jude Lopez, who worked for them, described Russ as "one of the most char-ismatic men I'd ever met." Russ ran marathons and was a pilot with a four-seater Citation. "Flying was his passion," said Lopez. "If we had a meeting in San Diego we'd take the jet."

By the time Russ met Becky (they were neighbors) he was on wife number four. For a while he lived in the Bahamas and owned a yacht that he sailed through the Panama Canal on extended vacations. As one friend put it: "Becky came into the picture as his secretary [book-keeper] and was promoted to wife and partner. He was tall and hand-some, and she didn't trust him any farther than she could throw him. They even shared the same office. If she saw a woman looking at him, she'd get someone to fire her."

Before Russ and Becky started Guardian Savings and Loan, he made a reputation for himself around Huntington Beach building four-plexes with a partner named Frank Mola. In his real estate office he had an old phone booth with a Superman outfit hanging in it. At their home there was a life-size portrait of Russ in knight's armor. It was the first thing visitors saw when they walked into the home.

Using Guardian's money (thanks again to the Nolan Act), the Jedinaks bought a 15-story office building on Beach Boulevard in Huntington Beach. The price: $55 million. (The building was—and still is—the only high-rise building on the boulevard and in most of Huntington Beach.) According to Rich Tachine, who worked as a broker for Guardian, the building was more than half empty. Lacking tenants, Russ and Becky decided to populate its floors with Guardian employees. They also were allowed to contribute the building's value (the $55 million the S&L had paid) to Guardian's capital. Deregulation could be a wonderful thing.

Instead of making "A" paper loans that could be sold to the government-chartered Fannie Mae and Freddie Mac, Russ and Becky jumped right into what they called "hard money" lending—making mortgages to consumers who were hard up for money. The Jedinaks focused solely on the value of the underlying house or the equity in the property. Guardian began using brokers, but limited the loan-to-value (LTV) ratios to 65 percent, 70 percent tops. "Russ had no problem taking back the property," said Tachine. "He was quite okay with that."

And Becky? She ran the collection effort, which included pouncing on borrowers the moment they were late. As a practice, Guardian, under Becky's watch, would send out a "notice of default" letter to the borrower after the mortgage became 30 days or more late—a practice unheard of in the subprime world of the 2000s. "You have to be aggressive—put the hammer down early," said Jude Lopez, who held the title of vice president at Guardian. "In this kind of business [subprime], if you get three months behind it's difficult to catch up."

One broker who worked with Guardian said of Becky Jedinak, "She was beautiful and she was tough." Employees who worked at the S&L knew her as a woman who watched Russ's money like a hawk. "The ex-wives burned through a lot of his money," said a business associate. She told employees to be careful how they spent the S&L's cash.

"One time she told me I was to make only half a pot of coffee to save money," said an employee who worked for the Jedinaks at one of their companies. Once he traveled with the couple to New York on business. At dinner Becky made him pay for his own beer and put him up in a low-rent hotel where he heard the elevator cables banging all night. One of her favorite sayings was "I worry about the pennies, and the dollars take care of themselves."

Guardian was not only the first S&L to aggressively move into subprime (hard money), but it was doing so with an army of unregulated loan brokers. As the S&L crisis worsened, state regulators from the California Department of Savings and Loans (CDS&L) began to take a close look at its operation. Examiners weren't so concerned about the subprime end of it, but the office building that Russ and Becky had contributed to the S&L as capital set off some alarm bells. Even though they had paid $55 million, state regulators valued the property, at best, at $38 million. Examiners from CDS&L "hated Russ and Becky for their arrogance and style," said a former employee.

On Christmas Eve 1991, regulators from the Federal Home Loan Bank of San Francisco messengered to the Jedinaks' home the legal documents removing them from Guardian's management.[11] Russ and Becky must've seen it coming to some degree. Eight months later Tachine ran into them in the fall at the annual convention of the Mortgage Bankers Association, which was being held in San Francisco. He was on his way to a cocktail party at the St. Francis Hotel in downtown. He stepped into the elevator and found himself face-to-face with the couple. "Russ was wearing a thousand-dollar suit, and on his breast pocket was one of those plastic name tags," said Tachine. "He had crossed out the words 'Guardian Savings' and written 'Quality Mortgage' in pencil." Becky was at his side, wearing a blue dress.

The Jedinaks were back in business, this time in nearby Irvine, a few miles to the south. Russ and Becky took their army of loan brokers from Guardian Savings and shifted them over to Quality Mortgage. Tachine and other brokers gladly followed. Guardian was now a ward of the government, but Quality Mortgage picked up where it left off, sans the office building on Beach Boulevard. An executive who

---

[11] Not only did the FHLB remove the Jedinaks from Guardian, but in 1995 the two signed a government consent order banning them from the S&L industry and agreeing to pay $8.5 million in damages in regard to Guardian's failure.

worked for Quality Mortgage noted that the Jedinaks didn't own Quality Mortgage outright, but through a holding company, "because of the Guardian thing," he said. (The regulators were after their money, but the two reportedly had pumped at least $2 million into Quality Mortgage to get it off the ground.) One manager later revealed to a reporter at the *Orange County Register* how a top executive at Quality Mortgage helped keep loan delinquencies low. "He backed payments off of current accounts at month's end, applying the money to delin-quent accounts. After the first of the month he would reverse the trans-actions." He added, "Russ and Becky always felt actions like that were signs of initiative and loyalty."

The Jedinaks were not alone in funding Quality Mortgage's start-up. One of their backers was the Wall Street firm of Donaldson, Lufkin & Jenrette.[12] DLJ provided Quality Mortgage with warehouse lines of credit and securitized most of its loans, according to Laura Pephens, an accountant who once did work for the Jedinaks. "DLJ was their pri-mary partner," said Pephens. After a few years, with so many new firms springing up and copying their model of using brokers to fund sub-prime loans, the couple decided to call it quits. In 1996 they sold the lender for about $65 million to Amresco Inc., a publicly traded sub-prime firm based in Dallas.[13] A private sale, it was unclear how much of the money wound up in the hands of Russ and Becky, but shortly thereafter the couple left California and moved to a ranch in Nevada, leaving the mortgage industry behind. "Vegas was really more of Russ's style, anyway," said Laura Pephens.

In 1991, the year the Jedinaks were thrown out of the S&L industry, Countrywide reached a milestone, one it happily added to its

---

[12] In 2000 DLJ was bought by Credit Suisse, which became a top-ranked securitizer of subprime loans as well as a leading warehouse lender.

[13] Amresco eventually ran into financial trouble and stopped funding loans. Lehman Brothers bought what was left of the company. Because of their regulatory problems concerning Guardian, the Jedinaks tried to lie low while managing Quality Mortgage. The two top day-to-day managers of the company were Evan Buckley and Neil Kornsweit. After the sale of Quality Mortgage, the two managers went their separate ways—Buckley launching BNC Mortgage of Irvine, which Lehman Brothers also eventually bought, and Kornsweit starting a subprime lender called One Stop. In the mid-1990s Aames Financial, Gary Judis's company, bought One Stop. When Judis retired, Kornsweit took over management of Aames.

growing corporate history in its museum lobby: It was now the largest residential lender in the United States. It reached that milestone for two chief reasons: It was picking up tons of new business because hundreds of S&Ls—especially in California—had failed. The other reason? It was now the largest originator of home mortgages using loan brokers. Other mortgage banking firms—banks, S&Ls, and nondepositories (Countrywide was still a member of the latter)—were imitating its lead. Where Mozilo went, others followed.

Loan brokers were now squarely on the map. If a residential lender wanted to ramp up its loan volume, there was one surefire way to do it: brokers. All a lender would need was a license to lend in a state and a loan broker on the ground to find customers. Dan Perl remembers when he first started out in the business in the mid-1970s. Brooklyn born and raised, he moved west as a teenager, where he became an avid surfer and then an English teacher at Santa Monica High. His best friend was William Ashmore, the same Ashmore who would rush to withdraw his money from Countrywide in the summer of 2007.

Ashmore was a professor teaching at the College of the Canyons. Perl, also the assistant baseball coach, was making $900 a month—chump change, he figured. With a part-time lifeguard job he pulled down a few more dollars a week, but it was no way to make a living or support a family, he thought. He and his friend took their real estate license test and quickly discovered that they could use it not only to sell homes but to broker loans. Perl learned that loan brokers working the California market could get by with a real estate agent's license. (To broker loans in the state, an individual needed a license of some type—either a real estate agent's license or another type.)

The two men started brokering loans for Anaheim Savings and then became broker representatives (reps) for All State Savings, another California S&L. Perl went door-to-door to different Realty firms in search of leads. Realtors sold homes. He, like Mozilo and others before him, figured their home buyers would need loans, right? In those early years, he would call on Realtors. "I'd tell them, 'I'm a mortgage broker,'" he said. "And they'd looked at me and say, 'What's a mortgage broker?'" They formed a small brokerage firm called Perl-Ashmore, and soon enough every residential lender on the West Coast began to realize what a mortgage broker could do for it, thanks in large part to Countrywide and Guardian Savings—Mozilo and the Jedinaks.

* * *

By the end of 2006 there were 53,000 loan brokerage firms open and operating in all 50 states. By comparison, the Mortgage Bankers Association had just 2,300 members—and its dues-paying companies were the ones actually funding the loans brought to them by brokers. When Countrywide—thanks to brokers—became the number-one home lender in the United States in 1991, there were just 14,000 brokerage firms in existence. Those figures came from David Olson, an economist who made his living conducting research on the loan brokerage industry through his firm Wholesale Access of Columbia, Maryland. Olson had actually started his career in the industry at Household Finance in the early 1970s. "I'm the one who got them into mortgages," he later recalled. "Back then Household's largest consumer loan was $600." From there he moved on to Commercial Credit of Baltimore (which Citigroup eventually swallowed), working in planning and research, advising the subprime and consumer finance company on acquisition targets.

Any mortgage executive or company that was seriously interested in brokers or subprime lending turned to Olson,[14] who launched his research firm just as the subprime and brokerage industries were beginning their ascent. According to Olson's calculations—disputed by few—sometime in the early 2000s brokers accounted for 60 percent to 70 percent of residential loans originated in the United States. Under his definition, a loan brokerage firm included companies that acted as intermediaries in the mortgage process (using money delivered at the closing table by giants like Countrywide) and small mortgage banking firms that actually funded the loan themselves and then sold it right away to an investor such as Countrywide, Citigroup, Wells Fargo, or any other of a number of wholesale giants. In the new century, the days of savings and loans dominating the home lending process were long gone. It was now a business that George Bailey would hardly recognize—one

---

[14] Olson's client list read like a who's who of the mortgage banking industry's elite, including Fannie Mae and Freddie Mac.

where a broker took a loan application, sent the paperwork (usually electronically) to a wholesaler (which underwrote it to some degree), and then arranged for its sale into a large security through Wall Street. It was, as Mozilo would declare many times, a "capital markets"–driven business, one that danced to the tune of Wall Street.

Loan brokers dominated the business on the front end, Wall Street on the back end. In the late 1990s there was concern that as lenders began to market loans over the Internet, brokers might go the way of the horse and buggy. In theory, a lender could go directly to the consumer, cutting out the broker entirely; but it didn't turn out that way. Brokers started advertising and listing their rates (which came from a wholesaler), too. Mozilo was a fierce defender of brokers, telling the trade press, "Listen, you can have all this Internet stuff, but they're not going anywhere. They go out there and they find the customer and they say, 'Don't waste your time—I'll find you the best rate.'"

When Dan Perl and Bill Ashmore became brokers, they could get by with a Realtor's license. By 2006 all states required individual loan brokers (a flesh-and-blood loan officer) to be licensed or registered—but that didn't mean they were regulated. Unlike banks and S&Ls, which took federally insured deposits from the public and were regulated by the Federal Deposit Insurance Corporation, Federal Reserve, or another agency, mortgage brokers reported to no one. They had no regulator. The only one loan brokers reported to was their wholesaler, their Countrywide.

Brokers and the firms they worked for were not publicly traded. They also did not disclose their loan originations or income to any agency or regulatory body. In 1998 mortgage lending became a $1 trillion a year business—that's a lot of loans. If loan brokers earned on average one point (1 percent) and accounted for 70 percent of all loans originated each year (Olson's estimate), that worked out to $7 billion a year in fee income. At the beginning of 2007 there were roughly 200,000 individuals who worked for those 53,000 loan brokerage firms that Olson spoke of—and they were earning a lot more than one point per loan. On subprime loans, the fees paid to brokers were a lot higher than the old standard one point. When Dan Perl graduated from Perl-Ashmore and moved on to managing a series of subprime lenders, some brokers he dealt with in California wouldn't do a deal unless they could make at least $10,000 on a loan. "Then on top of that they'd throw in $1,800 in junk fees, adding in bogus stuff like processing fee and delivery fees."

The income of individual loan brokers became the talk of the industry, with some intermediaries supposedly earning $1 million a year or more. No one knew for sure, because brokers didn't disclose that type of information to the public. (The negative PR implications of a broker earning $1 million making subprime loans to the public is self-evident.) One way a broker could earn large fees was through an arrangement with the wholesaler called a yield spread premium (YSP). Yield spread premiums had been around for years but didn't become a popular practice until subprime lending volumes began to accelerate in 2003. A YSP worked like this: A consumer (usually subprime) buying a home or refinancing and trying to keep closing costs low would agree to pay a higher interest rate on the mortgage in return for paying no points (or fewer points) at the closing table. The higher yield on the loan made that mortgage more valuable to the wholesaler (Countrywide, Wells Fargo, Washington Mutual), because the wholesaler could sell it to Wall Street at a better price than a lower-yielding loan would garner. In the world of Wall Street, the higher the interest rate on a loan, the more valuable it became. Why? Answer: because the loan would be pooled into a bond, and bond investors loved higher-yielding assets. A higher yield of even just 1 percent more on a billion-dollar bond would translate into millions extra in income for the bondholder.

To compensate the broker for that higher-yielding mortgage, Countrywide and others would pay the broker additional points—two, three, sometimes even four. (On a $500,000 mortgage, three points would work out to $15,000 in income for the broker—on just one loan.) It also gave brokers an incentive to talk customers into deals where they could save money on the closing by agreeing to a higher interest rate.[15]

---

[15] In the fall of 2007, in an op-ed piece in the *Boston Globe*, Harvard law professor Elizabeth Warren likened YSPs to a "bribe" being paid to brokers from wholesalers, setting off a firestorm in the mortgage brokerage industry. Thousands of brokers took to Internet sites and message boards, calling for the professor's scalp. Warren would later become chairman of a congressional oversight panel whose mission was to keep tabs on the $700 billion Troubled Asset Relief Program (TARP), a late Bush era piece of legislation whose initial goal was to buy troubled mortgage assets from the nation's financial institutions but later morphed into a government program whereby the Treasury Department would buy ownership stakes in banks to prop them up financially, assuring that they would not fail.

The YSP paid to the broker for arranging a higher-yielding loan was disclosed in the loan documents the customer signed, but it's questionable how much customers understood that the broker had a real incentive (the YSP) to bring in the loan at a higher note rate.

But who were these millionaire earners? One was Joyce Jenise Jackson, a former stripper turned loan broker.[16] Jackson, a curvaceous African-American woman who ran a small loan brokerage company called the Metropolitan Money Store (MMS)[17] in suburban Lanham, Maryland, specialized in brokering loans to subprime borrowers who were in danger of losing their homes. Business appeared to be good for Jackson. In June 2006 she threw an $800,000 wedding for herself and husband Kurt Fordham, also her business partner. At the historic Mayflower Hotel on Connecticut Avenue in Washington, she played host to 300 guests who sipped Moët and Cristal champagne. A friend with a video camera captured the 38-year-old as she descended the Mayflower's ballroom stairs in an elegant handmade silk wedding gown and gold tiara. During the reception, singer Patti LaBelle serenaded Jackson and her new husband with "Lady Marmalade" and other hits.

Within a year of her nuptials, though, Jackson would be out of business and accused by criminal investigators of running an equity-stripping scam on hundreds of homeowners, buying their houses on the cheap and taking out larger, new mortgages, walking away with at least $60 million. The Metropolitan Money Store advertised on roadways in predominately black communities in Prince George's County, Maryland, which bordered the nation's capital near the Anacostia River. One loan that MMS facilitated was to the Proctor family of Fort Washington. Melvin Proctor and his wife, Nadine, who were having

---

[16] According to the *Washington Post*, Jackson worked as a stripper in the Legends nightclub in Temple Hills, Maryland, from 1997 to 2003. She danced under the name "Night Rider." One of her most popular routines was riding into the club on a white stallion à la Lady Godiva.

[17] The Metropolitan Money Store had no business ties to the Turtletaubs' The Money Store. In 1999 First Union Bank of Charlotte, North Carolina, bought the Turtletaubs' company for $2.1 billion and then a year later wrote down the entire value of the lender to zero, making its investment practically worthless. The bank closed The Money Store in June of 2000 and First Union's longtime CEO, Ed Crutchfield, resigned. The reason: The Money Store acquisition.

trouble making their home payments, spotted one of MMS's roadside signs and then heard an ad on the radio. Jackson, who worked the deal herself, laid out to the family how the foreclosure rescue would work. It went like this: The family, who owed about $163,000 on the house, would transfer ownership of the house to a friend of Jackson's. (The friend, Linda Jones, was later accused of being a so-called straw borrower or a front for MMS and Jackson.) The Proctors were allowed to live in the house for at least a year until they repaired their credit. Then they would get their house back. The Fort Washington home was worth about $327,000. Jackson and her future husband, Fordham, then went out and remortgaged the house for its true market value, paying off the family's original loan, which was in danger of going delinquent. The profit on the transaction was $164,000 ($327,000 minus $163,000). The Proctors, according to a lawsuit they later filed, saw little of that money. Jackson, Fordham, and MMS walked away with at least $100,000. (Affiliated companies and a handful of title firms shared in the largesse.) Jackson and Fordham had no intention of rescuing Melvin and Nadine, but as part of the transfer to Jones (fronting for MMS) they executed a loan document where it appeared the Proctors were getting some of the money—via a loan where the interest rate was an eye-popping 40 percent.

When enough families began losing their homes to MMS, state and federal investigators began looking into the loan broker's supposed rescue operation. (The scheme worked only if the troubled homeowner had a decent amount of equity in the house.) By the summer of 2007 Jenise and Fordham were nowhere to be found, and even the Secret Service was taking an interest in the case. The Metropolitan Money Store was not your typical loan brokerage operation. There were many legitimate brokerage firms pounding the pavement, offering subprime and conventional loans to borrowers like the Proctors.

During the housing and mortgage booms, millionaire brokers were not necessarily the norm, but they existed, according to several interviews conducted by *National Mortgage News* and highlighted in some of its stories. Few brokers were willing to admit they earned $1 million or more a year. A survey conducted by the newspaper found that 25 percent of brokers it surveyed claimed earnings of between $200,000 and $400,000 in 2006. Eight percent said they earned north of $400,000. A broker named Kelly Stanfield contacted the newspaper and told a reporter the story of her company, Lake Mortgage. "I personally have not been lucky enough to get in on it, but we have a 'winners' list in our company," she said. "Some made over $100,000 a month. During the boom it was $200,000 [a month]."

The rescue mission that MMS was peddling could not have come about without a wholesale lender bringing money to the closing table. Without closing table funding from bigger fish, brokers would not exist. In the case of the Proctors of Fort Washington, the mortgage banking firm providing the check at the closing table was an Orange, California–based lender called Argent Mortgage, a company controlled by Roland Arnall.

And therein lies another story.

Chapter 4

The Beach Boys
of B&C

*How Roland Arnall Became the
Johnny Appleseed of Subprime*

We've got to stay under the radar.
—AMERIQUEST OWNER ROLAND ARNALL
TO CRAIG COLE, ONE OF HIS EXECUTIVES

A ngelo Mozilo doesn't remember the exact date he entertained a competitor named Roland Arnall in his Calabasas office, but he recalls that the meeting took place in either 2001 or 2002. "He came up to my office with some of his people," remembered Mozilo. "He came to talk to me about the business, how I did business. He was here for quite a while. I'll do that from time to time, talk to people even if they're my competitors. It was the strangest conversation I'd ever had. He thanked me for my time and then said good-bye."

Mozilo had met Arnall a few times before, and took an interest in him for two reasons: One of Arnall's former companies, Long Beach Mortgage, had run into problems with regulators who were trying to hold it responsible for what Mozilo called "disparities in loan pricing" on loans made to whites versus minorities. To hear Mozilo tell it, Long Beach was being held responsible for the behavior of one of its free-lance loan brokers. "He eventually won the case," said Mozilo. As the century turned, Countrywide had retained its title as the biggest user of loan brokers in the United States. Anything that might damage its lock on that business was of paramount concern to Mozilo and his cadre of senior executives.

The other reason Mozilo took an interest in Arnall was that Arnall's current lending venture, Ameriquest Mortgage, a retail nondepository based in nearby Orange, was beginning to accumulate a huge market share in subprime mortgages, a product niche that Countrywide had avoided for most of its 30-plus-year history but was now slowly but surely gaining traction in. Arnall was also on the verge of launching a nationwide wholesale lender called Argent Mortgage that was gearing up to sell subprime loans through loan brokers in as many states as possible—and as quickly as possible. If there was one thing that Mozilo paid careful attention to, it was market share. It was a given that he was going to let Arnall have some of his time. It also didn't hurt that Arnall was politically well connected, having donated hundreds of thousands of dollars to federal and local politicians over the years. Former California governor Gray Davis officiated at his wedding in 2000. It was the second trip down the aisle for Arnall, a middle-aged mortgage executive who looked a bit like retired Dodgers manager Tommy Lasorda.

"I'll do that," Mozilo said about the meet and greet. "I'll talk to competitors. There always could be something in it for me. I believe that on a level playing field, even if you know what I'm doing I can still beat you. Even if you know my play, I'm not afraid of any opponent."

★   ★   ★

Roland Arnall was not just any opponent. Like Mozilo's grandfather, he was an immigrant to the United States, but Arnall took a slightly more circuitous route. Only one thing seems certain about his early years: that he was born in 1939 in Europe. His family was Jewish, which meant their lives were in danger as Hitler came to power and Nazi Germany expanded its borders by invading other nations. His official

bio has him born in Paris on the eve of World War II. An unconfirmed press report says it was Poland. (Arnall has never given any type
of extensive interview about his past, or about anything else for that
matter.) To avoid detection by the Nazis, the family said they were
Catholic, according to one attorney who did business with Arnall. After
the war his family moved to Montreal and then immigrated to the Los
Angeles area in the late 1950s. Southern California was on the rise.
During those early cold war years the defense and aerospace industries were thriving in nearby Long Beach, one of the largest deepwater
ports in the United States. The Brooklyn Dodgers had decamped to
Los Angeles from New York, which at the time was in somewhat of
an economic decline. The New York Giants left as well, breaking the
hearts of Yankee haters in all five boroughs. In his teens Arnall and his
brother Claude began selling flowers on the streets of Los Angeles. In
time they parlayed it into a flower shop. That's where the public information about his early years ends.

In 1979, four years before the Nolan Act became law (which led to
the stampede of real estate developers owning S&Ls), Arnall obtained
a thrift charter from the state of California. His shop was called Long
Beach Savings (LBS), reflecting the hometown of its headquarters. By
1983 the Jedinaks were in nearby Huntington Beach, 15 miles to the
south. While Russ and Becky toiled with a handful of small commercial projects and then went full force into subprime residential lending, Long Beach concentrated on mostly commercial lending—projects
that Arnall was involved in as a real estate developer. Thanks to the
Nolan Act, developers could own an S&L and use its deposits to fund
office buildings, apartments, whatever they liked. "Roland was a vision-
ary guy," said Craig Cole, who once worked for him. "He saw a lot of
things in the business before the other guys did."

Long Beach Savings embarked on a business plan of funding mostly
commercial loans—apartments and office buildings—leaving the residential business to the state's George Bailey–like thrift owners, the ones
who still liked housing, people like Herb and Marion Sandler up in
Oakland, who operated World Savings. According to Cole, a former
Freddie Mac executive, LBS "was used for the personal development of
its owners." That would be Arnall. "He used it as a piggy bank. But it
made a lot of money."

Unlike some new thrift owners who also happened to be real estate developers (or wannabe developers), Arnall knew how to read a balance sheet. He didn't like losing money and he didn't cook the books (engage in financial fraud) of the S&L. Those who worked for him back then said most of his commercial projects at LBS made financial sense. "His were actually viable," said Cole.

But as the S&L industry began its historic collapse in the mid to late 1980s, Arnall became nervous. He saw too many developers with S&L charters, few of them doing well. One of his employees characterized Arnall's mood like this: "He wasn't thrilled with guys getting into his business, and the regulators kept getting younger and younger."

The "regulators" meant the examiners at the Federal Home Loan Bank of San Francisco, one of 12 regional branches of the Federal Home Loan Bank Board[1] in Washington. Arnall began to see developer-owned thrifts being taken over by the government and feared that even though his projects were mostly viable, he might be next. According to friends, he made the only sensible decision available to him—he took his S&L charter and turned it in to the federal government, or, as one employee bluntly described it, he told the examiners at the Federal Home Loan Bank of San Francisco to shove it.

"He actually burned the charter, lit it on fire," said Cole, who went to work for Arnall in 1995. Cole remembers walking into Arnall's office in Orange, California, and seeing a large urn on the credenza behind his new boss's desk. "I asked him what it was," said Cole. The response: the S&L charter of what used to be Long Beach Savings. "He was very proud of that urn. People would ask him about it and he would tell them."

In 1994 when LBS went up in flames (so to speak), Arnall named the new company Long Beach Mortgage (LBM) and began borrowing

---

[1] Prior to 1989 the 12 Federal Home Loan Banks served a dual role of both being a regional regulator of S&Ls and serving as a cooperative wholesale bank where each S&L could borrow money. In 1989 president George H.W. Bush passed the Financial Institutions Reform, Recovery, and Enforcement Act, which split the functions. The FHLBs became the wholesale lenders to thrifts in their geographic regions, while a new regulatory agency, the Office of Thrift Supervision (OTS), a successor to the Federal Home Loan Bank Board in Washington, was given the task of being the chief regulator. The OTS has six regional offices.

money through Wall Street and commercial banks. He was now the owner of a nonbank that had just about no regulators to deal with, only bankers to answer to. When he burned his S&L charter he also burned his bridge to using low-cost federally insured deposits. That was just fine with Arnall, Cole said. Before LBS was transformed, Arnall had already begun to dabble in subprime lending, partly because of the success he saw down the coast at the Jedinaks' Guardian Savings. (Remember that Guardian's downfall was its commercial loans, not its subprime residential business.) "He was segueing into subprime," said Cole. "The way the regulators saw it, he was exchanging one risky venture [commercial] for another [subprime]. They didn't like it."

Without federal examiners to worry about, Arnall hunkered down and began to work on what Cole called his "vision of mortgage lending." Arnall liked the subprime business, said Cole, because LBM could charge eight or nine points on a loan and make a ton of money. (Eight points on a $100,000 loan would be $8,000.) "Roland thought big," Cole said. Asked why any borrower in their right mind would pay eight points to LBM, Cole painted a picture of a borrower in distress, saying, "People wanted the money [that LBM could provide]. A lot of these were refis. In some cases borrowers wanted to strip out the equity in their homes." LBM was more than happy to please the borrower, he said. Some of the lender's customers would come in and make their payments in cash—"with wads of cash," remembered Cole. "We had a very good collections department."

Long Beach Mortgage under Arnall became obsessed with avoiding loan delinquencies. "We had a loan committee of four to five top executives," said one LBM officer. "We were expected to look at every deal. Roland liked to be able to kick a limited number of asses if things were not up to his expectations." His top secondary market manager (the one responsible for selling loans to investors) was a man named Yankee Dinovitz, an Orthodox Jew with a penchant for guns. Dan Perl, who did business with Arnall, remembered visiting LBM and being invited out to the shooting range with the secondary chief. "Yankee said, 'Let's go shooting,' so we did."

Arnall also liked technology, a trait that he had in common with Mozilo at Countrywide. Running LBM, it is believed that Arnall was the first mortgage executive to take subprime borrowers and break them down into subcategories that would one day result in them being considered A–, B, C, or D—just like a student's report card. LBM's customers were no longer thrown into a big bucket and labeled "people with bad credit." Arnall, according to Cole, built an Excel spreadsheet on his computer. "He created a system to grade loans," said Cole. "He put them in risk buckets. What bucket you were in determined the rates and fees."

Putting borrowers into certain risk categories appealed to Arnall's sense of order, said Cole. Arnall, he noticed, was a creature of habit who ate the same Chinese meal every day for lunch: orange chicken with rice. "He did this like clockwork," said Cole. (Another employee remembered Arnall's favorite lunchtime culinary dish somewhat differently as "sautéed vegetables over white rice. He would put this hot, red, oily sauce on it. He would put spoonfuls in his mouth and sweat profusely. I think he was on a kick to lose weight.")

Cole was hired in 1995 to help Arnall launch a wholesale "A" paper network that would originate government-insured and prime loans for sale to Fannie Mae and Freddie Mac, the two congressionally chartered mortgage investing giants. What better person to hire than a former salesman at Freddie Mac? After Arnall tossed the S&L charter overboard, he relied mostly on freelance loan brokers to bring mortgages into LBM, another practice he copied from the Jedinaks. Cole had been a top salesman at Freddie Mac whose job it was to keep the customers of that government-chartered enterprise happy while convincing them to sell as many loans as possible to Freddie, as opposed to its chief government-chartered rival, Fannie Mae.[2]

The name Arnall had picked for the new "A" paper wholesale network that Cole would help manage was Ameriquest Mortgage. His marketing department chose the name because, according to Cole, it sounded "like a good old-fashioned American name" (the *Ameri-* part) and described Arnall's "quest" to be national in scope. Long Beach

---

[2] Fannie Mae was chartered by the U.S. Congress in 1938, Freddie much later in 1970. Their mission, according to their charters, was to free up capital for residential finance by purchasing mortgages from lenders. The lender would then use that cash to make new loans. These government-sponsored enterprises (GSEs) would both securitize and hold mortgages on their books (balance sheets) and place their guarantee on mortgage-backed securities (MBSs) held on the books of other financial institutions, including commercial banks, savings and loans, and credit unions, among others.

Mortgage's wholesale division, headed by Jack Mayesh (and later on by Wayne A. Lee), would concentrate solely on using brokers to find subprime customers. By 1996 LBM, through a network of 7,500 freelance loan brokers, was "table funding" loans in about 30 states. It recruited brokers by holding parties at regional trade shows and taking out advertisements in industry magazines and newspapers.

Cole's job was to help put Ameriquest on the map in "A" paper wholesale. One of the first people at the company he got to know after being hired was Loretta, Arnall's secretary. "She protected him like a mother hen," said Cole. Arnall wanted the former Freddie Mac salesman to grow the new "A" paper wholesale network quickly. "Roland would call you days, nights, weekends. It would always start with Loretta saying, 'It's Mr. Arnall.' Whenever he had an idea about something, anything, he would call."

To those who worked for Arnall at his various mortgage companies over the years, there was one trait that stood out: his ability to manage what appeared to be one of the most successful mortgage companies in the nation and avoid the media entirely—including the California dailies, the *Wall Street Journal*, and the trade press. Until the early 2000s he was for the most part invisible, keeping his picture out of the papers as best he could. On occasion there might a story about the Los Angeles–based Simon Wiesenthal Center,[3] which Arnall helped found, but not much else. His avoidance of the press was intentional. Arnall, to the dispute of no one, shunned publicity with an almost religious zeal. Cole, an LBM employee for just under two years, remembers a conversation he had with Arnall when he said, "We've got to stay under the radar." Added Cole, "He was very secretive. He shunned publicity. Roland does not give press interviews."

★   ★   ★

The best way for a man to avoid public scrutiny is to not take his private mortgage firm into the public market. In 1997 a company called

---

[3] The Simon Wiesenthal Center, which has offices in Los Angeles, New York, Toronto, Palm Beach, Paris, Buenos Aires, and Jerusalem, is an international Jewish human rights organization dedicated to defending the safety of Jews worldwide and teaching the lessons of the Holocaust.

Long Beach Financial Corporation (LBFC) sold 22 million shares on the New York Stock Exchange, raising roughly $141 million. But Arnall was nowhere to be found in the IPO documents. Jack Mayesh, his right-hand man at LBM, was now in charge of the company. Years earlier the two had met in the flower trade; Mayesh's father was a wholesaler. Jack Mayesh's first line of work was politics. He started his career as a staffer to California assemblyman Howard Berman, managed a few political campaigns, and became reacquainted with Arnall just as he was starting LBS. Arnall hired him as a political consultant, doing what one source called "advocacy" work in Washington.

Long Beach Financial Corporation's chief asset was Long Beach Mortgage, Arnall's company. Prior to LBFC going public, he had created a holding company (Old Long Beach Holdings) and put LBM under it. He then took the subprime wholesale operation—which Mayesh ran—and isolated it into LBFC, the unit that was going public. Long Beach Financial Corporation was now funding $1 billion a year in subprime loans, most of it through loan brokers. Arnall kept the holding company, the retail division, and the servicing operation (which processed the monthly mortgage payments from consumers). When all was said and done, the holding company owned 70 percent of LBFC. When it went public, the holding company (which Arnall controlled) walked away with $100 million and Arnall got to keep his name out of the public record.

Coincidentally, or maybe not so coincidentally, Arnall was in the process of divorcing his wife of 37 years, Sally. The couple had two children. Executives who worked for Arnall described her as a stay-at-home mom who didn't know much about her husband's business or what it was really worth. When they divorced, Sally walked away with about $11 million, a fraction of what Arnall's holding company made on the LBFC IPO.[4]

When LBFC first filed its registration papers with the Securities and Exchange Commission, it initially had hoped to raise $300 million by selling 25 million shares at $12 apiece. By IPO time the price was down to $6 a share and the number of shares trimmed. But two years after going public, Mayesh turned around and sold LBFC—in a crumbling

---

[4] In 2005 Sally Arnall sued her former husband to reopen the divorce case. A trial was scheduled for October 2007. According to her attorney, Vicky Greene, Roland Arnall settled after the third day of trial. Both parties agreed to keep the settlement private.

market—to Washington Mutual (WaMu) of Seattle, a publicly traded savings and loan that was about to embark on a five-year buying spree of gobbling up a dozen or so mortgage companies or S&Ls. LBM would be Washington Mutual's first foray into subprime. The purchase price was $360 million. Kerry Killinger, WaMu's chairman and CEO at the time, was fast gaining a reputation in the mortgage industry as someone who would buy almost anything that was presented to him.

Mayesh was able to sell the firm at double its IPO price because LBFC had avoided the carnage suffered by its competitors. By early 1999 publicly traded subprime lenders—Cityscape Mortgage, First Plus, The Money Store, and many others—were sliding toward bankruptcy because they had securitized hundreds of millions of dollars in mortgages using gain-on-sale accounting where they overestimated the longevity of their bonds. All the future income they had anticipated never arrived. But under Arnall and Mayesh, LBM (and LBFC) had avoided the securitization market entirely. Mayesh was close to Greenwich Capital in Connecticut, an investment banking firm. Instead of securitizing mortgages through Greenwich (or another Wall Street firm), Mayesh (with Arnall's blessing) cut a deal to sell its subprime mortgages to Greenwich on what's called a "whole loan basis." This meant that LBM received cash right away for its subprime loans and didn't have to play around with assumptions about how long the loans would stick around on its books. (That would be the problem of Greenwich and the institutional investors that bought the bonds issued by Greenwich.)

When Washington Mutual bought LBFC, Mayesh hung around for a few months in a transitory role, signed a three-year noncompete clause with the S&L, and then left. By the time Arnall showed up on Angelo Mozilo's doorstep early in the next century, LBFC was now a wholly owned subsidiary of WaMu, which was also a competitor to Countrywide both in California and nationwide, vying for the same customers in 50 states. WaMu kept the Long Beach Mortgage name and continued its strategy of using loan brokers to originate subprime loans. Not only did Mayesh have a three-year noncompete agreement that prevented him from getting into the subprime wholesale business, but Arnall had a noncompete, too (in regard only to subprime wholesale).

The year 2000 was a particularly bad one for the residential loan industry. In one interview in the summer of that year Mozilo, when asked how things were, put his Bronx spin on the situation, telling a reporter from *National Mortgage News*: "It sucks." Countrywide was funding mostly "A" paper loans—a business it dominated—but had slowly risen in the rankings among subprime originators. Among A– to D lenders, it ranked seventh nationwide with originations of $5 billion, which gave it a market share of 4 percent, about half of what it had among prime lenders that sold to Fannie Mae and Freddie Mac. Countrywide was originating subprime loans, but only through retail branches of a division it had created called Full Spectrum Lending.

In the post-LBM era, Arnall's Ameriquest Mortgage was originating "A" paper loans through its wholesale network (using brokers) and whatever retail offices it had retained when Mayesh and LBFC were spun off from the mother ship. But because 2000 was such a bad year for originating new loans ("A" paper mortgage rates were at 8 percent), Ameriquest's profit margins suffered. "Roland threw in the towel because of the margins," said Cole. He converted Ameriquest from a wholesale "A" paper lender into a mostly retail one, with one important difference: It was now funding only subprime loans. (When he spun off LBFC, Arnall's noncompete didn't prevent him from owning a subprime retailer. In that regard he could do whatever he liked.) Conventional lending, as almost any mortgage executive knew, was a sucker's bet; it was a business rife with razor-thin profit margins. There was just too much competition.

Arnall and his executive team, which included Kirk Langs as the head of subprime retail, began expanding its reach into new states as quickly as possible. Langs, like his boss, was not the loquacious type, at least when it came to giving press interviews. He was a relatively young man, mid-30s, and did exactly what Arnall asked of him—grow Ameriquest quickly into the largest originator of subprime loans in the United States. "Kirk was our leader," said one area sales manager who worked under him. "He was charismatic. He knew the industry inside and out. He pushed growth."

Just two years after Ameriquest had begun opening retail branch offices to sell subprime loans directly to home buyers (and homeowners looking to refinance), the company had almost 40 regional sales managers spread out across the United States. But opening offices was only part of the equation. Now it had to motivate the retail loan officers (LOs)—the men and women who worked with the public. The best way to do that? Offer incentives. "Incentives" meant commissions. The more loans retail LOs brought into Ameriquest, the more money they made. It was as simple as that.

The process of making mortgages at LBM and the new Ameriquest was all about selling. When it came to sales—the origination of mortgages through brokers or LOs—Arnall was hardly a patient man. Early on, Cole remembers giving the LBM chief a status report, informing him that the new company had opened eight new offices, equipping each with new computer systems. "That's not good enough," Arnall said. "I want to be in all 50 [states]." Another sales manager remembers that Arnall was always thinking broadly—he wanted the lender to be a one-stop shop for all types of loan products, not just subprime. He wanted it to be like Countrywide.

Arnall also could run hot and cold with his senior executives. Pat Flanagan, who ran some of LBM's branches, was one such executive. One day he got a better job offer and went to tell Arnall about it. "Arnall suddenly decides he can't live without him," said another executive familiar with the story. "He says, 'What can I do?' And Flanagan says, 'Pay off my house.' So Arnall cuts him a big check. Later Arnall fired him."

The men and women who brought in the loans using brokers were called account executives (AEs). During their best years, wholesale AEs at LBM and other Arnall affiliates might earn anywhere between $30,000 and $50,000 a month, or $600,000 a year—and that didn't even include bonuses. Throw in the bonus money, and some AEs earned anywhere from $1 million to $2 million. If that couldn't incentivize the troops, then nothing would.

Arnall also believed in rewarding his top performers with junkets. It was a sales culture where the company's top AEs (the ones who brought the most loans in through brokers) were treated like royalty, being wined and dined at four-star hotels. Those who didn't perform either quit under pressure or were fired. Long Beach Mortgage, Ameriquest, and Argent employees were treated to weeklong cruises in the Caribbean. "It was nonstop drinking, gambling, and partying," remembered one former executive. Loan volumes (and profits) were so good during those years, he said, that Arnall threw a huge bash in Las Vegas for the company's top salespeople, giving away $1 million in cars, motorcycles, and cash.

Tim Hughes, an account executive at one of Arnall's shops, remembers what he calls "lavish three-day sales meetings" where once a quarter the top AEs dined on shrimp and filet mignon "with all the alcohol that one could possibly want to drink." He remembers a sales meeting where the company flew in 700 AEs "and we weren't exactly staying at a Motel 6. My boss told me that each sales meeting would cost well over $2 million." When it came time to give out the sales awards, salaries weren't mentioned but the loan volumes that the AEs had brought in using loan brokers were openly displayed on a large scorecard for all to see. "I did the simple math. A few of the AEs were earning a couple of million dollars a year."

For Ameriquest's retail loan officers, the event of the year was a party at the Atlantis in Las Vegas called "The Big Spin." Arnall would start the event off with a short, 15-minute speech and then leave the honors to his top lieutenants, including Langs, the head of retail. At one "Big Spin" party, an Arizona sales manager witnessed the company giving away 10 cars, including Porsches, and $10,000 in prizes. Depending on the year, the entertainment included a cross section of singers and actors, including LL Cool J, Penn & Teller, and comedian Jay Mohr. The motivational speakers—designed to prime the sales pump— included former New York mayor (and eventual presidential candidate) Rudolph Giuliani, Buffalo Bills quarterback Jim Kelly, boxer Sugar Ray Leonard, and others. But Arnall would rarely stick around for the show. He would make a short speech, start the event, and be on his way. "He was not a partier," said Cole. "He shunned the limelight. When it came to speaking he was quite awkward."

"It was all about selling," said a regional sales manager who worked the Southwestern states for Ameriquest. The manager, who didn't want to be identified, painted a portrait of Ameriquest's retail operations as such: "The idea was to fill every desk in your branch [with loan officers], whether it was three desks or 18 desks. It was high pressure on sales." To incentivize area managers, Ameriquest paid them on head count. The more LOs that managers had under them, the more they earned. Area managers could earn well over $1 million a year, he said.

But because the pressure to push loans to the public was so great, employee turnover could be tremendous. "I was interviewing people all the time for jobs," the regional sales manager said. Ameriquest even had what were called "internal recruiters" whose job it was to hire new loan officers (and processors who actually handled the loan application files) using the web site Monster.com. The internal recruiters screened prospective LOs over the phone. If they passed muster, the branch manager took over the hiring process.

If the LOs and sales managers made their sales goals, they got to stay and were rewarded. "If you had a good month and did $10 million in loans, he [Arnall] would say, 'Great. When are you going to do $20 million?' That was the new benchmark." This sales manager said that one month he missed his sales quota by one loan and was let go.

★ ★ ★

Arnall's timing concerning Ameriquest's rapid expansion into subprime retail couldn't have been better. The Russian debt crisis and abuses of gain-on-sale accounting (booking tomorrow's profits today on loan securitizations) that blew a hole in the subprime industry in 1998 and 1999 had decimated the ranks of subprime originators across the land. The lenders that escaped relatively unscathed from this minicrisis were the old-line consumer finance companies: Household Finance (which now owned Beneficial Finance); Associates First Capital Corporation, which had just been bought by Citigroup; and Arnall's old firm, Long Beach Mortgage. The market was wide open. Wall Street firms—Bear Stearns and Lehman Brothers being the most aggressive—had dusted themselves off from those bad subprime days of 1998 and 1999 and begun lending money to the nonbank subprime lenders, Ameriquest being at the top of the list.

There was one other thing Arnall had going in his favor: the recession. Shortly after President George W. Bush took the oath of office, the nation found itself mired in a recession, which was partly caused by the dot-com bubble. High-flying Internet firms with interesting ideas on commerce (but little or no revenue) began to fail—many of them publicly traded. To head off this economic flu, the Federal Reserve, chaired by Alan Greenspan, began to cut short-term interest rates. When short-term rates go down, long-term rates (like mortgage rates) always follow. It never fails. In 2000 the average rate on a 30-year fixed-rate loan for Americans with good credit was 8 percent. In 2001 the rate was at 6.91 percent and dropping fast (and would continue to fall for the next three years).

In the mortgage business, recessions are good for two things: refinancing booms and creating more subprime borrowers. A bad economy creates financial problems for consumers, causing them to go late on any number of bills, including credit cards and their existing mortgages. To Arnall, the immediate future probably never looked brighter. He had been a pioneer in using Excel spreadsheets to grade customers in the mid to late 1990s; he now had some new technology tools to play with: automated valuation models (AVMs) and underwriting software that relied heavily on FICO scores. AVMs were electronic appraisals based on property information gathered on the ground in neighborhoods and then disseminated over the Internet.

Seeing that the market was about to turn, Ameriquest's executive team tweaked its business strategy. It would continue to make subprime mortgages to home buyers with bad credit, but it liberalized how much equity or down payment they would need. Documents the company had given to its investment bankers at Bear Stearns showed that in 2001 its average loan-to-value (LTV) ratio was 74 percent. Two years later it was 81 percent. Gone were the days when a subprime lender wanted a cushion of 40 percent to 50 percent in a home before it would extend a mortgage.

But that wasn't the biggest underwriting change Ameriquest had made under Arnall and Langs. It had begun originating a brand-new type of home mortgage, basing its decision to originate on those much-loved technology tools: the AVM and the FICO score. It was called a stated-income loan. If a customer came into an Ameriquest branch and told a loan officer he or she made $100,000 a year (even if he or she might be a truck driver, gardener, or waitress), the company would fund the loan as long as the FICO scores, AVM, and whatever real appraisals the LO ordered up checked out. Ameriquest believed in technology. "Roland loved technology," said Cole. Technology didn't lie. That might be so, but people lied. In time, stated-income loans would earn the industry nickname "liar loans" because the borrower could claim to earn $200,000 even if he or she didn't, and the loan would go through as long as the FICO scores checked out.

In 2001 Ameriquest had funded $6 billion in subprime mortgages— 28 percent of them either stated-income loans or a similar product called limited-documentation mortgages. In other words, Ameriquest's trusting executives had given their blessing on $1.7 billion worth of loans (mortgages that would be packaged into bonds and sold on Wall Street) because borrowers said they earned a certain amount of money and they believed them.[5] Not even George Bailey of Bedford Falls was that trusting.

By 2003 Ameriquest and its various affiliates were originating $40 billion a year in mortgages across the nation—30 percent of them stated-income or limited-documentation mortgages. In dollars and cents that came out to $12 billion. Mozilo, who prided himself on knowing the lay of the land in the mortgage industry, took note. Speaking about Arnall he said, "He plays by his own rules. He's the guy who started stated-income [loans], the guy who started no-documentation loans. All his people were on commission." It irked Mozilo. Countrywide was the top banana when it came to funding all types of mortgages, but in the subprime sector—which was beginning to account for a bigger piece of a $2 trillion a year pie—it was far behind Arnall's shop. Mozilo didn't like it. He also discovered that some of his top LOs and AEs were being wooed away by Ameriquest. "We were losing them in substantial numbers," he said. Countrywide's troops were being raided by Arnall.

★   ★   ★

By paying a retail loan officer a commission to bring in mortgages, a lender walks a tightrope: The bonus money spurs the LO to produce, which is great for both the company and the LO. But the incentive money has the potential to corrupt the process, because it offers cash rewards for volume. It stands to reason that when you have thousands of salespeople peddling loan products in 50 states, somewhere along the line LOs will jam loans through the system regardless of the borrower's ability to repay. When a company makes a loan without caring about being repaid (it earns points and fees on the mortgage before selling it to an investor in the secondary market), this is often referred to as "predatory lending."

---

[5] Ameriquest spokesman Chris Orlando denied that Arnall was an innovator in stated-income loans. However, company figures released by Ameriquest at a Bear Stearns conference in late 2004 highlighted its involvement in stated-income lending as far back as 2001, with originations in that category increasing each year up until (at least) 2004.

In 2001—just as the lender's loan volume was beginning to take off—federal prosecutors in San Diego indicted seven Ameriquest loan officers for arranging fraudulent appraisals on 64 home loans in the San Diego and Riverside areas. The total dollar amount was $9 million. All seven were friends brought to the company by Chris Zennedjian, who was the first to become an LO there and then graduated to branch manager in San Diego. Prior to working at Ameriquest, one of the friends had been selling sunglasses on the street. After a year on the job, the group's members were driving around in BMWs and earning $20,000 a month. Zennedjian and another LO, Jarrett Pugh (and others), allegedly created false values on the homes by forging appraisal forms—but used the name of a real appraiser who had been approved by Ameriquest management. They were also accused of forging documents that overstated how much the borrowers earned.

Why would the defendants overvalue the homes? Answer: because the higher the house value, the larger the loan Ameriquest could fund. The larger the loan, the higher the commission the friends could earn. On $9 million in retail loans that Ameriquest had extended on the 64 homes, the seven friends earned $172,400, which works out to almost two points (2 percent) per loan. The loan officers, most of whom were in their 20s, found the borrowers by going through the company's "turn-down files" where LOs stored the names of customers who had previously been rejected for loans. But the borrowers didn't receive kickbacks from the LOs—they were just happy to get a mortgage.

Ameriquest sold the mortgages to WaMu, the S&L that was kind enough to pay $360 million for Long Beach Mortgage back in the spring of 1999. WaMu conducted a follow-up review on the loans, and discovered that the home appraisals on some were too high. The S&L wasn't happy. Executives there told Ameriquest and asked for their $9 million back. Many of the loans went into foreclosure. Ameriquest told the FBI and then sued its former employees, whom it had (of course) fired. All things being normal, the story should have ended there; but it didn't. It's not uncommon in the mortgage industry for loan officers or brokers to bend or break the rules so they can make more money. In an industry where 10 million new loans are funded every year, there are bound to be bad apples. All of the defendants in the San Diego case either pleaded guilty or were convicted—except for Carlos Campillo.

Campillo was friends with the others; that's how he had been brought into the company in the first place. But according to his attorney, Kevin Elmore, the young man was dragged into the case only because of his friendship with the group and because on one of the loans where he served as LO he used an appraiser whose name had been forged on a document. All of Campillo's friends were convicted or pleaded guilty, and settled the civil charges Ameriquest filed against them. Campillo, though, walked away from the criminal case with the allegations against him dismissed—as long as he completed one year of community service.

In trying to work out a deal with Ameriquest, attorney Elmore said he sat down with Adam Bass, an outside attorney for Ameriquest, and Wayne Lee, a top executive at the company. Bass, who chaired the mortgage and litigation practice at the Los Angeles law firm of Buchalter Nemer, was also Arnall's nephew.[6] Elmore said he and his client told Bass and Lee that the lender had major quality control problems. "We said managers at Ameriquest condoned and promoted fraud," said Elmore. But Bass, according to Elmore, was a bit taken aback by what the two had to say. "He refused to believe a word of it. His attitude was: 'None of that goes on here.' Normally in mediations, attorneys can see their client's weaknesses; not the case with this guy. The documentation and testimony of fraud my client had from working in the branch for just six months were astounding."[7]

★   ★   ★

---

[6] Bass is the son of the sister of Arnall's first wife. As a technical matter, he was Arnall's nephew prior to the divorce.

[7] Adam Bass declined to comment directly on Elmore's characterization of the meeting. However, Chris Orlando, a spokesman for Ameriquest Capital Corporation, disputed Elmore's version of the meeting. He said Ameriquest provided "significant assistance" to the FBI in the case. "To say the company was 'not responsive' or 'dismissed' the claims is patently false and defamatory." Joanne Davies, an attorney at Buchalter Nemer, also questioned Elmore's opinion of Bass's reaction regarding the matter. Elmore later clarified that Bass "refused to believe Ameriquest and its policies, procedures (or lack thereof), and climate contributed to fraud." Carlos Campillo, according to Elmore, to this day continues to be employed in the mortgage industry. Elmore served as Campillo's attorney during the early stages of the case before another lawyer, Todd Moore, took over the matter. Moore said he does not think Ameriquest executives turned a blind eye to fraud but said, "They took a hands-off approach as long as the loan met their guidelines. Ameriquest's reputation was such that they'd make a loan to anyone with a pulse as long as the LTV was okay."

By 2004 Roland Arnall's world had changed. He and his second wife, Dawn, were gaining attention as major political donors to both parties. His three-year noncompete agreement that prohibited him from entering the subprime wholesale business had ended. Shortly after his powwow with Mozilo, he launched Argent Mortgage, which, like Ameriquest, was housed in Orange. A few miles away was the city of Irvine, the financial epicenter of Orange County, California. Arnall had been in the savings and loan or mortgage business for well over a decade, and many of his former employees were following his lead by launching subprime firms of their own. "Ameriquest became a spawning ground for others who go on to start their own subprime companies," said Cole.

As the Federal Reserve continued to lower interest rates in the wake of the terrorist attacks of 9/11, new subprime companies swelled across Orange County. With office rents down amid a still somewhat weak economy, many of these upstarts could afford premium office space normally reserved for corporate lawyers and accountants. Arnall housed Ameriquest (a subprime retail lender) and Argent Mortgage (a wholesaler using loan brokers) under a holding company called Ameriquest Capital Corporation (ACC). He was its chairman. The company boasted at least 14,000 employees. It also had expanded its brands. Besides Ameriquest and Argent, it started other mortgage affiliates that funded, more or less, the same type of subprime and stated-income loans as Ameriquest/Argent. One was called Town & Country Credit, and another Olympus Mortgage, the latter of which was managed by Roland's brother Claude. (There was also an auto lending division called Long Beach Acceptance Corporation.) And Adam Bass, the lender's outside counsel? He was now working for ACC as well—as a top executive.

The formation of Olympus caught some of Argent's wholesale AEs by surprise, so much so that many found themselves competing against Olympus salespeople without even knowing that this new competitor was also owned by Arnall's ACC. Higinio Mangual, a former Olympus AE, said Olympus was Arnall's "brainstorm" to get his brother involved in the red-hot wholesale business. After several months, Argent AEs began complaining to their boss, Wayne Lee, that with Olympus now in the market they were competing against themselves. Lee eventually convinced Arnall to merge Olympus into Argent. Claude left the company (with an undisclosed payout) and opened the Punch Grill in Los Angeles.

While the subprime business boomed, Claude Arnall joined his brother and sister-in-law in donating thousands of dollars to politicians' campaigns. Their largesse to candidates would make Charlie Keating's donations during the S&L era look like peanuts. Dawn Arnall donated $5 million to the Progress for America Voter Fund, a political group backing the reelection of President Bush. Dawn, who was given the official title of co-chairman of ACC in mid-2002, was also a Bush "ranger," having raised at least $200,000 for the Bush campaign. A search of federal campaign databases shows such generous gifts at these: $1 million (Republican National Committee by Dawn Arnall); $360,000 (Democratic National Committee by Roland); and $250,000 (DNC by Dawn). The list went on and on.

On occasion all three Arnalls and their employees gave to campaigns of the same politicians, some of whom sat on committees overseeing their business, and some didn't. However, on the federal level, the Congress, Senate, and White House were of no real threat to Ameriquest and Argent. There were occasional discussions of federal legislation that might crack down on the lending practices of subprime firms, but as far as a bill actually passing (even on the committee level) was concerned, nothing came close. And if something did actually pass, Arnall had a friend in the White House.

It was on the state level that Ameriquest, Argent, and Countrywide faced their biggest threat to doing business. One way to influence the debate was to donate money to state candidates. In 2001 Georgia passed the Fair Lending Act, which required residential lenders to prove that on a refinancing that was less than five years old the new mortgage would provide what was called a "tangible net benefit" to the borrower. Ameriquest and other subprime lenders began lobbying state politicians to remove that provision. They feared it would harm their business. (In the early days of subprime lending, when consumer finance companies dominated the industry, most of the loans originated were either second liens or refinancings. In the modern era of subprime, lenders still relied heavily on refinancings, though the purchase of new houses was a growing part of their business. Ameriquest, by pioneering the use of stated-income and limited-documentation loans, created a whole new class of borrowers who could buy homes without having to prove they actually earned what they stated on their loan applications.)

Georgia State Senator Vincent Fort would later tell the *Wall Street Journal* that "Ameriquest was very, very engaged," adding that Adam Bass, Arnall's nephew, who was now on board at the company full-time, lobbied him directly. Senator Fort said he accused Bass of victimizing minorities, which, according to the newspaper, angered the attorney. Ameriquest's spokesman would only say of the meeting that it was "a very candid conversation about complex policy issues." After the Georgia law passed, Ameriquest began donating money to state legislators. One donation, for $2,500, went to Lieutenant Governor Mark Taylor after he emerged as a pivotal figure in the debate over whether parts of the bill should be overturned.

Many subprime lenders were threatening to pull out of Georgia, Ameriquest among them. Rating agencies Standard & Poor's and Moody's Investors Service said they would have trouble putting a rating on subprime mortgage-backed securities (MBSs), because any loan that violated the new law might spur litigation, thus tainting these bonds. (The last thing in the world an investor wanted was to buy a bond that might be the subject of litigation.) Within a few months, a new law was passed that neutered the tangible net benefit clause. Ameriquest and its competitors won. Money, in this instance, talked. Over the next few years the same scenario would play out in other states—Illinois, New Jersey, New York, and Pennsylvania, to name a few—with antipredatory lending laws being either passed or discussed, and lobbyists from subprime companies or trade groups trying to kill or beat back regulations that hurt Ameriquest and their competitors, including Countrywide.

One lobbyist fighting the good fight for subprime lenders was Wright Andrews, an attorney who ran a Washington-based lobbying shop called Butera & Andrews. (Andrews, a portly man with ruddy cheeks, was directly involved in beating back the Georgia bill.) According to the *Wall Street Journal*, the attorney also managed three different subprime-related trade groups: the National Home Equity Mortgage Association (Ameriquest was a member), the Coalition for Fair and Affordable Lending, and the Responsible Mortgage Lending Coalition. A cynic might argue that the names of the last two groups were a bit ironic given all the allegations of abusive lending practices that subprime firms like Ameriquest were being slapped with—outrageous points and fees and questionable appraisal practices among them. Besides his partner James Butera, Andrews had another ally in representing the industry, his wife Lisa. In 2003 Ameriquest hired Lisa Andrews as its senior vice president for government affairs, a fancy way of saying she was the subprime lender's top lobbyist.

At this point Arnall had plenty to protect. Ameriquest was the largest retail subprime lender in the land, funding about $30 billion a year in new loans through its 230 retail branches and thousands of loan officers. Argent, the wholesale division that relied exclusively on loan brokers, was originating just as much. Arnall's entire ACC empire (most of which was Ameriquest/Argent) was earning $1 billion a year pretax.

Wayne Lee, who had risen in the ranks at Long Beach Mortgage, had molded Argent into an origination giant by hiring aggressive account executives who gathered loans from a nationwide network of loan brokers, many of whom were already familiar with the company because they did business with Arnall's LBM. Ameriquest was spending millions of dollars in ads each year on television, radio, and the Internet. One series of TV commercials was called, "Don't judge too quickly. We won't." In one ad a teenage girl and her friends are on the way to a concert, the middle-aged father driving. The daughter asks the father to pull over at a convenience store so she and her friends can get some gum. As the girls run into the store, the father yells out that she'll need some money. The daughter, wearing a feathery pink waistcoat and a short skirt—and looking like a young hooker—leans into the car as the father, who's waiting at the curb, hands her a $20 bill. Just as he's doing this a police car pulls up behind him. The dad, with an embarrassed look on his face, and thinking what the cops are probably thinking, mutters to the camera, "I'm her daddy."

The ads—all of which portrayed situations that looked bad (but had innocent explanations)—aired in selected markets but without 800 numbers or web site addresses. The idea was to brand the Ameriquest name on anything that would give the company maximum exposure and make its telephones ring. (As Cole had noted, it was all about selling.) Over the years Ameriquest bought the naming rights to the Texas Rangers baseball stadium, and advertised on the walls of major and minor league stadiums. It sponsored a tour by the Rolling Stones, and even topped that by hiring (Sir) Paul McCartney to play the halftime show at the Super Bowl—the Ameriquest name emblazoned over the TV screen as the former Beatle finished "Live and Let Die."

Argent, even though it didn't deal directly with the public but through loan brokers, sponsored NASCAR race car drivers Dario Franchitti and Danica Patrick, the Argent name printed proudly on their cars and uniforms. It sponsored athletes far and wide—Jim Furyk, Chris de Marco (golf), Michael Phelps and Amanda Beard (the U.S. Olympic team), among others. Terry Rouch, who worked for several of Arnall's mortgage companies over the years, noted that the Ameriquest/ Argent name was "truly everywhere," saying the company's plan was to create instant name recognition "not to just brokers and borrowers but literally to the world and with all 50 state attorney generals."

The mention of the AGs by Rouch was a joke, but that's exactly what happened. Ameriquest/Argent was nothing short of a mortgage juggernaut. Not only was it the largest subprime lender in the nation, but it now ranked 10th among all residential lenders. The industry knew it, Mozilo knew it, investment bankers knew it. Managing directors from Bear Stearns, Lehman Brothers, and Friedman Billings Ramsey had all knocked on Arnall's door trying to convince him to take the company public through an IPO. Year after year he resisted, but then in late 2004 he began to think otherwise. Around this time both the press and several AGs' offices (California, Connecticut, Iowa, and New York) began paying attention to a growing pile of allegations against the company—that some of Ameriquest's retail loan officers were a little bit too high-pressure on the sales tactics, convincing homeowners to take out loans they couldn't afford. It was also around this time that Arnall's retail production chief, the man in charge of all the LOs on the street, Kirk Langs, announced his retirement. Langs was 40 years old. The company, true to form, said little about the retirement. Rumors began to circulate in the industry that Langs might have walked away with a retirement package worth $17 million. He, like his boss, wasn't one to give interviews.

A few years earlier, Elmore allegedly had warned Bass and Lee that the company had major quality control issues—and that management either didn't know what was going on or didn't take it all that seriously. The branch manager who worked in the Southwestern region for the company swore that his employees were clean but admitted that elsewhere in the company "there was blatant fraud going on," particularly in its Florida office. Mozilo, who was always looking to buy branches of competitors, said he hired a bunch of Ameriquest retail LOs who worked in the lender's New York area offices. "What I saw after a few weeks led me to turn it over to Spitzer," he said. (Mozilo declined to elaborate. Spitzer was Eliot Spitzer, the New York AG at the time.)

The *Los Angeles Times* published a story quoting Lisa Taylor, a former LO who worked in Ameriquest's Sacramento branch, saying the atmosphere was similar to that portrayed in the movie *Boiler Room*, where actors Vin Diesel and Giovanni Ribisi played young hotshot stockbrokers working for a corrupt investment banking firm selling worthless stocks to customers who were rubes. "That was homework," said Taylor, "to watch *Boiler Room*." She said Ameriquest had a do-anything-to-get-the-deal-done mentality. One time she walked in on co-workers who were using a brightly lit Coca-Cola machine as a tracing board where loan agents were copying borrowers' signatures onto blank documents. In other offices, LOs were chugging down silvery cans of Red Bull, working the phones deep into the night using lead-generation sheets that the company had bought from outside vendors. (Lead-generation sheets carry the names of potential customers.)

After a while the consumer complaints against Ameriquest started to pile up. Chief among them was that Ameriquest executives had built a sales machine where the selling of loans was paramount, and the ability of a customer to repay not so important. Between 2000 and 2004, customers had filed about 460 complaints with the Federal Trade Commission concerning how it did business. Countrywide's retail subprime division, Full Spectrum Lending, was a somewhat distant second with 100. California newspapers like the *Los Angeles Times* and the *Orange County Register* began investigating the complaints, which ranged from charging excessive and hidden fees and closing costs to pressuring appraisers into inflating home values they were reviewing. Loan officers sometimes would then convince borrowers to take out larger mortgages than what they needed. Larger loan amounts meant higher points and fees for the Ameriquest LOs.

While all this was going on, *National Mortgage News* reported that Ameriquest had scrapped its plan to go public but was now considering an option that would allow Arnall to take cash out of the company by selling $1 billion worth of bonds to institutional investors. Friedman Billings Ramsey, a small boutique firm based in Arlington, Virginia, right across the Potomac River from Washington, had pitched the idea, its founder, Eric Billings, initially leading the negotiations. Ameriquest, through a spokesman, declined to comment. It also declined to talk about another rumor making its way through business and political circles in the summer of 2005: that Arnall, a big supporter of the president, was seeking an ambassadorship, preferably to Israel, Sweden, or the Netherlands. (Friends of Arnall's told *National Mortgage News* that Israel was his first choice.)

By this time, the IPO was definitely off. Wall Street firms had made well over $100 million in fees from Ameriquest, Argent, and affiliated lenders over the years by lending them money and securitizing their subprime loans,[8] but the biggest payday of them all—underwriting fees from an IPO—likely would never materialize. Word of several state AG investigations concerning its lending practices had killed that hope.

In late July the Bush White House made it official: Arnall was being considered for the ambassadorship to the Netherlands. This time, Ameriquest's spokesman, Chris Orlando, finally decided to say something: "Mr. Arnall would be willing and honored to serve his country in any way he might be asked." Even though Arnall and his wife had made large donations to the Democratic National Committee over the years, all eight Democrats on the Foreign Relations Committee, which had the first vote on ambassadorships, said they would vote no because of the abusive lending allegations hanging over the company. Republicans were inclined to vote yes. Republican Senator Norm Coleman from Minnesota said of Arnall, "His personal actions had never been called into question."

In January 2006, and after several more months of rumors about what the AG offices were up to, Ameriquest made it official, agreeing to pay 49 states $325 million to settle charges that it engaged in abusive lending practices. (Virginia was excluded from the settlement because

---

[8] Even though Arnall's previous subprime company, Long Beach Mortgage, avoided securitizing subprime loans in the 1990s, Ameriquest was an active securitizer in the new decade, using Greenwich Capital of Connecticut, which eventually was bought by Royal Bank of Scotland (RBS). In 2008, RBS was taken over by the British government.

Ameriquest didn't lend there.) It was the second largest home lending settlement in U.S. history.[9] Roughly 750,000 loans that Ameriquest had made through its *Boiler Room*–trained LOs were affected by the settlement. On average, each Ameriquest customer would get $600. One of the most damaging charges against the company was that its LOs had engaged in a practice called upselling where the loan officer was compensated extra money to originate mortgages at a higher note rate or more points. In settling, the company admitted no wrongdoing and boasted to the press that the settlement with the states in no way restricted its ability to lend.

The deal also cleared the way for Arnall's ambassadorship to go through, though the vote was narrow. Shortly thereafter his wife Dawn was named chairman of ACC, the holding company that oversaw Ameriquest and Argent. Argent, the wholesale arm that used brokers, wasn't part of the settlement, though Iowa AG Tom Miller told reporters that the states would begin investigating wholesalers and brokers.

Adam Bass, who was now senior vice president of Ameriquest and vice chairman of the holding company, told *National Mortgage News* that the practice of upselling had ended three years earlier when the company had installed new software to prevent it. He said some of the company's "bad apples" had been fired, but wouldn't elaborate.

In May 2006 Ameriquest closed all 229 of its retail branches and fired 3,800 workers, including a few thousand LOs. (Argent continued to fund loans and was unaffected by the job cuts.) A few months later, in May, Bass and company spokesman Chris Orlando visited *National Mortgages News'* Washington office to pitch a story idea to executive editor Paul Muolo and bureau chief Brian Collins about a new retail strategy Ameriquest was embarking on. The retail offices had all been shuttered, but Bass said that by using technology and advertisements on television and the Internet, the lender would be born anew with four large call center operations that would handle applications over the telephone. While he was talking about the plan in a conference room, Bass's cell phone rang. It was his wife. "Honey, I'm here with *National Mortgage*

---

[9] In late 2002, Household Finance—which now owned the old Beneficial franchise—agreed to pay $484 million to several states to settle charges that it talked consumers into taking out larger loans than they needed while saddling them with higher rates and hidden costs.

News explaining to them our great new retail system." To Muolo it sounded like a staged phone call. Four months later the call centers were struggling, funding hardly any loans at all. Employees began sending e-mails to reporters that they were sitting around in offices the size of football fields doing nothing. The phones weren't ringing, even though Ameriquest was still running commercials on television and the Internet. By early 2007 the call center experiment would be deemed a failure and ended. Ameriquest retail was no more. Argent continued on for a few more months, trying to switch from originating subprime loans (which Wall Street was no longer paying top dollar for and in some cases was shunning entirely) to a new product called a 40-year loan where the loan payments were lower than on an old-fashioned 30-year fixed-rate loan, the kind that George Bailey used to make. Rumors began to circulate in the industry that by midyear ACC's mortgage operations had lost half a billion dollars, but because it was privately held the company didn't have to disclose anything to the public.

In January 2007 Wayne Lee sued Arnall's holding company, ACC, accusing the firm of reneging on a $50 million consulting agreement. When Langs had quietly retired in mid-2004, Arnall had promoted Lee to CEO of ACC, giving him responsibility to oversee both Ameriquest and Argent. He'd already been managing Argent, the wholesale arm, but the Ameriquest assignment was new. Shortly after taking control of management responsibilities for Ameriquest, Lee didn't find the situation to his liking. In his lawsuit, he said he tried to bring to Ameriquest "the legal protocol and financial discipline that had characterized Argent's superior performance in past years." In other words, Lee felt that Argent (which used outside brokers) was a clean shop that wasn't gouging consumers on points, fees, and appraisals. (Investigators and people who did business with Argent would later question this assessment.) But Lee did have one thing in his favor: Argent had not been mentioned in the Ameriquest AG settlement or been a party to it all—which left many professionals wondering.

Lee blamed Arnall for blocking his efforts to clean up Ameriquest. Even though Arnall had appointed him to head the retail arm, a few months later he told Lee that he shouldn't "involve himself in the affairs of Ameriquest." In June 2005 Lee resigned, 11 months after being promoted. Arnall was not a defendant in the lawsuit, though he was mentioned prominently. Upon Lee's resignation, Arnall offered him a $50 million consulting contract. ACC paid him a lump sum of $20 million, promising to pay five more installments of $6 million each. Lee said when the first installment was due, the check never arrived. He got tired of getting the runaround and sued. As usual, Arnall had no comment, but ACC's attorney, Bernard LeSage, did. He called Lee's claims "a ridiculous work of fiction."[10]

★ ★ ★

In the spring of 2007, after months of sale rumors, ACC made it official: It was selling Argent and what was left of Ameriquest's loan servicing operation to banking giant Citigroup for an undisclosed sum.[11] As a processor of loan payments, Ameriquest received a fee for doing the monthly paperwork on $60 billion in subprime mortgages, most of which had been originated by Ameriquest and Argent. On April 17, at Citigroup's annual shareholders meeting, chairman and CEO Charles Prince stood alone on the stage of Carnegie Hall—just as his predecessor Sandy Weill used to do—and took questions from shareholders and members of the community. Matthew Lee of Inner City Press, a consumer advocate who had made it his mission in life to expose both predatory lenders and companies overcharging minorities on loans, questioned Prince about Ameriquest's track record of abusive lending and whether Argent might have similar problems. Prince,[12] who was

---

[10] As this book went to press the lawsuit had been settled with neither side disclosing the terms.

[11] Once again, Citigroup was rolling the dice on subprime even though two years after buying Associates First Capital Corporation it paid $215 million to the Federal Trade Commission to settle abusive lending allegations against the company.

[12] Among other jobs he held before he worked for Citigroup, Prince was general counsel for Commercial Credit of Baltimore, a nonbank subprime lender owned by Travelers, the insurance company giant. In April 1998 Travelers and Citigroup announced a historical merger (via a $70 billion stock swap) that would create a commercial bank/investment bank/insurance conglomerate. The investment bank piece of the deal was Smith Barney, which Travelers owned. Smith Barney included the old Salomon Brothers franchise, Lew Ranieri's old company. Shortly after the Citigroup-Travelers merger was announced, Congress neutered the Glass-Steagall Act, which, in place since 1933, banned the combination of banks with investment banking houses.

caught off guard by the question, said, "We're not going to buy anything unless it's cleaned up."

The sale of Argent and the Ameriquest servicing operation closed
in the fall of 2007—with no details revealed, especially price. Nine
months earlier Citigroup, under Prince, had gone dark to the trade
press, refusing to tell *Inside Mortgage Finance* and *National Mortgage News*,
the two trade publications that each quarter collected subprime origination and servicing figures, what Citi was producing in the way of
A– to D loans. For 10 years Citi had gladly given over the figures. Here
Citi was buying Arnall's last remaining subprime company—and acting
a bit like the ambassador himself, disclosing little. Argent was no more.
Citi dismantled the name. Arnall was now officially out of the mortgage business, hosting cocktail parties at the embassy in The Hague, far,
far away from the cities and beaches of Orange County.

★   ★   ★

When it comes to producing prodigies, Southern California is known for
two things: baseball prospects and subprime mortgage companies. At the
beginning of 2006—when the business of making loans to Americans
with bad credit still looked like a safe bet to many Wall Street firms that
were lending money to firms like Ameriquest—eight of the nation's
top 15 subprime firms were headquartered in Southern California, the
land of the Beach Boys. Seven of the 15 were nonbanks that survived on
warehouse lines of credit from the likes of Bear Stearns, Credit Suisse,
Lehman Brothers, and Merrill Lynch. The rest were owned by banks.

Part of the reason was the weather. "Heck, it's warm here," said Dan
Perl, the subprime executive who started out his career as a loan broker, briefly managed an S&L, and then launched his own firm, only
to pull the plug and then become a bottom fisher who bought delinquent mortgages on the cheap. "You can go surfing in the morning and
then drive 50 miles east and be in the mountains." Perl, who had been
nicknamed The Big Kahuna by some of his employees, was born in
Brooklyn into a conservative Jewish family. Like Arnall, he moved west
in search of a better life. "There was no cabal here. We were all disen-
franchised. In the 1970s and 1980s if you wanted money you had to go
to Wall Street with your hat in hand. The Street had the power, but a
bunch of guys who got into the business started by grabbing an S&L."

Arnall was one of those executives, as were Russ and Becky Jedinak. They entered the business using the cheapest way they knew how: getting their hands on a savings and loan and then benefiting from deregulation. When regulators made it too difficult for them, they did the only sensible thing an entrepreneur could do—they got out from under the watchful eye of the examiners and started a nonbank. Luckily for them, Wall Street had warmed up to the business, realizing it could make big money by securitizing their mortgages—even if they were made to homeowners and home buyers who had bad credit.

Even though Arnall was out of the business by 2007, he (as well as the Jedinaks) had left behind a family tree of executives and loan officers who had worked at one of his companies and then decided to either start their own subprime shop or work for an existing one, taking along with them the tricks of the trade—not all of them good. In a way, Arnall had served as the Johnny Appleseed of the industry. Jack Mayesh, Arnall's right-hand man at Long Beach Mortgage, stayed out of the business for three years after the company was sold to WaMu and then reemerged with a brand-new lender called Residential Mortgage Assistance Enterprise or ResMAE for short. (Note how it sounds like Fannie Mae.) It was based in Brea, nestled in the foothills of north Orange County, 20 miles from the Pacific. Its specialty—to no one's surprise—was subprime lending. Mayesh's backers on Wall Street? Lehman Brothers and Greenwich Capital, which promised to lend him money and either buy or securitize his loans. Joining Mayesh in his new venture were two other former executives who had worked for Arnall: Edward Resendez and William Komperda. In its first year of operation ResMAE funded $1 billion in loans, a phenomenal sum for a company that a year earlier didn't even exist.

Another former Arnall acolyte at Long Beach Mortgage was Steven Holder, who went on to help start New Century Financial Corporation, a nonbank that eventually supplanted Ameriquest/Argent as the largest subprime funder in the United States. Holder eventually left New Century and formed yet another company, Encore Credit, which Bear Stearns backed. Also out of Long Beach Mortgage came Frank Curry, who formed Acoustic Home Loans. LBM alumni Pat Rank and Bob Dubrish launched Option One Mortgage, which eventually was sold to Fleet Bank of Boston, and then to H&R Block, the tax preparation giant. (In time Option One became a top five ranked subprime originator.) Arnall employee Tim Walsh launched the retail arm of First NLC Financial Services of Deerfield Beach, Florida. Eventually, more than 100 Ameriquest employees, including several top sales managers and LOs, would join him.

The action was in Irvine and Orange or nearby edge cities, not too far from the Pacific Ocean. New Century favored the commercial hub between Orange County's modest airport and the sprawling campus of the University of California at Irvine. This large commercial district, one of two in Irvine, has none of the density or hyperactivity of New York or Chicago. The district was meticulously planned, with each glass office building placed as carefully as a piece on a chess board. Intermingled with the offices are French and Italian eateries, upscale Mexican grills, luxury apartments and condos, and executive gyms. On any given day a subprime office worker might go out to lunch and run into three or four of his or her competitors. Though mortgage companies occupied dozens of floors in various office towers, they crammed in as many warm bodies as possible. Everyone was making good money—off of people who *weren't* making good money or had bad credit. As subprime lending boomed, the parking lots of those office buildings increasingly were littered with the latest Porsches, Ferraris, Mercedeses, and BMWs. And it was all located five minutes from the beaches of the Pacific Ocean, and 30 miles from Angelo Mozilo, who was battling all of them to be the king of subprime.

Chapter 5

Angelo Rising

The Son of a Bronx Butcher Makes Good

There is a certain amount of hubris there. In terms of arrogance, Countrywide is at the top.
    —FORMER SANDLER O'NEILL ANALYST MIKE MCMAHON,
        WHO COVERED THE COMPANY FOR NINE YEARS

Physically speaking, Angelo Mozilo is not an imposing man. He is no taller than 5 feet 10 inches at most. There's a tightness to his skin that suggests that somewhere along the line there was cosmetic surgery—nothing radical, just a nip or tuck here or there. He has crow's-feet at the corners of his eyes, but what 69-year-old doesn't? And there's that ever-present tan, the butt of jokes even by friends who've known him for years. Few see him sitting on a beach in Malibu, earning his George Hamilton copper skin tone the natural way.

He has a confident smile, and a voice that carries the intonation of knowledge, one that suggests he knows more about one thing—the residential mortgage business—than you will ever know, even if you had 100 years and he had just one. Those close to him know that he loves the business, often referring to Countrywide as his "baby" or his "daughter," the latter a word he used when talking to politicians while his company's fortunes crumbled.

He is not the kind of man to chuckle at a joke to make you feel good. He doesn't need that, not in the twilight of his career, which was fast coming to an end in early 2008. If you had seen him the year before in Washington at the spring forecast conference of the National Association of Home Builders—politically speaking, one of the most powerful trade organizations in America—you would see a man dressed in a suit and tie, sitting at lunch with home building executives, picking their brains about a deteriorating market, one in which home prices were falling and the inventory of homes for sale was quickly rising. His suit jacket might be off, his sleeves rolled up. He wanted to hear it from the builders themselves straight up—about declining sales, rising lumber prices, data points that would harm his business. He has always been that way: not afraid to hear the worst of it. He believes if there's a train about to jump the tracks he wants to know so he can get Countrywide safely out of the way. He has always been prepared for a fight, prepared to survive.

Angelo is thin and trim. At 69 (in early 2008) he looked much the same way he did 20 years earlier and even 20 years before that. As a boy he had what's called an asthmatic condition, and sometimes had to stay in bed for a week until it passed. "There were no effective medications for asthma in those days," he recalls.

His hair is a silvery gray, closely cropped, combed from left to right. It has been that way for decades. Even though he is not tall or powerfully built, after a few minutes of talking to him you realize that he's tough and afraid of nothing. He has a quick answer to most questions—at least from stock analysts and reporters. That toughness started back in the Bronx, the poorest of New York City's five boroughs, a place where poor Irish, Italian, and Jewish immigrants settled during the turn of the previous century.

He tells a story of his youth: He was a young boy, two years old. He had ear infections that wouldn't clear, a mastoid infection that wouldn't subside. "There was no penicillin in those days," he says. The first operation didn't work. There were more. They didn't work, either. His father, first-generation Italian, owned two butcher shops in the Bronx. When those early operations failed, the senior Mozilo sold one of the shops to pay for another operation. This one was done on the kitchen table at the Mozilo household. This time the surgeon cut deep. "They had to cut away part of it," Angelo says and stops. "There was no penicillin," he repeats. "That's why I have holes behind my ears. That operation worked."

He didn't learn the story of how his father had sold one of his butcher shops to pay for the surgery until much later, when he was 14 or 15 years old. By that time he'd been working in the remaining butcher shop, sweeping the floors and learning the trade, which included cutting up chickens and making sausage. He wasn't afraid to get blood on his hands. Butchers who were afraid of blood were worthless. "I was a pretty good butcher," he says.

About his father, an Italian immigrant, he will say this: "He was a terrific man. He'd drive around the neighborhoods in the Bronx, giving out packages of meats to the seniors who could no longer make it into the shop." He remembers it clearly.

About his mother, he would note her love of higher learning and her insistence that her children should graduate from college. "She was obsessed with education," he says, an obsession he remembers when he talks of his friend Lew Ranieri, the former Salomon Brothers bond trader who started in the mail room and rose to the trading desk, then became vice chairman of the firm. "I was awed by him. Here was a guy who had raw intelligence. He never finished college and he was a genius."[1]

By his own account, Angelo enjoyed helping out in the butcher shop but had other ideas about a career. On his 14th birthday his father woke him early and drove him down to the health department so he could get his working papers. He became a messenger for Lawyers Mortgage and Title, a Manhattan mortgage company on West 43rd Street, continuing to work for his father on weekends. He attended public school until the eighth grade, then switched to a Catholic school, which meant there was tuition to pay—and he'd be paying it, not his father. When it came time to attend college, he had to ask his father for permission, which was reluctantly granted. "He wanted me to work with him in the butcher shop," Angelo said. His father died in the shop,

---

[1] After being promoted to the Salomon Brothers trading desk, Ranieri had not yet earned his college degree. A few years later he finally took night classes, earning the final credits he needed, including a language credit in Italian.

never having enjoyed retirement. "An inspector came in and he had a heart attack right there," says Angelo. "He leaned against the counter and fell." Angelo attributes it to fear.

Any young man who grew up in the New York metropolitan area before 1960 (and perhaps even after that to some degree) defined himself by his ethnic heritage. Mozilo was no different. He was Italian, and when he traveled outside his neighborhood he was sensitive about how he was regarded. (Despite all the jokes about his tan, Mozilo has a dark complexion.) He worked at Lawyers Mortgage in midtown from the time he was 14 to age 21, learning the business of funding residential loans from the ground floor up. "I worked in every single department—title, closing, and insurance. I ran the cash cage." He was the only Italian working at the company. "Everyone else was Jewish," he remembers, "but I felt no discrimination."

In 1960 he attended night school at New York University while still working at the mortgage company. He ached to be a trader on Wall Street but was concerned how he'd be treated. "Italians on Wall Street were relegated to one thing," he said of the time, "Jews to another, the Irish. The WASPs did the relegating. I felt it was an uphill battle."

It was that year his boss, Edwin Katz, decided to merge Lawyers Mortgage with a Norfolk, Virginia–based lender called United Mortgagee. The owner of the company arrived in Manhattan to talk details with Katz. "He sees this one goy kid running around the office," says Mozilo. "That was me. He looks at me and says, 'I want that kid to merge the two companies.' So I have to go down to Norfolk." The man who struck the merger was named David Loeb, who just so happened to be a Bronx native as well. "I didn't want to go. The Bronx was gang-infested at the time, but to go down South? I'd never left New York. I thought, why me?" Katz offered Mozilo a deal that was hard to refuse—he offered to pay his night school tuition.

Within a few days Mozilo, who was engaged to his girlfriend Phyllis, found an attic apartment and began the task of combining the two firms' files and accounting records. He returned to New York, where Loeb was now based, and declared to his new boss, "The job's done. They're merged." He wanted to stay in Manhattan. Instead, since he'd done such a good job of combining the two companies' operations, Katz told him to stay down in Norfolk and originate "spot loans," which was the jargon used to describe mortgages on existing houses. Loeb's business was centered around making mortgages to buy houses in newly built subdivisions. Angelo reluctantly complied.

He wasn't sure where to start, so he began knocking on the doors of realty firms. "I started calling on Realtors," he said. To his amazement he found that "no one had ever done this before" in Virginia. He worked until two and three in the morning, and presented his bosses with what he called "a box full of loans." They were pleased. This time they sent him even deeper South, down to Orlando, Florida, where there was a mini housing boom under way. With his new wife in tow— "crying all the way," he recalled, because she, too, wasn't fond of that part of the country—he began calling on both builders and Realtors, but this time he came up snake eyes. "This was the deep South," he recalled. "I was making no progress." He started to wonder if his last name and the way he looked (a sharp-dressing Italian from New York) had something to do with it.

He had a small office in Orlando. Across the way was an accountant who saw him working late each night. "He was Jewish and asked me how business was. I told him not good. He replied, 'It's because you're Italian.'" The next week the accountant introduced him to some builders he knew who were Jewish and happened to have developments under way in nearby Brevard County, home to Cape Canaveral. The year before, President Kennedy had announced the mission to the moon. Space science engineers were pouring into the area along with their families and needed housing. "They were literally living in tents on the beach," he said.

Mozilo got an idea: Why not finance a new subdivision to take advantage of the land rush and make the mortgages on the homes? On the day the subdivision was set to open models for viewing, heavy rains pounded the coast. Furniture was floating in the models. Mozilo feared that the idea would bankrupt the company or at the very least get him canned. (His wife was now pregnant with the couple's first child.) But the demand for homes was so great he caught a break. The home-buying engineers, according to the future Countrywide chief, rolled up their pants and signed on the dotted line anyway. "They needed a place to live," he said. "I couldn't take their loan applications fast enough." It cemented his reputation within the company.

In time, Mozilo worked his way up to executive vice president, but never owned a stake in the firm. United Mortgagee belonged to David Loeb and Edwin Katz. In 1968 the two men sold out to a conglomerate. "They didn't know anything about the mortgage business," Mozilo said of his new owners. "Among other things, they were in the bra business." When Loeb quit in disgust with management (over the issue of them wanting to raid the lender's escrow funds,[2] as well as other differences), Mozilo hung on for a few months and then resigned as well. He was 30 years old and had three kids. Almost immediately he and Loeb teamed up to form Countrywide. Mozilo once again became an advance man, but at least it was in California, whose warm, sunny climate he quickly fell in love with.

One of the first branches Mozilo opened up for the young company was in Orange County, the future home of Arnall's Ameriquest and countless other subprime lenders. He legged it around Southern California highways, interstates, and boulevards looking for shopping centers with For Lease signs. He met with landlords and negotiated the lease contracts. In the company's formative years, he and Loeb paid Countrywide's loan officers on commission. Soon enough he discovered that "if the salesmen left us we'd lose business, because they took it with them."

In 1974 Mozilo was earning $2,000 a month. His only promise of wealth, according to him, lay in whether Countrywide could prosper. The young company had a handful of offices but was looking to expand into Arizona, Florida, and North Carolina. Loeb was still back in New York, serving as the firm's trader, disposing of its loans in the secondary market. (The *primary market* is the phrase used to describe the origination of a loan to the consumer. When a mortgage is closed and then changes hands, it is considered a *secondary market* transaction.)[3]

---

[2] Escrow funds include money set aside in advance by the borrower to pay real estate taxes and insurance. The money is held by the lender or servicer of the loan.

[3] Not all mortgage originators sell their loans into the secondary market. Some— depositories mostly (banks, S&Ls, credit unions)—might keep the loans on the institution's balance sheet, offsetting these assets with liabilities (deposit accounts). Secondary market investors might include, but are not limited to, other banks, S&Ls, Wall Street firms, Fannie Mae, and Freddie Mac.

Mozilo had a formula for opening the offices. Each would employ three to four workers—mostly women. Mozilo will tell you that he is a happily married man. "It wasn't what you might think," he said. There was a method to his madness. Early on, the lender was producing only one type of loan—a mortgage insured by the Federal Housing Administration or Veterans Administration (FHA/VA), the federal government. "I wanted them to type well, and women could do that," he explained. "There were a lot of forms and a lot of typing. To process loans, they had to type. That's what I was going after. Guys? All they wanted to do was sell, but they couldn't type. Back then the FHA/VA did all the underwriting for you."

Finding women to "man" the offices could prove difficult. Mozilo was driving around the state opening up new branches in towns and cities where subdivisions were quickly sprouting up. He would conduct employee interviews in motel rooms. "I set the interviews up in motel rooms because I was coming into town and needed a place to stay," he said. "Sometimes, the rooms would have suites, but not always. I had to laugh. A lot of time there'd be men standing in the doorways, pacing. I remember one guy—I thought he was going to lose it, hit the wall with his fist or something." Employees in the early offices did exactly what Mozilo first did when he arrived in Virginia—call on Realtors because that's where the home-buying process began.

The offices that Mozilo set up did everything from taking applications to underwriting and funding the loan. "It was a hub-and-spoke approach," said Mike McMahon, the Sandler O'Neill analyst who made it a point to personally know Mozilo and study his methods. Countrywide had a four-person office approach. "Once that office couldn't handle the volume anymore, he'd find a new location two miles down the road and open another one to see if they could make a go of it," he said.

Because FHA/VA loans accounted for just 15 percent of all mortgages originated in the United States, Countrywide could grow only so much. Prior to the savings and loan (S&L) crisis, thrifts still dominated the business. But all that changed in 1970 when President Nixon signed a bill that allowed Fannie Mae, the congressionally chartered secondary market agency, to begin buying conventional loans— that is, mortgages made to consumers with good credit who didn't necessarily need FHA or VA coverage. Suddenly things were looking up for the company, as well as for every nondepository mortgage banking firm that was tired of being kept down on the farm, making only government-insured loans.

★ ★ ★

James A. Johnson had a blue-chip resume when it came to politics. Born and raised in Minnesota, he was the son of a state house speaker whose circle of friends included a onetime presidential candidate and icon of the Democratic party, Hubert Humphrey. Before he was even old enough to vote, he volunteered for his first political campaign. He became a top aide to Senator Walter Mondale, Democrat of Minnesota, and served under him for many years, eventually chairing the politician's 1984 bid for the White House. After Mondale's loss to Ronald Reagan, Johnson married Maxine Isaacs, the campaign's press secretary. They became well known in Democratic circles. Columnist Matthew Cooper of *Slate* once likened them to James Carville and Mary Matalin, calling them a "hot political" couple. Cooper's comparison, however, was a bit off. Whereas Carville and Matalin might be viewed as attention-seeking TV pundits, Johnson and his wife didn't exactly live to be in the media limelight. They had serious political connections inside the Beltway and could peddle influence plenty, but Johnson was someone who expressed his views in private and went public only when it made political sense. Of Norwegian decent, Johnson was tall, trim, and fit with an intelligent face. He was also a heck of a lot better looking than the cue-ball-headed Carville.

In 1980, after Jimmy Carter lost to Reagan, the Minnesota native founded Public Strategies, a Washington consulting firm that gave advice to business clients, including investment banking firms. His partner was Richard Holbrooke, the diplomat. Eventually, the practice was bought by Shearson Lehman Brothers and Johnson became employed by the investment banker, working alongside David Stockman, a former budget director in the Reagan administration. One of their clients was Fannie Mae.

Johnson was not a businessman himself—he never ran anything but a consulting firm and political campaigns. But those who worked for him describe him as someone who thought like a businessman.

"He's gifted," said one former Fannie executive. "He has a strategic mind. He understands how business works." In the late 1980s Johnson became a consultant and then a top executive at Fannie Mae, mostly because of his political connections. The man who recruited him was Fannie Mae chairman and CEO David O. Maxwell, a former mortgage insurance company president and a past general counsel at the Department of Housing and Urban Development, the cabinet-level agency that administered the FHA program and also served as regulator of sorts to Fannie Mae and its sibling company Freddie Mac. (The two men had been introduced by a mutual friend and hit it off.) Maxwell had one other distinction—he had once written a letter of recommendation for an up-and-coming mortgage banker named Angelo Mozilo and his partner David Loeb. Ticor Mortgage Insurance, where Maxwell had served as president, had its headquarters just down the road from Countrywide on Wilshire Boulevard. When Maxwell, nearing retirement age, was searching for a successor to head Fannie Mae, he looked no further than down the hallway toward Johnson's office. There were no other candidates for the position. Maxwell worked the company's board of directors, convincing them that the silver-haired Minnesotan with the oversize horn-rimmed glasses was their man. Case closed.

When Johnson officially took over as chairman and CEO in February 1991, he hit the road, spending much of his first two years traveling the nation, meeting the company's clients, who weren't consumers (though Fannie Mae wound up owning their loans) but mortgage banking firms and their top executives. "Jim," said a friend, "wanted to go out and learn the industry." Inevitably, his travels took him to California for the same reason any mortgage executive with an ounce of business sense catered to the state: It had a huge market share and a growing population that needed some place to live—which meant mortgages. Mozilo's Countrywide was already doing business with Fannie Mae, selling its conventional loans to the government-sponsored enterprise (GSE). "The Countrywide account," as it became known inside the GSE, was baby-sat by John Fulmer, who ran Fannie Mae's West Coast office on Wilshire Boulevard, conveniently located right across the street from Countrywide's headquarters and not too far from the old Ticor office where Maxwell had once worked. Fulmer and Mozilo were somewhat tight. Johnson wanted to be tight with him, too.

One thing that Jim Johnson was known for—besides his political talents—was his personal radar. A Fannie Mae executive who worked under him for many years described him this way: "He knows how to pick the right person who's on the ascendancy. It's a rare talent." Or maybe not that rare. The new CEO and the bean counters who tracked the millions in loans the GSE bought each year spotted the fact that Countrywide had been growing quite rapidly over the years and was about to achieve the one milestone that any good mortgage executive could dream of: becoming the largest residential lender in the United States. And Countrywide wasn't even an S&L.

With savings and loans continuing to fail at a record rate, Fannie Mae executives knew the mortgages they'd be buying in future years wouldn't be coming so much from S&Ls but from nonbank mortgage companies like Countrywide and a growing number of large commercial money center banks—like Norwest (later to merge with Wells Fargo)—that after years of ceding the business to the S&L industry finally realized that home lending, if done properly, wasn't so bad after all. And what a business it was becoming. In 1991, in the post-Reaganomics era, interest rates began to fall, which sparked both home building and mortgage lending. It didn't take long for Jim Johnson to realize that Mozilo "was the guy," said one of Johnson's aides. "Jim knew that he had to do everything he could to make Angelo think, 'I'm his best friend.' If Jim was traveling to the West Coast he'd say, 'We need to call Angelo and set up a golf game.' He became a student of Angelo. He knew his routine—that he'd be up at four in the morning, head to the gym, and start watching FNN."

Johnson wasn't looking for friendship alone; he wanted Countrywide to sell all, or at least most, of its billions in loan originations to Fannie Mae—and not to its crosstown competitor, Freddie Mac. Fannie Mae's executive team, Johnson included, knew that with the S&L industry shrinking and loan securitizations through Wall Street becoming a reality, they could benefit greatly by placing mortgages and mortgage-backed securities (MBSs) on their balance sheet. They needed volume, and Mozilo was the man who could deliver it. Johnson's goal was to cement the relationship between Countrywide and Fannie Mae for years to come. "When Jim realized how much volume Countrywide was taking down, especially in California, he made it his mission to get to know Angelo," said the Johnson aide.

Being the fierce competitor he was, Mozilo could smell a snow job a mile away. He knew exactly why Johnson was warming up to him. He once told a reporter that Johnson was so slick "he could cut off your balls and you'd still be wearing your pants." He meant it as a compliment. (At the time he made the remark, Countrywide was having some minor loan buyback disputes with Fannie Mae.) Over the years he continually referred to Johnson as a "great guy" and a "good friend." Johnson, as he had planned, had become one of Mozilo's closest confidants. But if his friend wanted Countrywide's business, Fannie Mae would have to pay for it in the form of lower fees. When Countrywide, or any lender, sold a loan to Fannie Mae, the GSE subtracted from the price paid what was called a "guarantee fee." Typically, that fee would be 23 basis points (0.23 percent) of the loan amount. Mozilo wanted volume discounts from Johnson. He got them.[4]

Over the next 15 years Countrywide and Fannie Mae—Mozilo and Johnson and then Mozilo and Franklin Raines, Johnson's successor—would be linked at the hip. Johnson invited Mozilo to attend and speak at retreats for Fannie Mae's top executives and sales team. The Fannie Mae chief, in turn, frequently flew on the Countrywide corporate jet. Johnson and other Fannie Mae executives were recipients of "Friends of Angelo" loans where Countrywide made them mortgages at discounted rates and fees. They played golf together. Later on when Johnson retired from Fannie Mae to chair the Kennedy Center, who would be sitting in the box with him at plays and performances but Angelo Mozilo? As Countrywide's loan originations soared into the stratosphere, so did Fannie Mae's on-balance-sheet assets. As one firm's earnings rose, so did the other's. Depending on the year, Countrywide might account for 10 percent to 30 percent of all the loans Fannie Mae bought. One joke making the rounds in the industry was that Countrywide was really just a subsidiary of Fannie Mae. When General Electric, Wells Fargo Bank, Household Finance, American International

---

[4] The guarantee fees that Fannie Mae charged to individual lenders it bought loans from were a closely guarded secret; however, executives close to the company said at one point Countrywide was being charged a guarantee fee of just 13 basis points, but only if it delivered sizable volume. It was, if true, the lowest "g-fee" deal Fannie had ever granted.

Group, and two other financial service giants formed a lobbying group called FM Watch to fend off Fannie and Freddie's efforts to enter other mortgage-related businesses that they dominated, Mozilo refused to join the group, defending the GSEs. "They [the FM Watch group] don't know what they're doing," he said. "If Fannie and Freddie catch a cold, I catch the fucking flu." He was afraid that if anything happened to the GSEs it would screw up his business as well, because he sold all of his conventional "A" credit quality loans to the two.

In 1992 Countrywide finally rose to the top of the heap. It funded $30.5 billion in mortgages (thanks in part to its use of loan brokers), becoming the nation's largest originator. Mozilo was now king of the industry and was crowned (elected) president of the Mortgage Bankers Association (MBA), an annual honorary position where he toured the nation making speeches about industry issues, reminding listeners (including the media) how mortgage bankers were an integral part of the "American dream of home ownership." (A constant political battle for the trade group was shooting down any effort to eliminate or curtail the tax deductibility status of mortgage interest payments, a favorite target of Republicans.) The MBA was the largest trade association serving and lobbying on behalf of residential lenders to make sure Congress didn't pass any laws that might hurt their profits or prospects. Mozilo took the job seriously (not all do). Frank Hattemer, a warehouse lending executive who worked for Bank United of Houston, an S&L controlled by Lew Ranieri, remembers attending the MBA convention in Boston when Mozilo was installed as president. The convention officially started on a Sunday and ran to midday Wednesday. Many conventioneers arrived on Saturday to set up trade show booths or play tourist. "A lot of us were out the night before, drinking too much," said Hattemer. "I came down for breakfast all bleary-eyed around nine in the morning. There was Angelo in the lobby wearing a suit and Gucci loafers, greeting people and shaking hands. He had that smile on his face and looked like a million bucks."

★　★　★

As the 1990s progressed, Countrywide and Fannie Mae (as well as Freddie Mac) continued to grow rapidly. After costing U.S. taxpayers $150 billion (not including interest payments), the S&L industry had been reregulated back into making mostly home mortgages. The old-fashioned Bailey Building and Loan styled lender was still around, but their numbers were greatly reduced. Thanks to mortgage securitizations—pioneered a decade earlier by Lew Ranieri at Salomon Brothers, as well as First Boston and Credit Suisse—the home lending industry had been transformed into one where huge national lenders like Countrywide could set up shop in any state by obtaining a low-cost license, originate mortgages (through either non-deposit-gathering branches or loan brokers), and sell them to Fannie Mae or Freddie Mac, receiving cash for their loans. The cash would be used to make more loans. Wall Street firms would sell the Fannie/Freddie-guaranteed MBSs to institutional investors, which meant pension funds, life insurers, commercial banks, or even S&Ls.

The securitization of mortgages, as well as the trading of MBSs, was a huge profit center for the likes of Bear Stearns, Lehman Brothers, Merrill Lynch, and several other traditional Wall Street firms that had what were called "fixed income" departments. Fixed income meant bonds. Not only did Bear, Merrill, and the others sell Fannie/Freddie MBSs, but they also had set up business desks in New York where traders would buy whole loans (unsecuritized mortgages) from nonbank lenders, S&Ls, and others, packing the mortgages into MBSs. Each time a bond was sold, an investment banking firm made a commission. Wall Street couldn't compete against Fannie and Freddie for "A" paper loans, since the GSEs had government charters, allowing them to borrow money at a cheaper cost, so instead they went after non-conforming loans, which included jumbo mortgages and the growing subprime sector. Each year the GSEs' regulator would set a loan limit based on the average median home price in the nation. Anything under that limit the GSEs could buy. Anything over it was considered jumbo, which left that business to Wall Street.

Mozilo got an idea. He and one of his young lieutenants, David Sambol, decided to open up a trading desk at the Pasadena headquarters to buy and sell (i.e., trade) jumbo loans and Community Reinvestment Act (CRA) loans. (Under federal laws, banks and S&Ls had to have a certain percentage of their assets invested in loans backed by real estate within a few miles of their headquarters and outlying branches.) Countrywide hired a bond salesman named Jonas Roth, who had worked for regional brokerage houses, to run the operation. "You couldn't do whole-loan trades on Fannie/Freddie mortgages because you couldn't beat their prices," Roth later recalled. It was also part of Angelo's plan to get a 10 percent market share, he noted. (In the 1990s Mozilo wanted a 10 percent share. By the next decade his dream had grown to 20 percent, then to 30 percent.) Under Sambol and Roth, Countrywide would originate jumbos and other nonconventional loan types and sell them to the highest bidder.

Typically, a mortgage firm that engaged in this strategy to originate nonconventional (nonprime) loans would use Bear Stearns, Merrill Lynch, Lehman Brothers, or another Wall Street firm for its trades. But Mozilo, who was by no means a fan of the Street, wanted to play in their game. Enter Roth. "On our first deal we sold $12 million in Alaska loans to Goldome Bank, which needed loans for CRA purposes. We made double the profit we could've made by selling to Goldome. We made a killing. Goldome needed those CRA credits. We knew we had something there." The unit's profit goal that year was about $30 million. The whole-loan trading desk brought in a net profit of $95 million.

From 1993 to 2000 Roth served as Countrywide's national sales manager. The traders working under him could earn three to four "sticks a year." One stick was equal to $1 million. It didn't take long before word got out to Countrywide's senior managers elsewhere in the company that whole-loan traders working in its capital markets group under Roth were raking in the dough, thanks to their commissions. "There was some resentment on the part of the managing directors," said Roth. "Angelo was hearing a lot of complaints about it."

Roth was summoned to Mozilo's Pasadena office along with Sambol. "We're going to put a cap on what the salesmen can make," Mozilo told him.

"You can't do that," Roth implored him. "You can't tap out the salesman." Mozilo stood up and walked over to the window. He signaled for Roth to come over. "You see that street down there?" Mozilo asked. "That ain't Wall Street, that's Lake Street. We do things our way."

Roth said the cap was placed on the whole-loan traders, but not for long. "They found another way to pay by putting the money in a separate account for them."

Shortly after Roth arrived on the scene in Pasadena, Countrywide began dabbling in subprime. At first, Mozilo doubted the product. "It was a different business than what we were doing," he said. (Peter Cugno, the former Beneficial manager who ran his own subprime company, recalled that Countrywide had brokered a few loans to him during the 1980s but never got very involved in the credit-impaired business.) In 1994, while Long Beach Mortgage, The Money Store, Aames, ContiMortgage, and others were beginning to ramp up their subprime operations (including securitizing the loans they produced through Wall Street), Mozilo stayed on the sidelines. In 1995 he stepped into the game but Countrywide originated just $93 million. The next year its subprime originations quadrupled.

Jonas Roth walked out of Countrywide's headquarters, which had been moved to nearby Calabasas, in 2000. "After a while they started hiring a lot of Wall Street people," said Roth. "I felt the Street people were brought in to take over the trading desk."

He didn't feel comfortable at the new headquarters, the former Lockheed Martin building, which included a large campus with a running track and an in-company restaurant that Roth described "as one of the best restaurants in Calabasas." (The traders had to have somewhere good to eat so they wouldn't stray too far from the trading desk.) In came traders and sales managers from Bear Stearns, Morgan Stanley, and UBS Securities. (Ron Kripalani from Chase Securities eventually took over as sales manager when Roth left.) "When I started, there were five people in the department. When I left there were 700." Mozilo may not have liked Wall Street so much, but he had no problem hiring its top guns.

Initially, Roth missed the "sticks," the action. "The money was good," he said. He missed the sales retreats, staying at the best hotels, and the rest of it. "The best beaches, the best food," he said. Like Roland Arnall, Mozilo treated his salespeople well. The one thing Roth didn't miss was the basement conference room in Calabasas. The former owners, Lockheed Martin, fearing a nuclear attack, had built a bomb shelter down there. Mozilo had it converted into a conference room. "It was like a vault," said Roth. "The doors were two feet thick, airtight. When they closed them you couldn't hear a thing. It was strange."

As the century turned, the mortgage market got strange, too. In 1998 mortgage bankers enjoyed their best year ever, originating a record

$1.5 trillion in home loans as rates on conventional "A" paper loans fell to under 7 percent for the first time in three decades. Countrywide and its competitors ramped up to take refi applications, but then volumes fell off the next two years as rates crept up again. There were massive layoffs throughout the industry, including job losses at Countrywide. Lenders folded. Loeb was now in retirement, chairing a competing company—called IndyMac—that he and Mozilo had helped start. (Based in Pasadena, IndyMac's CEO was Mike Perry, a dark-haired and handsome young executive who reminded Mozilo of a younger version of himself. IndyMac emulated Countrywide in many ways, including the use of loan brokers. And like Countrywide it started out life as a nondepository only to later on convert to a savings and loan charter. Perry also had a loan program similar to Mozilo's "Friends of Angelo" effort, but his was appropriately called "Friends of Mike." By this time Mozilo and Loeb were no longer so close.)

In the summer of 2000 when Mozilo was asked how the market was, he gave his best Bronx spin: "It sucks." Countrywide's share price fell, as did that of just about every lender associated with the mortgage industry. The hangover caused by the Russian debt crisis and subprime meltdown lingered. For the first time in the history of the company, he was seriously thinking about selling Countrywide. There were two companies whose offers he contemplated: Wells Fargo of San Francisco, which was managed by Richard Kovacevich, and Washington Mutual, which had been growing rapidly in recent years by gobbling up other savings and loans. Its CEO was Kerry Killinger. WaMu, as it was known, was headquartered up in Seattle. Both had nationwide mortgage franchises, as did Countrywide. Mozilo also had bought a small bank in Virginia to expand his funding sources for mortgages. Instead of relying on just warehouse lines of credit and commercial paper borrowings from banks, he was now using federally insured deposits.

Enter Warren Buffett, the venerated value investor who controlled insurance conglomerate Berkshire Hathaway. Mozilo had gotten to know Buffett because their insurance companies did business together. In his efforts to mold Countrywide into a financial services giant, Mozilo a few years earlier had bought Balboa Casualty & Life. To sell life insurance, companies needed to maintain a triple-A rating (meaning they had the best credit in the world). To achieve triple-A status,

Balboa needed to take out an insurance policy itself. It got two bids—one from American International Group (AIG),[5] the other from Berkshire Hathaway. Before Buffett would grant the policy, his analysts at Berkshire did what was called a "mark" on Countrywide. A mark meant that Buffett's bean counters went over the lender's books with a fine-tooth comb. Buffett liked what he saw. The policy cost Mozilo $2 million. AIG's quote was $10 million. According to Mike McMahon, the Sandler O'Neill stock analyst who was then covering Countrywide, Buffett then personally bought two million shares in the company because he felt it was undervalued. (Berkshire Hathaway also owned positions in Fannie Mae and Freddie Mac.)

The two men became friends. When both WaMu and Wells Fargo came courting, Mozilo flew out to Omaha to see the "Oracle." Buffett put him up in an Embassy Suites Hotel. Mozilo was a Four Seasons kind of guy. They met for breakfast at the hotel, standing in line in the cafeteria with their trays. People were staring. (Mozilo later learned that the reason Buffett wanted to meet at the Embassy Suites was that as a frequent guest of the hotel chain he was entitled to a free breakfast once a month. This was Buffett's once-a-monther.) After breakfast they went out to Buffett's car, a Lincoln Continental. Tapes were scattered about the dashboard. "The car was a dirty mess," Mozilo said of the visit. The Lincoln wouldn't start. Buffett didn't have a cell phone. He called a tow truck by using a pay phone inside the hotel.

---

[5] AIG's CEO was Maurice "Hank" Greenberg, considered by some to be a legend in the insurance business for making AIG a giant in that field. However, Greenberg resigned in 2005 after AIG admitted to giving intentionally false information to regulators during an inspection of its property-casualty business. AIG was also a founding member of FM Watch, the anti–Fannie Mae/Freddie Mac group. Mozilo was a key ally of the two GSEs and preferred not to give AIG any business if he could avoid it. During the subprime boom AIG also wrote insurance policies on subprime mortgage-backed securities. These insurance policies, which covered the investor in the event of losses, were called credit default swaps (CDSs). AIG also owned a subprime lender of its own called American General Finance Services, which, unlike many lenders of the time, kept its mortgages on its balance sheet. In the summer of 2009 AGFS began liquidating some of its $20 billion balance sheet of subprime mortgages. By this time AIG was mostly owned by the U.S. government. Also, when AGFS began liquidating some of its mortgages, it sold the loans initially to Credit Suisse, which chose PennyMac, Stan Kurland's new company, to service the loans.

Back at Buffett's office in Omaha, Mozilo noted it didn't have a computer in it. The two men talked about who might make a good acquirer for Countrywide. Buffett advised him that the number-one thing he should worry about was his people—his employees. Mozilo feared that if Wells Fargo—his closest and toughest competitor—bought Countrywide, Kovacevich would move to cut duplicative jobs (potentially, there would have been thousands), which meant his people would be out in the cold. The idea didn't thrill him. He had about two dozen top executives who had been with him 20 years or more. Some of his kids worked there. "Angelo is extremely loyal to his people," said McMahon.

Mozilo, after hiring Goldman Sachs & Company to be his advisor, turned down Kovacevich's overtures. When he looked at WaMu's offer closely, he didn't like the idea that the giant thrift's stock looked a bit overvalued to him, trading at about 20 times earnings.[6] He saw little upside if he took WaMu's stock in exchange for Countrywide's undervalued shares, which were trading at their book or liquidation value. Over the prior three years WaMu had bought several other S&Ls. Word had spread in the industry that Killinger in some cases had overpaid and was having a tough time merging all the different computer systems that the S&L used to originate and service its loans. Plus there was management to think about. Mozilo, for the most part, respected Killinger, but wasn't too keen on some of the executives running the mortgage department. Mozilo wouldn't say, for the record, what he thought about WaMu's mortgage chief Craig Davies, but executives close to him said Davies was the S&L manager that Mozilo thought so little of he wouldn't even let him run one of his branches. According to McMahon, the Sandler O'Neill analyst who had grown somewhat close to Mozilo ("He always returned my phone calls," said McMahon), WaMu sent a team of executives in to analyze Countrywide's books. (Wells Fargo never even got that far.) Ultimately, though, Mozilo decided to keep Countrywide.

His decision not to sell the company was a stroke of good timing. (Rumors about Wells Fargo, WaMu, and other potential suitors

---

[6] Twenty times earnings meant 20 times the earnings per share (EPS) calculation. Earnings per share is derived by taking a company's profit and dividing it by the number of outstanding shares. On Wall Street it is standard practice to measure performance based on EPS.

eyeing Countrywide would persist for years, some true, most not. Mozilo would listen to offers plenty, but rarely did he take them seriously.) Interest rates began to fall in early 2001 and kept right on dropping year after year. Each year was better than the one before right on through to 2003. Countrywide followed Arnall and the rest of his competitors into subprime, starting slowly at first and then ramping up by funding loans through the company's wholesale division. He was now using independent loan brokers to bring subprime mortgages into the company. Countrywide also bought already-funded loans from other originators on a so-called correspondent basis, offering smaller nonbank firms a warehouse line of credit.

By 2004 Countrywide was funding—through its retail, wholesale, and correspondent channels—$40 billion a year in subprime loans. Its share price had more than doubled from two years earlier. Not only was Mozilo's company the largest lender and servicer of mortgages in the United States (and the entire world), but it was now a top-five subprime originator, encroaching on Arnall's perch. Home prices kept rising in the nation's most populous markets: New York, Los Angeles, Boston, San Francisco, San Diego—places where there seemed to be too many home buyers and not enough reasonably priced houses for middle-income Americans. The coasts, as mortgage and housing economists liked to call them, were on fire, values rising 15 percent to 25 percent a year, in some places even higher.

With Countrywide's stock price almost quadrupling in value since 2000, some of Mozilo's top lieutenants became millionaires (easily), at least on paper: Stan Kurland, David Sambol, Carlos Garcia, Eric Seraki, Kevin Bartlett, and Ron Kripalanni.[7] The list went on and on. When talking to stock analysts and mutual fund chiefs who loaded up on Countrywide's stock, Mozilo liked to brag that many of the company's top executives had been with the lender for 20 years. He spoke of the company's "culture" where executives strived to be the top lender in every major city it had branches in or brokers on the ground. If Mozilo and his origination managers heard word of a loan officer or broker at another company who was a top producer (who took in a dizzying

---

[7] Kripalanni's first name was really Ranjit, but he shortened it to Ron.

amount of loan applications each year), they would make the LO an offer he or she couldn't refuse. Stories began to circulate about million-dollar signing bonuses for LOs who would jump ship for Countrywide.

A woman who ran a small mortgage banking company in Fairfield, Connecticut, recalled getting a recruiting call from a Countrywide manager (a woman also) in 2005. Countrywide hadn't yet expanded into the southern coast of the state that gripped the I-95 corridor from New York up to Rhode Island. "The recruiter told me that 'we're going to dominate from Greenwich to Canaan, and we need managers.'" The starting salary to manage a branch—excluding bonuses—was almost $400,000 a year. "She warned me that it would be time consuming and stressful and that if I couldn't handle stress I shouldn't take the job." The woman passed on the offer.

Within a year she saw Countrywide keep its promise about invading Fairfield and many of the suburbs that served as bedroom communities to commuters traveling both to New York and to New Haven and Hartford, Connecticut's largest city and its capital, respectively. A Countrywide branch manager in nearby Danbury was reportedly making $1.4 million a year. She also saw the company's loan officers cozying up to Realtors, taking a page from Mozilo's early playbook, on being there first where the rubber met the road—when the home buyer signed on the dotted line to buy a house. She remembered dropping by a condo project to leave her card and was shown the unit by a woman she thought was a Realtor. "She actually worked for Countrywide," said the woman.

Mozilo's walking orders to all his managers boiled down to this: dominate your markets. Roth, who ran the trading desk for seven years, described it as "drinking the Countrywide Kool-Aid. When you go to work there, it's an amazing transformation. Angelo is a tremendous leader, a tremendous motivator. It's a proud, proud thing to work for that company. Of course, a lot of people think it's a sweatshop."

★   ★   ★

In the modern era of mortgage banking—as opposed to the Bailey Building and Loan days of yesteryear—it's all about selling loans to the home buyer or refinancing an existing customer. But originating loans is only part of the equation. How mortgages should be origi-nated, what standards a company uses, and what loan brokers a lender chooses to do business with—the policing of all this falls on the com-pliance department. Any mortgage professional who ever attended a compliance workshop or trade show hosted by the Mortgage Bankers Association would, after sniffing an abundance of perfume in the air, quickly realize one thing: It's a field dominated by women, totally dominated by women. Most of the men working in compliance are there to manage the women.

Earlier in his career Mozilo saw the value of women in mortgages because they could perform a key task very well: type information onto paper loan applications a heck of a lot faster (and more accurately) than most men. In Mozilo's world back then, all guys wanted to do was sell mortgages, but someone had to do all that typing. By the early 2000s women increasingly were joining men in the ranks of professional loan officers and brokers, but when it came to compliance departments—and every lender had one—they remained mostly female.

Betsy Bayer started out her career in home finance working for Belair Savings in 1982. "It was the S&L to the stars," she recalled. Movie producers Jon Peters and Peter Gruber were on Belair's board of directors. During her career she worked at First Interstate (where she met Mike McMahon) and then later on at IndyMac of Pasadena.[8]

The idea of the compliance department at Countrywide (or any lender) was to make sure that its loan officers played by the rules. Bayer was hired by Countrywide in 2004. As first vice president, her turf was the lender's wholesale department. "I was the rules person," she said.

As for Countrywide being a great place to work—as Roth and others might testify to—she isn't so sure. "It was a sweatshop," she said. "They had these posters all over the office. They were 'work/life bal-ance' posters, like they were concerned about your well-being. What a load of bullshit. It was a sweatshop." Even though many of Mozilo's

---

[8] IndyMac was formed in 1985 by Mozilo and Loeb as a side project, of sorts, to Country-wide. Its mission in life was to be a conduit—a legal entity through which Countrywide could securitize jumbo mortgages above the Fannie Mae/Freddie Mac loan limit. At the time, Countrywide had no balance to speak of and could not hold jumbo loans for investment purposes.

senior executives had been with the company 20 years or more, the Countrywide she worked for had a high turnover rate where many employees would leave before two years were out. "That's a fact that never gets published," she said.

Bayer said that during the boom years from 2002 to 2006, new hires at the company weren't exactly handed a road map on the Countrywide culture. It took employees "at least a year to learn the company. By the end of the second year you learn that change does not come easily." Managing wholesale compliance, she—and others—learned that the idea was to produce as many loans as humanly possible. Bayer, being the company's "rules person" for loans brought in through its broker network, didn't think compliance was being taken all that seriously by Mozilo and his senior managers.

Chris Goode, who worked in compliance for the correspondent group (the division that bought loans from other lenders), found the same thing. "As a due diligence person you don't want to say 'The sky is falling,'" said Goode. The idea, he said, was to produce volume—as much as possible. "The due diligence folks were steamrolled by the enormity of the money in the business." His division, in particular, was in charge of looking at all the subprime loans the company was buying from other lenders.

Countrywide was producing plenty of subprime loans, all right. Between 2004 and the end of 2007 the company originated $150 billion in mortgages rated A– to D. Of these, it was doing the monthly processing (servicing) on $100 billion, collecting fees from the investors to whom it had sold the loans. Countrywide even securitized its own subprime loans through its capital markets group, which acted more or less like an investment banker—like a Merrill Lynch or Bear Stearns. (It can be argued that Countrywide had a Wall Street firm inside its own walls: itself.)

Betsy Bayer looked at what was going on inside the company and didn't like it. When it came to using loan brokers, Countrywide had a hard time turning them down. "There were 44,000 brokers in the U.S.—38,000 were approved and signed up to do business with Countrywide," she said. When it came to checking out loan brokers, "It was fill out this application and we'll approve you in 72 hours." (Some of the company's background checks had been outsourced to a contractor in India. Data input on brokerage firms was done in India, said

Bayer, but the decision to approve brokers still remained at company headquarters in Calabasas.) Not only was Bayer wary of subprime, but increasingly so was Stan Kurland, Countrywide's president. Remember that Kurland started out his career as an accountant, and true to form, according to those who worked under him, Kurland fit the stereotype; that is, he was somewhat conservative when it came to numbers and loan underwriting standards. In particular he didn't like the idea that Countrywide was funding subprime mortgages where the loan-to-value (LTV) ratio was higher than 80 percent. "When Stan found out that we were doing subprime loans with LTVs over 80 percent he went ballistic," said a company manager. "He was a very conservative guy." Then again, stereotypes go only so far. David Sambol, who was competing with Kurland to be Mozilo's eventual successor, also started out as an accountant. Sources both inside and outside the company said Sambol was pushing Countrywide into funding more subprime loans. "Dave was the guy who drove the bus off the cliff into subprime," said the manager. "Kurland wanted to pull back."

Executives watching the horse race between the two men began to see a split between Kurland and Sambol. The two men had always been on friendly terms with each other. "Angelo was in the middle," explained one senior executive at the company. "It was like Dave was the Devil on one shoulder and Stan the angel on the other. Who would Angelo listen to? We were all watching."

Mozilo, in his thirst for market share, had followed Arnall's company into the business of originating stated-income loans (where home buyers state their income and the lender believes them as long as their FICO score checks out). Stated-income loans came in two types: prime and subprime. But when it came to the "A" paper credit quality stated-income loans, Fannie Mae and Freddie Mac (for the most part) wouldn't touch them because of the lack of underwriting. Countrywide also followed the crowd in originating another popular loan of the 2004 to 2007 period: payment option ARMs (adjustable-rate mortgages) (POAs), a product where the consumer was offered four different payment plans each month. One of these options included negative amortization, where borrowers could keep their payments artificially low by delaying large interest payments each month, thus adding new debt onto the loan amount. It was what some lenders called an "I'll

worry about it tomorrow" option. By 2006 Countrywide was the largest payment option ARM lender in the nation, originating $11 billion
worth a quarter.

"When you go for quantity, quality is what you give up," said Bayer.
"To get volume, you lose quality—that's what they did." When she arrived
in 2004, the company's compliance department was in what she called
"complete turmoil." When pressed further, she said Countrywide wasn't
doing its homework when it came to underwriting. "They were relaxing
credit guidelines."

She said that inside the company compliance staffers had a term for
stated-income loans: "liar loans." Bayer said the only ones in the company who called them that were members of the compliance staff. No
one else in the firm used the phrase, at least not within earshot of the
production chiefs.

Chapter 6

The Holy Roller
of REITs

REITs? They're like pigs with lipstick.
—ANGELO MOZILO

Of the things that Patrick Flood loved the most in his life, there were Jesus Christ, his wife and family, and baseball. As for real estate investment trusts, or REITs as they are commonly called, he wasn't so sure.

In the mortgage industry Flood was known for his religious fervor—he was a born-again evangelical Christian—but also as a hands-on manager who had the ability to ride the cyclical waves of the home lending business, usually coming out on top. After graduating from Winthrop University in Rock Hill, South Carolina, where he played second base for the Eagles in the Big South Conference, he had done nothing but mortgages. He worked in the residential loan department of a small Atlanta-based savings and loan (S&L) called Home Federal Savings of Atlanta, originating paper and working his way up to sales manager and then chief operating officer. His college degree was in communications, not finance or business administration. "I'm what you call a people person," he would say of himself.

Under Flood's stewardship, the tiny S&L grew to seven branches and 120 employees. When it came to housing and mortgages, the South (Georgia in particular) was a great place to be. The coastal city of Savannah had one of the fastest growing deepwater ports on the East Coast, and the state, thanks to a low corporate tax rate, boasted of its "strong, vibrant business environment." Georgia was home to the headquarters of Coca-Cola, CNN, and Home Depot. Its climate was warm, attracting retirees and baby boomers. As the population grew, so did the housing and mortgage markets. Atlanta was a cosmopolitan city. (Heck, even singer Elton John had a house there.) Home Federal's lending business performed so well that its owners sold off its branches and converted the lender into a nonbank that relied on warehouse lines of credit to originate loans.

The new company was called HomeBanc Mortgage. Year after year it ranked among the top home lenders in the Atlanta metropolitan area. People in the mortgage industry began to notice. In 1996 the nonbank was sold to First Tennessee, a money center bank based in Memphis. Then the national market began to sour in late 1998 as the Russian debt crisis and the failures of dozens of subprime lenders began to take their toll. In 1998 residential lenders originated $1.5 trillion in home loans, their best year ever. By 2000 volumes were down by a third to $1 trillion. Suddenly the business didn't look as good, but Flood thought otherwise. Using private equity money from a Chicago hedge fund called GTCR Golder Rauner, he bought HomeBanc from First Tennessee for $60 million. In the wake of 9/11 the Federal Reserve began cutting interest rates, and suddenly Flood looked like a genius. His timing couldn't have been any better.

HomeBanc was now his shop. Out from under First Tennessee, he began to grow the lender as he saw fit. He had a few chief business tenets, one of which was to avoid wholesale lending through mortgage brokers. "I see no value in wholesale," he told a reporter. "None." Another was to hire employees that he considered "ethical."

Flood weeded out nondesirables by having applicants take a written test that was custom made for him by a consulting/head-hunting firm called Talent Mind. To zero in on which applicants might have the ethics he was looking for, he gave Talent Mind 100 personal disciplines that he considered essential. He didn't ask about their religious backgrounds, but did ask questions that zeroed in on character. One question HomeBanc asked was this: Would you call in sick on a Monday in order to get a three-day weekend? "It was a 'values' test," said Flood. "We wanted to find out what their idea of 'trust' was. No one else in the industry was doing this." HomeBanc also asked applicants whether they did volunteer work.

As HomeBanc began to grow, it went through a handful of human resources (HR) directors before settling on Ike Reighard, a friend of Flood's who had attended bible studies at the company in the late 1990s. "We had been searching for an HR director for a year," said Flood. "We had gone through executive search firms and everything. I couldn't find anybody I liked." Reighard was also a minister who had founded the North Star megachurch in suburban Kennesaw (Cobb County) outside of Atlanta. He had no financial services or HR experience, but to Flood that didn't matter much. When asked about it, the HomeBanc CEO replied, "He was a pastor. What's better than that?"

As HR director, Reighard (and other chaplains) would visit HomeBanc's retail branches weekly. Some employees sent out daily e-mail devotionals, and bible studies before work and during lunch were not uncommon. The *Atlanta Journal-Constitution*, which once did a story on HomeBanc, quoted a sales manager as saying the lender presented itself "as a faith-based organization but by no means did they require or force anybody to follow their beliefs."[1] Or as Flood once told the *National Mortgage News*: "We weren't all a bunch of bible thumpers. We spent a lot of time finding people to be LOs [loan officers] who shared our values. I'm first a God-fearing Christian man, but I don't require people to be what I am." That said, one investment banker who worked with Flood noted that "Pat liked to cite from scriptures in business meetings." The investment banker added that Flood also was fond of spending HomeBanc's money on "extravagant things" like corporate suites at Atlanta Braves and Falcons games.

---

[1] CNN once aired a special report on religion and corporations. HomeBanc was one of the companies featured.

For retail (direct-to-consumer) lenders selling mortgages to the public, loan officers are a company's most important asset. By Flood's own account, some 90 percent of all HomeBanc's employees had no prior mortgage experience. Using a sports metaphor, he said proudly: "We acquired through the draft." In the mortgage industry there are two schools of thought when it comes to hiring LOs. Some executives believe it's preferable to hire LOs with experience, because they already know the ropes, so to speak, of taking applications and working with the public, particularly on making legal disclosures about rates and terms. Others see no problem with training workers from scratch, because it gives lenders the opportunity to teach what they think are good business habits and avoid undesirable skill sets that might have been taught at other companies.

Flood and his staff trained HomeBanc's LOs, focusing on service. "We were competing against national banks. We had to treat the customer better than everyone else." But before he would sign off on an LO hire, the applicant had to provide a list of 150 contacts or what the company called a "sphere of influence." The contact sheet was considered a list of leads—people who might one day need a mortgage.

As HomeBanc expanded into other southeastern states, including Florida and the Carolinas, it needed more capital to grow. During 2002 and 2003 Flood spent time toying with the idea of HomeBanc buying an S&L but said federal regulators from the Office of Thrift Supervision in Washington weren't keen on the idea. "They didn't want a private equity partner involved with an S&L," he said. (The mortgage company was majority owned by GTCR Golder Rauner though Flood had a stake as well.)

Instead, he found a man he likened to a preacher in his beliefs: Eric Billings, the co-founder, chairman, and CEO of Friedman Billings Ramsey (FBR), a boutique investment banking firm based in Arlington, Virginia, a 15-minute car ride—depending on traffic—from the nation's capital. If HomeBanc couldn't buy an S&L (using its federally insured deposits to fund loans), then it would go public—through either a traditional C corporation structure or a real estate investment trust (REIT). What exactly was a REIT? It worked like this: A company had shareholders. If those investors owned shares in a C corporation (a plain-vanilla ownership structure used by most public firms), they weren't necessarily entitled to receive dividends each quarter. But a REIT existed *to* pay dividends. It was a dividend junkie's sexiest dream come true.

By design, REITs had to pay dividends—90 percent of their earnings had to be paid out to shareholders each quarter. In exchange for giving away that much of their earnings in the form of dividends, REITs caught a huge tax break from the federal government. If they doled out their corporate earnings in dividends, they avoided paying taxes to Uncle Sam. In theory, a REIT was a valuable ownership structure, because by paying out that much in earnings each quarter (while avoiding a huge tax liability), it would attract investors who would line up to buy not only the initial public offering (IPO) but additional offerings of stock. At least that's how it was supposed to work. And that's how Billings and other executives explained the idea to dozens of mortgage executives over the years, Patrick Flood being just one of them.

In late 2003 when Flood finally made the decision to take HomeBanc public through an IPO, J.P. Morgan Securities[2] was the lead underwriter in the deal, but Flood had heard so much talk in the industry about FBR's expertise in mortgage REITs, he insisted that Billings' firm be brought in to assist.

When it came to REITs, Billings was the mortgage industry's go-to guy, said Flood. "If you said the words 'mortgage' and 'REIT' in the same breath, FBR was clearly the company that came to mind in the mortgage industry. We looked to FBR for validation."

Regarding Billings, one of the firm's founders, Flood likened him to a preacher. "Eric was passionate about the whole thing," he said. "I love people who are passionate about their beliefs."

For some of J.P. Morgan Securities' bankers on the deal, Billings was a little bit too passionate. According to Flood, J.P. Morgan's chieftains in its financial institutions group (FIG) discouraged FBR's coming on board. "They were concerned that they might steal the lead away from

---

[2] In 2000 J.P. Morgan Company merged with Chase Manhattan Bank. The amalgam of a traditional Wall Street firm and a commercial bank was called JPMorgan Chase & Company. Early on, after the merger, the name J.P. Morgan Securities was still in use.

them," said the HomeBanc executive. "It was fascinating to watch them fight. Investment banking firms have personalities. Some are like golden retrievers; some are like pit bulls." FBR was in the pit bull camp, he said.

Flood wanted in the worst way to grow HomeBanc into a major force in mortgage banking. And even though he admired Billings' passion in regard to REITs, he later admitted to having major doubts about the REIT structure. "I remember going on the road show to sell the IPO to investors, and one of them [from FBR] said to me, 'You have to punch them in the head with it.'"

One of Flood's concerns was the complexity of the REIT structure and something Billings and his executives called the "toggle" concept, which Flood admitted he never fully understood. For one meeting before going public, Flood and some of his top officers flew into Reagan National Airport in Washington and then cabbed it to Arlington where FBR had its headquarters. It was raining that evening and the group arrived after six o'clock. "Manny [Friedman] and Eric were sitting across from us at the conference table," said Flood. "They weren't happy with us, because we were late. But they then went on reassuring us about REITs, explaining the 'toggle,' how you can move back and forth with a REIT. It gave me the willies." (Three years after going public, Flood was still at a loss to explain how a REIT "toggle" worked. It was a term used by FBR to explain how a mortgage-lending REIT can set up two subsidiaries—one taxable, one not, but both with identical lending licenses. Depending on a lender's strategy of originating and selling loans to Wall Street or holding them in its portfolio, it can switch or toggle between the two units to minimize how much in taxes in might have to pay.)

In the end, HomeBanc's transformation into a publicly traded REIT did not go smoothly. The company was hoping to bring its IPO to market in the early spring of 2004. John Simmons, J.P. Morgan's banker in charge of the deal, told Flood in February that the IPO was a "slam dunk." Flood and his team went on what he called a "brutal" two-week process of selling the deal to institutional investors such as the Fidelity and Franklin mutual funds. (When a company sells shares to the public, its goal isn't to sell 100-share lots to individual investors, but to get mutual funds to buy huge blocks of stock.) In the spring, unemployment figures showed stronger than expected job growth, which meant the Federal Reserve might start hiking short-term interest rates—which always spelled bad news for mortgage lenders.

Flood's HomeBanc was a bit of an anomaly among nonbanks going public using the REIT ownership structure. Most of the mortgage-related REITs that had come to market were for subprime firms. HomeBanc was mostly an "A" paper lender with one slight twist: It specialized in interest-only loans where the customer didn't pay off any of the loan's principal, only interest. It sold some of its mortgages to Fannie Mae and Freddie Mac, but a good many of its loans were sold to Bear Stearns. "About $15 billion over eight years," estimated Flood. HomeBanc was not your typical prime lender, but it certainly wasn't subprime, either. It went public at $7.50 a share instead of its offering range of $14 to $16 a share. Still, Flood wasn't totally disappointed. HomeBanc had raised $290 million, not bad for a small regional lender that was funding only $4 billion worth of loans a year. It also meant that a company he and his partners had bought just a few years earlier for $60 million was now worth more than four times that amount.

★   ★   ★

To those who have seen Eric Billings and FBR executive Rock Tonkel run their REIT road show, or sales pitch, it's an impressive sight. In some cases 50 people would be in the room—10 from FBR; 10 from the lender going public; an army of attorneys from FBR's law firm, Hunton & Williams; and accountants from Ernst & Young. If Billings couldn't be there himself, he would set up a live conference call where attendees could see him on-screen. The idea was to convince mortgage company executives and/or their owners to either convert into a REIT ownership structure (if their firm was already publicly traded) or go public using a REIT. The other part of the road show was selling the concept to the mutual fund managers who would sign up (subscribe) to shares before the IPO ever came to market. "It was like a revival meeting at a Southern Baptist church," said a former managing director from Bear Stearns who witnessed Billings' pitches several times. "You walked out of there, your hands in the air, shouting, 'I believe! Hallelujah!'"

One attorney who worked for a Virginia-based subprime lender and sat in on most of the meetings before his firm went public through a REIT brought to market by Billings described the FBR chief in evangelical terms: "He was the Holy Roller."

It wasn't just Billings' sales pitch, his passion for REITs, as Flood and others would call it. FBR did not belong to the New York club of investment banking firms that included Bear Stearns, Lehman Brothers, Merrill Lynch, and others. Unlike those firms—most of which had long pedigrees, some as many as 150 years—FBR was less than 20 years old. It was a newbie among decades-old giants, and to some investment banking veterans, the firm never stood a chance. One Wall Street managing director who caught some of Billings' REIT pitches remembered quietly laughing at the presentation. "But Eric believed in it," he said. "He was the lead. After they took you public they wanted to do M&A [mergers and acquisitions] for you. They thought they owned you."

The biggest problem with the whole REIT concept? It sounded democratic on paper (the earnings trickled down to every single shareholder), but when you gave away 90 percent of your net income, it left little money for capital expenditures or future growth. Or maybe that was the point. A mortgage REIT would have to keep on borrowing to stay afloat and to grow—and where would a REIT turn to borrow? Answer: (likely) to the same investment banker that took it public: FBR. Angelo Mozilo once looked at the concept and was floored by it—and not in a good way. "REITs?" he once said of the idea. "They're like pigs with lipstick." In one interview with *National Mortgage News* he likened REITs to a coot. "Do you know what a coot is?" he asked the reporter. "It's a bird that shits and eats at the same time." The reference was to the fact that mortgage-lending REITs are forced to pay out 90 percent of their earnings to shareholders, taking away most of their ability to retain cash—cash that might be used for M&A or to weather a cyclical downturn in mortgages.

★   ★   ★

Friedman Billings Ramsey was the brainchild of Emanuel J. Friedman, or "Manny" as everyone called him. Friedman was the son of a Wilmington, North Carolina, rabbi. When he was 13 he used his bar mitzvah money to buy 10 shares in P. Lorillard Company, a tobacco company. Two months later he sold the shares at a $60 profit. He attended the University of North Carolina at Chapel Hill and then moved to the Washington, D.C., area and began taking night classes at Georgetown Law School. To support himself he taught middle school geography. In 1972, the Vietnam War still in progress, he tried to land a job with a brokerage house but had little luck. Finally, in 1983 Legg Mason Wood Walker of Washington hired him.[3]

Friedman's first assignment was selling stocks in oil, gas, and casino companies. (This was before the era of a revitalized Atlantic City, Donald Trump, and Indian casino gambling in Connecticut and Mississippi.) By his own admission he did not fare particularly well, later telling the *Baltimore Business Journal*, "I had years of failure until I turned 37 when I met by partners." In 1982, Eric Billings, a Boston native, joined Legg Mason but left two years later, jumping ship for Johnston, Lemon & Company, which also was headquartered in Washington. Friedman followed. Within a few years both men had worked their way up to become senior vice presidents in Johnston Lemon's institutional sales group (selling stocks to pension and mutual funds, the trust departments of banks, and the usual corporate suspects). During his five years there, Friedman was one of the firm's top revenue producers. In some of those years he accounted for up to 40 percent of the firm's revenue.

At Johnston Lemon the two men met Russell Ramsey, a former salesman for Pitney Bowes who had attended college at George Washington University. (Even though he was from Massachusetts, Billings had graduated from the University of Maryland in nearby College Park, right inside the Capital Beltway.) In 1989, two years after the stock market crash of 1987, the three men left to start their own firm, borrowing $1 million to get it off the ground. They spent $5,000 on used furniture that had been abandoned by another area brokerage firm. Friedman Billings Ramsey Group, Inc. was born. Friedman was the senior partner among the three, owning the largest stake.

While still at Legg Mason, Friedman—after not doing so well with energy and casino stocks—began to focus on analyzing the shares of small savings and loan companies, developing an expertise in the sector.

---

[3] The historical information on FBR was culled by the *International Directory of Company Histories*, Vol. 53 (St. James Press).

During its early years, FBR made a market in trading bank stocks but also focused on being an asset manager for wealthy individuals and institutional clients. (When the three men left Johnston Lemon, they took with them a large chunk of that firm's 25-person sales department. Chuck Akre, a well-regarded manager and stock picker, was invited to join them but declined, only to be snatched away by FBR a few years later.) In the 1989–1990 time frame, the nation's S&L crisis was accelerating. Because many troubled S&Ls had invested billions of dollars in commercial real estate (Charlie Keating and Lincoln Savings being just one of many), Friedman made a bold prediction, telling clients to avoid or even short vulnerable banks and real estate stocks. (Short sellers make money by betting that a stock's price will decline.) He was right.

But Friedman also had enough smarts to realize that the downturn wouldn't last forever. When the White House and Congress pledged $150 billion to clean up the nation's insolvent S&Ls, FBR jumped on the bandwagon, or as one FBR executive put it, "They joined the vanguard of those raising capital for troubled institutions. Originally they were on the short side. Now, they were going long."

While at Johnston Lemon, Friedman had become familiar with a large California S&L called Glendale Federal Bank, which had $18 billion in assets on its books, some of them in the form of bad commercial real estate projects. Even though the publicly traded Glendale had $18 billion in assets, its market capitalization (stock price multiplied by number of outstanding shares) was just $30 million. The nation was in the throes of a recession, due in part to the S&L mess. S&Ls and commercial banks had supplied billions of dollars in easy loans that spurred overbuilding by developers. Southern California, in particular, had been hit hard by defense industry cutbacks, especially in aerospace. But Friedman figured that something with $18 billion in assets, even at a discount, had to worth more than a $30 million market cap. FBR raised $450 million to help rescue Glendale Federal, saving it from a takeover by federal regulators.[4] (FBR also raised additional equity for

---

[4] In 1998 Glendale Federal merged with another large California S&L called CalFed. Four years later Citigroup bought CalFed.

other struggling S&Ls, including Dime Savings and Brooklyn Federal Savings, both based in New York.)

The three men realized that their expertise in banking, S&Ls, and real estate was a way for the young firm to make a name for itself among the Merrill Lynches and Lehmans of the world. FBR became one of the first investment banking firms to take the REIT concept, convincing investors that they could use it to buy commercial real estate properties of almost any type. After the government bailed out the S&L industry,[5] providing $150 billion worth of taxpayer assistance, commercial real estate markets began to improve.

In the mid-1990s lenders learned their lesson in regard to commercial real estate. Like the S&L business, the commercial property market (offices, hotels, shopping malls, and the like) regained its health—but only after the days of easy credit (loans from banks and thrifts) ended and executives once again began making their business decisions based on the cash flow of a commercial property. Office buildings, hotels, shopping malls, and another nonresidential projects all generated revenue from the rents they took in from the businesses that wanted their space. In commercial lending there was a simple equation called "minimum debt service ratio" that loan officers used in determining how much money they would be willing to lend on a property. If the owner of an office building had a mortgage, for example, that cost $100,000 a year, the commercial mortgage bank (or Wall Street firm) might require that the property generate in rental income at least $120,000, which meant the property had a minimum debt service ratio of 1.2. Less conservative lenders might allow for a ratio as low as 1.1. In the world of commercial mortgage lending, it was all about cash flow. The beauty

---

[5] The nation's commercial banking sector also suffered during those years, with the Federal Deposit Insurance Corporation coming within a few billion dollars of going broke. Banking executives, though, were a little brighter than their counterparts in the S&L industry. Banks and S&Ls had different charters. The S&L depository insurance fund was called the Federal Savings and Loan Insurance Corporation (FSLIC). Banks, by design, made many types of loans, including commercial real estate and business loans. Up until the Garn–St Germain Act of 1982, S&Ls did one thing and one thing only: make home mortgages. After Congress realized what a disaster it had made of the industry with that bill, it reregulated all S&Ls, forcing them to put a majority of their assets into home mortgages. This happened in 1989 through the passage of the Financial Institutions Reform Recovery and Enforcement Act, signed into law by George H.W. Bush.

of owning an office building in a hot property market was this: Once the lease expired, the landlord or building owner could jack up the rent, increasing the cash flow. Increased cash flow from rents meant that a property could support an even larger mortgage.

Billings and his partners at FBR were among the first to realize that with all the cash flow (rents) that office buildings, hotels, and the like were throwing off, commercial properties were perfect vehicles for REITs. In 1994, FBR, with Billings as its point man, raised $350 million for Prime Retail Corporation, a Baltimore-based shopping center owner. The REIT business quickly became a major part of the young investment banking firm's menu of activities. The firm was now 200 employees strong. Manny, Eric, and Russ, as they were known to their workers, were in their early to late 40s. Thanks to commercial property REITs, the young firm had gained a reputation for being an innovative investment banking boutique that didn't need a New York address to thrive. It attracted young deal makers and fostered a culture where the dress code was ultracasual—jeans and shorts even—complete with a company health club, sauna, and masseuse. The average age of its employees was under 30. Employee turnover was light.

Friedman, meanwhile, began focusing his attention on what Wall Street liked to call "specialized finance companies," a code phrase for residential subprime lenders. Prior to the Russian debt crisis of late 1998, which also hammered many publicly traded subprime lenders, FBR took a handful of mortgage lenders public (including Long Beach Financial, which had been spun off by Roland Arnall). According to one senior Long Beach executive, FBR's point man on the IPO was Rock Tonkel, a former top regulator from the Office of Thrift Supervision (OTS) who had left the world of government agencies behind in 1994 and joined FBR. "When it came to REITs, Rock was completely on board," said one former FBR manager.

Tonkel, a heavyset man, had actually met Friedman while he was still a regulator at OTS. One of his assignments was Glendale Federal. (Tonkel's nickname in the industry was "Rock Steady" Tonkel.) Another was Dime Savings. Tonkel tried to push Long Beach president Jack Mayesh to convert into a publicly traded REIT, but Arnall's right-hand man wasn't buying into the idea, primarily because mortgage-lending REITs had absolutely no track record whatsoever. Mayesh knew Billings and admired his capabilities as a salesman but ignored Tonkel's suggestions on becoming a REIT. Mayesh went for the standard C corporation structure, tax breaks notwithstanding.

★   ★   ★

The downturn in the subprime market of the 1990s lasted roughly two years. By cutting short-term rates dramatically, the Federal Reserve under Alan Greenspan helped to prop up a struggling U.S. economy that wasn't quite in a recession but surely wasn't booming and adding jobs fast enough to please both the Fed and the Bush White House. In 2003 when 30-year "A" paper loans could be had for 5 percent with just about no points paid up front (for a consumer with good credit), residential originations by lenders of all different stripes (banks, S&Ls, nonbanks, and credit unions) reached a record $3.9 trillion. Subprime originations, for the first time ever, topped almost $400 billion a year—or 10 percent of all home loans funded in the United States, also a record. Suddenly, a business that had looked doomed just five years earlier appeared to have a bright future. After all, if as a nonbank you couldn't make money by borrowing money from Wall Street at, say, 3 percent and lending it out to consumers with bad credit at 8 percent, something was definitely wrong. In between the 3 percent and the 8 percent was a total of 500 basis points (5 percent) of gross profit, and no matter how bad some of these borrowers were, there was plenty of cushion to buffet delinquencies.

Thanks to their knowledge of how S&Ls (and therefore mortgages) worked, Friedman and Billings as well as Rock Tonkel recognized the potential and began pushing the REIT concept hard to the owners of subprime lending companies. (However, they were now doing so without the services of Ramsey, who had resigned from the firm to start a venture capital fund that specialized in Washington-area technology, telecommunications, and media firms.[6]) Even though the REIT market for mortgage lenders did not exist after the 1998 crash, FBR had established itself as the premier investment banking firm when it came to using commercial property REITs to buy buildings, raising

---

[6] Ramsey left the firm but remained as a director with a 12 percent share. FBR did not change its name.

billions of dollars for investors through either IPOs or secondary offerings of stock.

★   ★   ★

When it came to mortgage REITs, Billings—according to both mortgage executives who listened to his pitches and former employees—was a true believer. One former FBR manager remembers hearing Billings singing the praises of mortgage REITs on several occasions. "Eric would argue for REITs until he was blue in the face with veins popping out of his head." In one company strategy session he remembered Billings saying, "I will REIT-up commercial, I will REIT-up stadiums, I will REIT-up telephone towers."

Pat Flood clearly remembered Billings' zeal. "Eric would tell you that REITs made sense. He was adamant, convinced that this was the best way for mortgage bankers to get out of the cellar."

The "cellar" referred to the second-class citizen status of nonbank mortgage lenders—subprime and prime alike. Investment banking firms like Merrill Lynch, Lehman Brothers, and Bear Stearns would take nonbank lenders public from time to time, but few managing directors on Wall Street who worked at these firms seriously believed that these nonbanks had much in the way of long-term viability. The idea was to take nonbanks public and then eventually sell them to federally insured banks or S&Ls, institutions that took deposits from the George Bailey crowd in Bedford Falls.

Besides the ability of REITs to avoid a huge federal tax bill, Billings heavily promoted one other aspect of the REIT ownership structure: their ability to hold assets (bonds backed by subprime loans) on their books. When a subprime lender went public it raised capital. That capital could be use as a cash cushion. A REIT could originate loans, sell them to Wall Street, create a bond, and then put that bond on its books, by calling it a "financing," which meant it had a loan, or debt, against the bonds it held. Plain-vanilla C corporations that were nonbank mortgage lenders for the most part originated loans and sold them off immediately (or securitized them) while retaining the right to service the loans or bonds, which gave them the ability to receive fee income on mortgages they originated but no longer owned.

Nonbank C corporations tended not to have large balance sheets.[7] But Billings had a phrase for REITs that had the ability to create multibillion-dollar balance sheets; he called them "unregulated banks."

The heyday of Wall Street firms taking nonbanks public occurred in the 1980s. In the 1990s and early 2000s few IPOs for nonbank mortgage firms came to market. If a company was going to be a serious player in mortgages, it had better own a bank or a thrift. Using deposits to fund mortgages was generally cheaper—and a more stable source of funding. Countrywide's Mozilo saw the writing on the wall and bought a small bank in 1999, which he promptly began to grow. But with FBR and Billings aggressively singing the praises of REITs, and investors thirsting for yield in a thriving post-9/11 economy, all that changed. Billings also began focusing on converting lenders to REITs through a private placement of stock called a 144-A filing. (The name comes from the form a company has to file with the Securities and Exchange Commission [SEC].)

In June 2003, with subprime lending volumes poised to take off, FBR converted a Maryland-based lender called Fieldstone Investment Corporation to a REIT using the 144-A form. "Eric focused on 144-A placements because you could raise equity first and then file with the SEC later," said one FBR official. The Fieldstone placement was a resounding success, raising roughly $700 million. Over the next 18 months FBR went on a tear, taking subprime nonbanks public, raising equity through private placements (in anticipation of an IPO), or selling additional shares for lenders that focused on originating non–Fannie Mae/Freddie Mac loans (not necessarily subprime), including American Home Mortgage Investment of Long Island ($360 million), New York Mortgage Trust ($135 million), HomeBanc, Saxon Capital of Virginia ($386 million), New Century Financial of Irvine ($783 million), Aames Financial ($342 million), People's Choice Financial of California ($407 million), Encore Credit of Irvine ($386 million), and MortgageIT Holdings of New York ($200 million).

---

[7] C corporations, if they wanted, could hold assets, too, and treat them as a financing; but REITs, because they could set up both taxable and nontaxable affiliates, had certain advantages over them. According to Sandler O'Neill analyst Mike McMahon, the key advantage was that it made the earnings of a REIT appear less volatile when they really weren't.

Besides these lenders, Billings, Friedman, and Tonkel crisscrossed the nation, pitching the REIT story to as many subprime executives as would listen. Barney Guy, chief financial officer for MILA Inc., a privately held nonbank lender based in the Seattle suburb of Mountlake Terrace, met with Billings and Friedman. The pitch he heard was slightly different. "They told me if I do it, we'll drive everyone else out of business," said Guy, who had worked in the subprime industry for well over 20 years. But Guy and his boss, company founder Layne Sapp, weren't buying. "I told Eric we don't like the idea of paying out 90 percent of our earnings," said the CFO.

Also on FBR's list of subprime firms to pitch the idea to was Aegis Mortgage of Houston, which was owned by Cerberus Capital, one of the nation's largest hedge funds. Aegis was the creation of Rick Thompson, an attorney with an accounting degree. Thompson had made a name for himself in the industry by joining forces with investor Gerald Ford, who bought an insolvent Texas S&L called Gibraltar Savings. Gibraltar (like Keating's Lincoln Savings) was saddled with millions in overvalued commercial real estate, but after being recapitalized by its new owners changed its name to First Gibraltar and bought a profitable mortgage company called Troy & Nichols of Monroe, Louisiana from the government. Thompson ran Troy & Nichols for a few years and then sold it to Chase Manhattan Bank. The sale netted Ford and his investors a nice chunk of change—about $210 million. In the mid to late 1990s Thompson had built Aegis up from scratch, buying subprime branches belonging to dead lenders felled in the 1998–1999 crash. He sold most of Aegis to Cerberus, which had a reputation of being both a notorious bottom fisher (buying ailing firms with potential) and an investor that liked to buy young companies on the ascent. Aegis fit the latter bill.

By 2003 Aegis was funding $10 billion a year in subprime loans and a similar product called "alt-A." (Alt-A loans were made to home buyers with good credit but who had characteristics that turned them off Fannie Mae and Freddie Mac. Alt-A could be stated-income loans or loans made to borrowers who despite having good credit also had run up a lot of credit card or auto loan debt.) From time to time, Tonkel and another FBR executive named Henry Fan would show up on Thompson's doorstep, preaching the word about converting to a REIT. Tonkel was the FBR principal who came to Houston repeatedly trying to talk Thompson into a REIT IPO. Billings would follow up with several phone calls. By 2004 FBR was not alone in the REIT game. Even though many traditional Wall Street firms had turned up their noses at the concept (because of the huge dividend payouts), all that was in the past. Subprime was hot. Bear Stearns, Lehman Brothers, and the investment banking side of Bank of America all began talking to Thompson and his boss at Cerberus, Steven Feinberg, about taking Aegis public—either through a C corporation or through a REIT. Billings again took the lead, traveling to Houston, telling a group of Aegis executives, "You're nuts if you don't this." The meeting lasted almost three hours. Friedman was there as well. Thompson would not talk about the meeting, but one Aegis executive described it as a "high-energy show. It was high volume."

By the spring of 2005 the IPO market for subprime lenders began to turn sour for two reasons: First, the Federal Reserve had been hiking short-term interest rates over several months, which began to cut into the profit margins of most subprime lenders for one simple mathematical reason: When short-term rates went up, the rates on warehouse loans Wall Street was extending to them (that they would use to originate mortgages to people with bad credit) also rose. That necessarily would not spell disaster because, in theory, they could increase the interest on the mortgages they made to the public. But that was no longer the case. Short-term rates were rising but mortgage rates were not. There were now so many nonbank and bank subprime lenders making loans that competition prevented everyone from hiking their rates. The first lender to hike its rates—even by just half a percentage point—suddenly saw its applications fall through the floor.

The other reason the IPO market began to dry up? Rumors were swirling around about Arnall's Ameriquest being the subject of predatory lending investigations in multiple states. The last thing in the world the market liked was an investigation about a mortgage firm's lending practices—even if it was an aberration. And it was doubly bad that the rumors concerned the nation's largest subprime lender: Ameriquest.

Thompson, according to those close to him, stopped listening to FBR's IPO pitches—REIT or otherwise. He, too, didn't like the idea of paying out 90 percent of his earnings to shareholders. Two Lehman Brothers managing directors, Bill Curley and Tony Viscardi, were now pitching the IPO idea directly to Cerberus chief Steven Feinberg.

Lehman Brothers told Feinberg that even though the IPO market was beginning to move away from subprime lenders (again, due partly to Ameriquest's troubles with the states), Aegis might be able to raise between $600 million and $1 billion. Feinberg was itching to do a deal. "He wanted to cash out of Aegis," said an executive close to him.

Meanwhile, back at FBR, Tonkel, who had been promoted to president and put in charge of investment banking, was given the task of landing the biggest fish in the IPO pond—Arnall's Ameriquest. "It was Rock's job to court Arnall to try to get Ameriquest or Argent to go public through FBR," said one manager at the company. "If he had done it, it would've been a major league home run for the firm." But investors were growing skittish. Rates were rising, competition was stiffening, and there was Ameriquest itself. What type of investor would take a chance on a firm that was being investigated for its lending practices by attorneys general far and wide?

Both Billings and Friedman had mentioned the possibility of taking Ameriquest public to Mozilo over at Countrywide. "Roland was looking for an exit strategy," Mozilo later recounted. "He wanted out." Ameriquest and its wholesale sister company Argent, combined, held the number-one perch among all subprime lenders. Together, they were a downright volume hog. By the time 2005 ended, Ameriquest/ Argent had funded almost $75 billion in subprime loans, a record for any lender. Its two closest competitors: New Century in Irvine, which had been launched by one of Arnall's proteges (Steve Holder), and Countrywide. Among the nation's 20 largest subprime originators, just two were privately held: Arnall's company and Aegis.

To investment bankers at FBR, Lehman Brothers, and Bear Stearns, and to the other money men of Wall Street, it was inconceivable that two companies so large were not publicly traded on a stock exchange. Mozilo was no longer so jealous of Ameriquest, which by then had stopped raiding his top producers. If FBR wanted to do an IPO for Ameriquest or Argent,[8] then let them, Mozilo thought. The way he

---

[8] At various times between 2003 and 2005 Arnall contemplated taking Ameriquest and/or Argent public as part of his exit strategy from the mortgage industry. Arnall would never address the issue, but Mozilo and investment banking officials, including one from FBR, said an IPO was seriously under consideration even though ACC never filed any paperwork with the SEC.

saw it, Billings "was taking companies that were failing, or had no long-term chance of making it, public. I felt there was no way a REIT would help." He made it perfectly clear to anyone who would ask him about REITs, citing their perpetual disgorging of 90 percent of their earnings: It was the stupidest idea going.

By the fall of 2005 the IPO market for nonbanks, through REITs or otherwise, had dried up. But that didn't stop FBR from making one last-ditch attempt at taking Aegis public. "FBR called us and said, 'I know the market is moving away, but we think we can raise $400 million for you,'" said one Aegis executive. "They went to Feinberg personally. They said, 'Give us a few days.'" After a few days nothing had happened. The Aegis executive described FBR's overtures during the time as "fake it until you make it."

★   ★   ★

By the fall of 2005, FBR had become a different place, partly because the market for mortgage REITs had just about dried up, but also because Manny Friedman, 58—the man who had pioneered the investment bank's foray into subprime—suddenly announced his retirement from the firm amid an SEC probe that included insider trading allegations against him. The agency was examining the company's role back in 2001 of marketing shares of Annapolis-based CompuDyne Corporation to a group of hedge funds. By year-end 2005, even though Friedman had not been formally charged, FBR offered to settle the case for $7.5 million.[9] When the retirement announcement came, many company employees were caught off guard. As much as Billings, he was the public face of FBR. Billings put out a statement thanking Friedman for his "countless contributions to the firm." He and his friend had shared the titles of co-chairman and co-CEO, but now Billings was the only one left of the investment bank's three founders,

---

[9] When the hardcover edition of this book was first published in July 2008, the SEC probe of Friedman still had not been officially settled. Billings and FBR declined to discuss the matter. CompuDyne, which merged with another company in late 2007, was a technology firm specializing in (among other things) institutional security systems. According to a report by the *Washington Post*, Friedman eventually settled the matter by paying a fine without admitting or denying wrongdoing.

even though the firm retained their names. Friedman issued a statement saying he had "great confidence in FBR's future."

Between the beginning of 2005 and the end of 2006, the dozen or so publicly traded subprime/nonprime REITs that FBR had taken public or raised equity for originated $329 billion in home loans, or one out of every five subprime or nonprime (alt-A, stated-income) mortgages made to home buyers in those years. By the fall of 2007 most of these FBR-sponsored lenders had filed for bankruptcy protection or had been sold to other owners—including Wall Street firms Morgan Stanley and Bear Stearns, which had bought, respectively, Saxon Mortgage of Virginia and Encore Credit, the latter being yet another Southern California firm in the basket of subprime lenders started by an Ameriquest alumni: Steve Holder, who had co-founded New Century, also co-founded Encore. Morgan Stanley and Bear Stearns would eventually shut down these lenders.

The failures of all these firms followed pretty much the same pattern: The loans they extended to consumers with bad credit would go delinquent at a higher rate than they ever dreamed. The buyers of these loans in the secondary market—which were always Wall Street firms like Bear Stearns, Merrill Lynch, Lehman Brothers, Deutsche Bank, or the rest of the New York club—would ask the lender to repurchase the bad loans or give them additional money for their troubles. But if the lender happened to be a REIT paying out 90 percent of its earnings to shareholders, it didn't have that kind of money. And it wasn't just a few bad mortgages; it was thousands upon thousands, totaling hundreds of millions of dollars. Eventually, it added up to billions of dollars.

Mike McMahon, the former Sandler O'Neill analyst, surveyed the carnage in late 2007 and wasn't exactly perplexed by what he saw. He had left Sandler the year before, having grown disgusted with, among other things, the twin accounting scandals at Fannie Mae and Freddie Mac. Both these congressionally chartered mortgage giants had bookkeeping problems, relating to how they hedged their mammoth mortgage portfolios, which consisted mostly of "A" credit quality MBSs but also a growing pool of alt-A and subprime loans that had been securitized. (A hedge was a financial bet that compensated them in the event of rising or falling interest rates, which affected the values of the mortgages or MBSs they held. To please Wall Street, both GSEs wanted to have steady, not wildly fluctuating, earnings. But being that their business involved buying residential loans—a highly cyclical business reliant on low interest rates—having a steady anything was next to impossible.) Freddie Mac, under its chairman and CEO, Leland Brendsel, had understated its earnings by about $5 billion—on purpose so it could save that money to help in future periods when earnings were light. Fannie Mae had done the opposite: It overstated earnings to please Wall Street.[10] Fannie's scandal claimed the job of its politically well-connected chairman and CEO, Franklin Raines, who was forced out by the board a few days before Christmas 2004. (A former investment banker with Lazard Freres, Raines served as budget director in the Clinton administration.) It would not be the last time these two congressionally chartered companies would be in the news making headlines.

As an analyst at Sandler O'Neill, McMahon had followed Countrywide, Fannie Mae, Freddie Mac, and a handful of mostly community banking companies, writing research reports on these publicly traded lenders and advising the firms' institutional clients whether they should buy or avoid the stocks. A month before McMahon left Sandler in the fall of 2006, he said to a reporter, "How can I cover these firms when I can't believe anything they're telling me?" He was talking mostly about Fannie Mae and Freddie Mac. But he also had taken a close look at mortgage REITs and, like Mozilo, saw no sense in the structure—unless you happened to be the investment banking firm taking them public. "A REIT is an investment banker's dream client," said McMahon. "When rates are low [and originations boom], REITs have significant growth and always need to raise equity. It's a virtuous cycle."

Many of the mortgage executives who listened to Billings' REIT pitches, including HomeBanc's Flood, didn't doubt Billings' sincerity. He so believed in REITs that he even converted part of FBR into a REIT and began investing in subprime mortgage-backed securities. In

---

[10] It would take Fannie Mae and Freddie Mac almost four years before they would fully recover from their respective accounting scandals, putting in place accounting systems and practices that allowed their regulator, the Office of Federal Housing Enterprise Oversight, to fully understand just how much they were really earning or losing from their hedging practices. However, once the two solved the problem of their antiquated systems, they would have another problem on their hands: growing delinquencies in their subprime, alt-A, and even "A" paper holdings.

2004, one of the peak years for subprime originations and a year in which FBR raised equity for at least seven subprime lenders, the firm started by Eric, Manny, and Russ earned a record $350 million. But by 2007 all of the earnings would be wiped out and then some. FBR lost $660 million in 2007, due in part to its investments in subprime MBSs and the purchase of a subprime lender in Florida called First NLC Financial Services. Its stock price would fall to a dangerously low $1.50 a share, compared to an all-time high of almost $30, leaving investors wondering about its long-term viability.[11]

A former FBR manager who saw the writing on the wall and left the firm put it like this: "Eric's hubris did him in. Once he likes something, he does not understand that sometimes markets can change. He became convinced that he is right and the market is wrong."

---

[11] In January 2008, shortly after Fieldstone filed for bankruptcy protection, Walter Buczynski, a top executive at the company, killed his wife by breaking her neck. He then drove to the Delaware Memorial Bridge where he leaped to his death. His suicide note blamed personal and not financial problems for his actions.

Chapter 7

The End of the
(New) Century

I f there was one central reason for Friedman Billings Ramsey's
(FBR's) success with REITs, it was because of a company called
New Century Financial Corporation, which (not surprisingly) was
headquartered in the mecca of subprime: sunny Irvine, California. "In
2004 New Century raised almost $1 billion with their REIT offering,"
said subprime industry veteran Barney Guy, who was working for a
competitor up in Washington state. "Everyone in the industry looked at
that and said, 'Jeez. They're bulletproof.' Because of that offering, New
Century had so much capital." (Guy was off by about $200 million, but
his point was well taken.)

Two years later, New Century had supplanted Roland Arnall's
Ameriquest/Argent empire as the top residential subprime originator
in the United States. A nonbank that was barely a decade old, New
Century—thanks to the REIT conversion by FBR—was the largest
publicly traded subprime lender on the planet, bar none. Its share price:
$52 a pop. Since being founded in 1995, the lender had had a stel-
lar growth record, expanding exponentially as interest rates plummeted
in 2002 and 2003 and continuing to balloon even as rates climbed

in later years. By 2006, it did business with up to 47,000 mortgage brokers scattered around the country and sported a retail network of 222 branch offices. New Century took pride in calling itself "A New Shade of Blue Chip," in reference to the blue-chip stock of the most established companies on the New York Stock Exchange. (The blue chip is the most valuable chip in a casino.) Even Angelo Mozilo, whose sales staff was being raided by New Century, had something nice (sort of) to say about the company: "They were the hottest game in town."

Yet in 2006, there was some transition among New Century's highest ranks. Brad Morrice, the company's long-standing president, was set to become its chief executive as well, replacing longtime CEO Robert Cole. But Morrice was an unlikely candidate to head a high-octane sales machine like New Century. The mortgage bank lived to churn loans for sale to Wall Street, and its sales staff had the strongest voice in its decision making. Morrice, who became CEO a week before turning 50, was nothing like the young, hardworking, hard-living salesmen who brought in loans by networking with mortgage brokers. Overweight, with thin gray hair and glasses, he was a man who devoured books. Morrice was an intellectual who enjoyed debating theories and sometimes analyzed decisions to death, former colleagues said. He had one nervous tick: constantly saying "um." Before co-founding New Century, he had had little experience running a mortgage bank. His biggest detraction: he wasn't a salesman.

In May of that year, before taking control, he addressed shareholders at the company's annual meeting at its Irvine headquarters. First he apologized for not wearing a tie. He was still waiting for construction of his new multimillion-dollar home in nearby Laguna Beach to be finished and forgot to pack a tie in his suitcase. During his speech, he warned of the worst pitfall that could befall a home lender: "The history of the mortgage business generally suggests that companies that run into big trouble and in some cases go out of business don't do that because they run out of customers. They do it because they run out of money."

Morrice's ascension to the top job at New Century marked the pinnacle of a winding career that began on a completely different track. Morrice was a former corporate attorney with a law degree from the

Boalt Law School at the University of California, Berkeley. He also held an MBA from Stanford University, which was no slouch among business schools. He worked his way up to partner in the Los Angeles law firm that eventually became known as King, Purtich & Morrice. His specialties: assisting mortgage bankers with their legal affairs, digesting complex legal documents in a short time, and explaining the ramifications to his clients in simple, clear language.

★   ★   ★

In the 1990s, one of the clients of Morrice's law firm was Plaza Home Mortgage in Santa Ana, near Irvine. Plaza Home Mortgage owned a midsize savings and loan (S&L) and also borrowed money from other bankers to make loans it would later sell. Jack French headed Plaza. A veteran of the Korean War, French was a motivational leader whom colleagues described as loyal and tough but with a sensitive side—he once cried while praising employees at a company Christmas party. One day in 1992, French had a late-afternoon meeting with his lawyers in a Los Angeles high-rise. After the meeting broke up, Morrice escorted French to the elevator. It was getting dark. They were alone. Surprising French, Morrice said he would be interested in coming to work at Plaza Home Mortgage. French looked him over. It was the first time Morrice had ever mentioned ditching his legal career and coming to work for French as an executive. If Morrice was nervous about making such a bold play, he didn't show it. Morrice was cool. "Give me a call," French said. "We'll talk about it."

French hired Morrice, who had zero experience running a mortgage company, as an executive vice president in February 1993. It was the kind of snap judgment French occasionally made. He recognized Morrice's intellectual gifts and decided to see what he could do. In the beginning, Morrice didn't do much. As one executive at Plaza Home Mortgage later noted: "He spent all day writing on a legal pad. He didn't know the mortgage business."

Another snap judgment French made was to enter the subprime business by forming a new but separate affiliate. He called it Option One Mortgage Corporation. The idea actually came from a friend of his, Ed Gotschall, an executive who helped keep the books over at Guardian Savings—the Jedinaks' S&L. In the world of mortgage banking, secrets were few and far between, and word began to spread that Guardian Savings was making a ton of money by originating subprime first lien mortgages and securitizing the paper through Wall Street. Roland Arnall noticed, as did Jack French.

Gotschall wanted to head the new venture, but French decided on two other executives instead: Pat Rank and Bob Dubrish. Both had helped Arnall get Long Beach Mortgage off the ground. But grateful for Gotschall's assistance, French made him Option One's chief financial officer. When French told his financial backers at First Interstate Bank about his plan to launch Option One, they balked. As the lead warehouse lender to Plaza Home Mortgage, First Interstate wasn't interested in offering credit so Option One could gamble on home buyers with a history of payment problems. French insisted to his bankers, "We're not lending money to criminals." But First Interstate didn't care. They cut him off.

French found a more willing audience on Wall Street. Salomon Brothers had securitized subprime mortgages with Guardian Savings and was hungry for more business. In a deal that would become a prototype for subprime lenders, Salomon agreed to provide Option One with both a warehouse line of credit and securitization services. A decade earlier, Salomon had been the king of the MBS market thanks to mortgage trader cum vice chairman Lewis Ranieri. However, by 1993 Ranieri and all his top traders had departed Salomon, and the firm's MBS business—which catered only to "A" credit quality loans—was in tatters. Salomon's staff introduced Rank and Dubrish to credit rating agencies and bond insurers and let them know what types of questions they might ask. Salomon's guys "held our hands," said a former Option One executive. In December 1993, Option One sold $80 million in subprime mortgages to Salomon, which then packaged the mortgages into bonds. It was one of the largest subprime deals up to that time. Option One was on the map.

The growth of Plaza Home Mortgage—including Option One—soon became a headache for French, who found day-to-day operations tedious. In the summer of 1993, French and the president of Plaza Home Mortgage, James Weld, agreed to part company. Brad Morrice was itching to get the president's post, but French had his reservations. For one thing, Morrice, though smart, had been with Plaza for only about a year and was still green. About this time, a lawyer friend of French's told him about a real estate development company executive named Robert Cole who had experience in banking and wanted to jump back in. Cole was an impressive speaker with banking experience, but French wasn't sure he was the right choice. Former colleagues described Cole as a "stuffed shirt," very conservative in appearance and behavior but good at raising money. "He painted a picture with words. He had credibility," one former colleague said. In the end, French and the board of directors of Plaza Home Mortgage struck a compromise—they made Cole and Morrice co-presidents of Plaza in 1994. The duo weren't in charge of Plaza for long before French and the board decided to sell the company. A year after Cole and Morrice took the helm, Plaza was sold to Fleet Financial Group, a commercial bank, for $88 million. Cole and Morrice were out of a job.

★   ★   ★

When mortgage executives in Orange County were out of work in the 1990s, they would hang out at the Irvine, California, offices of headhunter Lee Hecht Harrison. It became known as the "halfway house" for the mortgage industry. It was there that Cole and Morrice teamed with another Plaza refugee, Ed Gotschall, the numbers cruncher. They began plotting a new mortgage company to focus exclusively on subprime: New Century Financial Corporation. Their plan was to borrow money from Wall Street using warehouse lines, just like Arnall's Long Beach Mortgage, and originate loans to consumers with bad credit.

New Century would sell the loans back to Wall Street. It would operate like Option One but without a sister S&L to help fund loans. New Century would rely entirely on borrowed money—warehouse lines. But there was a hitch. The former Plaza trio had special skills but not much experience running a staff of loan officers. They decided to take a chance on a fourth partner known for his drive and ability to motivate sales staff, someone with years of experience in consumer finance and subprime lending. Steven Holder became the fourth co-founder of New Century. Holder, six feet four and a college dropout, was described by one former

New Century employee as "a charismatic SOB who wooed everyone." He, like many subprime executives, also came from Long Beach Mortgage and was in charge of production—the origination of mortgages using loan officers and brokers.[1]

The four partners had the right idea and skills, but they needed money. They counted on Bob Cole to work his magic with potential investors. Cole was a perpetual networker who had a slew of contacts with money or working for firms that had money. Cole tapped a former colleague, Michael Sachs, an attorney who had been legal counsel for a self-storage company while Cole was an executive there. Sachs, who was confined to a wheelchair as a result of suffering polio as a child, made up for his lack of mobility by sharpening his mind. After listening to Cole, Sachs called a venture capitalist he knew: John Bentley, a partner with Cornerstone Equity Partners in Arizona.

In the fall of 1995, Sachs and the four founders flew to Cornerstone Equity Partners' headquarters in a modest office building in Phoenix. They were ushered into a conference room, and Bob Cole launched into his pitch about New Century. He handed John Bentley a binder with rosy projections about the future profits to be had from subprime lending. Bentley later said that Cole was a passionate speaker when it came to New Century and that he always carried promotional materials on the company. "It was his job to raise money. He never missed an opportunity," Bentley said. Bentley and his partner, Sherman Chu, who had a background in mortgage banking, liked what they heard. And they were pleased that three of the founders had worked together at the parent company of Option One, a profitable subprime start-up. They felt that Holder stood out from the other three, Bentley said. Without him, New Century wouldn't fly. "They needed a production guy, and Steve is all about production," Bentley said.

Bentley and Chu agreed to invest $2 million and took a 63 percent stake. They also got the right to name five people to the company's nine-member board of directors. Sachs invested $250,000, and the four founders agreed to invest $425,000, Bentley said. Holder didn't have the cash and the others pitched in for him, something that never sat well with

---

[1] Prior to working for Long Beach Mortgage, Holder was a manager at two consumer finance companies: TransAmerica and Nova Financial Services.

Cole or Gotschall, Bentley said. It later came out in Phoenix's *New Times* newspaper that the money Cornerstone invested in New Century came from a unit of the Baptist Foundation of Arizona, which allegedly ran a Ponzi scheme that targeted many elderly Baptists. The foundation, which had made a series of risky real estate investments, filed for bankruptcy in November 1999 owing investors close to $600 million and having assets of just $200 million. Around that time the Baptist Foundation unit sold its stake in New Century to raise cash, and Bentley resigned from New Century's board, since his venture capital firm no longer had a stake in the lender.[2]

With seed money in its pocket, New Century began in 1995 in a small office in Newport Beach, a posh coastal town later made famous by the teen TV drama *The O.C.* From the beginning, the four founders had difficulty managing their egos. Each bore the title of president and chairman, making New Century perhaps the only company in the United States (and probably the world) with four presidents. The rivalry was strongest between Morrice and Cole, who had been forced to share the president's title at Plaza Home Mortgage. In their new headquarters, they moved a wall about a foot so they would each have the exact same size office. They also hired career coach Vance Caesar to help them work together. Caesar held a series of team-building exercises, including hand-holding and pep talks.

Once again Salomon Brothers elected to support a start-up subprime lender. In November 1996, Salomon agreed to lend New Century up to $175 million, and in return it got first peek at 70 percent of the lender's first $500 million in loans for sale. New Century could borrow up to $105 per $100 of loan balance. In other words, Salomon was lending New Century an extra $5 to pay its operating costs. One former New Century executive later said that was a sweetheart deal since any credible lender should keep its expenses to less than $3 per loan. Since subprime loans were so profitable, Salomon provided New Century with a generous margin for error.

★   ★   ★

---

[2] Bentley later said Sachs was the one who introduced him to the unit of the Baptist Foundation.

The early days of New Century were known as the Steven Holder era, former executives said. He immediately began recruiting and training an army of account executives (AEs) whose job it would be to convince mortgage brokers to send loans New Century's way. The company grew quickly and soon moved to an 11-story black high-rise near John Wayne Airport in neighboring Irvine,[3] a city about 45 miles south of Los Angeles with a burgeoning professional services industry, the largest university in the county, and lots of pricey new home developments popular with young families.

The irony of being headquartered in upscale cities like Newport Beach or Irvine while making loans to folks struggling to break into the middle class either was lost on the founders of New Century or they didn't care. Indeed, as office rents dropped in Irvine following the recession of 2001 it became common for mortgage companies to lease space in office towers once reserved for corporate law firms and accountants. In 1996, the first year New Century funded mortgages, the company originated or bought from other lenders $357 million in subprime loans. The following year its loan volume increased more than fivefold to nearly $2 billion.

Holder, the salesman, pushed his staff to keep up the pace. When things were slow, he got creative. He invented special days when he would review loan files. Some sales staff dubbed the days "signing parties." At mortgage banks like New Century the account executives brought in the loans, earning big commissions and all the glory. But loan underwriters had to approve each loan file, ensuring all the documents were in order. Only then would the bank fund the loan and the account executive get a commission. If Holder noticed loan volumes dropping, he would announce a day when he and other top managers would personally review problematic loans. "If loans were stuck, it was a way to get them unstuck," one former sales manager said.

On the morning of a signing party, sales staff buzzed at New Century. Any ambitious AE with a problem loan whipped out the file.

---

[3] Irvine was once the home of Charlie Keating's Lincoln Savings. In the postsubprime crash era, Orange and the surrounding counties became the home to several mortgage vulture funds that sprang to life to bottom-fish in delinquent mortgages. One such firm was Stan Kurland's PennyMac.

Holder rounded up a few sales managers, and they strode floor to floor, creating a whirlwind of excitement. Holder stopped at any object in the center of a room, whether a table or file cabinet, and set up shop. Account executives quickly gathered in lines eager to show him their problem files. They hurriedly explained why their loans were really okay, despite not fitting into the company's underwriting guidelines. Holder would lay on the charm, smiling and coaxing them while simultaneously grilling them with questions to see if they knew their stuff. If they gave reasonable answers, his pen flew. Loan approved.

The signing parties raised eyebrows among the company's more conservative executives, who worried Holder let poor-quality loans get funded. However, his supporters said he would not sign every loan, and that not every borrower fits into a simple underwriting box. But one former executive said the ability of senior sales managers to overturn the objection of a loan underwriter was risky and undermined the motivation of underwriters to tackle difficult files. Why object to a loan if some sales guy's boss would just override your objection? But the fault did not rest solely on Holder's shoulders, this executive said—the other three founders had failed to create a proper system of controls on the approval of loans. According to the executive, the company lacked a counterweight to Holder's powerful sales team.

With Holder heading loan production, Cole handling Wall Street, Morrice heading administration, and Gotschall keeping the books, New Century climbed in the origination rankings. As it did, the four founders began to contemplate selling shares to the public. Being publicly traded would open the company to more scrutiny, but it was also a way for the original investors to have a means of cashing out some of their holdings and for the founders to make money via stock options. In addition, New Century could issue more shares to pay for its expansion. However, venture capitalist Bentley said the company couldn't go public with each founder having the title of president and chairman. That would be ludicrous. The founders' egos had to be massaged. Eventually, the investment bankers handling the initial public offering (IPO) convinced the founders they needed more rational titles, Bentley said. But who would be CEO—Cole or Morrice?

After some debate, they agreed on Cole, who was the best speaker of the bunch (he didn't say "um" as much); he also had experience with Wall Street, and so was the best choice to be the lender's public face. The other three let Cole have the top job.[4] New Century had a modest but respectable IPO in June 1997, raising about $30 million at $11 per share—not bad for a company that was only two years old. Then the Russian debt crisis struck in the fall of 1998, sinking the fortunes of almost every single subprime firm that was both publicly traded and securitizing mortgages through Wall Street. Several subprime lenders were failing, and New Century executives were getting worried. The company's stock was tanking. It fell to a paltry $2.50 on October 6, 1998, and employees began looking for new jobs. Cole, though, managed to save New Century by convincing a commercial bank, U.S. Bancorp of Minneapolis, to invest $20 million in the company's preferred stock and to buy most of its loans for a year. Instead of securitizing its subprime mortgages though Wall Street, New Century would sell them in whole-loan form to U.S. Bancorp for cash—which is exactly what Arnall's Long Beach Mortgage had done. The alliance with the bank was announced on October 19, 1998. New Century's stock immediately rebounded. It was saved.

★   ★   ★

One day Steven Holder walked into the office of Greg Schroeder, head of sales training at New Century, and said, "What if we hire Tommy Lasorda as a pitchman?" Schroeder, six feet two and overweight, went way back with Holder. They had worked together at Long Beach Mortgage. When Schroeder heard the idea he groaned. Hiring the former manager of the Los Angeles Dodgers baseball team was just the latest in a string of random proposals sales managers were throwing his way. To Schroeder it seemed as though every loan production chief at the company fancied himself a marketing expert. But Schroeder handled his boss with tact. He countered, "If we are going to do this let's be scientific."

New Century hired a market research firm and an advertising agency. They scrapped the Lasorda idea and told Schroeder, who eventually

---

[4] Even though Cole was now the CEO, all four founders continued to receive exactly the same pay and bonuses each year. In 1998, the year after the IPO, each earned a salary of $281,600 and a bonus of $600,893.

became head of marketing at the company, that New Century should brand itself as a provider of "fast financial solutions." In the mortgage market, and particularly in the subprime space, consumers wanted their money quickly. And loan brokers wanted to help the consumer—quickly. (It was all about making the sale.) Schroeder mulled it over and eventually hit on the concept of a computer system that would accept or reject a borrower's application without any human reviewing the file. Fannie Mae and Freddie Mac, the largest buyers of home mortgages in the country, had created such systems, which were used by their customers that were "A" paper lenders, like Countrywide, Wells Fargo, Chase Home Finance, and others. Could New Century do the same for subprime?

Holder approved, and Schroeder needed to figure out how it would work. One night, after a sales meeting in St. Louis, Schroeder and Dan Sussman, another sales manager, were sitting outside a restaurant in a shopping mall converted from a train station, and they began envisioning how the computer system would function. The conversation grew spirited and soon they were sketching the design on cocktail napkins. It would be a web site for mortgage brokers who would enter key details on a borrower. Each loan customer would be broken down into a series of numbers: a FICO credit score, a debt-to-income ratio, the number of missed payments on loans or bills, and whether or not there were any public filings against the borrower, such as a notice of default on a mortgage. Every borrower would be evaluated by the numbers.

They decided to allow New Century's loan brokers to pull a credit report on each borrower for free—saving the brokers a few dollars. New Century ran its own report anyway if the file got to final review, so why not do it at the beginning instead? But the software would limit how much information each broker could see on the credit report, to discourage the broker from shopping the loan file around the industry to other subprime wholesale lenders. The concept was easy, but getting the system built proved a challenge. Schroeder found that New Century's tech department and budget had been slashed during the financial crisis of 1998, which meant he had to convince Holder to let him hire staff. To boot, the tech department would allow Schroeder the use of only one computer server, which he had to stick in an empty closet. "We had to prop the door open and put in a box fan to keep the server cool," Schroeder said.

Despite the headaches, Schroeder completed the project in six months. It was dubbed "FastQual" and promised to render a decision on a borrower not in minutes but in 12 seconds. The next obstacle was marketing it—getting New Century's brokers (who dealt with the public) to use it. Among other things, New Century promoted the FastQual brand by sponsoring race cars and inviting its loan brokers out to the track for the day. But Schroeder felt he needed something more. In 2002, he hired Dan White to find the way. White, six feet five with a completely bare scalp and facial hair just around the mouth, had bounced around small radio stations in Los Angeles as a disc jockey and worked as road manager for Fleetwood Mac and Santana. In his first week on the job, Schroeder took White to a broker trade show in Cleveland, Ohio. New Century had a booth in the city's convention center to show off FastQual, and was one of hundreds of companies with booths. White observed they were getting little attention. Another company that had hired some sexy models got more visits.[5]

"What did this booth cost you?" White asked.

Schroeder's reply: about $50,000.

"What's your return on investment?" White then asked.

Schroeder wasn't sure. "Some things are hard to quantify."

"That's not acceptable," White said. "I think what you need to do is take New Century on the road like Aerosmith."

Instead of using "booth babes" at a mortgage industry trade show, White said New Century needed "to be the show." New Century should take FastQual on a road show across the country—and not share the spotlight with anyone. Schroeder proposed it to New Century's management committee, which included the company's founders. The committee was divided on the proposal. Gotschall, the company's numbers whiz, decided to back it, becoming the swing vote. Schroeder later recalled Gotschall saying, "It's not should we do it, but what will happen if we don't do it." New Century was in stiff competition for subprime borrowers with Mozilo's and Arnall's firms. They were looking for an edge.

---

[5] A favorite way for mortgage lenders and vendors to attract visitors to their trade show booths was to staff them with so-called "booth babes"—attractive young women who didn't necessarily work for the firm.

Everything—attendance, food, and even alcohol—would be free to mortgage brokers. The road show was named "Close More University" and featured a dozen top sales coaches sharing techniques and advice with brokers. White ran everything like the rock concerts he was used to managing with 84-foot screens, aerial lighting, and surround sound. The shows started in hotel ballrooms but grew so large they migrated to convention centers. The first year's budget totaled $5 million. The budget expanded each year until it hit $20 million. One of the largest shows was at the Los Angeles Convention Center. It featured four 30-foot screens. One area was sectioned off and set up with 100 laptops running FastQual. New Century software trainers, who were budding account executives, wore bright red shirts and gave FastQual demonstrations. Before the show started, one of New Century's board members, Fredric Forster, showed up. The shows had become so big the board's interest was piqued.

Forster, a former president for H.F. Ahmanson and Company, once one of the state's largest S&Ls, stood next to Cole as Schroeder welcomed them. "How many people does this place hold?" Forster asked.

"We have reservations for five thousand, but I expect about half," Schroeder said.

"You'll never fill it," Forster predicted.

"Care to bet on that?" Schroeder said. The two men wagered $10. Forster, the director, thought New Century was throwing money away and that not enough brokers would attend to make it worthwhile. But the brokers came—nearly 3,000 strong. At the end of the day, Forster paid the $10 and said he was impressed. The cost of the Los Angeles show: $650,000.

The biggest measure of the road show's success was the expanding popularity of FastQual to brokers who were hunting for subprime borrowers on the streets. It was marketed as "prequalification" software, since New Century didn't issue consumer disclosures until the physical file arrived (such disclosures are required by law when offering a consumer a home loan). About 86 percent of loans approved by FastQual were funded as is, no changes. Before the road shows, FastQual was reviewing up to $100 million a day in loans. After a few years of road shows, FastQual reviewed up to $3 billion in loans in a single day. To be sure, it rejected many loans, too. But one company executive said that saved the sales staff time by eliminating "garbage loans" that came into New Century from brokers.

★　★　★

In late 2000 New Century co-founder Steven Holder left the company after a rift developed between him and the other three founders. His detractors say he was forced out because it became clear to the others that under him New Century had funded too many mortgages that were winding up delinquent. ("Shitty" was the word some of them used.) The other three believed that Holder cared only about sales—to the point of recklessness. But Holder had supporters at the company who believed that he was the real force behind New Century's phenomenal growth, single-handedly creating the sales infrastructure that led to the company going head-to-head with Ameriquest and Countrywide. Within a month Morrice, who held the president's title, also become chief operating officer, a position formerly shared by Holder. Morrice was beginning to assume total control of New Century.

After Holder's departure, the three remaining founders invited Mike McMahon, then an analyst with investment bank Sandler O'Neill, and an old acquaintance of theirs, to visit New Century so they could discuss the lender's future and see if the two firms could do business together. The reason McMahon knew the three: He was one of First Interstate's warehouse lending executives who had lent money to Plaza Home Mortgage, where Cole, Morrice, and Gotschall all had once worked. McMahon and a colleague flew in from San Francisco and went to New Century's headquarters near John Wayne Airport. In the company's boardroom one afternoon, they all munched on chips and sandwiches and batted around ideas. The founders said they had "survived death" in 1998 and now needed to figure out a game plan.

"I know what you should do," McMahon said. He suggested using some of the $100 million or so the company had in cash to buy back stock "every single day" until they and he were the only shareholders left. They laughed, but McMahon was serious. He owned a few thousand shares and thought the company buying back its own stock would boost the share price, because the earnings per share would increase with fewer shares outstanding.

Gotschall told the analyst that the company wanted to become a major financial player like Household Finance, revealing the colleagues' ambition.[6] Then someone said, "What do you think of REITs?" (That meant FBR and Billings.) McMahon objected to the REIT idea. It would require building a huge portfolio of loans on New Century's books, which McMahon said would become problematic if delinquencies ever rose higher than anticipated. He also didn't like the idea of paying out 90 percent of a firm's earnings to shareholders, because doing so prevented the company from building up capital— money it could use for a rainy day. (When it came to REITs, the analyst and Mozilo were on the same page.) McMahon said New Century should stick to selling loans for cash, which had enabled the firm to survive the credit crisis of 1998. Besides, having a large portfolio on its books while also running a major loan-making operation would be a complicated story to sell to Wall Street, McMahon said.

Bob Cole, then chief executive, said, "Do you mean having a big mortgage portfolio would be a detraction?" McMahon said it would, and that was not all. As a REIT, New Century would be constantly spending its money on buying loans and paying nearly all of its profit to shareholders as dividends. Thus, it would constantly need to sell shares to raise cash for expansion, McMahon said. Yet if interest rates ever rose, stock of a mortgage REIT would likely fall, since New Century would earn less of an interest spread on its loans. It would have to pay more to borrow money, but it would take longer to raise consumer rates, or the money coming in the door. Investors would anticipate that, expect a cut in dividends, and so sell shares, he said—not to mention the fact that fewer homeowners refinance when rates rise. "If you convert to a REIT, you'd better hope rates go down forever," McMahon said.

The REIT idea stayed on ice. But as subprime lending boomed, Eric Billings of FBR became more persistent in his REIT pitches, spending much of his time visiting mortgage companies or chatting up their executives over the phone or in person on the virtues of converting to a REIT. Despite McMahon's warnings, Cole, Morrice, and Gotschall

---

[6] In 2002 British bank HSBC bought Household Finance, one of the nation's largest subprime lenders, for $14 billion.

warmed up to the idea. They even paid Billings' firm $250,000 to study how New Century could make the switch to a REIT.

In October 2003, the founders were ready to take the plan to their board of directors. A series of meetings ensued in which the complicated proposal was explained again and again. Eventually, Bear Stearns, then a warehouse lender to New Century, agreed to play devil's advocate at a board meeting so directors would get more than FBR's rosy picture. At a two-day meeting in March 2004 at New Century's headquarters, Bear Stearns officials warned—as Mike McMahon had previously done— that converting to a REIT would make the company reliant upon issuing additional stock to raise money. They also cautioned the board that a liquidity crisis would be more likely for the firm as a REIT, since New Century would be paying out nearly all of its income to shareholders. It would not be setting aside money for a rainy day. And, finally, Bear Stearns officials predicted that being a REIT would limit the potential for New Century to be acquired one day by a bank. Whatever New Century wanted to do, it didn't need to be a REIT to get it done, they said.

The board ignored Bear Stearns' pleadings and in April 2004 approved the REIT conversion. Billings had won. FBR would get its payday by handling the public offering of stock. Six months later, in October, New Century introduced itself to the world as a mortgage-lending REIT, raising close to $800 million in an initial public offering—an incredible capital gain from the lender's first IPO in 1997 when it raised $31 million. The REIT idea looked like a golden egg. In addition to FBR, other companies assisting in the IPO and collecting fees included UBS, Merrill Lynch, and Morgan Stanley.

In the weeks before the REIT conversion and in the first month after it, New Century's stock rose by 50 percent from around $40 per share to more than $60 per share. But the novelty soon wore off and the stock fell back to $40 by April 2005, just six months after the change to a REIT and one year after the board of directors approved the switch. That month David Einhorn, head of New York–based investment firm Greenlight Capital, surprised New Century management with a public filing with the Securities and Exchange Commission that said New Century's strategy of building a portfolio of loans to boost its stock had failed. At the time, Einhorn owned 9.1 percent of the company's stock, or 5 million shares. He meant business.

Behind the scenes, Einhorn had never liked the idea of building a portfolio of loans and had let the New Century trio know his thoughts, former New Century executives said. But, as with the warnings of analyst Mike McMahon and Bear Stearns, the founders ignored Einhorn's concerns. They remained convinced that building a portfolio of loans made long-term sense because the loans would guarantee income over time. To build the loan portfolio, New Century set up a hybrid REIT structure, which sounds complicated and was complicated, critics said. As simply put as possible, New Century became two companies, one at the top and one at the bottom. At the top was a REIT that would buy loans at fair market value from a subsidiary unit that made loans. The parent made money from the interest on the loans it bought, and the subsidiary unit made money by selling loans either to the parent or to investment banks. Critics said the complexity of the structure made New Century's stock unappealing to Wall Street investors, even though investment banks were eager to lend it money to make loans and to later buy the loans so they could turn them into securities. Wall Street wanted to do business with New Century but lost the desire to own it.

Einhorn supposedly was impressed by Gotschall's brains but never thought much of Cole's leadership. At one meeting in Manhattan between New Century's top management and Einhorn's people, Einhorn stared coldly at Cole and rarely spoke. Einhorn, who grew up in Milwaukee, built a reputation as a shrewd Wall Street investor, sometimes going short on companies, betting they would fail. But he had become an early believer in New Century's ability to make loans and had gone long on its stock.[7] Einhorn declared war on New Century's management. He threatened to run his own slate of candidates for New Century's board. Eventually, the company founders reached a compromise and gave Einhorn one seat on the board.

★   ★   ★

---

[7] Einhorn previously owned a stake in another Irvine-based subprime lender, BNC Mortgage, before Lehman Brothers funded a management-led buyout of the lender. Einhorn had made a bid for BNC but later dropped it. He wanted to see New Century buy back stock instead of using cash to buy its own loans, former New Century executives said.

In 2005, at the peak of the housing boom in the United States, New Century was the largest publicly traded subprime lender in the nation, originating $56 billion in loans. That year its profits hit a company record of $416 million. New Century's founders were getting seriously rich. Cole, Morrice, and Gotschall each earned $1.6 million in salary and bonuses for 2005 and were awarded $769,992 worth of stock plus options to buy more. But the real money was in stock sales and dividends. That year Cole sold $9.4 million in stock and via stock options bought $1.9 of stock at discounted historical prices. Morrice sold $11.6 million and bought $3.1 million, and Gotschall sold $9.3 million and bought $1.5 million. And they raked in dividends on the shares they owned, earnings millions more. (Cole and Morrice, combined, earned $17 million in dividends that year.) Gotschall, the son of a coal miner, became the co-founder best known for philanthropy. He pledged $3 million to Mission Hospital in Mission Viejo and led a fund-raising drive for $50 million. He told a reporter that his son had had his ear fixed there after it was bitten off by a dog and that his daughter went there once for a broken arm.

As the company's profits exploded, Wall Street grew more eager to lend it money. In 2001, Salomon (now owned by Citigroup), Morgan Stanley, and other companies extended $2.1 billion in warehouse credit lines to New Century. By 2005, at the peak of the housing boom, Morgan Stanley had upped the credit line to $3 billion, and Bank of America, Barclays, Bear Stearns, Deutsche Bank, and Credit Suisse joined the party. In all, Wall Street was bankrolling New Century to the tune of $15 billion. One executive at New Century who worked with Wall Street firms said companies that lent it money weren't supposed to get privileged peeks at their loans, but they would "whine and cry" if they didn't. The whiners included Bank of America and Bear Stearns, this executive said. When interest rates were falling in 2002 and 2003, a pool of loans being collected for a future securitization by an investment bank could increase in value by the simple fact that other debt on the market offered lower yields. That trend "forgave a lot of evil," this executive said.

New Century's success as a publicly traded company brought it more prestige than any other firm that focused exclusively on subprime loans. Its executives spoke at conferences hosted by Wall Street investment bankers such as Morgan Stanley and Piper Jaffray, and the founders became financial sponsors of various community groups. New Century spurted cash in all directions. It wasn't just top management getting rich. The best salespeople earned $1 million to $3 million a year. Loan processors who never graduated from college and did little more than check paperwork on loan files earned up to $100,000.

"Alex"—his name has been changed per his request to remain anonymous—talked about life inside the company. He was a top account executive at New Century. In a good year, he earned $2 million in commissions. Account executives were the star employees at New Century, convincing mortgage brokers to bring them customers. They worked on a monthly schedule. At the beginning of each month things were slow, and Alex and his colleagues would golf. They frequented Pelican Hill in Newport Beach, Orange County's top public course with $200 greens fees and a view of the Pacific Ocean at nearly every hole.

Each month started with regular 9 A.M. to 6 P.M. hours for Alex. But as the weeks rolled by the hours become longer and AEs hustled like mad. At lunchtime they grabbed tacos off the "roach coach" that drove by the office. They chatted up brokers on one side and tried to push loans through New Century's underwriting staff on the other. "We would do everything we could do to get the deals done," Alex said. "Sales had the final say on anything." Indeed, sometimes AEs applied a little extra pressure on other employees to get loans approved. In one office, a salesman whacked the top of an appraiser's desk with a baseball bat and screamed at her for killing his deal, according to a report in the *Washington Post*. Every month morphed into a race, Alex said. AEs were under constant mental and physical strain. "I grew old at New Century," Alex said. When housing prices were rising, "There weren't any bad loans," he said.

Like Ameriquest, Argent, and Countrywide, New Century rewarded its top wholesale AEs, taking them on a Princess Cruise to the Bahamas for four days of heavy drinking. Actor Tom Arnold, formerly of Fox Sports Net's *Best Damn Sports Show Period*, did a "Best Damn Mortgage Company" routine on the ship, quizzing top executive Patrick Flanagan. It was one big celebration of the AEs. "We were rock stars," Alex said. And good-looking, too. New Century liked to hire very attractive women. Two of the founders, Morrice and Holder, left their wives for New Century staffers whom they later married.

But the company's reliance on mortgage brokers also exposed it to fraud. New Century financed four properties in Colorado tied to a fraud ring that began when Torrence James and Ronald Fontenot met in federal prison and later decided to become mortgage brokers, according to the *Denver Post* newspaper. The state did not regulate brokers at the time, but has since passed a law that brokers be registered (but not licensed). The two former prisoners allegedly arranged for properties to be bought and sold at inflated prices. Marc Loewenthal, a senior vice president with New Century, later told *Orange County Register* reporter Mathew Padilla that his company bought back all four loans from investors. He said the company developed a computer system to detect potential fraud by identifying suspicious patterns, such as appraisers who tend to overstate the value of property. The system helped the company avoid making nearly $1 billion in suspect loans in much of 2006, he said. It was an impressive number but also implied many suspect loans may have been funded before the system was created.

★   ★   ★

In 2005 New Century had its most profitable year ever, but it was also a time when market forces began to turn against the lender. The rate of home price appreciation peaked, a bad sign for subprime lending, which lived off cash-out refis, when borrowers took the equity out of their homes, usually to pay off credit card debt or auto loans. At the same time, the Federal Reserve raised short-term interest rates to keep inflation in check. Because long-term rates remained low, lenders saw their profit margins squeezed. In a nutshell, they were forced to borrow high and lend low—a deadly combination.

Even as things were getting tougher, Brad Morrice, the president and chief operating officer, launched his campaign for control of the company. Taking the reins of day-to-day management was easy. Holder had left and the other two founders, Cole and Gotschall, were beginning to lack interest in tedious daily decision making, a former executive said. Morrice was the only founder who showed a steady supply of energy and enthusiasm for the company's day-to-day management. It came as no surprise when New Century announced Morrice would become chief executive on July 1, 2006, a little more than a week before his 50th birthday. Though giving up the coveted CEO title, Cole remained chairman of the board. Gotschall became semiretired, working more as a consultant, but also stayed on the board.

In January 2006—just a week before the company announced Morrice would soon take the helm of New Century—the company's media flack offered *Orange County Register* reporters Mathew Padilla and Jeff Collins a sit-down interview with the CEO-in-waiting. Padilla was intrigued. New Century had just come off a phenomenal year, making $56 billion in loans and netting $400 million in profit. Its stock price pegged the company's worth at more than $2 billion. But cracks were beginning to show in the mortgage banking industry. Home prices were losing steam, and mortgage companies were killing each other over customers. Over at Countrywide, Mozilo had been warning publicly that there were more lenders than consumer demand warranted.

Mozilo also said a price war between New Century and Ameriquest Mortgage was squeezing profit margins for everyone doing subprime, including his shop. In the mortgage industry a price war worked like this: A lender kept cutting the interest rates on the loans it offered until more business came its way. The lower the rates went, the less profit everyone made. Of Ameriquest in particular, Mozilo was quoted in the *American Banker* as saying about price cutting, "Not to demean them in any way, but they are clearly the aggressor." (To be sure, consumers should have benefited from such a price war except that they often got low teaser rates and later could not afford payments when the rates became adjustable.)

Padilla and Collins arrived at New Century's high-rise around noon and were shown to its boardroom, where they waited for a few minutes until Morrice arrived. When he did, the new CEO was in a jovial mood. He shook hands with the reporters and then sat at the head of the table and everyone began munching on sandwiches. Morrice soon launched into a history of subprime lending and rambled on about his old days at Plaza Home Mortgage in Santa Ana. He said it took several months for subsidiary Option One to collect enough loans to do its first big sale to Wall Street, and on the day the deal was set to close a fire broke out in Laguna Beach, threatening his seaside home. His wife, frantic, called him and he told her to toss whatever she needed into the car and drive anywhere. He couldn't go to meet her because he had to stay and finish the deal. Morrice said that was his "first wife" and then made one of several "uh-ums," seeming to chuckle at the implication of his remark. Morrice said he was hiring senior managers like Joseph Eckroth, a former Mattel executive, to raise the level of management at the company and make it more professional, more like other financial firms. (The suggestion here was that under Cole, New Century wasn't hiring the best people it could.)

New Century was also seeking to diversify beyond subprime whole-sale, which depended on loan brokers. For years it had a retail branch network, but storefronts accounted for less than 10 percent of its loans. In May 2004, it bought the rights to the retail brand Home123, and in January 2005 it began running Home123 ads on TV and the Internet with home improvement guru Bob Vila pitching the company. Yet retail remained a side business, largely overshadowed by the company's AE salespeople, who benefited from the FastQual road shows aimed at winning over brokers. New Century tried to expand retail and even branched out into "A" paper lending with the $81 million acquisition of the Houston, Texas–based mortgage origination operations of RBC Mortgage, a unit of Royal Bank of Canada, in September 2005, just four months before the company would announce Morrice's ascension to CEO. It was a gamble. RBC Mortgage had been trying to ditch the money-losing prime and alt-A business for a while. New Century thought it could make the unit profitable and was anxious to diversify into other loan types. It inherited 140 branches in the deal. Shortly after the purchase, New Century said in a filing with the SEC that the RBC operation was still losing money, though management remained optimistic it would eventually turn profitable.

During the meet and greet and later in a phone call with Padilla, Morrice said a price war with crosstown rival Ameriquest had gone too far: "We kind of played that game to the point where margins were really unacceptably low to our investors." His plan was to become the Wal-Mart of subprime lending—he could live with a lower margin on each loan but make it up in volume, a classic tactic in retail sales. He said if New Century did $56 billion in loans in 2005 it would do $100 billion in 2010. In short, he was optimistic. Still, he candidly admitted that home prices had to keep rising at least 4 percent annually for the company's business model to work. New Century largely depended on owners treating their homes like ATMs, withdrawing cash as home prices rose and their equity expanded. "There is a big generational change occurring from what was once the American dream of paying off the house to a much more prevalent mind-set today of living off the house," Morrice said.

By the summer, with Morrice finally ensconced as CEO, the company's profits hit a wall, and, worse, loans were beginning to go sour as soon as they were made. It was happening to all subprime lenders—some more than others. New Century was in the "more" category. Borrowers would go through the trouble of getting a new loan, and immediately default. Wall Street firms like Bear Stearns, Merrill Lynch, Credit Suisse, and others that had been extending warehouse credit and then buying the loans so they could securitize them finally began to take a closer look at what they were eating. It was as though Wall Street had woken from a five-year dream, discovering that loans they once believed in were suddenly (now possibly) tainted by fraud or sloppy paperwork, or were simply given to people who could not afford them and gave up trying as soon as they realized they would not be bailed out by rising home prices. Investment bankers began to send back to New Century any loan with a problem in its file or because the borrower had missed an early payment.

A former loan processor at New Century later said that good customers became scarce in 2006 as housing prices slid and that sales staff began ignoring the company's own guidelines, which already were fairly aggressive considering 40 percent of its loans at the time were stated-income loans, meaning a borrower could get a loan while providing little or no proof of income. She said bending the rules was the only way sales staff could get loans done. Another former employee who worked as a loan underwriter said that some of the "exceptions" included sticking elderly borrowers on fixed incomes into adjustable-rate loans that would eventually become unaffordable. "It got to a point where I literally got sick to my stomach," she said. "Every day I got home and would think to myself, I helped set someone up for failure." When Padilla and fellow reporter John Gittelsohn presented New Century with these statements from former employees, a company spokeswoman said borrowers went through an extensive review, including credit checks, and that New Century made sure people could repay the loans or increase their net worth through rising home equity.

By the fall of 2006, delinquencies were rising even more. Morrice had cause for real concern, because if his company lost money, if its profits reverted to losses for two consecutive quarters, then the Wall Street firms providing the $15 billion bankroll could cancel their credit lines. Their rights were clearly defined in the warehouse lending agreements with New Century. It simply had to make money. In July, August, and September of 2006, Wall Street firms that had paid cash for New Century's loans forced it to take back $182 million worth of them—more than five times what the company had to take back for the same period a year earlier, according to a company filing. Even more striking, for the first nine months of 2006, New Century sold $447 million worth of second mortgages at a discount. For the same period a year earlier, it did not sell a single second mortgage at a discount. It appeared that as soon as home price appreciation stalled, the dirt was crawling back out from under the rug.

Just four months after becoming chief executive, Morrice faced the uncomfortable task of presenting New Century's sliding profits to investors and analysts on a conference call. One former executive said Morrice, though sharp and confident, was not the same orator Cole had been. The executive said when Morrice spoke to investors and stock analysts, "They were screaming, 'Who is this guy?'"

From the company's dark office tower in Irvine, Morrice and chief financial officer Patti Dodge spoke to investors and analysts across the nation via telephone to discuss its third quarter 2006 earnings, which were down 45 percent from a year earlier. (New Century co-founders Cole and Gotschall were now out of the picture, connected to the lender as semiretired directors. They were not even on the call that day.)

Morrice, his voice steady, first declared his disappointment with the results. Next he said the lender planned to retreat from a focus on paying dividends—the very reason REITs existed—and would instead focus on returning $400 million to investors via a combination of dividends and share repurchases, which would boost the sagging stock price. In a 180-degree reversal from the company's previous stance, Morrice dismissed the REIT concept, and said New Century was "first and foremost" a mortgage banking company. Was the firm going to keep growing its loan portfolio? "We do not plan to add to the portfolio going forward, simply to support a specific dividend target," Morrice said.

It wasn't what analysts wanted to hear. Investment bankers on the other end of the line peppered Morrice and Dodge with questions. Morrice and Dodge stuck to their guns that they had the means of providing shareholders with $400 million in value and that the best course was to be "flexible" and either pay dividends or buy shares as market conditions warranted. When other executives at the company learned of the near-abandonment of the REIT status, they looked for an underlying reason, the real reason. One executive later speculated that Morrice struck a deal with Einhorn, who had never liked the idea of building a portfolio of loans on the company's books, something essential for a REIT. The executive further speculated that perhaps Morrice promised to back off the REIT thing if Einhorn would back him as CEO. Nobody knew.

As if all that wasn't enough for analysts and investors to digest on the call, Morrice also addressed a dramatic spike in the company's loan delinquencies. He said New Century was tightening its lending standards. Things had gotten a little too loose in the industry, with first-time home buyers not proving their income while borrowing heavily against the value of their homes. The trend in delinquencies wouldn't have a "meaningful" impact on profits, Morrice said. Morrice was backed up by Dodge, who said, in response to an analyst's question, "We've been planning for those higher levels of delinquency and losses all along." She said the company was setting aside sufficient funds to cover losses from sour loans. But was it?

Earlier that same day, the company had issued a press release detailing its profits for the third quarter of 2006. In one part deep in the release, the company changed the way it accounted for its reserve (called an allowance) for loan losses by merging two categories: money it set aside in case a loan went south and another category dubbed "real estate owned," for homes that the lender had taken back from tardy payers. The total of the combined categories was $239 million, making it appear the reserve had increased 14 percent. Just seven days after the release and conference call with reassuring words from Dodge and Morrice, New Century filed its official earnings report with the

Securities and Exchange Commission. This time the two categories were split as they always had been before, and it was clear that New Century had not set aside $239 million for sour loans, but instead only $192 million—a difference of $47 million. Considering that New Century earned only $67 million in profits that quarter, the $47 million difference in the two figures was very significant. As a lender adds to a loss reserve, it must lower its profit by an equal portion under generally accepted accounting rules. Further, despite a deteriorating housing market and rising loan delinquencies, New Century actually decreased its reserve from the second quarter (when it totaled $209 million) to the third quarter (when it totaled only $192 million). In the company's defense, as well as the defense of Morrice and Dodge, it should be noted that it made fewer loans in the third quarter and held less in loans on its books, which could justify a lower reserve.

In any case, of the handful of analysts who followed the company, only one caught the accounting anomaly with the mysteriously merged categories: Zach Gast, an analyst for the Center for Financial Research and Analysis in Rockville, Maryland. The month of the filing, Gast wrote a critical report on New Century, pointed out the strange accounting, and said its reserves were getting a little thin. Unfortunately, his report was only for paying customers of the Center for Financial Research and not for the general public or the media. Later, Gast said that he believes company officials intentionally misled people with the accounting anomaly. "That's clearly deliberate," Gast said. "It's a pain in the butt to pull together these earnings releases and [quarterly reports]. When a company goes out of its way to change disclosures to hide deteriorations, that's a huge red flag." He added that if the company had done things properly, "They would have lost a significant amount of money in that quarter, and that would have spooked the people they depended on for liquidity as well as investors."

★ ★ ★

New Century's dwindling prospects accelerated dramatically when the company dropped a bomb on Wall Street on February 2, 2007, saying that it didn't properly account for problematic loans it had to take back from investors in 2006 and that its quarterly profit statements for that year contained accounting errors and "should no longer be relied upon." Worse still, it said its profits that year were lower than previously reported. Brad Morrice read a brief statement to investors over the telephone. He did not take questions, and no one at the company would comment further on its earnings.

Morrice had to contend with a tidal wave of negative reaction to the news. The company's stock plummeted 36 percent the next day to close at $19.24, its lowest level in four years. The drop wiped out $600 million of the company's stock value in one day. Richard Eckert, at the time an analyst with Roth Capital Partners in Newport Beach, said that day, "Restating earnings is like telling your investors you lied to them." Eckert, who followed the company and had a "buy" rating on the stock before the news, seemed perturbed in a phone call with Padilla. He said it was no coincidence that the company was disclosing errors at about the same time it had to file its annual report with the SEC. The annual report must be independently audited, whereas quarterly reports do not. Morrice and other executives hunkered down after the disclosure. They declined all phone or face-to-face interview requests by Padilla and other reporters.

A month later, on March 2, New Century dropped another bomb. It said in a filing that it expected to report a loss for all of 2006, partly because it should have added to its reserve for loan losses (exactly as analyst Zach Gast had said). As if that wasn't enough, New Century also said that its $17.7 billion in credit lines could be jeopardized by its accounting errors and financial loss in 2006. New Century said that it had obtained some waivers from its creditors on such issues, but that if it did not obtain more waivers, then its auditor KPMG would question its ability to remain solvent. And to round out New Century's many interesting disclosures that day, the company said the United States Attorney's Office for the Central District of California was conducting a criminal inquiry in connection with trading in its securities and the irregular accounting for loan losses. Investigators did not disclose who they were looking at or what transactions. (A few months later New Century would disclose that the SEC had launched a formal investigation.) In the months before New Century's disclosure of accounting errors, Ed Gotschall sold a few thousand shares for $121,806. But in 2006, the year of the accounting errors, Gotschall, semiretired but still on the board, sold nearly $20 million worth of shares and exercised his rights to buy $4.6 million in shares at cheaper historical prices. Also in

2006, Cole, who remained chairman of the board but stepped down as CEO that summer, sold $7.4 million in shares and did not buy a single share. Perhaps to his credit, Morrice sold the least shares, $1.6 million worth, and spent $849,702 on discounted shares.

An analyst had raised the issue of stock sales during the company's conference call to discuss third quarter 2006 earnings. Since Cole and Gotschall weren't on the call that day, Morrice spoke for them, saying it had to do with their "personal financial planning." Morrice also pointed out that Cole and Gotschall had sold shares under predetermined plans. (When Angelo Mozilo of Countrywide was criticized for selling shares in his company while its fortunes waned, he, too, used the "predetermined plan" rationale.) That was also true, but the timing of the plans could be questioned. For example, Cole and Gotschall each sold 100,000 shares in August 2006 under plans adopted two months earlier.[8] By the time those plans were adopted, June 2006, it was clear the subprime industry and New Century in particular were getting rocked by falling profit margins and rising loan delinquencies.[9]

On the first business day following the late Friday filing with such devastating disclosures by New Century, a couple of analysts from Merrill Lynch issued a report saying the company was on the precipice of a "death spiral" and that its board of directors should consider bankruptcy to preserve whatever assets it could. As one might imagine, the company's stock tanked. It fell 69 percent to close the day at $4.59, erasing another $560 million in market value.

Morrice was getting desperate. The next day he hastily convened a conference call with 11 of the company's creditors—including Wall Street behemoths Citigroup and Goldman Sachs—who were holding its mortgages as collateral for $8.5 billion in debts, according to a story in the *Wall Street Journal*. Shareholder and board member Einhorn joined him on the call. Morrice sketched a plan he had concocted with Einhorn and Bear Stearns. If the investment bankers would release the mortgages to New

---

[8] Gotschall died on January 8, 2009, of natural causes while watching a replay of a college football game.

[9] In December 2009, the SEC charged Morrice, former CFO Patti Dodge, and a former controller with fraud. Their lawyers vowed to fight and Morrice's lawyer called the charges "flatly false."

Century, it would make new bonds to sell and repay the lenders. Einhorn said he would consider buying the riskiest of the new bonds, which likely would find few takers, and Bear Stearns bankers said the plan could work. The creditors hung up more concerned than before. Morrice had said the company's cash had dwindled to $40 million, down from $100 million a day earlier and $350 million at the end of 2006, according to the *Journal*. That night Citigroup bankers wrote a letter saying New Century needed to meet a margin call on its credit line and demanding $80 million by the next day. Citigroup also demanded it take back $717 million in loans. Other bankers followed, and New Century quickly got slammed with demands that it take back nearly $9 billion in loans.

Morrice was out of moves. Completely overwhelmed, New Century became the largest mortgage company to fail since the housing downturn began when it declared bankruptcy on April 2, 2007, and immediately fired 3,200 people, or more than half its workforce. Morrice delivered the dire news to employees during a conference call. He choked up, seemingly on the verge of tears, and then steadied himself. He stuck to his script, saying, "This was a very hard step for me personally and clearly not the outcome I would have preferred."

But there was an outcome that Morrice had passed on: About a year earlier Merrill Lynch & Company and its CEO, Stanley O'Neal, were in the hunt to buy a subprime originator, and not just any firm— they wanted a top-ranked lender. Even though its profit margins were starting to thin in early 2006, Morrice's company more than fit the bill. According to a report in the *Orange County Register* and later interviews, Merrill Lynch in early 2006 was talking to Morrice about buying the nation's largest publicly traded subprime lender for $52 to $55 a share. At the time New Century was trading just shy of $52. Morrice and the board balked. No deal. It was having some (profit) margin compression, yes, but to the former corporate attorney the future still looked mostly bright.

When the bankruptcy papers were filed, the mortgage industry expressed disbelief. The lender's fortunes had crumbled rapidly. Subprime loan brokers would have to find another wholesaler to deal with. Richard Wilkes, who had spent his career managing mostly "A" paper lending shops, noted that loan brokers weren't the only ones upset by New Century's collapse. "In Orange County all the Lamborghini dealers flew their flags at half-mast," he said.

Chapter 8

A Conspiracy by Merrill?

Oh, it just pissed him off.
—A FORMER BEAR STEARNS MANAGING DIRECTOR
WHEN ASKED ABOUT MERRILL LYNCH CEO
STAN O'NEAL AND HIS JEALOUSY OF LEHMAN'S AND
BEAR'S SUBPRIME SECURITIZATION BUSINESS

*The most dangerous moment in any financial market boom is the
one where the suppliers of funds stop paying attention.*
—PETER MARTIN, ECONOMICS EDITOR OF THE *CANBERRA TIMES*

W hen a mortgage trader from Wall Street gets on the telephone and calls the manager in charge of originations at a residential shop, he doesn't have time to ask about the lender's sick mother or how his kids are doing. It's not that kind of relationship. It is—and always has been—about getting the lender on that particular day to sell as many loans as possible (product) at the best possible price to the loan trader's firm. That's what mortgage trading is all about. Trading loans on Wall Street is, for the most part, a male-dominated business, and always has been. As sexist as it may sound, it's not a business fit for women "unless they have balls," as one former trader put it.

There will be a courting—a wining and dining of the mortgage banker. The man in charge of making the "sell" decision for the non-bank mortgage lender usually carries a title like "senior vice president in change of capital markets" or something with the phrase *secondary marketing* in it. (Once the consumer signs on the dotted line, the ink dries, and the loan is resold, it's considered a secondary market transaction—whether it's bought by Fannie Mae, Merrill Lynch, Lehman Brothers, or some other investor.) It stands to reason that when the lender's capital markets chief visits the island of Manhattan, he will be taken out to dinner at a fancy restaurant, attend a Knicks or Yankees game, or be put in a limo and driven down to Atlantic City to take in a show and spend the evening gambling at the blackjack or craps table. It's about winning over that executive, giving him something of value, and establishing a financial bond. But when that telephone rings between the hours of nine and five and the trader is on the other side, he doesn't necessarily care how your weekend was. He wants to know how much in product (loans) you'll be sending his way, either right away or in a forward commitment, a promise to deliver millions in loans over the next few months.

There's a reason for this, no doubt. The trader wants to take those mortgages and package them into a bond—and so does his competitor a few blocks away or in midtown at Bear Stearns on Madison Avenue. That's what Wall Street does. The higher the yield on that bond, the more money an issuer can make. It doesn't matter that the yield is only 1 percent or 2 percent above a comparable Treasury bond or a Fannie Mae or Freddie Mac security. When you're dealing with bonds worth millions, if not hundreds of millions of dollars, one point means a boatload of additional cash for the investor.

It just so happens that the highest-yielding mortgage bonds are collateralized by loans made to Americans with bad credit. A lender that plays in the subprime space—such as Angelo Mozilo's Countrywide, Roland Arnall's Ameriquest, or any number of other firms—charges the borrower more interest for that A– to D loan than they would on a Fannie/Freddie loan because of the risk involved in giving money to people whose credit histories suggest that paying their bills on time is not at the top of their to-do list.

Smart mortgage managers thoroughly review the borrower's credit history and appraise the house to make certain that if the loan goes south at least there will be equity there to serve as a buffer against losses. At least that's how subprime loans were made for decades until the modern era, which might be argued began in 2000 (or after the crash of 1998). When the modern era came along, going over the loan file with a microscope was out the door. Time-consuming and bothersome tasks like reviewing loan files could be outsourced to firms like Clayton Holdings of Connecticut, The Bohan Group of San Francisco, or Opus Capital of Chicago, among others. (Those are the three largest.)

Each and every Wall Street firm playing in the subprime arena from 2002 to early 2007—the largest gold rush in mortgages since the inception of the mortgage-backed security (MBS) two decades earlier—had a three-pronged approach to sucking as many subprime loans as they could out of nondepositories like Ameriquest, New Century, Ownit Mortgage (Bill Dallas's last company), Aegis (Rick Thompson/Cerberus), or any other B&C, alt-A, or stated-income lender, most of which were headquartered in Orange County, California. The approach started with salespeople.

"The sales guys from the Street would come talk to you and hype you up," said one subprime executive from Irvine. "They would try to get you to do something. From Monday to Thursday you would make the loans, put all the data in a spreadsheet, and send it to the Street, and they'd call you back with their bids. By Friday your mistake would be in the marketplace."

From 2004 onward Steve Hultquist, executive vice president in charge of capital markets for Aegis in Houston, Texas, was visited once a week by salesmen from Bear Stearns, Merrill Lynch, and other investment banking houses that were searching for mortgages to securitize. Hultquist was in charge of alt-A loans (subprime in nature but with good FICO scores) and payment option ARMs (loans where the homeowners could keep their payment artificially low by increasing their future debt). The privately held Aegis used mostly loan brokers to gather mortgages. Why? Because if the loan broker didn't produce, it wouldn't cost Aegis a dime. If the broker brought a fundable loan to the company, only then would Aegis have to pay. There would be no benefits, medical plan, or 401(k) to worry about. That was the beauty of loan brokers, as Arnall and Mozilo could attest: less overhead to worry about.

Each and every morning Hultquist's team of account executives (AEs) would e-mail or fax Aegis rate sheets to thousands of loan brokers across the nation, telling them what type of mortgages they were willing to originate, and on what terms. The lists of loans that Aegis would fund were referred to as menus and included such essentials as how high the loan-to-value (LTV) ratio and borrower's debt-to-income (DTI) ratio could be. Hultquist and his subprime counterpart at Aegis, Soc Aramburu, didn't create their loan menus in a vacuum. Aegis sold its subprime and alt-A loans to any number of Wall Street firms, including Bear Stearns, Credit Suisse, Deutsche Bank, Greenwich Capital, and Merrill Lynch. If the Street wouldn't buy, there would be no loans to originate. As a nonbank wholesale lender, Aegis' menu was shaped almost entirely by its investors on Wall Street—what type of mortgages they were willing to buy. "The salesmen from the Street would come and pitch their products," said Hultquist, "and we would listen."

The initial approach from a Wall Street firm to a subprime executive didn't always start with a salesman. Sometimes the trader would just cold call a subprime manager he had met at an industry trade show or look at a ranking of top subprime lenders and dial his way through an automated phone system (if he didn't have a business card). But the action (the three-pronged approach) always started with a salesman or trader. It's the job of the salesman to "make the bell ring," so to speak. Next came the quant, short for quantitative analyst. It was the quant's job to analyze the loans the Street firm was purchasing—to look at the Excel spreadsheets coming in and make sure the product (mortgages) was up to snuff. "The quants are the ones who tell you why they are kicking stuff back," recalled one subprime executive.

The quants act, more or less, like the compliance department of a lender such as Countrywide. On Wall Street the quant's job isn't to underwrite the loan. That's the mortgage banker's job, or at least it used to be before stated-income loans (borrowers state their income and the lender believes it as long as the FICO score is decent) came along and dominated the business. If a mortgage executive selling loans to Wall Street has a problem with what he's being told about the quality of the loans he's offering, he might complain to the quant; but the final decision whether to buy a loan pool rests with the loan trader, who nine times out of 10 carries the title of managing director. On Wall Street, managing directors are king—they share in the firm's profits. Some traders started out as salesmen and moved up. In time, traders (stocks or bonds—it doesn't matter) eventually become CEOs. Quants rarely take that route. As one loan trader put it: "Quants move on to hedge funds."

Once a Wall Street firm agrees to buy a large pool of mortgages from a nonbank, that's where the outsourcing firms come in: Clayton Holdings, Bohan, and Opus. It's their job to reunderwrite the file, to assure the investment banking firm that the file is fine—that it's the type of subprime or alt-A loan that can go safely into a security. But Wall Street isn't stupid when it comes to controlling costs. It uses outsourcing firms for one very practical reason: full-time equivalents (FTEs), or employees who are on the payroll, which means they are entitled to benefits. The goal of every good managing director on Wall Street is to keep down the number of FTEs unless they are revenue producers like salespeople and traders. Why? It's simple, says Richard Wilkes, who spent 30-plus years as a mortgage banker before starting a recruiting firm that helped Morgan Stanley staff up for a new mortgage conduit[1] during the subprime boom. "FTEs get charged against revenue," he said. "Bonuses are paid on revenue." No FTEs, and the revenue numbers look better—a whole lot better. "The Street didn't want to hire their own underwriters," he added. "They're traders, not originators. Hiring underwriters increases costs." Early on, when Morgan Stanley began staffing up its conduit, the total FTE allocation was $1.25 million: $1 million for the managing director in charge of the group and $250,000 for his secretary. That was it. Everything else was outsourced.

For Merrill Lynch, Credit Suisse, and the other investment banking firms thirsting after the subprime business, there was one last piece of the puzzle when it came to attracting mortgage lenders that they could buy mortgages from: warehouse lines of credit. In 2002, five of the seven largest subprime originators in the land were nonbanks

---

[1] A conduit is a legal structure, an entity through which a Wall Street firm buys loans from a lender and securitizes them into mortgage- or asset-backed bonds.

(Ameriquest, Household Finance, New Century, Option One, and Homecomings), which meant they needed to borrow large sums of money to originate loans either through their branches or through independent loan brokers. A warehouse line was a big loan—nothing more, nothing less—but without it there was no fuel to fire the origination machine that the subprime industry would turn into. And there were only two places to get warehouse credit: large banks (or thrifts like Washington Mutual) or Wall Street. According to Frank Hattemer, senior vice president in charge of warehouse lending at Washington Mutual (WaMu), the Street's game was this: extend warehouse loans to nonbanks at no cost in order to get their securitization business. There was nothing Hattemer could do about it. His department wasn't in business to offer something for nothing.

In 1995, two years before Arnall spun off Long Beach Financial into a publicly traded New York Stock Exchange company, the entire subprime industry originated just $35 billion in mortgages, or just 5 percent of the residential loans funded in the United States that year. After the Russian debt crisis of 1998 and the resulting meltdown of the subprime industry, which lasted about two years, the business came back, first gradually and then like a gale-force hurricane. "Wall Street ran away from the business during the Russian debt crisis but got right back in," said Hattemer.

As to why the Street had suddenly reversed course after a two-year lull in subprime, there are theories and there are facts. Fact: Interest rates were falling to historical lows. In June 2003 the Federal Reserve, nursing a recovering post-9/11 economy, cut short-term rates one final time, to just 1 percent, which meant subprime lenders of all stripes could borrow money cheaply and lend it out to consumers at rates not too much higher than what Fannie Mae and Freddie Mac were charging. Profit margins were huge. Fact: Home prices were rising steadily in several hot real estate markets like Boston, Los Angeles, New York, and San Diego. If a newly originated loan went bad in one of those markets, there would be 25 percent more in home equity to take away the blues of the foreclosing lender. Fact: Wall Street firms, which at first had encouraged overly optimistic gain-on-sale accounting (booking tomorrow's profits today on securitizations), were preaching to the new breed of lenders to be more conservative. Fact: Being conservative on gain-on-sale accounting wasn't a big deal anymore, because Wall Street had, finally, found a way to take the riskiest pieces of a securitization (the subordinated or "B" pieces) and put them into larger securities called collateralized debt obligations (CDOs). With CDOs the risk was transferred to institutional investors both in the United States and overseas.

The Street surmised that as long as home prices kept going up at a rate of 25 percent a year, there would be nothing to worry about. Fact: Eric Billings and Friedman Billings Ramsey (FBR) were converting dozens of new and existing subprime lenders into real estate investment trusts (REITs), which had balance sheets that could hold those risky subprime "B" pieces if need be. Theory: Starting in 2003 Fannie Mae and Freddie Mac—the government-chartered mortgage investing behemoths whose mission in life was to buy "A" paper loans and provide liquidity to all sectors of the market—were flat on their backs, dealing with multibillion-dollar accounting scandals. In the past, the two government-sponsored enterprises (GSEs) had been innovators, creating new loans that mortgage bankers could make to their consumer customers. With Fannie's and Freddie's top managers being given the boot and investigators and politicians breathing down their necks, Fannie and Freddie weren't innovating anything. Moreover, their ability to buy loans was hampered by their accounting problems. In stepped Wall Street, with Lehman Brothers and Bear Stearns leading the way, extending huge warehouse lines of credit to nonbanks (at dirt-cheap prices), buying their mortgages, securitizing them, and then selling the end bonds to pension funds, insurance companies, municipalities in Florida, and German banks (and others). It was all about yield. Subprime loans had yield. Yield made the phones ring and investors say yes.

In 2003, when "A" paper rates fell to 5 percent and consumers rushed to refinance their existing homes and buy new ones, loan originations in the United States reached a record $3.9 trillion, with subprime loans accounting for $390 billion or 10 percent. The next year, total home fundings fell to $2.8 trillion but subprime lending soared to $608 billion or almost 22 percent of the market—a record. Fannie and Freddie appeared to be fading fast. Bill Dallas, who had sold his first subprime company, First Franklin, to National City in 1999, remaining as chairman emeritus of the subprime lender, decided to go out on his own and start a new subprime wholesaler called Ownit Mortgage

Solutions, located close to his home in Agoura Hills (and not too far from where Mozilo had his mansion). Dallas, who had cemented his reputation in the industry by doubling his money on First Franklin, believed he could ride the mortgage cycle one more time. His private equity backer was once again CIVC Partners[2] of Chicago, which also had invested in First Franklin and shared the profits when National City bought the lender. Brimming with confidence, one of his bios read: "Bill Dallas is famous for his crystal-ball clairvoyance and cutting-edge approach to mortgage lending." When word got out that Dallas was back in business, Wall Street firms starting showing up at his office armed with their briefcases and league tables. "When they visit, they pull out the league tables and show where they're ranked," he later recalled. "They're always armed with those league tables."

In the case of subprime mortgages, a league table is a ranking of the top issuers of asset-backed securities (ABSs). All subprime mortgages are backed by homes, but to distinguish the business from "A" paper loans that Fannie Mae and Freddie Mac might purchase, Wall Street started using the term *ABS*.[3] When Dallas started Ownit Mortgage, Royal Bank of Scotland (which had bought Greenwich Capital) dominated the securitization business, along with Morgan Stanley, Credit Suisse, Citigroup,[4] Lehman Brothers, and Bear Stearns. "When the subprime business recovered, Lehman was making money hand over fist," recalled Dallas. "To many, Lehman owned the market." The one Wall Street giant buried in the rankings on the league tables being shown to Dallas was Merrill Lynch. "Merrill," as Dallas noted, "was late to the party."

★　★　★

The bread and butter of making money on Wall Street lies in selling stocks and bonds. Over the past century some firms have built their

---

[2] Bank of America, even though it took pride in having exited the subprime lending business in the previous decade, owned a stake in CIVC.

[3] Besides home mortgages, ABSs might also include credit card receivables, auto loans, or other consumer products.

[4] Citigroup Securities, the investment banking arm of the company, included Salomon Brothers Smith Barney.

reputations on being specialists in one or the other, but few have been kings in both of these lucrative sectors for very long. When E. Stanley O'Neal was promoted to CEO of Merrill Lynch in the summer of 2002, he aimed to change the perception among institutional investors that the firm—even though it had 15,000 retail brokers worldwide—was solely an expert in selling stocks. More than anything else, O'Neal, a native of Alabama and the only African-American ever to head a traditional Wall Street firm, wanted to expand the firm's presence in corporate finance—and bonds in particular. "He came from the bowels of the organization," said Angelo Mozilo, who counted O'Neal among his friends. (Countrywide was a corporate client of Merrill Lynch, borrowing money through commercial paper and warehouse lines. At various points in its history, Merrill had raised equity for Mozilo's company.) Unlike many of his CEO predecessors at Merrill, O'Neal didn't start out at the firm as a retail stockbroker.

Like Mozilo, the new Merrill CEO came from humble beginnings. His grandparents were slaves, his parents farmers. O'Neal himself worked on the assembly line at General Motors (GM) before moving up into the automaker's finance department and attending Harvard Business School, paid for by GM. "When Stan came in, there was a lot of angst in the organization," said Mozilo. "Stan came from corporate." Two factions developed at Merrill: corporate, where O'Neal had worked, and equities. Shortly after taking over, O'Neal moved to cut costs, and eliminated 24,000 positions, including hundreds of middle managers and senior executives he considered unessential. It was one of the biggest housecleanings ever on Wall Street—and had nothing to do with a market correction.

Pat Flood of HomeBanc Mortgage remembered the housecleaning well. He had been selling millions of dollars' worth of mortgages to Merrill's trading desk in New York. The relationship went back at least five years. "When O'Neal came in, the message we got from Merrill was that they didn't know what they were going to be doing in mortgages," he said. "There was a lull there for a while, and during that lull Bear Stearns starting paying up for our loans." So long Merrill. Hello Bear.

During that lull it didn't take O'Neal long to realize one central fact about the bond market. As a financier who headed corporate finance (lending money to companies and markets), he quickly did the math and came to know what every other top player in mortgages already had ingrained in their memory banks: Residential mortgages represented the largest debt market not only in the United States but in the entire world. Americans owed $8 trillion on their homes—even more than the federal government owed on all its Treasury bonds (even with record deficits during the Bush years). And with Fannie Mae and Freddie Mac ailing, subprime volumes were taking off. In 2000, Wall Street firms had securitized $74 billion in subprime ABSs, or just 7 percent of all home loans originated that year. Two years later that figure had more than tripled to $233 billion in ABSs.[5] When Bill Dallas looked at the league tables that year, Merrill Lynch was ranked fourth from the bottom with just $8 billion in subprime securitizations. According to Dallas, who had been in meetings with O'Neal, the new CEO of Merrill Lynch was not happy about his company's standing in the league tables. "They wanted in—in a big way," he said. "They felt left out."

But to get into mortgages, Merrill was missing two essential ingredients: an aggressive trading desk with salespeople and traders who could court firms like Dallas's Ownit; his former shop, First Franklin; as well as every other subprime lender, many of which had their headquarters in Orange County. Almost every Wall Street firm that ranked high in the securitization league tables had loan traders or salespeople who were well known among the lenders they were buying loans from. At Lehman Brothers there were Tim Fitzpatrick and Matt Miller. At Bear Stearns there were Mike Nierenberg and Jeff Verschleiser, with Baron Silverstein assisting on sales; at Deutsche Bank, Michael Commaroto and Paul Mangione, with John Groesbeck on sales; at Nomura Securities, Steve Katz; at Citigroup, Jeff Perlowitz was in charge of the desk. It was a club, and if they didn't personally know one another, they were, at the very least, aware of who the competition might be across town or two blocks to the south.

Traders, in the words of former Nomura executive Neil Spagna, "live in a small world" but control a huge business: mortgages. As Spagna once noted, "The traders put the deals together; they run the business. They're the ones responsible for the P&L."[6]

---

[5] According to ABS rankings compiled by Thomson Financial.

[6] P&L stands for profit and loss.

According to Dallas and others, O'Neal's message to Merrill's mortgage department was clear: Go after the subprime business. Be number one. By 2004 Merrill began to move up in the ABS league table rankings. It was in that year that Countrywide's capital markets group, Countrywide Securities Corporation, blew away the competition, securitizing $72 billion in subprime and nonprime loans. Mozilo, who at first had resisted the subprime business, was now the chairman and CEO of not only the largest prime lender, but the fastest growing subprime originator—plus the top securitizer of non-Fannie/Freddie loans.

O'Neal grew anxious about the business. He felt he was missing the boat. "Stan didn't want to get left behind," said Mozilo. According to Bill Dallas, O'Neal shoved aside the senior manager in charge of the mortgage department, replacing him with Michael Blum, who carried the title of managing director in charge of global asset-based finance. It was the job of Blum and his team to take pools of receivables (loans or similar debt instruments), including mortgages, credit cards, car loans, and even loans made to movie studios, and turn them into "investments for sophisticated investors." Sophisticated investors meant institutional investors—pension funds, insurance companies, and overseas banks and governments. Investments meant bonds. The message Dallas heard from O'Neal and the traders he was beginning to work with at Merrill was that the nation's number-one seller of retail stocks not only wanted to be number one in residential ABSs, but wanted to be number one worldwide. "Stan was the one driving it," said Dallas.

With Blum now in charge of Merrill's mortgage effort, things began to change. In April 2004 Merrill hired a trader named George Davies to help ramp up the volume of loans coming through the firm's trading desk. One subprime executive who did business with Merrill remembered getting a phone call from Davies in 2004. "Merrill was on the prowl then," said the executive. "Davies called me up and said, 'We're buying.'" And buy Merrill did. But it wasn't just the fact that Merrill was now in the market, getting the word out to every subprime lender that would listen; it began paying more for loans than every other Street firm. In the lingo of mortgage trading, a loan bought at par is sold for 100 cents on the dollar. But during the subprime boom of 2002 to 2006, no lenders in their right mind would accept par for their loans. The idea was to get as much as they could—102, 103, 104, sometimes even 105 cents on the dollar. (This was a great deal for originators like Dallas's Ownit Mortgage, because not only was the company making points and fees from the consumer getting the loan, it was also getting a premium from Wall Street.)

If Merrill Lynch agreed to buy a $100,000 subprime mortgage for 105 cents on the dollar, that meant the originator of that loan would receive $105,000 back from Merrill. Merrill and other investment banks, by practice, rarely bought one loan at a time—they bought them in huge pools. (A pool consists of many mortgages, totaling tens of millions, if not hundreds of millions, of dollars.) Why would the Street pay $105,000 for a loan that had a principal balance of only $100,000? There were two reasons: First, subprime mortgages carried higher interest rates than Fannie/Freddie loans, so investors would find the subprime bonds more attractive because of the higher yield and pay up for them. The other reason had to do with interest payments. During the first seven years of a loan, consumers pay mostly interest, and even on a $100,000 loan that can add up to thousands of dollars over time. Some of the loans the Street was buying carried prepayment penalties where the consumer was charged a large fee for refinancing the mortgage. When it came to subprime, the ultimate quest of Merrill, Bear, and the other firms was to create a bond that could be sold to another investor. Bond investors don't like surprises—but they do like yield.

To entice Bill Dallas and other subprime executives into selling their loans to Merrill, its salesmen offered them a deal: If you agree to sell your loans to us, we'll offer warehouse financing for next to nothing. Merrill's warehouse chief was Jim Cason, who had been with the firm for a couple of years. With O'Neal's edict to grow the firm's subprime business, Cason's unit, by 2005, became one of the largest warehouse lenders to nonbank residential lenders in the nation. "The idea was to create a one-stop shopping place for subprime lenders," said one warehouse executive familiar with Merrill's effort. "Merrill would make no money on their warehouse business, but it would do it to get the securitization business." As George Davies, the head trader, later admitted: "The idea was to secure product [mortgages]."

By the time 2005 ended, Merrill was the seventh largest issuer of subprime ABSs in the United States out of a growing field that now included 25 securities underwriters. That year Merrill had bought and securitized $30 billion in subprime mortgages, and was just a few billion dollars behind its archrivals, Bear Stearns and Countrywide. Even Washington Mutual, a thrift, had started a capital markets group to securitize all the subprime loans being funded by its Long Beach Mortgage subsidiary, the company it had bought a decade earlier, just 19 months after Arnall spun it off in an initial public offering (IPO). In April 2006 George Davies was hired away by WaMu, which was beginning to have its own ideas about becoming a major player in subprime securitizations. ("It was considered a major coup when we landed Davies," noted one WaMu senior vice president.) Replacing Davies as head trader was John O'Grady.

O'Grady, said one Irvine-based mortgage executive, was "gung-ho and bullish for subprime." He took O'Neal's edict on ABSs and ran with it. O'Grady didn't give the warm and fuzzies to some of the origination executives he was dealing with at the subprime shops, but most hardly cared—as long as Merrill kept paying more than anyone else for loans. "O'Grady looks like William F. Buckley with those glasses of his and all," said one manager who traded with him. "It was like he was talking at you, but as long as they were bidding stuff up we sold to them. We had a name for O'Grady—we called him 'The Irishman.' He had to sign off on any deal [trade] over $50 million."

★ ★ ★

By 2005, unbeknownst to most American borrowers, a handful of Wall Street firms had been in the business of actually originating residential loans for well over a decade. It was a well-kept secret—outside the mortgage industry, that is—because that's the way Wall Street wanted it. The last thing the brokerage side of Lehman Brothers needed was its equities business to be marred by negative headlines about its residential loan unit. In the previous decade Lehman had launched a residential loan division called Aurora Loan Services, headquartered in the Denver suburb of the same name. Bear Stearns was also in the business through a company called EMC Mortgage of Irving, Texas. No one at Bear even knew what the initials EMC meant, but the going joke was that it stood for "Ed's Mortgage Company." Ed was Ed Raice, EMC's president.

EMC was born in the ashes of the savings and loan (S&L) crisis and was started as a way for Bear to invest in delinquent residential and apartment loans from the government. Over time, as the S&L crisis waned, EMC morphed into a subprime lender. Working in tandem with its parent, Bear Stearns, EMC originated its own loans but also bought large bulk packages of mortgages through such lenders as New Century and Option One Mortgage. The mortgages—to no one's surprise—were securitized by Bear's capital markets group in New York. Oh, and there was one other thing: EMC and Aurora didn't exactly have retail loan offices where a home buyer could walk in off the street and fill out a loan application. Both lenders originated mortgages only through loan brokers and small mortgage banking firms (mostly nonbanks) called correspondents. Having retail employees to pay would result in more full-time equivalents (FTEs) on the payroll—and that would, of course, eat into a managing director's bonus money.

Merrill Lynch also owned a mortgage company, but unlike Bear and Lehman it actually put its own name on the subsidiary and wanted everyone to know it—as long as they were a client of the firm's retail brokerage unit. And being that Merrill had 15,000 stockbrokers, chances were high-net-worth individuals (rich people) who bought and sold stocks through the Wall Street giant knew about it. Based in Jacksonville, Florida, Merrill Lynch Mortgage Capital, managed for many years by CEO Larry Washington, specialized in making mortgages to its own brokerage clients—people with (presumably) very good credit. "They were going after high-net-worth individuals who were clients of its brokerage business," noted Mozilo. To many who worked at Merrill in the Komansky or Tully eras,[7] the idea that Merrill would originate subprime loans (much less lend money to nonbanks that played in the hard-money arena) was anathema. Merrill Lynch was about catering to the rich—not making mortgages to home buyers who lived from paycheck to paycheck. All that changed in October 2005 when Merrill revealed that it had invested $100 million in Bill Dallas's latest venture

---

[7] Dan Tully and David Komansky were O'Neal's predecessors at Merrill. Both came from the retail side of the business.

in subprime lending, Ownit Mortgage Solutions of Woodland Hills, California.[8]

"Stan wanted to be in the direct origination business," remembered Dallas, who, along with his partners at CIVC, were happy to take O'Neal's money. "They came and valued us at $500 million." Suddenly, Merrill not only was in the business of lending to rich people (its clients) but now also owned 20 percent of Ownit, the youngest and fastest growing subprime lender in the nation.[9] Dallas and his partners were hoping that Ownit, on track to fund $8.2 billion that year, would turn out to be another First Franklin, which under National City was coming off a $30 billion origination year. Merrill placed Mike Blum, the managing director in charge of global asset-based finance, on Ownit's board. As one Ownit executive noted: "Blum was intimately involved with us." Merrill was now on the hunt to purchase stakes in other subprime lenders as well.

Alexander "Zan" Hamilton, a former investment banker in the mortgage group of Credit Suisse, recalled sitting in the executive dining room with Merrill's Mike Blum in New York, listening to him talk about the firm's plans to buy stakes in other subprime lenders as well. "It was all about the trading desk owning the originators," said Hamilton. In 2003 Hamilton left Wall Street and became CEO of LIME Financial Services of Lake Oswego, Oregon, a nonbank mortgage lender started by Fred Baldwin, a former partner of Bill Dallas. Dallas had merged an early incarnation of First Franklin into Baldwin's company, Trillium Mortgage. Prior to the merger, Dallas's First Franklin was an "A" paper lender only. Trillium was subprime. "Fred was the guy who taught Bill how to make subprime loans," said Hamilton.

Meanwhile, Mozilo and O'Neal had become friends, serving on the President's Business Council and occasionally playing golf together. (In some press reports O'Neal, a member of at least four country clubs, had been described as a golf fanatic. His handicap was nine.) To those who knew him, O'Neal could be standoffish and had a reputation at

---

[8] Dallas and CIVC bought into a smaller nonbank lender called Oakmont Mortgage in December 2003. Dallas became its chairman and CEO and changed the name of the company to Ownit Mortgage Solutions.

[9] According to originations rankings compiled by SourceMedia.

times of being a bit of a loner, but he and Mozilo had a common bond: the mortgage business. Some analysts had even speculated that "Mother Merrill" (as the firm was once called for its maternal nurturing of executives) might even buy Countrywide.

Between 2003 and 2006, Merrill's operating profit averaged $5.2 billion, more than double the $2.1 billion average in the preceding five years. It looked as though the O'Neal years were going to be good ones for the firm. By mid-2006 Merrill's subprime securitization business was humming, and so was its collateralized debt obligation (CDO) business. Merrill had embarked on a strategy of buying subprime loans (providing warehouse lines to those same originators), securitizing the mortgages into ABSs, and then taking some of the riskier tranches of those securities and putting them into CDOs, selling the end bond to U.S. buyers or overseas.

Rumors began to surface that the investment bank was in the hunt to buy pieces of even more subprime firms or own a large lender outright. Two executives in Merrill's mortgage group, Matt Whalen and Vince Mora, had been put in charge of scouring potential candidates to purchase. For a while, Merrill courted New Century, which was second only to Arnall's Ameriquest in originating subprime loans, but the two sides couldn't come to terms. New Century's CEO-in-waiting, Brad Morrice, thought the offering price of $52 to $55 a share was too low, even though its profit margins were beginning to suffer, said a Morrice colleague.[10]

Merrill continued talking to other lenders. It wasn't content to own just 20 percent of Dallas's Ownit and parts of other firms. It was missing a key ingredient in its soup-to-nuts approach of creating subprime ABSs and CDOs: owning an actual lender that could absolutely guarantee Mother Merrill a steady flow of mortgages that it could package into ABSs and then carve up into CDOs. Even though Mozilo and

---

[10] In mid-2003 the Federal Reserve, under chairman Alan Greenspan, began increasing short-term rates, which also upped the borrowing costs for lenders using warehouse lines and/or deposits. Unlike in past mortgage cycles, this time long-term rates on mortgages did not rise in tandem with short-term rates. One reason lenders did not hike the rates on mortgages sold to consumers was the fear of losing business. Competition was stiff—from both new firms and "A" lenders entering the subprime niche.

O'Neal were golfing buddies, the Merrill CEO never once let on that the world's largest investment banking firm wanted to own a company that actually funded mortgages. "Never in my conversations with Stan did it come up," Mozilo later recalled.

In early September of 2006, Merrill announced it was buying Bill Dallas's old firm, First Franklin, from National City, the Cleveland-based money center bank. The price, which included two other related businesses (one that serviced loans on a monthly basis), was $1.3 billion—four times what National City had paid for First Franklin back in 1999. When the news reached Mozilo, he was taken aback. He asked O'Neal why Merrill was getting into his business. "It's part of our plan" was O'Neal's reply. Mozilo knew exactly what that "plan" was—it was his plan. Countrywide originated subprime mortgages and securitized them through its own capital markets division. The only thing that Countrywide didn't do was create CDOs. "They didn't want to come to us for loans," said Mozilo. "They thought they could manufacture it themselves."

Merrill issued a press release where Blum, the structured finance chief, was quoted as saying the purchase "fills an important gap for us." When Dallas heard the news, he was anything but happy. Ownit and First Franklin were fierce competitors—both in California and nationwide. Both used loan brokers exclusively to originate subprime mortgages to credit-impaired borrowers. Both lenders were originating some of the hottest mortgage products in the industry: ARMs that had initial low teaser rates that didn't reset for two, three, or five years and 80/20 loans where the borrower didn't have to make any type of down payment and instead took out a first mortgage for 80 percent of the purchase price and a second lien (deed of trust) for the remaining 20 percent. And they originated loans to people with bad credit—with FICO scores as low as 540. (Remember, to be considered a Fannie/Freddie "A" paper credit, a borrower had to have a minimum FICO score of 700.) The days of Peter Cugno's subprime industry, one where Beneficial Finance wouldn't extend a loan unless the borrower had at least 30 percent (preferably 40 percent), were long gone. At Ownit, Dallas and his chief operating officer, Bruce Dickenson, had given the lender's account executives a motto inspiring them to produce loans: "Go out and kill the bear and we'll skin it."

Dallas tried to talk O'Neal out of buying First Franklin. He remembered that a year earlier, when Merrill revealed that it had bought a 20 percent stake in Ownit, "their stock price didn't go up enough. They weren't happy." The way Dallas saw it, Merrill was "doubling down in subprime."

Merrill, though, wasn't the only one doubling down. Ownit, in its thirst to grow rapidly, was funding loans where consumers could have a debt-to-income (DTI) ratio of up to 60 percent, which meant 60 percent of their salary would be used just to pay their monthly bills. The standard DTI ratio for Fannie/Freddie loans was 30 percent. "'Go out and kill the bear,' they kept telling us," said one Ownit account executive. That fall the AE[11] was called into a meeting where Dickenson explained to a small group of senior executives that Dallas had just fired one of the lender's most successful AEs—who worked the Southern California market—because the company had discovered what they were told were "serious fraud" issues on brokered loans. The AE in question was producing $360 million a year in product—loans Merrill was ultimately buying and then securitizing. No details were provided on what type of fraud was involved, but one thing appeared certain: The loans this AE funded were going delinquent at a rapid pace.

Under O'Neal and Blum, Merrill had catapulted its way to the top of the subprime ABS rankings because it paid more than any other Wall Street firm for mortgages but it also had the most pro-lender policy when it came to loan buybacks and early payment defaults (EPDs). If a nonbank like Ownit sold a loan to Merrill and it went bad within 60 days, it was the lender's problem; it would have to repurchase (or buy back) the delinquent loan from Merrill. But if the loan went bad on the 61st day, it was Merrill's problem, not the lender's. Just about every Wall Street firm except Merrill made the lender buy back delinquent loans up to 90 days after the origination date. It was easy to see why Dallas and others might favor Merrill.

Merrill's trading desk didn't actually underwrite the loans they were buying. They told the lenders what type of characteristics the mortgage could have (LTVs, FICO scores, and the like), bought the loans, and

---

[11] The AE agreed to be quoted only under the condition his name not be used.

hired the outsourcers (Clayton, Bohan, and Opus) to conduct a final review, paying those firms about $150 per loan file. Again, the idea was to avoid hiring those FTEs. In 2004 and 2005, home lenders originated $1.4 trillion in subprime loans—almost all of it winding up in ABSs, with the riskier bonds going into CDOs. Reporters from *National Mortgage News* and the *Orange County Register* began to investigate the outsourcing firms, interviewing not only the executives at those companies but also their rank-and-file workers who were hired—on a contract basis—to sit in hotel conference rooms, armed with a laptop, with orders to review one loan an hour. Mortgages were given a rating of a one, two, or three. One meant pass, two meant so-so, and three meant fail. "You weren't supposed to fail loans unless they were horrendous," one contract underwriter told the reporters. He also confessed that they were told by their supervisors at Clayton never to use a certain word—"fraud."

Because competition was so stiff those years and because Merrill, Bear, J.P. Morgan, and other Wall Street firms were so hungry for product (which they could put into ABSs and CDOs), the goal, the underwriters said, was to pass as many loans as possible. Eileen Loiacono, a Bohan contract worker who worked on loans that Merrill and other Wall Street firms bought, told Padilla of the *Orange County Register* that the pressure was so intense to approve as many loans as quickly as possible that one of her supervisors (whom she would only identify as "Robert") would frequently stand up on a desk screaming at the laptop worker bees, "Work faster or you're going to get fired!" Another would scream, "Get your fucking act together!"

Loiacono singled out Merrill in particular. "They perpetuated the whole thing," she said. If she found a loan that might rate a three, a Merrill supervisor would find a way to get the loan approved.

Loan fraud is a fuzzy term that can mean many things, but in practice it boils down to two basic swindles: Either a borrower is lying about his or her income or the house is not worth what someone says it is. By late 2006 agents from the Federal Bureau of Investigation were describing loan fraud as pandemic in the United States, singling out stated-income loans (that is, so-called liar loans) being funded through mortgage brokers as a chief problem. Stated-income mortgages were on the product menu at Ownit.

In late November, Dallas had two major problems at Ownit: what Merrill's impending purchase of First Franklin might mean for him and the sad discovery that tens of millions of dollars' worth of mortgages it had originated through loan brokers and sold to Merrill were going delinquent just a few months after being originated. Not only was Merrill buying more loans from Ownit than every other Street firm (that's what happens when you own 20 percent of the company), but it was also providing warehouse financing to Dallas's shop. The CEO was starting to hear complaints about the delinquencies from Merrill, which wanted Ownit to buy back the bad loans. Around this time Dallas held a conference call with some of his top wholesale account executives. The topic of the conversation? What Merrill's purchase of First Franklin meant for Ownit. Some AEs believed Dallas feared that Merrill might merge the two companies and he'd be out of a job, but he told the AEs that Merrill planned to operate the two subprime wholesalers independently of each other even though they both were based in California and funded the same type of loans. One AE who was in on the conference call said Dallas took the opportunity to "tell us how ignorant some of his co-workers" were at his former company, First Franklin. During the call he kept referring to First Franklin as "First Fucking Franklin" and "First Fuckers." The AE said he came away from the call feeling secure about his future. "All seemed well," he said.

On Monday, December 4, Dallas spoke at an industry trade show in Las Vegas, giving his views about the future of the industry, signing copies of a book he'd co-written called *Strategic Financing: A Survival Guide for Loan Originators*. Roughly 2,000 mortgage professionals were in the audience at the Mandalay Bay Resort and Casino. Over the preceding week he had been haggling with Merrill over its request for Ownit to buy back millions in delinquent loans. When he went to Las Vegas to make his speech he thought he had a deal worked out on the buybacks, but Merrill, he said, reneged. Shortly after leaving Vegas, Dallas decided to throw the company into bankruptcy, sending out an e-mail to employees that started, "With deep sadness . . ."

The next day at a subprime conference in New York sponsored by SourceMedia, which owned *American Banker*, the *Bond Buyer*, and *National Mortgage News*, several Wall Street executives were in attendance, including top executives from Bear Stearns and Deutsche Bank, which a few months earlier had bought MortgageIT, a large alt-A and subprime wholesaler that had been a publicly traded REIT brought to market by Friedman Billings Ramsey. During one of the panel sessions at the meeting, Bern Amlung, a senior Deutsche Bank executive who had a thick German accent, was asked whether his bank might buy another subprime lender. He seemed noncommittal and slightly nervous. "Maybe," he said, "but we're still digesting what we have [MortgageIT]." At lunch that day news broke on Bloomberg that Ownit had closed. Amlung left the meeting early. (About nine months after the meeting it was revealed in the *Wall Street Journal* that a division of Deutsche Bank was shorting an index called the ABX; by doing so investors could profit if the value of subprime ABSs went down. Greg Lippmann, chief of global trading for ABS and CDO instruments, was advising some of the bank's hedge fund clients to bet against the housing market by shorting the index. Michael Commaroto, who oversaw Deutsche's mortgage trading operation, was none too pleased that while he was trying to buy mortgages from subprime lenders another part of the bank was betting against his clients. One lending executive close to Commaroto said Deutsche Bank itself had earned $700 million by shorting the ABX. "Lippmann bragged about it," said the executive. "Some of the bank's board members weren't all too happy, but even at $700 million it wasn't enough to make up for all of DB's mistakes in mortgages.")

Even though Ownit's collapse should have worried O'Neal, Blum, and others at Merrill, it didn't. Merrill planned to move ahead with its $1.3 billion purchase of First Franklin. Over at Countrywide Mozilo continued to be troubled at Merrill's purchase, telling one reporter that by acquiring First Franklin, "I guess they think they're taking a shortcut to the freeway of happiness." In late January 2007, during a conference call with analysts, Mozilo said all was not well in the subprime market, estimating that 40 to 50 mortgage banking and brokerage firms were closing their doors each day. Countrywide, he said, would weather the storm just fine—and would gain market share. Two weeks after he spoke to analysts, Merrill's Ken Bruce—the same analyst who in August would suggest that Countrywide might have to file for bankruptcy—issued a report warning that subprime loan delinquencies were accelerating.

In late February Merrill handed over $1.3 billion and became the sole owner of First Franklin, which had finished 2006 with $28 billion in subprime originations, seventh best in the nation. "With First Franklin they would be number one in ABS," Dallas said. In time most ABSs would be carved up and placed into CDOs. At about the same time a story appeared in *National Mortgage News* noting that Merrill's warehouse lending division, headed by Jim Cason, was making margin calls on several nonbank subprime lenders that had received large loans from the company. A margin call meant that the loans the nonbank had originated (and pledged as collateral for the warehouse line) were no longer worth as much. Merrill went to several of its nonbank warehouse customers, lenders like ResMAE (Jack Mayesh's company) and Mortgage Lenders Network of Connecticut, demanding that their owners pay Merrill more money. These same firms also were having loan buyback disputes with Merrill's trading desk over the issue of delinquent loans.

Rumors began to appear in the market that Merrill—now the proud owner of First Franklin—was engaged in a conspiracy to shut down competitors to its new acquisition by using margin calls and loan buyback requests to force competitors such as Ownit, ResMAE, and Mortgage Lenders Network into bankruptcy. Bill Haldin, a public relations executive working out of the investment banker's California office in Sacramento, denied that there was any type of conspiracy under way but would not provide any information on how many margin calls the firm had made. He would only say that margin calls "are something we do on an as-needed basis." An account executive who worked for Ownit said he was told by Dickenson that the reason Merrill closed Ownit was "to make more market share for First Franklin." (Dickenson declined to comment on the story, but didn't deny it, either.)

A California subprime president who sold millions in loans to Merrill the previous two years didn't quite see a conspiracy but admitted that the Wall Street firm, to feed its CDO pipeline, "was throwing its clout around. It's a full-court press to get more business in the door. Hey, man, that's capitalism." However, he also noticed something else: Merrill's trading desk was starting to get pickier about the loans they were buying from firms they didn't own a piece of. Also, Merrill had given new orders to its underwriting outsourcers, Clayton and Bohan:

Start sampling a greater percentage of the loans we're buying through the trading desk. Neil Spagna, the former Nomura executive who also once worked at Clayton, noted that typically, Wall Street firms (Merrill included) would sample only 20 percent or 30 percent of the loans they were buying. "On a billion-dollar pool it would only be 20 percent."

Smaller lenders, like Sunset Direct in Oregon, a company managed by Bob Howard, who had been in the business for two decades, were actually seeing Merrill review 100 percent of their loans. In other words, it appeared that the larger the lender (and loan pool size), the less Merrill looked at the loans. The smaller the lender, the more Merrill looked.

In the months ahead, at least three dozen nonbank subprime lenders (and about 400 loan brokerage firms that fed mortgages to them) closed their doors, the victims of margin calls and loan buybacks. There was talk that Merrill might close its warehouse lending division to nonbanks. Bill Haldin, Merrill's PR man, denied it.

By midyear five different investment banking firms—Merrill, Lehman Brothers, Bear Stearns, Morgan Stanley, and FBR[12]—owned seven different subprime or alt-A lenders, which in turn accounted for about 15 percent of the market. To Mozilo, who was still funding and securitizing subprime and alt-A loans at Countrywide, it certainly looked like Wall Street was building a machine to "go from origination to securitization to servicing." Most of the subprime lenders owned by investment bankers also were in the business of servicing subprime loans on a monthly basis, controlling the monthly payments on about $240 billion in mortgages—20 percent.

Having a large market share can be a wonderful thing—as long as that market doesn't go into a skid. In July 2007 when Mozilo described housing as being in the worst shape since the Great Depression, he wasn't just giving his opinion. Loan delinquencies on subprime mortgages were rising rapidly. At Countrywide almost 20 percent of the A– to D loans it was servicing on a monthly basis were late. It stood to reason that if Countrywide was having problems with its subprime loans, then the Street-owned lenders—and just about every other firm—were

---

[12] In 2005 FBR bought First NLC Financial of Deerfield Beach, Florida, for $88 million.

likely having problems, too. But something else was going on at Merrill: Just as it was handing over $1.3 billion for First Franklin, the company's bond salespeople were having a harder time selling all the CDOs it was producing—especially to overseas investors. (On each CDO bond Merrill sold, it reportedly earned a commission of 1.25 percent, or $12.5 million for each $1 billion bond.) When Mozilo's comments were publicized in July the CDO bond market began to dry up, which meant if Merrill couldn't find buyers for the bonds it would have to invest in them itself—using its own money.

In early October, Merrill disclosed to its investors (and to the public at large) that it would take a $5 billion charge when it released third quarter earnings in a few weeks, because it had to revalue some of its CDOs—in particular those that included subprime bonds. The billions in A– to D quality loans that its trading desk had been buying the past few years (and then giving to the structured products group to securitize) were going bad just as quickly as Countrywide's. But when the real number came out three weeks later, the actual CDO charge was much higher—$8 billion. For the quarter it had lost $2.4 billion, the only major Wall Street firm to lose money that period. Standard & Poor's, the rating agency, called the write-downs "staggering," blaming the mess on "management miscues."

On Sunday and Monday, October 21 and 22, Merrill's board met to review the results, grilling O'Neal and his top executives. The *Wall Street Journal* quoted a top executive as calling the meeting "definitely tense and very testy," but the newspaper predicted that O'Neal's job "doesn't appear to be in immediate jeopardy." A week later the 56-year-old CEO resigned, the *New York Times* reporting that his fall "is a reminder of how dangerous it is to tinker with a firm's culture." A few years earlier when O'Neal became head of the company, he called the notion of a nurturing "Mother Merrill" passé. He aimed to diversify Merrill away from its core business of selling stocks. He had succeeded, thanks in part to Merrill's foray into subprime. Merrill and Citigroup were now the largest CDO issuers in the world, but the assets underlying the bonds they had issued—and invested in themselves—were rapidly falling in value.

In November Angelo Mozilo received an e-mail from O'Neal, who told him he was doing fine and that he had always admired what the founder and CEO had made of Countrywide. (His retirement and severance benefits from Merrill were worth $160 million. He could afford to be fine.) But Mozilo now had his own problems: continuing delinquencies in subprime and a share price of under $10. Countrywide was now worth a quarter of what it had been valued at a year earlier.

In the fourth quarter Merrill posted the largest loss in company history: $8.6 billion, with $12 billion set aside to cover expected losses on its subprime CDO bonds. The total damage from its investment in subprime was now over $20 billion—and that didn't even include what it cost to buy part of Dallas's Ownit and First Franklin. And what about First Franklin? Since O'Neal's departure, the lender had been quietly laying off wholesale AEs and closing offices. By early 2008 it was funding very few subprime loans—and only if they could be sold to Fannie Mae or Freddie Mac, which still hadn't fully recovered from their accounting scandals of four years before.

Dave Duffy, a wholesale AE for First Franklin in its south New Jersey office, e-mailed a reporter at *National Mortgage News*, telling the newspaper he didn't have any loans to sell, adding that Merrill was "starving us out." It was late December, and the AE was making a base salary of just $2,000 a month, a fraction of what he used to earn. He added that Merrill wouldn't even give him car expense money anymore. It was too depressing to go to work, he said. An almost four-year veteran of the lender, having relocated from Georgia, he was now working from home. Every time he went into the office, the few remaining employees would "just play Scrabble and PlayStation on the conference room monitor all day." Duffy predicted that things were so bad that Merrill would probably close First Franklin by January or late February. He was off by only a few days—Merrill pulled the plug on its $1.3 billion investment in early March.

Chapter 9

A Warning from Lewie

CDOs, SIVs, and Other Things No One Understands

If you didn't have your shit together, Lewie would destroy you, tear you apart. I was in a meeting once and he did it to me. I went downstairs and felt like crying, quitting, but people said, "Don't worry about it. He does that to everyone."
—A FORMER SENIOR EXECUTIVE OF BANK UNITED,
A LEW RANIERI JOINT

Will I be a bull in a china shop? Yeah, absolutely, without a doubt. I don't care for people telling me what I can't do.
—LEW RANIERI

For those who have worked under him, the world is full of Lew Ranieri stories. Frank Hattemer, who ran warehouse lending for Ranieri when he controlled Bank United of Houston in the 1990s, remembers eating dinner with a client in downtown Houston. They were in the Renaissance Hotel's restaurant, right across the street from the bank's headquarters. "It was nine o'clock at night," says Hattemer. "We were sitting in the restaurant and who comes down for a late snack but Lewie, wearing his PJs, slippers, and a bathrobe. He sees me and sidles into the booth, sitting next to the client. I think he had a part of a submarine sandwich in each hand. He must've spent two hours with us, telling stories. The client was fascinated by him. He couldn't believe how amazingly smart this guy was, dressed in his bathrobe, eating subs at nine o'clock at night."

Headquartered in Houston, United Savings was a savings and loan with assets of $5 billion that failed during the height of the S&L crisis. In 1988 the federal government, in its desperation to clean up the nation's S&L mess, began selling hundreds of failed thrifts by giving away billions of dollars' worth of tax breaks to any investor who was willing to take on the carcass of any of these failed institutions. One year after departing as vice chairman of Salomon Brothers, Ranieri and his new company, Hyperion Partners, bought United Savings and changed its name to Bank United. Not only was he the co-inventor of the mortgage-backed security (MBS), but here he was the proud owner of United, one of the largest thrifts ever to fail in the Lone Star State. (Included in the carcass of this failed thrift might be such assets as junk bonds, raw land, even a taxicab company. Ranieri wound up with at least one taxicab company.) The biggest tax break the government gave away, which Ranieri noticed (along with many other business-men, including Revlon chairman Ron Perelman[1]), was the ability of the new owners to deduct from their future earnings the losses of pre-vious years. Not only could they deduct these past losses from future earnings of their newly acquired S&Ls, but they could shelter the earn-ings of their other companies as well. What was there not to like?

About two months after Ranieri acquired United Savings from the government, he thought it would be a proper idea to review the troops of the S&L that he had just purchased from Uncle Sam. He planned to bring along his friend Tony Nocella, whom he had hired as a manage-ment consultant to help run the institution. The ultimate goal was to jettison certain executives who probably should have been fired from the institution long ago. According to Hattemer, a few weeks prior to Ranieri's arrival at the thrift's headquarters, some of the lifelong Texans

---

[1] During the 1980s Revlon, with the backing of Drexel Burnham Lambert, attempted a hostile takeover of Salomon Brothers, Ranieri's old firm, only to fail. Salomon's white knight was Warren Buffett.

who worked at the S&L starting making cracks that Ranieri and Nocella "from the Mafia were coming to town."

Ranieri got wind of certain remarks about his Italian heritage (and the Mafia comment) and thought it might be a fun idea for him and Nocella to dress up in zoot suits straight out of *Guys and Dolls*. Wearing spats and pinstripes, he and Nocella sat in the boardroom, the lights dimmed, with a poster of Frank Sinatra on the wall. At one end of the long conference room table was a statue of the Virgin Mary, at the other end a statue of Jesus. One by one Ranieri and his friend, wearing red roses in their lapels, called in executives whose futures hung in the balance. Ranieri sat at the end of the table near Jesus, Nocella at the other end, near the Virgin Mary. (One employee who witnessed the show said Ranieri also placed a plastic horse's head on the floor, a nod to the movie *The Godfather*.)

When Ranieri addressed the executive in question, he would stare at the statue of Jesus. He would then bark, "Why are you turning your back on the Virgin Mary?" When the executive would swing around to face the other way, he would shout, "Why are you turning your back on Jesus?" It went on all afternoon until he and Nocella had cleaned house of all the undesirables who had toiled for Charles Hurwitz, the man the government held responsible for United's collapse.

Twelve years later Ranieri sold Bank United—then a publicly traded S&L—to Kerry Killinger's Washington Mutual for $1.2 billion. Financially speaking, it would have been (perhaps) the pinnacle of his career except for one thing: Ranieri was the man universally credited with helping create the mortgage-backed security while working at Salomon Brothers in the late 1970s. Arguably, the emergence of the MBS was the most important invention in the history of the U.S. financial system since the creation of stocks and bonds themselves. The argument goes like this: What's the largest debt market in the world? Answer: The U.S. residential mortgage market. At $9 trillion (as of early 2008), U.S. consumers owed more money on their homes than the federal government owed on all its Treasury bonds—even after the record deficits of the Bush administration (George W.).

In 1977 when Salomon Brothers began toying with the idea of creating a bond backed by mortgages, U.S. consumers owed about $1 trillion on their homes. Back then, mortgage debt also outstripped government debt. It seemed like an obvious thing to do—except for the fact no one had ever done it before. According to Ranieri, the idea to create a mortgage bond was actually sparked by Salomon Brothers chief economist Henry Kaufman.[2] "It was Henry's research that drove it," said Ranieri. Kaufman looked at the demographics and concluded that the savings and loan industry (which then kept most of its originations on its books) didn't have the capacity to hold all the mortgages coming down the pike when baby boomers (a tidal wave of 80 million Americans) would reach peak home-buying years.

After starting his career in Salomon's mail room, Ranieri worked his way up to the trading desk—the utilities trading desk, that is—before being handpicked by Salomon Brothers partner Bob Dall to work on mortgages. Dall once told writer Michael Lewis that Ranieri "had the mentality and the will to create a market. . . . I have never seen anyone, educated or uneducated, with a quicker mind. And best of all he was a dreamer." Together, the two men (and others) toiled with early MBS structures, before Salomon issued the first pass-through bond, in 1977, securitizing mortgages for Bank of America. (With a pass-through bond the investor actually owns a share in an underlying pool of mortgages. With later versions of the MBS investors were paid through a trust, which administered the cash flows generated by the underlying loans.) But Ranieri considered the Bank of America security a failure. "It was a difficult sell to institutional investors," he said.

The biggest problem that he and Salomon faced was the fact that securities backed by mortgages were not legal investments in many states. To alleviate the problem, Salomon (under Ranieri's tutelage) lobbied successfully for changes in blue-sky laws, which suddenly made MBSs acceptable investments. Problem solved. (Blue-sky laws refer to state laws that regulate what types of securities can be sold to the public and to public institutions. The laws can vary from state to state.) A market was born.

---

[2] Kaufman, who eventually became vice chairman of Salomon before leaving the firm in 1988, was known for his bearish forecast on interest rates. He often predicted that rates would rise, thus hurting bond prices. His constant gloomy prediction on rates earned him the nickname "Dr. Doom." Along with Salomon Brothers, Crocker National Bank was involved in creating early MBS structures.

But it wasn't just that. Creation of the first private MBS[3] allowed ailing savings and loans the ability to pool all of their low-yielding mortgages into bonds and get them off their books. (A tax break passed by the federal government allowed S&Ls to write off their losses over several years, which helped thrifts tremendously.) Ranieri was seen as a hero to the industry. When he spoke to S&L executives at trade shows or private meetings, they hung on his every word, taking what he had to say as near gospel. Salomon dominated the MBS market from 1978 to the mid-1980s. (In the 1980s one of Ranieri's best friends was Stan Strachan, founder and editor of *National Thrift News*, an industry trade newspaper that catered to S&L executives. The two men were as close as brothers. Neither had finished college; they were loud, bearded, and liked to eat. Both were incredibly sharp. Strachan, half seriously, used to joke to his staff of reporters that he was going to leave the newspaper to work as an MBS trader at Salomon.) Ranieri went from head trader on the mortgage desk to the vice chairman of the company.[4] During its fattest years of dominating the MBS business, the mortgage trading desk under Ranieri earned upwards of $200 million a year, accounting for 40 percent of the firm's revenues. At the time it was a phenomenal amount of money.

While trading mortgages, Ranieri also was helping S&Ls securitize their old conventional "A" paper quality loans into bonds. (S&Ls originated "A" loans, government-insured mortgages, and jumbo loans.[5]) Ranieri first convinced Freddie Mac to place its guarantee on the mortgage bonds. Fannie Mae then followed along. Because these two were chartered by Congress, investors treated the bonds as though they were backed by the U.S. Treasury. This spurred other Wall Street firms—First Boston and Drexel Burnham Lambert being the toughest

---

[3] The first MBS created by Salomon was modeled somewhat after Government National Mortgage Association (Ginnie Mae) securities backed by the federal government. Ginnie Maes were bonds collateralized by mortgages backed by the Federal Housing Administration and Veterans Administration.

[4] Among Ranieri's contemporaries at Salomon was John Meriwether, a bond trader (not on the mortgage desk, though) and arbitrage specialist who founded Long-Term Capital Management, the hedge fund that went under in 1998.

[5] A jumbo loan is any mortgage that is greater than the annual Fannie Mae/Freddie Mac loan limit, which is based each year on median home prices across the United States.

competitors of Salomon—to start their own mortgage trading desks and mine for the same gold as Ranieri.

Ranieri—who prefers to be called Lewie—once aspired to be a chef (as did his brother Salvatore). He majored in English at St. John's University on Long Island before landing a job in the mail room at Salomon. "When they offered to put me on the trading floor I was about six credits short of a college degree," he recalled. "One of them was an Italian credit I needed." He delayed graduating to become a bond trader. He was self-taught in three computer languages, Fortran, Basic, and Cobol, and claims credit for getting Salomon to computerize its trading operations. "I started the Salomon Brothers computer room," he says. "I was the one who first set it up."

When he wasn't on the road selling the firm's MBS services to thrifts and banks, most mornings he would have breakfast with Salomon CEO and chairman John Gutfreund. "John had been like my dad," said Ranieri. "My own dad died when I was young." It was believed that Gutfreund was grooming Ranieri to be his successor—the Brooklyn-born Ranieri who once aspired to be a chef, majored in English, never attended business school, and grew up on the streets of Brooklyn. Ranieri (like Mozilo, Arnall, and Stan O'Neal) came from next to nothing. Unlike Merrill Lynch, whose reputation was built on the retail sale of stocks, Salomon's was built on bonds. He once boasted that in 1984 (the height of Salomon's dominance of the mortgage market) his mortgage trading desk had made more money than all of the rest of Wall Street combined that year.[6] Even though it looked as though Gutfreund was considering Ranieri to be his heir apparent, that's not how things turned out. When Salomon's mortgage profits began to wane later in the decade and its top traders departed for the competition, Gutfreund fired Ranieri in July 1987, three months before the stock market crash of October 19. To this day Ranieri isn't sure exactly what happened. "He always had me clean up his messes—like the Phibro deal.[7] When John decided I was too big for the company it broke my heart," he said.

[6] According to the book *Liar's Poker* by Michael Lewis.

[7] In 1981 Salomon merged with a commodities trading firm called Phillips Brothers or Phibro for short. Gutfreund believed that Salomon needed Phibro's capital and commodities business, but after profits exploded in its mortgage department (under Ranieri) it became clear that the deal was unnecessary. With commodities profits lagging, Salomon eventually sold the Phibro unit.

His expulsion from Salomon is a topic that Ranieri still is not happy talking about. "I thought I was going to have a breakdown," he said. Ranieri had spent his entire professional life at Salomon. "He absolutely loved the place," said one of his former employees. "He was crushed." Two years later, in 1989, a former bond trader at Salomon named Michael Lewis wrote a book, *Liar's Poker*, that chronicled Salomon's rise to prominence during the decade—first and foremost in mortgages. Lewis didn't work in the mortgage department, but with chapters entitled "A Brotherhood of Hoods" and "The Fat Men and Their Marvelous Money Machine" he captured the *Animal House*–like atmosphere of the firm's mortgage trading desk, portraying Ranieri as a John Belushi type of character who was loud, lovable, and among all else sloppy in appearance. "He owned exactly four suits, all polyester," wrote Lewis, noting a few sentences later that as he grew rich at Salomon, Ranieri "continued to own four suits," quoting the MBS co-inventor bragging that he owned more power boats than suits. (Ranieri says he has hardly any recollection of ever talking to Lewis or meeting him. "I never read the book, but people told me about it. You have to remember that I was brokenhearted around that time, and the last thing I wanted to do was read a book about Salomon Brothers. I mean, I started in the mail room when I wasn't even 18 years old." Even though he may not have talked to the writer/former trader, a careful read of the book suggests that at the very least Lewis had access to several top employees at Salomon—including Dall—who were close to Ranieri on his ascent to the vice chairmanship.)

Liar's Poker went on to become a national best seller and turned Ranieri into something of a Wall Street folk hero. One of the most important things Lewis established about Ranieri was his intolerance for the pretense of investment bankers on Wall Street. Ranieri was from Brooklyn and started in the mail room—and he was proud of it. That intolerance also included financial services executives of most types. "He has a great bullshit detector," said Frank Hattemer, who worked for him.

Hattemer, the warehouse chief who worked at Bank United in Houston, remembers attending a dinner thrown by the thrift's CEO, Barry Burkholder, at a Houston country club in the 1990s. "Lewie hated that striped-pants kind of stuff," said Hattemer. "Burkholder was the kind of guy who enjoyed good wine, and if he didn't like it, he sent it back. Lewie hated that, too. So during the dinner, he started a food fight.

You should have seen the look on the faces of Burkholder and his wife. They were aghast."

Ranieri served as chairman of Bank United and wasn't necessarily involved in the thrift's day-to-day management, but he made his presence known throughout the organization. "He had pet names for people—and they weren't always good," said one former manager. "We created an organizational chart where 'Fucking Dough Boy' was in charge of this, and 'Shit for Brains' was in charge of that. The 'Cretin' was in charge of another department. Stuff like that. We wrote it all down in a big chart." (Some of Ranieri's former acolytes have suggested that the practical joking portrayed in *Liar's Poker* was merely a warm-up for what went on at Bank United.)

But Hattemer and many others who worked for Ranieri at Salomon, Bank United, and other companies are clear about one thing: The Brooklyn native may have been loud, brash, and (like Mozilo) known to spit out expletives, but they believe when it comes to mortgage finance he is incredibly smart—that he sees things in the market before anyone else. And most of them loved him (still do) for his lack of pretense and for, above all else, his honesty. In 2000 when Washington Mutual bought Bank United, they kept Ranieri on retainer as a consultant, paying him $500,000 a year. One time the thrift actually paid him twice. Ranieri called the company's accounting department and said he was sending the check back. "That's the kind of guy he was," said Hattemer.

★ ★ ★

Bill Campbell, a public relations executive for a small PR firm in New York, once had this to say about the growing mortgage crisis in the fall of 2007: "If only we had built a time machine, went back to 1980, and knocked off Ranieri, none of this would ever have happened." Campbell, whose clients included several mortgage firms, was joking. But his point was that the mortgage securitization had run amok—that subprime mortgages were going delinquent at record rates, causing dozens of firms to fail and threatening a whole industry whether they were in subprime or not.

Ranieri's legacy was the MBS. When he and Bob Dall launched Salomon's mortgage desk in the late 1970s, they didn't even know what the word *subprime* meant. By 2006 Ranieri, at 59, was a well-respected elder statesmen of both Wall Street and the mortgage industry. He donated generously to the Republican party and New York state politicians alike as well as a handful of Democrats. Banking regulators and members of the Bush administration regularly sought out his advice on financial matters, especially if they had to do with Fannie Mae and Freddie Mac, two institutions whose health he believed were paramount to keeping the U.S. mortgage market strong—that is, liquid. Ranieri was a member of the Grand Old Party, and even though some Republicans made a sport of publicly bashing Fannie Mae and Freddie Mac because of the power they held in the "A" paper business, he wasn't in their camp on this issue. He knew that without Fannie and Freddie's early support there would be no MBS market; that was something he had never forgotten.[8]

Retirement is not a word that people associate with Lewie Ranieri. Even though he had sold Bank United six years earlier, he kept active in the market, managing Ranieri & Company, the small boutique investment banking firm that he started after leaving Salomon. He had his hands in several other investments as well—some successful, some not. As one former employee remembered, "Lewie made a lot of money and lost a bit of money for investors, but overall he's in the black. Not everyone can say that."

When the century turned, Ranieri bought a small community lender called Franklin Bank of Texas, which, like Bank United, was based in Houston. He served on the board of Computer Associates of Long Island, one of the nation's largest software companies, and helped the firm survive after it was revealed that two of its top executives had been cooking its books. Ranieri, who joined the board after the financial fraud was well under way, once told a friend of the executives in question, "These are either the smartest guys I've every met or they're crooks." The latter turned out to be true. (A fan of the ballet, he also helped straighten out the finances of the American Ballet Theatre of New York.)

---

[8] When Freddie Mac's accounting scandal broke in June 2003 and the firm cleaned house, Ranieri was mentioned as a candidate to run the place. He didn't want the job.

By the fall of 2006 Ranieri was not happy. He was the chairman and largest single shareholder in the publicly traded Franklin Bank. Even though he no longer traded loans himself, Franklin's employees did. Regulators at the Federal Reserve and other banking agencies, including the Federal Deposit Insurance Corporation and Office of Thrift Supervision,[9] had just released a working paper called "Guidance on Non-Traditional Mortgages." What the heck was a nontraditional mortgage (NTM)? Answer: subprime loans, payment option ARMs, stated-income loans—the types of mortgages that Ameriquest, Argent, Countrywide, First Franklin, and many other originators were still funding as though the good times would last forever. The message from Washington to the residential lending community was this: You had better start disclosing more about these loans—especially the ARMs— to your home-buying customers, because we're starting to hear a lot of complaints that you aren't telling them how their loan payments might go through the roof when the interest rate adjusts.

Ranieri knew the guidance meant that his traders at Franklin Bank would have to carefully review the loans they were buying, which was fine with him. (They more or less did that anyway.) But in the summer and fall some of the loans Franklin was trading "made us hold our nose." At Bank United and then Franklin Bank, Ranieri had avoided the subprime business entirely. "We were just plain old mortgage guys," he said. "We never even looked at getting in." (Even though the bank avoided nonprime residential loans, it was a national lender to home builders, a business that would suffer greatly in the years ahead.)

But the loans Franklin Bank was being offered had what Ranieri called "layered risk," which meant the mortgages were ARMs, were made to borrowers who had low FICO scores, were originated to too many first-time home buyers, had exceptions (certain underwriting rules were waived), and had a number of other characteristics that made the co-inventor of the MBS queasy. "The stuff we were seeing was just getting worse and worse." He told the trading desk at Franklin in Houston to stop buying.

---

[9] The Office of Thrift Supervision (OTS) regulates all lenders with a savings and loan charter. The Federal Deposit Insurance Corporation (FDIC) regulates commercial banks, as does the Federal Reserve. The Office of the Comptroller of the Currency (OCC) regulates commercial banks with a national charter.

On December 5, 2006, Bill Dallas sent out his company-wide e-mail telling his employees at Ownit Mortgage—as well as its independent loan brokers—that he was pulling the plug on the company. (In the e-mail he didn't mention the loan buyback disputes he was having with Merrill Lynch, though that would be reported by the press in just a matter of days.) Less than a week later, on Monday, the 11th, the Office of Thrift Supervision held what it called a "Housing Summit" at the National Press Club in Washington. The conference's goal was to bring the public up to speed on what the agency felt were some of the key issues affecting the housing market, chiefly declining home prices—which since the Great Depression had never declined, at least on a national basis—and the regulators' "Non-Traditional Mortgages" guidance. Invited speakers included a local lending executive from B.F. Saul Mortgage; David Berson, chief economist at Fannie Mae; Kathy Dick, a top regulator from the Office of the Comptroller of the Currency (OCC)—and Lewie Ranieri. Even though it was a public forum, most of the attendees were regulators from the various Washington agencies, as well as members of the press.

Berson talked a bit about declining home prices, noting that investors (people who speculate on the values of homes increasing, including so-called flippers) are more likely to use ARMs than are regular home buyers, and reminding the audience that "about 80 percent of what we purchase are fixed-rate loans." (A month later, speaking once again at the Press Club, the Fannie Mae chief economist predicted that when it came to falling home values the "biggest declines are behind us." His prediction would later prove to be a major embarrassment to Fannie Mae.)

Dick from the OCC talked about the NTM guidance, which was relatively new, noting that the NTM market "is a young one without a lot of history." What she didn't mention was that the NTM guidance was just that—guidance. Bank executives could throw the guidance in the trash can. It wasn't a rule or regulation. She also didn't mention that half the subprime market—ARMs being a key product for A– to D lenders— was controlled by nonbanks like Ameriquest, New Century, WMC Mortgage,[10] Option One Mortgage, and others. If they were nonbanks,

---

[10] WMC Mortgage was owned by General Electric, which had bought the subprime lender a few years earlier for about $500 million.

that meant the OCC or any other regulator in Washington couldn't touch them. Bank regulators had oversight only over federally insured institutions that took deposits. Bank and thrift regulators didn't regulate mortgages per se—they regulated institutions. Then up stepped Ranieri.

Two decades earlier, when Lewie spoke, thrift managers were eager to listen. He was a near celebrity. This time, the nation's banking regulators were the ones doing the stargazing. Here, in front of them, was the man mainly responsible for the creation of the MBS—but with one important footnote. When Ranieri, Dall, and others invented the MBS, the idea was to securitize loans backed by plain-vanilla "A" paper mortgages. "There was 40, 50 years' worth of historical data on those types of mortgages," he later recalled. "You had a pretty good idea how they would behave." He had never dreamed that Wall Street would be so stupid as to securitize a bunch of mortgages that had no history to them. The modern subprime mortgage was 10 years old at most. The loans that Ameriquest, First Franklin, New Century, and others were funding had no resemblance whatsoever to the second deeds of trust that Peter Cugno used to underwrite and fund for Beneficial Finance back in the 1960s. Cugno's loans at least were backed by homes with 40 percent equity in them. The loans being funded by First Franklin (which Merrill was about to buy) and Arnall's company were made to people with little in the way of down payments and who were stated-income borrowers. They told the loan officers how much they made, and the loan officers believed them—as long as their FICO scores were decent.

Looking a bit overweight and frumpy in a loose-fitting suit, the first thing Ranieri did was remind the regulators of the "staggering changes" in the mortgage business over the past two years—from one where Fannie/Freddie loans used to dominate to one where a "powerful MBS sector was untethered in its enthusiasm." Without saying it directly, he hinted that Wall Street had gone gaga securitizing subprime mortgages without paying much attention to quality, and there wasn't a whole lot they, as regulators, could do, because most of the loans were being originated by nonbanks. Subprime and nonprime loans now accounted for a record 25 percent of all mortgages funded in the United States—and the growth looked unstoppable. He noted that at least when Fannie Mae and Freddie Mac dominated the mortgage business "they played the role of gatekeeper"; the government-sponsored enterprises (GSEs) had loan underwriting standards—things like minimum down payments, two-inch-thick loan documents, and mortgage insurance that covered potential losses. "Those standards have been pushed aside," he said, looking over the top of his oversized glasses. And what was worse, he told his audience, 80 percent of the loans he was talking about were being funded through loan brokers over whom they, the regulators, had no control whatsoever.

Lewie was just getting started. He said the loans that families were using to buy homes weren't Fannie/Freddie loans but "stated-income, 'neg-am,' 80/20 loans," which meant the consumer had made no down payment and instead borrowed 20 percent of the purchase price by taking out a second deed of trust home equity loan on top of an 80 percent first mortgage. ("Neg-am" was short for negative amortization, a feature of risky payment option ARMs that Countrywide and others were originating by the billions of dollars' worth. Neg-am meant the borrower was actually adding onto the debt instead of paying it down a bit each month.) Then he moved on to the end investor—the institutions buying the bonds. Investors, he said, were used to getting data on the securities they were buying, but not in this new market.

"The rating agencies are playing the role of quasi-regulator," he said. "They've been cast into this role." The rating agencies meant Standard & Poor's, Fitch, and Moody's. It was their job to look at the loans backing the subprime bonds to make sure the investor was getting a quality product. It was up to the rating agencies to grade the bonds; that's what the securities underwriter paid them for. In a nutshell, Ranieri felt that investors—including overseas buyers—weren't getting enough information. He mentioned collateralized debt obligations (CDOs), which were securities made up of other securities, all subprime. During the question-and-answer period with regulators, he told them the "subordinated tranches of MBSs are being put into these CDOs. Generally, they're being sold to nonbanks and foreign banks." In general, he believed that investors weren't being told enough information about the loan-to-value ratios backing the mortgages that had been securitized. "This is a public securities market," he said, "and investors, foreign investors, don't have a clue."

Then he started on the Securities and Exchange Commission (SEC) (in a nice way). "They're the regulator of the capital markets—they can make a difference," he said. He told the audience that his bank had stopped trading in ARMs—that when they looked at the loans being sold in the secondary market "about 40 percent" of them didn't meet the new NTM guidance issued by the federal regulators. Of course, it didn't really matter because the guidance had no teeth. The Federal Reserve, OCC, and other agencies were just suggesting; they weren't dictating. Either way, Ranieri didn't like what he was seeing in the mar-ketplace. "You can't do business this way," he concluded.

Ranieri's comments were based on his knowledge of the market and his analysis of CDO bond disclosure documents. "I exactly read this stuff," he said. But he was also supplied research on ABS bond dis-closures by Mark Goldhaber, a friend of his who was an executive at Genworth Financial, a financial services company that owned a mort-gage insurance division. Genworth, which had been spun off by General Electric a few years earlier, was the most conservatively managed of the nation's seven mortgage insurance companies. For years Goldhaber, who served as both a lobbyist and a public relations man for Genworth, was a behind-the-scenes player in Washington who both scoured pending financial legislation for nuances that might help (or hurt) Genworth and read actuarial tables.[11] He was also an active member of FM Watch, a lobbying group trying to contain the powers of Fannie Mae and Freddie Mac. (Ironically, he used to work for Freddie Mac.)

Afterwards, a reporter went up to Ranieri and asked him whether he was blaming the SEC for not having a handle on the subprime MBS market. "This isn't an indictment of the SEC," he said, checking his BlackBerry. He looked up at the reporter and said, "The transpar-encies are not what they should be." Translation: this was an indictment of the SEC.

It would seem that when the man who helped invent the MBS warns about a market where $1 trillion in loans had been securitized over the previous two years (subprime ABSs) that it would get a lot of media attention. It didn't. Bloomberg and *National Mortgage News* wrote about Ranieri's remarks, but it wasn't exactly front-page cover-age in the *Wall Street Journal* and the *New York Times*. Then again, the

---

[11] In the summer of 2007, Goldhaber privately predicted that the subprime losses would probably rival the cost of the S&L crisis: $150 billion.

wreckage in the subprime market had barely started. Bill Dallas's Ownit Mortgage had just gone under, but Merrill Lynch was moving full speed ahead with its purchase of First Franklin. It appeared that despite Ranieri's warning about loan quality and bond disclosures on subprime ABSs, whatever was occurring in the market was perhaps a blip—and over the next few months things would turn around.

In the months ahead, Ranieri would make similar speeches, including a talk at the Milken Institute in Los Angeles. (Ranieri counted Michael Milken, the former junk bond king, among his friends. He said that when it came to poor bond disclosures on subprime securities, "Mike was on my side.") One of his biggest problems with CDOs was the "B" pieces of subprime ABS securitizations. The "B" pieces were the subordinated parts of the bonds—the ones that took the first losses in the event of loan defaults by subprime borrowers. According to Ranieri's research, many of these subordinated bonds (the riskiest ones) were not really public securities that had any genuine scrutiny behind them. "A lot of these were 144-A's," he later said. "These were private securities." By that he meant the issuer (Merrill and Citigroup being the two largest issuers of CDOs in 2006) had registered the securities, but the bonds were sold through a private placement. The 144-A route was exactly what Eric Billings of FBR was doing in regard to converting certain subprime mortgage REITs into stockholder-owned companies: public registration with private ownership. The advantages of using a 144-A filing were less paperwork and less scrutiny by the SEC.

Why would an investor in a subprime CDO such as a German bank like SachsenLB or an Australian beach town community like Manly (a suburb of Sydney) invest in a bond that included the riskiest pieces of a subprime ABS? The answer was that they wanted a security that yielded more than a U.S. Treasury bond. (Both SachsenLB and Manly bought subprime-related CDOs and lost huge sums of money by doing so.) U.S. Treasuries are considered the safest fixed-income investments in the world, but in the 2004 to 2007 time frame—the height of the CDO issuance, when well over $1 trillion in securities were sold to investors worldwide, not all of them backed by home mortgages, mind you—the yield on a 10-year Treasury bond might be only 4.5 percent. The yield on a CDO might be two or three percentage points higher, and when an investor is dealing with a bond that might have a face value of $100 million, an extra percentage point or two translates into tens of thousands of dollars in additional income. It wasn't just the money, though. The investor, the suburb of Manly for instance, trusted the investment banker that was selling them the CDO. "These bonds are sold without much disclosure because they pass the sophisticated investor test," said Ranieri. "Merrill and Citi put them into CDOs. Then they take these CDOs and sell them to nontraditional mortgage guys."

The two largest investment banks that issued CDOs were, as Ranieri noted, Citigroup and Merrill.[12] It wasn't just that they sold the bonds; in the case of Merrill, the investment banking firm would provide a loan to almost any investor that wanted to buy a CDO from it. In short, Merrill was providing warehouse financing to CDO investors. And Merrill, of course, was providing warehouse financing to nonbank subprime lenders like Ownit, a company (like many others) that was gathering mortgages from independent loan brokers. This warehousing on top of warehousing was what investment bankers liked to call leverage. Not only did Merrill own 20 percent of Ownit, it was lending money to the company to originate mortgages to the public and then on the back end it was financing the purchase of CDOs by investors. The CDOs included securitized subprime loans that came out of a lender it owned 20 percent of: Ownit. It was a perfect chain: Merrill was profiting every step of the way.

Ranieri looked at the whole process and concluded that by using 144-A's and putting the securities in CDOs, Wall Street firms like Merrill "were circumventing the system, which meant that anyone who might stand up and yell 'bullshit,'" like the SEC, was absent from the process. Ranieri knew that the CDO business was making "big, big money" for Stan O'Neal, the head of Merrill Lynch. "If you were Stan O'Neal you drank the Kool-Aid," said Ranieri. "Of course, Angelo [Mozilo of Countrywide] was out there trying to convince

---

[12] In the first half of 2007, before the subprime ABS market began to crumble, Merrill Lynch and Citigroup ranked first and second, respectively, among all CDO issuers in the United States, according to *Asset-Backed Alert*, an industry newsletter. Merrill issued $33.4 billion in CDOs, a 46 percent increase from the previous year. Citigroup ranked second with $28 billion, a 45 percent gain.

everyone that 100 percent LTV loans were okay." And Ranieri liked Angelo. In some of his speeches during the previous two years Mozilo had been a big proponent of no-down-payment lending, believing that if home prices kept going up at a rate of even just 5 percent a year, borrowers would quickly have equity in their newly purchased homes. Mozilo had met Ranieri while Countrywide was still a young company using Salomon to securitize loans for it. "I would come up to Salomon and have lunch with him," Mozilo recalled. "Lew and I used to bet each other on when the FHA would raise its rates. Back then the FHA set its own rates—it didn't matter what the Fed was doing."

By the summer of 2007 losses on CDOs by foreign investors were beginning to get coverage in the *Wall Street Journal* and other newspapers. The term *CDO* had suddenly become part of the financial lexicon to describe what exactly was happening on the back end of the mortgage food chain (so to speak). When it came to subprime originations, the front end entailed loan brokers finding a customer, and a wholesaler like Argent, Countrywide, or First Franklin funding that loan at the closing table.[13] The back end of that mortgage food chain entailed the reselling of that loan, its securitization, and then the slicing and dicing of its cash flows into different bonds. Mortgages weren't just being securitized into ABS bonds; they were being resecuritized and put into CDOs. Keep in mind that when a subprime ABS is created by a Wall Street firm (such as Merrill), it has different tranches, meaning the cash flow is divided into smaller bonds, each with different risk characteristics, maturities, and yields. All of the tranches are rated by S&P, Moody's, or Fitch. As Ranieri once noted, "These deals are structured backwards. They sell the support tranche first. If you don't have it, you can't do the deal."

The support tranche was the "B" piece or subordinated tranche—the one where all the losses were taken first. During the subprime boom of 1995 to 1998, the "B" pieces were sold to hedge funds or held on the balance sheet of publicly traded subprime lenders. How did the lenders manage to keep the risky bonds on their books? They

---

[13] When a wholesale lender like Countrywide funds a mortgage using a loan broker, the transaction is sometimes referred to as "table funding," because a check is delivered by the provider of funds (Countrywide) to where the closing is being held.

borrowed money from Wall Street to finance these holdings. A slightly different twist on the CDO was an invention called the structured investment vehicle (SIV) that had one key difference: SIVs were investment funds and didn't necessarily have ratings from one of the big three rating agencies (though the underlying securities in the fund might).

In 2007 the biggest player in the SIV market was Citigroup. According to the *Wall Street Journal*, Citigroup was the largest participant in the $350 billion SIV market, managing seven funds with a combined value of $80 billion. But the beauty of SIVs—at least for the investment bankers that managed the funds—was that they were off-balance-sheet investment funds, which meant Citigroup collected a fee as manager, arranged for investors to buy into the fund (using short-term loans called commercial paper), and didn't have to tell its regulator anything about what it was doing because SIVs, as a technical matter, were owned not by Citigroup but by outside institutional investors. In the beginning of 2007, Citigroup—without offering an explanation—stopped disclosing to trade newspapers like *Inside Mortgage Finance* and *National Mortgage News* how much in subprime loans the company was originating and servicing each year. The only way to ascertain the information was to wait for the annual loan origination figures to be released by the Federal Reserve under a law called the Home Mortgage Disclosure Act (HMDA).

It was generally assumed that Citigroup's subprime division, CitiFinancial of Baltimore, was the tenth largest originator of subprime mortgages in the United States. The nation's largest commercial bank had an interesting pedigree. Its CEO was Charles Prince. His predecessor was Sandy Weill, who became the head of Citigroup shortly after Citibank merged with insurance giant Travelers Group. Travelers was Weill's company. The former number-two executive at financial services giant American Express, Weill in 1986 had bought a struggling midsize consumer finance company, Commercial Credit Company of Baltimore, fixed it up, and eventually parlayed that acquisition into several others, which is how he wound up with Travelers. Commercial Credit's general counsel was Charles Prince. By the time Citibank merged with Weill's insurance giant in 1998 (thus creating Citigroup), Travelers also happened to own an investment banking company called

Salomon Smith Barney—which included the remnants of Ranieri's old firm, Salomon Brothers.

By the time Ranieri made his speech at the Press Club in Washington, Citigroup was originating subprime loans coast to coast through retail loan offices that once belonged to both Commercial Credit and Associates First Capital Corporation,[14] the subprime giant it had bought back in 2000. It also was using loan brokers and buying already originated subprime loans from other lenders. It was then taking the loans, securitizing them through Citigroup Securities (the old Salomon Smith Barney), and putting them into CDOs and SIVs. Under Weill and Prince it had created a beginning-to-end subprime mortgage factory—one that resembled what Bear Stearns had and what Stan O'Neal over at Merrill Lynch was trying to build.

★　★　★

In the summer of 2005 Karen Weaver went on a tour of Southern California. She wasn't a pop star—she was managing director in charge of global securitization research for Deutsche Bank in New York. Her mission: to interview subprime executives on how they did business—how they underwrote the billions in loans they were churning out each month. Southern California, Orange County in particular, was subprime central. It seemed like a logical place to start. In the fall of that year she issued a report noting that subprime mortgage securities increasingly were being thrown into CDOs. Historically, residential loans were never placed in CDOs. CDOs were originally created by Drexel Burnham Lambert as a way for investors to buy a basket of junk bonds backed by companies in different industries. The idea was to diversify risk. In the early 2000s CDOs consisted primarily of corporate bonds and loans, credit card receivables, and aircraft leases and receivables. The idea, as Michael Milken envisioned, was diversification. But beginning in 2003, Wall Street underwriters, led by Citigroup,

---

[14] Before going public a decade earlier, Associates First Capital was owned by Ford Motor Company.

threw the diversification model out the window by creating CDOs that contained mostly mortgages—subprime mortgages, that is.

One of Weaver's conclusions was that housing prices just couldn't possibly keep rising so much year after year. She predicted that in the years ahead "subprime mortgage losses will increase significantly." A few months after the report came out, Greg Lippmann, Deutsche Bank's global ABS chief, began shorting the ABX index, betting that subprime bonds (ABSs) would decline in value. Lippmann's bet against subprime was made a full year before Ranieri made his remarks to regulators in Washington. Of course, Lippmann's goal was to stay under the radar; he didn't want the publicity to ruin his bet, which turned out to be hugely successful. His actions later came to light well into 2007, first in the *Wall Street Journal* and then in the *New York Times* and other newspapers. Lippmann declined to comment. But Lippmann wasn't the only one shorting the ABX. John Paulson, 51 (no relation to the Bush Treasury secretary), a little-known hedge fund manager who grew up in Queens, later said he made $15 billion by betting against subprime. A handful of Street firms were doing the same—but keeping their investments out of the public eye: Goldman Sachs, Lehman Brothers, and Morgan Stanley.

By early 2006 most mortgage executives who were selling loans to Merrill and Citigroup had a good idea that not only would their mortgages fuel ABS issuance (that was a given) but they would feed the growing CDO market. "The entire [subprime] industry knew that Merrill was putting the product into CDOs," said Ownit's Bruce Dickenson.

The feeling among lenders and investors was that as long as the three rating agencies gave the CDOs an investment-grade rating (BBB or higher), then there should be no worries. Treasuries, the best credit in the land, were AAA rated. But many CDOs actually were rated AAA by Moody's, S&P, and Fitch. This was accomplished by the Wall Street securitizer obtaining bond insurance from one of the three big bond insurance companies—Ambac Financial Group, MBIA Inc., and Financial Guaranty Insurance Company (FGIC). If the loans underlying the CDO went bad, the bond insurers would pay. In the new modern era of subprime finance, it appeared that Wall Street had all the to-do boxes taken care of with a check mark in each. An investment banker like Bear Stearns owned the actual originator of the subprime loans.

Check. If it didn't own the originator, it bought mortgages through the trading desk. Check. It securitized the mortgages into subprime MBSs (ABSs). Check. It took out bond insurance. Check. It obtained investment-grade ratings from either Fitch, Moody's, or S&P. Check. It found domestic or foreign investors. Check.

What could go wrong? Was Ranieri (and Weaver) overreacting? One thing was certain: Wall Street firms like Merrill Lynch and Bear Stearns—as Ranieri would later come to realize—were not carefully reviewing the billions in loans they were buying each day. These weren't the "A" paper loans of yesteryear, a product that had made Salomon (and Ranieri) rich. These were modern-day subprime loans— a whole new breed of animal. As Ranieri once joked, "There's nothing wrong with mortgages—it's an unstable asset."

Chapter 10

Deep in the Belly of the Bear

The long-held dream of "Carl Chamberlain"[1] was to work on the mortgage trading desk at Bear Stearns, Merrill Lynch, Lehman Brothers, or any of the other Wall Street firms that were doing a brisk business in subprime lending during the years 2004 to 2007. It was a gold rush, and he aimed to be in on the action. A Manhattanite, he had a degree in paralegal studies with a specialty in foreclosures and litigation. For a while Chamberlain worked as a frontline loan analyst at First Franklin's Garden City office in Nassau County out on Long Island, underwriting so-called liar loans (stated-income loans), taking a careful look at verification of employment (VOE) forms on potential borrowers. He was asked to leave after he raised a stink about some of the lender's underwriting practices, which included a manager encouraging certain borrowers to take out cash advances on their credit cards and use the money for a down payment. "The reason they needed

---

[1] This contract underwriter, who worked for Clayton and other outsourcing firms, requested that his name be changed for publication in this book. He continues to work in the mortgage industry.

the advance was because they had no money," he said. Then he discovered Clayton Holdings and a practice called "rolling."

Based in suburban Shelton, Connecticut, Clayton was the largest
of a half-dozen or so due diligence firms that vetted subprime and
alt-A mortgages being funded by lenders like Aegis, Ameriquest, First
Franklin, Ownit, and the rest of the nonbanks churning out $2.4 trillion
in mortgages during those years. In 2006, rank-and-file clerks hired by
Clayton vetted a million individual mortgages for Wall Street firms,
chief among them Merrill and Bear. Even though these loans supposedly had been already underwritten by the lenders originating them,
the Street (intelligently) wanted a second opinion—at least on some of
them. Depending on the lender and the size of the loan pool being
sold, Clayton might review just 5 percent to 20 percent of the mortgages they were buying. In the fast and furious days of the boom
years, underwriting, especially on liar loans, might only include minimum documentation. Since many nonbanks like New Century, First
Franklin, and Ownit knew their loans would be vetted a second time
by the Street, they would create what were called "thin files" on loans.[2]
These paper files might include only a pay stub and a credit report. As
for Clayton, its clients included Bear Stearns, Merrill Lynch, Morgan
Stanley, Citigroup, and just about every other investment banking firm
that was buying whole loans through their trading desks with the ultimate goal of creating subprime bonds, some of which would wind up
in CDOs. As one executive vice president who sold to the Street noted:
"They were not set up for the long haul or to generate quality. They
were designed to generate revenue."

There were two reasons the Street firms reviewed only a small
sample of the loans they were buying, said Chamberlain. The most
important reason was the relationship with the lender. "The lower
the sample you requested [of the lender], the more likely it was that

---

[2] The thin files were given to Clayton, Bohan, and other contract underwriting firms by
the lenders selling the loans to the trading desk. They pertained mostly to stated-income
loans, but not always, according to different underwriters. One Clayton underwriter noted
that on one of the loans she reviewed, instead of a formal appraisal from a professional
appraisal firm there was a statement "from the borrower saying what he thought the
property was worth."

you'd win the bid," he said. Lenders like Aegis and First Franklin had so many Street firms interested in buying their subprime and alt-A mortgages they could tell potential suitors that if they wanted to win the bid for the loan pool they should agree to review just a fraction of the mortgages.

In early 2005 an executive from Washington Mutual visited Aegis in Houston. WaMu was warehousing Aegis and wanted to buy some of its loans, but one of its managers told the lender that WaMu insisted on reviewing 100 percent of the loans it was buying. The Aegis executive turned to him and said, "See that conference room? Bear Stearns is in there looking at some of our loans. They're only reviewing 20 percent. If they're comfortable reviewing 20 percent, you should be, too." The WaMu executive left Houston without a deal.

Over a two-year period Chamberlain underwrote hundreds of loans for Bear Stearns but never met its chairman and CEO, James Cayne. He also never met Cayne's top lieutenant (and presumed heir apparent), Warren Spector, co-president of the firm, nor Ralph Cioffi, senior managing director in charge of two Bear hedge funds, whose job it was to invest in bonds created from mortgages that Chamberlain reviewed on his laptop. Throughout its history in mortgages, which dated back to the mid-1980s, Bear Stearns prided itself on being one of the most astute risk managers in the business. Jess Lederman, a former managing director who worked for the firm during those early mortgage-backed security (MBS) years, described the company as having "tremendous disciplines." When it came to assessing trouble with the riskiest of certain financial instruments—especially mortgage-backed bonds—Bear was supposed to be among the best.

That said, just because Bear was supposed to be one of the best risk managers on Wall Street (a good risk manager is someone who can spot trouble a mile away), that didn't mean Bear wanted to actually employ a bunch of grunts who sat in a big conference room all day long look-ing at the loan files of the mortgages it was buying. "We were grunts—that's what we were," said one woman who worked on assignments for Clayton in the New Jersey area. Hiring and keeping hundreds of underwriters on the payroll would just result in the creation of more full-time equivalents (FTEs). As Richard Wilkes had pointed out, FTEs cost money—and more important, when it came to executive bonuses, FTEs were charged against revenues.

In the modern area of mortgage finance—one where Wall Street was in control of the nonprime sector—the idea was to keep the head count lean. If Bear Stearns was going to hire people to work in its mortgage department, it would much rather employ managing directors who could bring in mortgages through the trading desk—people like Mike Nierenberg and Jeff Verschleiser. The clerical work of actually reviewing the loans they were buying through the desk fell to contractors who worked for Clayton, The Bohan Group of San Francisco, or Opus Capital Markets of Chicago. It was the type of work that Carl Chamberlain and hundreds of others did. They were the grunts looking over the files. Over a three-year period the Carl Chamberlains of the world reviewed thousands upon thousands of mortgages bought through the trading desk of Bear Stearns.

Even though he'd had a bad experience at First Franklin, Chamberlain figured if he worked as a contract underwriter for a year or so he could latch on to a mortgage job in New York where he lived. After signing on at Clayton, the first thing he learned was that he wasn't working for Clayton at all. He was working for the PCI Group, an employment agency based in northern New Jersey. (Wall Street firms weren't the only ones concerned about FTEs.) " 'You work for us,' Clayton always told us, but PCI was the actual employer," Chamberlain said. "That was the name on the paycheck."

In 2006—the second busiest year ever for subprime lenders (and the Street firms buying their loans)—he spent six months, on and off, holed up in Orange County hotels, working in rented conference rooms with hundreds of other grunts, reviewing the loan files to make sure there was nothing wrong with the mortgages the Wall Street client had contracted to buy. He would fly into John Wayne Airport in Santa Ana (near Irvine), immediately report to the Hilton or Radisson, and be handed a laptop and a box of loan files. The goal: to review one loan an hour, assigning each a grade of one, two, or three. "My quota was one loan an hour," said Chamberlain. "If you can't do that, you won't get called again for work." Bill Holtz, a career underwriter who did some work for Clayton, seconded Chamberlain's assessment of the pressure they were under. "It was very common to hear one per hour or one every 45 minutes," he said. Holtz said the message from the supervisors boiled down to this: "'Don't reunderwrite the file, people. The borrowers are in the home and the electricity is on.'"

Each investment banker using Clayton or Bohan would give the contract underwriter a set of guidelines, contained in an Excel spreadsheet, to measure the loans against. "There are 600 pages in a guidebook," noted Chamberlain. "You don't have time to do it over."

A rating of a one or two meant the loan was good, and the Street firm would buy the mortgage. A three meant fail, with a recommendation not to buy. But sometimes Chamberlain's supervisor on the job would overrule his three ratings. "They would make it a one or delete your comments," he said. "There were compensating factors or CFs. If it does not meet [the investor's loan] guidelines you can say it's a two because it has CFs." When a reporter from *National Mortgage News* asked Chamberlain what a compensating factor might be, he laughed. In one case, a CF was granted because the borrower had been on the job 20 years and was applying for a loan where the debt-to-income ratio was too high. But his favorite CF was one where his supervisor granted an exception because the house had what he called "curb appeal." Chamberlain chuckled. "Curb appeal. Funny, a house doesn't pay the mortgage; the borrower does. So I never quite understood how this was reason enough to push the loan through."

Mortgages that received ratings of one or two from Clayton's grunts were bought without question. The idea, according to several contract underwriters interviewed by reporters Muolo and Padilla, was to pass as many loans as possible.

Over at Bohan, a top executive there told Padilla that some of the due diligence firm's Wall Street clients had a "history of overturning a lot our 'red Xs.'" A red X meant loan rejected, that the Street firm shouldn't buy it. "You need to keep volumes up," said the executive. "Originators were going public. There were large investors. Rates started rising. How do you keep volumes up? You get creative."

For all the work that the grunts were performing, Clayton and Bohan received about $150 per loan file. (The cost might vary, depending on how much the Street firm asked of Clayton.) The grunts, in turn, could earn $30 to $40 an hour. "You got a per diem of $40 per day for food, $80 on the weekends," he said. "That's what the 'rollers' did. Some of them were making $125,000 per year when you factored in the per diems."

Rolling, Chamberlain soon learned, was the practice of staying over on the weekend, instead of returning home and then coming back to Orange County on a Monday. During the boom most of that action was in Orange or the surrounding counties, thanks to the presence of Ameriquest, Argent, Accredited Home Lenders, Option One, Ownit, and New Century. The grunts working in the conference room lived all over the United States. "They were like the gypsies of the indus-try," he said. "It's cheaper to put you up in a hotel than fly you back home and out again. It's called 'rolling.'" (He also mentioned there was "hanky-panky" going on in those hotel rooms, adding, "That's what happens when you live in hotels.")

Sometimes, Chamberlain would roll over, whereas other times he'd fly back to New York. On the job he met all sorts of fellow laptop grunts and fellow industry gypsies, most of whom didn't have much mortgage experience. It wasn't exactly a young person's game, either. He met retired schoolteachers, single mothers, people look-ing to change careers, workers with only high school degrees, college graduates. "I don't mean to sound mean," said Chamberlain, "but some were lacking when it came to intelligence. On a refi versus a 'cash-out' refi they'd ask, 'What's a cash-out?'" Holtz said some of the under-writers he worked with were on their "second or third marriage" and had a tendency to drink too much. He was even less charitable than Chamberlain: "They were just plain broken in spirit and body. I didn't really fit the part. I don't drink and I'm happily married."

Before setting its grunts loose on a box of loan files, Clayton put them through a two-week training course. The number of loans the grunts would review could be as few as 800 or as many as 8,000. The number varied depending on the size of the loan pool the Street firm was buying. The grunts answered to a lead supervisor. Some of the leads, unlike the contract clerks (the grunts), worked directly for Clayton. The lead interfaced with a transaction manager (TM) who also worked for Clayton. It was the transaction manager's responsibility to work with the Wall Street client, who also had a TM on the job. "If Bear had won the bid for the loan pool, the TM would be a vice presi-dent from Bear Stearns," said Chamberlain.

On large loan pools totaling hundreds of millions of dollars, at least 100 grunts would be working in a hotel conference room, trying to keep up with the quota of reviewing one loan an hour. "You might work past midnight sometimes, which was ridiculous because by that time your brain was mush," said Chamberlain. "As an underwriter I would point out stuff to the leads. They would basically tell you to keep your mouth shut. 'Make it pass,' I was told by a Clayton lead."

Holtz said the leads played a key role in making loans better than they were. "Leads or the QC [quality control] staff would just delete your comments and change the grade to say a '2' with compensating factors. Clayton didn't want to pass off the lenders or the investor/client. They were making money from all sides of the deal."

When Chamberlain went through Clayton's two-week training course, one of the first things he was told by his instructor was never to use the "f-word." *Fraud* was the f-word, he said. "*Fraud*—don't ever say that word."

Eileen Loiacono, a contract underwriter who worked at Bohan, remembered that her supervisor (a former nurse with one year's experience in underwriting) argued repeatedly with her that fraud could not be proven so the word should not be used, and overturned Loiacono's objections. The former nurse was married to an operations manager at Bohan. Once she was put in charge, the former nurse hired her best friend as an underwriter, said Loiacono. "Subprime loans flooded the market," she said. "Bohan didn't have enough people, so they grabbed them from anywhere."

Disgusted by what she saw, Loiacono left Bohan in 2007. "This whole subprime thing has left such a vile taste in my mouth," she said. "I was not allowed to do my job properly." Her new chosen profession? "I'm going to work for a health insurance company."

As for the leads who oversaw workers like Chamberlain and Loiacono, they were the managers in charge of the underwriting job. They were in charge of the grunts, holding a metaphorical whip over them. A grunt working for Bohan told the reporters that some leads "used bad language to try to control the contractors—such things as standing up on tables, telling them, 'If you don't get your fucking act together and get this job done, I will send each and every one of you home tomorrow.'"

Leads, as Chamberlain and grunts working for Bohan said, were paid bonuses for finishing underwriting jobs early. Job turnover among the grunts was a problem. Wall Street was buying so many loans that many contractor underwriters realized if things didn't work out at Bohan they could move over to Clayton or Opus, which offered the exact same services to Bear Stearns, Merrill Lynch, and the others. According to Loiacono, at one point Bohan's web site boasted that its underwriters (the grunts) each had five to seven years of underwriting experience. She highly questioned those numbers.[3]

Over at Clayton, Chamberlain came away none too impressed with the two-week training course it gave the grunts. "It wasn't formal training," he said. "Clayton does train but offers no type of certification. There is no recognition by a trade organization." Quality control supervisors also took a two-week training course "even if they'd never been in the business before," he said. Still, Chamberlain kept working as an underwriter because the money was good and he hoped for a valued job on a Wall Street trading desk.

But there was one lead in particular he wasn't crazy about (Chamberlain would only identify him as "G"), who had joined Clayton after serving as a manager at Wal-Mart. For some reason, he said, Bear Stearns always requested "G." "He pushed everything through," said Chamberlain. "He was chummy with the Bear people. He called them a lot." As to who "G" spoke to at Bear, he had no idea. For whatever reason, Bear Stearns always wanted him on their jobs.

One former managing director who worked at Bear said, "Bear didn't really care about quality. They wanted volume." But Clayton was hardly an innocent party, said the managing director. "They told the client [Bear] what they wanted to hear."

But Bear knew that the loans that Clayton was looking at would wind up in the subprime bonds it would be issuing. Neil Spagna, the former investment banker who also worked at Clayton, remembered, "Since Clayton underwrote the loans, we'd be asked to talk to the investors who were buying their ABS bonds."

★   ★   ★

---

[3] By the spring of 2008 Bohan's web site boasted that its underwriters have 10-plus years of experience.

For most of the 1990s, if you asked a mortgage banking executive who the go-to guy at Bear Stearns was in regard to mortgages, the answer, nine times out of 10, would be Warren Spector. He wasn't exactly a household name on Wall Street, but he had quietly risen in the ranks at Bear, spending almost his entire career at the firm. He grew up in suburban Bethesda, Maryland, a few miles from Washington. He attended Princeton University in the late 1970s, then transferred to St. John's College. According to Dan Phillips, who founded First Plus, the high loan-to-value (LTV) ratio lender, Spector was so studious that as a child he went to math camp during the summer while other children were playing sports.

During his junior year at St. John's, Spector wrote to Alan "Ace" Greenberg, then a managing partner at Bear Stearns,[4] asking for a summer job. According to a report in the *Wall Street Journal*, Spector was offered a summer position at the firm but then turned it down, saying he couldn't afford to live in Manhattan on $125 a week. After graduating from business school he once again asked Greenberg,[5] who had ascended to the CEO slot, for a job, and this time accepted when a position was offered. He spent time on the government bond trading desk and then moved over to the mortgage desk where he, as well as others, made their mark by establishing Bear's research credentials— especially in MBSs. Bear, like Salomon Brothers, was known as a fixed-income shop, and fixed income, of course, meant mortgage bonds—the hottest product on the Street in the 1980s.

Jess Lederman, who worked as a managing partner at Bear during that era, remembered, "There was a lot of analytic brainpower at the firm during that time. There was Chuck Ramsey, who did spread analysis on mortgage pools." Bear, along with Salomon, was among the first Wall Street firms to carefully analyze all the underlying mortgages in the MBSs

---

[4] Bear Stearns went public in 1987. Up until then, the privately held firm had managing partners who shared in the investment bank's yearly profits. As a publicly traded company, the title "managing director" replaced "managing partner."

[5] Greenberg worked on Wall Street for 50 years and is credited with turning Bear Stearns into an investment banking powerhouse. But he wasn't without his quirks. Among the legendary things he said was this: "I will fire you if you so much as throw out a paper clip." Under Greenberg, Bear's bond and mortgage traders had a reputation—deserved or not—for being among the best in the business. "His sales force was second to none," said Jonas Roth, a former national sales manager for trading at Countrywide.

they were trading with an eye toward how quickly the bonds would pre-pay. An investor who had a good idea how long the bonds might stick around had an advantage over buyers—and sellers—on the other side of the trade who didn't have access to this research. "Bear was extra aggressive when it came to extreme analytics," said Lederman.

Among the whiz kids working on Bear's calculations was Spector, the math camp veteran. (As Lew Ranieri had once observed, "Mortgages are about math.") With Bear establishing itself as a force in MBS research and trading, Spector moved up in the ranks and became a managing director. He also had become somewhat close with Bear's new CEO, James "Jimmy" Cayne. Among other things, the two men shared an affinity for both golf and bridge. (Ace Greenberg was also a bridge devotee.) Both Spector and Cayne were tournament-quality players. (Cayne was a bit better—he was a champion on the U.S. National Bridge Team.) Spector had once told a reporter, "Bridge is a game of drawing conclusions from incomplete information. What doesn't happen is as important as what does." Such a description might also apply to bond trading. (However, when Spector was socializing with Dan Phillips at his homes both in New York and on Martha's Vineyard, the card game of choice was poker.)

As a managing director, Spector was put in charge of all fixed-income instruments, including mortgage bonds. One managing director who worked with him offered this praise: "Warren knew what was in every tranche." How he rose to head the fixed-income department is a matter of some conjecture. His predecessor was a managing director named John Sites. Because he was close with Cayne (never underestimate the bonds of bridge players), supposedly, Spector played a central role in the firm pushing Sites to the side so he could have his job. "Warren made a few enemies on that one," said one co-worker. (It wouldn't the first or last time a senior executive lost his or her job based on personal ties.)

Spector became head of the department just as the subprime boom of 1994 to 1998 was cresting. On a daily basis he was overseeing $10 billion in bond trades a day. He, as well as other managing directors at Bear, was well aware that one of the best ways to convince non-bank subprime (and high-LTV) lenders to sell their mortgages to the firm was to offer other services as well—like warehouse lines of credit.

Bear's financial institution group (FIG), which concentrated on raising equity and offering other traditional banking-related services to mortgage lenders, was run separately from the trading desks. (At some Wall Street firms, that's not always the case.)

Even though Spector didn't directly oversee the mortgage trading desk, he knew its value to the fixed-income group. "He wasn't directly involved in MBS but he negotiated the credit lines," said Phillips. He also would frequently socialize with some of the firm's clients, such as Phillips, a practice that led some to believe that he very well might have been privately anointed by Cayne to one day be his successor. "Warren," said a former Bear trader, "put on the charm offensive with Jimmy."

One California mortgage banker remembered being flown to Las Vegas in early 1998 by Phillips to attend what he called a "Frank Sinatra memorial tribute" at the MGM Grand. "Frank's kid was running the orchestra," said the executive. "Paul Anka and a few singers from the Fifth Dimension were performing. At the table right next to mine was [Robert] DeNiro. I also met Spector and Kevin Ingram[6] from Deutsche Bank. Phillips had flown them all in for the event." The little math genius from Bethesda had come a long way. By then Spector, known for wearing oversized horn-rimmed glasses, was married to Margaret Whitton, an actress who had a supporting role in the steamy movie *9½ Weeks* starring actor Mickey Rourke.

★ ★ ★

---

[6] Back in 1998 Ingram was in charge of Deutsche Bank's mortgage trading desk in New York. Deutsche Bank was also a warehouse lender to Phillips's First Plus, a high-LTV lender that was dabbling in subprime as well. Sometimes featured in the pages of *Black Enterprise* magazine, Ingram, an African-American, was known for wearing black leather pants, throwing lavish parties, and showering his girlfriends with expensive gifts. He got the heave-ho from Deutsche Bank when the subprime market began to crater in the fall of 1998. In 2001 he was indicted on money laundering charges in connection with a plot to sell illegal weapons to foreign entities that might have ties to terrorist organizations. Ingram pleaded guilty to money laundering charges after cutting a deal where he testified against two New Jersey men, Diaa Moshen and Mohammed Rajaa Malik. He served 18 months in prison and was released in 2004. He also worked as a bond trader for Goldman Sachs, and according to *Black Enterprise* was mentored by Goldman Sachs chief Jon Corzine, who was elected to the U.S. Senate and then became governor of New Jersey. One mortgage executive who did business with Ingram when he was at Deutsche Bank described him as "a short, stocky black man working for a German bank. He stuck out."

By the mid–1990s there was only one major Wall Street firm that actually owned a subprime lender—Bear Stearns. Bear had launched EMC Mortgage earlier in the decade to buy delinquent loans (at bargain basement prices) from the Resolution Trust Corporation, a special government agency chartered by Congress to liquidate $300 billion in commercial and residential assets owned by failed S&Ls. The inventory included both loans and real estate (not to mention a few billion dollars' worth of junk bonds sold to thrifts by Drexel Burnham Lambert and Michael Milken). During its early days, EMC was a servicing company only, meaning it tried to bring delinquent loans current by working with borrowers to restructure their payments. If a loan workout wasn't possible, the next step would be to foreclose, take over the property, and then resell it—at a much higher price, it was hoped, than what Bear had paid for the delinquent loan. The company was started from scratch (de novo) and headquartered in Texas because, as one Bear official said, "They didn't want to put it in New York because of the taxes they'd have to pay there, plus no one puts a servicing operation in an expensive place like New York anyway."[7]

Ed Raice was an accountant by training who came out of Bear's back office to manage EMC. To those who knew him, the last thing in the world Raice wanted to do was relocate to Irving, Texas, near the I-30 corridor, a strip of highway made infamous during the S&L crisis because of all the failed townhouse and condo developments alongside it. (Many of the condo units were never completed. One U.S. attorney who saw the poured concrete foundations that had never been built upon called the slabs "Martian landing pads.") Raice was not leaving New York for Irving.

"Ed did not live in Texas," said a friend at the firm. "He didn't want to move to Texas. He didn't want anything to do with Texas. He stayed in New York and ran the thing from there. He never went to Texas unless he really had to."

The S&L crisis did not last forever, and by 1996 Bear, gingerly, started using the company to originate subprime loans—but only through loan brokers and small mortgage banking firms called "correspondent

---

[7] The servicing operations of most mortgage companies are usually housed in suburban or rural areas where office space and housing costs are cheap. Over the past five years some functions have even been outsourced to India. Rarely is a major servicing operation located in a major city.

lenders." By then Neil Spagna had left Kidder Peabody, whose trading desk had been competing against Bear's, and had gone to work for Clayton—which began analyzing loan files for EMC. Back then, said Spagna, Clayton was reviewing 100 percent of the subprime loan files that Bear was buying from lenders. "By 1996 Bear was huge in subprime," he said. "EMC would buy bulk loan packages from Option One and New Century." In New York, Bear had set up conduits (legal entities) to buy mortgages from other subprime lenders as well. It had taken First Plus public and was securitizing its loans. Then the bottom fell out of the subprime market in the fall of 1998. By mid-1999 First Plus was bankrupt and Phillips's days of traveling to New York to play poker with Spector and Dan Marino were over.

EMC and Bear were left (more or less) unscathed by the subprime mess of 1998–1999. Unlike lenders like First Plus, The Money Store, ContiMortgage, and others, EMC was smart enough to avoid the phony-baloney machinations of gain-on-sale accounting in regard to its bonds. When dozens of subprime lenders went bust during those years, Raice and the folks at Bear realized that when the business returned it would leave less competition and more opportunity for EMC. "Ed understood the loan business," said Spagna. "He knew the risks and pitfalls. He also knew that to be in this business you had to grow it—you had to be aggressive."

★　★　★

Ralph Cioffi of South Burlington, Vermont, was a product of Catholic schools—first Rice Memorial High School and then St. Michael's of Colchester. He was a running back, fullback, and offensive guard at Rice. When he attended college he concentrated on bodybuilding and had a reputation as being quiet and not very outspoken, according to a report by Bloomberg. He graduated in 1978 with a business degree. By 1985 he was working for Bear Stearns in its Chicago office as a bond salesman in mortgages, where he got noticed "because he was a salesman who knew the product and he was smarter than most salesmen," said one colleague. Among the traditional Street firms, Bear had one of the lowest turnover rates among its executives and managing directors. Under both Greenberg and Cayne the firm liked to reward smart, hardworking young managers. Like Spector, he moved up in the organization, became a managing director in 1996, and found himself working in the fixed-income side of the business (bonds) in New York under Spector.

By 2003 Spector was now co-president of the company, and many assumed that Cayne, who was then 69, had placed his bridge-playing friend at the top of the short list to succeed him. By this time the subprime residential business had indeed recovered, and Bear, thanks to its trading desk and EMC, was among the top issuers of subprime ABS securities. In 2003 Wall Street firms had purchased and issued $233 billion in subprime bonds—almost twice what it had the year before. With Fannie Mae and Freddie Mac ailing from their respective accounting scandals, the nongovernment business looked wide open.[8] Cioffi approached the firm's top executives—including Cayne and Spector—about starting a Bear-sponsored hedge fund to invest in subprime bonds, including ABSs and CDOs. He received their blessing, and in March of that year the High Grade Structured Credit Strategies Fund was born. The name of the fund was a mouthful to say. Internally, it was referred to as the High Grade fund, which was somewhat ironic given that it was investing in bonds backed by people whose credit was anything but high grade.

And that's where Clayton and Bohan and grunts like Carl Chamberlain and Eileen Loiacono came in. It was their job to review the mortgages that Bear was buying from Aegis, Ownit, First Franklin, and the rest of the industry to make sure they wouldn't blow up down the road. But the last place you would find Jimmy Cayne, Warren Spector, and Ralph Cioffi was in the conference room of an Orange County hotel, looking at the raw product of what they'd be securitizing and putting into bonds. Based on what the High Grade fund was returning for its investors it might be argued: Why should they bother? According to a report on the wire service Bloomberg, Cioffi's High Grade fund supposedly returned 46.8 percent from October 2003 to early 2007.

---

[8] During the 1980s General Electric's financial services unit in Stamford, Connecticut, had talked to a handful of Wall Street firms about starting an "A" paper conduit that would compete against Fannie Mae and Freddie Mac. However, the idea was shot down because all the parties involved believed that the government charter of the two allowed them to borrow money more cheaply in the capital markets. In other words, no matter how well GE might run its "A" paper conduit, the quarter- to half-point borrowing advantage of Fannie and Freddie would put it at a competitive disadvantage.

Of course, hardly anyone at the firm, unless they worked for Cioffi, could tell you exactly what type of subprime assets were in the High Grade fund. But that was sort of the point. Hedge funds are private, and even though Bear Stearns was a publicly traded company with an 85-year history behind it, it wasn't obligated to disclose a whole lot about the High Grade fund—except of course to its investors, who included some of its own senior managing directors, among them Cioffi. Part of the reason it didn't have to disclose anything about itself to the public was that as a legal matter the hedge fund was headquartered in the Cayman Islands, whose secrecy laws are legendary. (Court documents later revealed that its "unaffiliated directors," meaning no Bear Stearns or related personnel, were based in Ireland and then later on the Caymans. No individual names were revealed.)

What also was legendary was the fund's rate of return (and Cioffi's reputation as its manager). William Burrell, a regional manager for Bear in California, never met Cioffi while he was at the firm but described his reputation as being "the magician." The magician, according to Burrell, "lived in a black box where no one evaluated him. And that's because he was the one who understood these weird arbitrages with option vehicles where he was leveraged 30 to 1, but as long as his returns were good it didn't matter."

Burrell knew one thing, though: that Cioffi's delinquency models assumed that subprime loans would not go bad at a rate of more than 1.5 percent. In 2006 those models were thrown out of whack when subprime delinquency rates began to creep up and a chorus of concern about the United States possibly being in the early stages of a housing bubble grew louder. In April of that year a little-known lender called Acoustic Home Loans was forced to close its doors after two of its Wall Street warehouse lenders—Bear Stearns and Merrill Lynch—asked Acoustic to buy back a few million dollars' worth of delinquent subprime loans. The story made the front page of *National Mortgage News* but got little play elsewhere. However, Acoustic was the first subprime lender to fail because of loan buyback requests from Wall Street firms. Acoustic was yet one more subprime lender based in Orange County. Its CEO was Frank Curry, who had cut his teeth on subprime lending at Long Beach Mortgage, Roland Arnall's company.

Even though the public had no idea what Cioffi's hedge fund was investing in (why should they care, really—hedge funds were for rich investors only), court documents would later provide a glimpse of the "high grade" bets he was making with the $930 million of investors' money. Management of the fund was housed under Bear Stearns Asset Management (BSAM for short), which Warren Spector oversaw. Cioffi was using the millions raised and borrowing even more money to buy not only subprime ABSs and CDOs, but credit default swaps, interest rate swaps, futures, options, and even positions on currencies. All of these investments were bets (for lack of a better word) that the subprime residential business would stay on an even keel and that home prices would not collapse. Cioffi and his management team at the fund—which included Bear managing director Matthew Tannin and vice president Joanmarie Pusateri—were using derivatives that paid off like insurance policies—that is, as long as the subprime market stayed healthy. Downtown at Deutsche Bank, Greg Lippmann, managing director in charge of global trading for ABSs and CDOs, was betting the opposite by shorting the ABX index. Lippmann's bet was now the better of the two.

In the fall of 2006, Cioffi's bets on subprime began to lose money. That year BSAM, which Spector oversaw, also signed off on the creation of two more hedge funds. Not only was Bear an investor in the funds, but so was the London-based Barclays Bank, which also was lending money to the High Grade fund. In April 2006 Tannin shot off an e-mail to two Barclays executives, Ram Rao and Edward Ware, assuring them that things were well: "I don't want to sound like a broken record but the value of this transaction lies in the transparency of credit information on high underlying credit quality assets." Those underlying assets would be the ones the grunts at Clayton and Bohan were jamming through the system at the rate of one an hour.

Just because Bear had taken in $930 million of investors' money and another $600 million on the second subprime hedge fund created by Cioffi, that doesn't mean its total exposure was $1.530 billion. Reports varied, but the two largest subprime funds under Cioffi's management had investments (bets) totaling anywhere from $10 billion to $40 billion. In the spring of 2007 when word leaked out that the funds were losing money, Bear promised to lend the funds $1.6 billion. But the pledge hardly stabilized matters. As it turned out, Merrill Lynch had lent the funds $850 million and, nervous that it might lose money, made a margin call on Bear. (In the world of investment banking, a margin call translates into: "Give us more money.") Merrill officials gave Bear a couple of days to pony up more money, then took control of its collateral—$850 million worth of subprime bonds. Merrill immediately sold the bonds, a company spokeswoman telling reporters that they were "not unhappy" with what they'd received for the bonds—which they wouldn't disclose.

Not only was Merrill margin-calling subprime lenders, but it was now margin-calling a subprime hedge fund managed by one of its fiercest competitors. Investment bankers who worked in mortgages began to view the drama between the two firms with some amusement. "I think it's fascinating when you have one Wall Street firm go after another," said a former Bear executive who managed his own investment company in Manhattan. "I've never seen one dealer seize another dealer's assets like that."

A few months before Merrill seized its bonds, Bear had actually filed an S-1 statement with the Securities and Exchange Commission to take public a company called Everquest Financial. Everquest's co-CEOs were Cioffi and a former Morgan Stanley and Smith Barney executive named Michael J. Levitt. In the filing, Bear, the only underwriter on the deal, bragged about the "strong track record of our managers" (Cioffi and Levitt) and "attractive opportunities" in the CDO market. Nowhere in the filing was anything mentioned about the troubles facing Cioffi's hedge funds. It just so happened that Everquest's portfolio included $720 million in CDOs, two-thirds of which had been purchased from Bear's BSAM unit, which was under Spector (and included Cioffi).

In the midst of all this, Bear also bought a nonbank subprime company called Encore Credit, based (of course) in subprime central: Irvine of Orange County. Encore was yet one more subprime firm started by an executive who used to work for Roland Arnall—in this case Steve Holder, who also helped start New Century. Two years earlier, Encore's parent company, ECC Capital, had gone public through Friedman Billings Ramsey, raising $354 million. (It was another Eric Billings REIT deal.) Bear was one of Encore's warehouse lenders. In the fall of 2006 Bear agreed to pay a fraction of its initial public offering (IPO) price—just $26 million—for the company. Why? Because Encore had sold Bear millions of dollars in mortgages that were now delinquent. When asked about all the loan buyback requests between Encore and Bear, Renu Aldridge, a Bear spokeswoman, told *National Mortgage*

News that "those problems are in the past." Maybe so, but Bear was now forcing buybacks on so many lenders that one joke making the rounds in the industry was that Bear didn't actually buy loans, "it rented them."

Even though Bear had EMC, it felt confident enough about the future of subprime that, like Merrill, it wanted to assure its trading desk (and Cioffi's hedge funds) a steady flow of product from another friendly source—Encore. (Ed Raice, the head of EMC, had left the company about three years earlier in a contract dispute. One investment banker who worked with Raice described the situation: "Ed thought he was the smartest guy in the world. He asked Bear for $10 million [a year]. They said, 'How about $6 million?' He said no and walked.")[9] When Bear finally closed on its purchase of Encore in February of 2007, it no longer had to worry about giving its shareholders any money. Encore had so many unfilled loan buyback requests from Bear that the nonbank wound up paying Bear $7 million to take the lender off its hands. (Some investment bankers were calling it an "anti-purchase," because the new owner was actually getting paid to take over the company.)

By the beginning of the summer the hedge funds were on the verge of collapse. Bear wasn't saying how much the funds had lost, but the sub-prime industry was going in the exact opposite direction from what Cioffi had bet on. Investors wanted their money back. Bear, though, wasn't telling reporters anything about the funds—and the media (as well as the public) couldn't really figure out what was in them, because they were based in the Caymans. The *New York Times* focused one of its stories on BSAM executive Richard Marin, noting that during one weekend while Bear was trying to salvage the hedge funds the executive was busy adding to his personal Internet blog, which he had dubbed "Whim of Iron." Marin had blogged about how he "stole away" from the "crisis-hedge-fund-salvation-workaholic weekend" to take in the new Kevin Costner murder thriller *Mr. Brooks*. His recommendation: skip it. (The blog embarrassed Bear, which strongly encouraged Marin to block access to it.)

In late July, after haggling with other lenders (including Barclays), Bear threw both funds into bankruptcy, disclosing that the newer fund, the one called "Enhanced," was worthless. In the weeks preceding

---

[9] Raice, like many Bear (and ex-Bear) officials contacted by co-author Paul Muolo, declined to comment about anything having to do with Bear or EMC.

the crisis, the investment banking arm of JPMorgan Chase, another lender to the funds, had at least one conversation with Spector, urging Bear to lend more money to the funds. According to the *Wall Street Journal*, Spector told the JPMorgan executives that they were "naive," reminding them of Bear's expertise in the mortgage business. Later that evening JPMorgan sent a lawyer to Bear's midtown headquarters, armed with an official default letter. Like Merrill, JPMorgan wanted its money back. The newspaper also noted that Spector, with the hedge funds' future hanging in the balance, had spent several days in Nashville playing in a national bridge tournament, as did Cayne.

On Wednesday morning, August 1, a day or so after the funds' bankruptcy filing, Cayne called Spector into his sixth-floor office. Bear's share price had fallen almost 30 percent since June. Not only had the hedge funds collapsed, costing investors (including several managing directors at the company) hundreds of millions, perhaps billions, but Bear itself, a firm that had built its reputation on its analytical ability and sound risk management practices, was looking at potential losses totaling billions because the firm, too, had bought subprime CDOs for its own account. Cayne, who was more or less forced to talk to the media about the hedge fund debacle, said the firm had suffered a "body blow of massive proportion." In Cayne's view, Spector was at least partly responsible. Even though he wasn't the one making the trades for the hedge funds, he was ultimately responsible for BSAM—and for what Cioffi had done. The 73-year-old Cayne asked for Spector's resignation.

A friend of Spector's described him as "devastated," adding, "You have to realize—Warren grew up at the company." Spector, who was 49, had spent his entire 24-year career at Bear, starting out in government bonds and then mortgages—a product that was now the reason for his demise. (Even though he was devastated, his severance package was $23 million, money that would help heal his psychic wounds.) Friends came to his defense, portraying him as the fall guy for Cioffi's mistakes, but not all of his colleagues were sympathetic. "Warren is not a hands-off boss," said one. "You don't fool Warren."

A trader who was close to Spector, though, said that he had warned him about what he called the "cascading risk" the hedge funds were taking on. "Warren had taken his eye off the ball." The "cascading risk" comment was a reference to all the trades Cioffi was making on the hedge funds' behalf. Cioffi, though, was not fired along with Spector, but the firm was now saying little about exactly what he was doing for Bear. The firm couldn't afford to get rid of Cioffi, at least not right away, because he was the manager of the two funds—the one making all the trades on their behalf. (Cioffi was also carrying the title of co-CEO of Everquest, whose IPO was now deader than dead and whose future was in doubt.)

A few months later, Massachusetts sued Bear Stearns Asset Management, accusing Cioffi of making hundreds of trades on behalf of the hedge fund without receiving the approval of the fund's independent directors.[10] In 2003 when he first convinced Bear's board to let him start the High Grade fund, 20 percent of his trades had not been signed off by the directors. By 2006 the number was markedly higher—80 percent didn't have prior approval. By November it was common knowledge that the U.S. attorney's office down on Foley Square was now taking an interest in the two funds.[11] If a U.S. attorney was looking at the hedge funds, that meant it was now possibly a criminal matter. Apparently Cioffi, according to one lawsuit, had been making "optimistic forecasts" about the hedge funds even though he had withdrawn "millions of dollars" of his own money from one in February and March of 2007. Supposedly, the reason Spector got the boot so soon after the funds' collapse was that so many senior managing directors at Bear had invested their own personal money in Cioffi's creation. Arturo Cifuentes, the CDO expert who used to work at Wachovia, said he counted among his friends "a few top" Bear Stearns executives who did just that. "I can say this," he told reporter Paul Muolo. "I know they bought into those funds with their own money." He laughed. "You might say that they bought their own shit."

In December Cioffi resigned from Bear, *resigned* perhaps being the official word for fired. He remained as a consultant to the firm as Bear began to sift through the funds' bankruptcy and all the related lawsuits from investors who had seen their millions evaporate. Cayne announced

---

[10] Massachusetts staff attorney Michael Regan would only say that 10 to 15 individuals, family trusts, or partnerships located in the state had been investors in the High Grade fund.

[11] Bear disclosed that the hedge funds were the subject of a criminal investigation in an October 10, 2007, filing with the Securities and Exchange Commission.

his retirement as CEO in January but remained as chairman. A few weeks earlier Bear disclosed an $850 million loss for the fourth quarter, adding that it had to write down its mortgage investments (the hedge funds) and other ABSs that it couldn't off-load to investors by almost $2 billion. Alan Schwartz, a veteran in the firm's mergers and acquisitions (M&A) group, was named the new CEO. Historically, roughly 30 percent of Bear's revenue had been tied to mortgages in some fashion or other. "Does Schwartz have any mortgage experience?" asked one Bear shareholder, laughing. "Not even a little." One of Schwartz's first decisions as the firm's new CEO was to shut down Encore. As for Bear, the market wasn't quite done with it. The next few months would decide its future.

As for Carl Chamberlain, the grunt who had been working for Clayton, reviewing subprime loans that Bear and other Street firms purchased, in late 2006 he finally landed his dream job with a mortgage trading desk of a foreign bank. (He named the firm but didn't want it publicized.) The bank decided to close the desk the next summer just as Cioffi's hedge funds collapsed.

Chapter 11

Armageddon Times

The Tan Man Departs, Bye-Bye Bear

> *This is Armageddon.*
> —CNBC STOCK PICKER JIM CRAMER, TALKING
> ABOUT THE GROWING CREDIT CRISIS
> IN THE SUMMER OF 2007

O n June 8, 2004, Angelo Mozilo stood at the podium of the National Building Museum in the heart of Washington a few blocks from the National Mall. His wife Phyllis and some of his grandchildren were in attendance to see him receive a lifetime achievement award from the National Housing Conference, a 75-year-old nonprofit group whose mission for most of its life was to promote affordable housing through lobbying. For several years running, Countrywide had been the largest originator of home mortgages to minorities, a notable achievement. Politicians and regulators were on hand as well. Before Mozilo rose to speak in the cavernous building, some of his best friends in the industry made testimonials about his rise from the streets of the Bronx to create Countrywide, a lender that helped to house millions of Americans over four decades, earning billions of dollars in the process and making its shareholders—including Mozilo, his family, and all his top executives—wealthy.

Lewie Ranieri told the audience of 200 or so how Angelo was one of the few who would listen to his "crazy ideas" when he was a young bond trader at Salomon, toying with early versions of the mortgage-backed security (MBS). Jim Johnson, the former Fannie Mae chairman and CEO, made glowing comments about Angelo's business acumen and work ethic; and Howard Levine, a commercial mortgage banking executive who was one of his best friends, cracked jokes about Angelo's love for tailored shirts and custom-made suits. (Levine also joked how Mozilo had fired him a few times.) When Mozilo stood up to thank the audience for their kind words and jokes, three F-18 fighter jets flew overhead—as though on cue. Their roar could be heard throughout the building, the jets' silver wings outstretched, visible through the skylights above, stark against a late afternoon blue sky. But the F-18s weren't there for Mozilo's anointing by the National Housing Conference. It just happened to be the day that the casket of former president Ronald Reagan was being wheeled down Pennsylvania Avenue before it came to lie in state in the Capitol rotunda. The F-18s were flying in formation for the 40th president of the United States. But Mozilo had been in the right place at the right time. It would be hard for him not to think of it as a beautiful moment.

Two years later in the fall, the *American Banker*, a 100-year-old daily newspaper that was the *Wall Street Journal* of the financial services industry, bestowed upon Mozilo its lifetime achievement award.[1] In a special issue, the newspaper recapped the highlights of his career, accompanied by a photo spread featuring Mozilo decked out in casual fall clothes looking very much like a man who knew how to dress in season. A few months after that Mozilo began working with a free-lance writer on his autobiography. Several interviews were done and shown to a literary agent. It was to be his life story—a tale of how the grandson of immigrants rose from the streets of New York to create the largest home lender in the history of the world. It would be

---

[1] In late 2007 when Countrywide's problems worsened even more, one *American Banker* editor in Washington would occasionally joke, "I'm so glad we gave him that lifetime achievement award. I wonder if we can take it back." *American Banker* and *National Mortgage News*, as of late 2009, were owned by SourceMedia.

his story, capping a 40-year career. And then he would (presumably) retire. But in July of 2007 Mozilo, without explanation, pulled the plug on the project. Then in mid-August Merrill Lynch analyst Ken Bruce issued his report entitled "Liquidity Is the Achilles Heel," suggesting that Countrywide might even go bankrupt.

The $2 billion investment that Countrywide received from Ken Lewis and Bank of America on August 22 looked, initially, like a steal ($2 billion for 16 percent of a company that was recently worth $40 billion). What Lewis didn't know was that earlier in the year Mozilo had been holding private talks with Sandler O'Neill chief James "Jimmy" Dunne about Countrywide buying the boutique investment banker. Besides offering stock research, Sandler O'Neill was trying to make its mark in initial public offerings (IPOs), private and public equity placements, and mergers and acquisitions (M&A) work. In the spring Mozilo had told *National Mortgage News* that he was in the hunt for a "broker/dealer," but didn't let on it was Sandler O'Neill, where Mike McMahon used to work.

Mozilo and Dunne belonged to the same golf club, the Quarry. Plus, Sandler O'Neill now employed Brian Sterling, a former top executive at Merrill Lynch who had managed the Countrywide account for the investment banking firm. (When Stan O'Neal took control of Merrill, Sterling was one of thousands who lost their jobs in his housecleaning effort to streamline management.) If Countrywide had bought Sandler O'Neill—which had been founded by Herman Sandler,[2] a former top executive at Bear Stearns—it would have put him in a business he had once loathed: Wall Street (though it can be argued that through its capital markets group, which securitized subprime and nonconforming mortgages, Countrywide already was, in part, an investment banking firm).

By the early fall of 2007 Mozilo had other problems to worry about. Ken Lewis and Bank of America had stepped in and calmed investors' fears (and the fears of JPMorgan's Jamie Dimon) about Countrywide's cash position, but there were other concerns in the marketplace.

---

[2] Company founder Herman Sandler lost his life along with 65 other employees in the terrorist attacks of September 11, 2001. Sandler O'Neill had its headquarters in the Twin Towers of the World Trade Center.

The 50-year pattern of home prices going up (on a national average) had reversed. Now prices were going down and it didn't look like the trend was about to abate any time soon. Late payments on all types of mortgages—"A" paper loans sold to Fannie Mae and Freddie Mac as well as subprime loans—were rising. After the Bank of America announcement, Countrywide's stock rose a few points but then began to drift down again. The two Bear hedge funds started by Ralph Cioffi were wrangling with creditors in bankruptcy court in the Caymans, and the general media were beginning to jump on the "subprime contagion" story with a vengeance. The *Wall Street Journal* and the *New York Times* had, combined, at least 20 reporters (counting their wire services) working on various mortgage-related stories.

Even though Treasury secretary Henry Paulson (on behalf of the Bush White House) was trying to reassure world financial markets that the country's worsening subprime crisis was contained, it didn't exactly look that way. Over in the United Kingdom, Northern Rock, a large mortgage lender headquartered in Newcastle in northeast England, was the subject of depositor runs after rumors began to spread that its bankers would no longer lend money to the company. Northern Rock's specialty was lending English home buyers up to 125 percent of the value of their homes—just like First Plus had done in the United States the decade before. To boot, Northern Rock, a top 10 lender in the U.K., resembled Countrywide in that it was both a depository and a borrower of warehouse lines from other banks. Its bank lenders, after seeing what had happened to both Countrywide and the two Bear Stearns hedge funds, suddenly had become skittish about extending more loans to it. (This was also around the time CNBC stock picker Jim Cramer was hopping around the set describing the situation as "Armageddon.")

Mike McMahon, who had left Sandler O'Neill the year before, looked at the situation and Ken Bruce's "sell" rating on Countrywide and wondered whether Countrywide was going to make it—and he had been a longtime fan of both the company and Mozilo. "Ken Bruce's 'sell' rating was right on," he told a reporter. McMahon—who on occasion had referred to Mozilo as "The Tan Man" (in a kind way)—noted that the "sell" rating made by his former intern was not made lightly. "It had to be approved by a supervisory analyst—one person or a committee of people." He also noted that by issuing the "sell" rating on Countrywide, "Merrill was kissing off" any potential business it might be doing for Mozilo's company in the future, including debt and equity offerings. "By Bruce issuing that report, they were going to lose business," said McMahon. (Bruce's "sell" rating also fueled rumors that Merrill was continuing to do anything it could to eliminate competition to its subprime lending affiliate, First Franklin.)

By early October Mozilo was still angry with Merrill Lynch (and to some degree Stan O'Neal) for the damage Bruce caused, but he could no longer explain away some of the stark facts affecting his company. Countrywide's loan delinquencies were rising rapidly, especially on the $118 billion in subprime loans it was servicing (though didn't necessarily own) on a monthly basis. (As a servicer it received fee income off of the loans for processing the monthly payments.) In a few weeks the company was set to release its third quarter earnings, and when it did it would reveal that almost 24 percent of its subprime servicing portfolio ($28 billion in mortgages) was delinquent. A year earlier the ratio was 16 percent. Countrywide was not only the largest residential servicer of all types of home mortgages, but two years earlier had become the largest servicer of subprime loans. Mozilo had conquered yet another market—but it was a business now crumbling. He was trapped.

Increasingly, the Countrywide founder was becoming agitated by the press coverage of his company. Over the years he had generally had a good relationship with the media, especially CNBC and the *New York Times*, which a few years earlier had done a glowing feature on him. But late in the summer *Times* columnist and reporter Gretchen Morgenson wrote a story called "Inside the Countrywide Lending Spree," which quoted former loan officers and brokers who told the reporter that Mozilo's creation—which a decade earlier hadn't even been in subprime—was now steering customers into high-cost mortgages so it could maximize profits. The allegations were no different than what some public interest groups had been saying on and off over the years, but now that the accusations were published in the *New York Times* it was as though they had been validated. (Mozilo and company spokesman Rick Simon declined to talk to the reporter.)

Mozilo was so angry with the *Times* and the negative publicity it had generated that he shot off an e-mail to his workers, rebutting the story, telling his workers that Countrywide's business practices "prohibit steering borrowers who qualify for prime loans into subprime loans." In an interview with *National Mortgage News*, Mozilo called the story "99 percent inaccurate," adding that "the press has a tremendous amount of power and no one to answer to."

But Betsy Bayer, the Countrywide compliance executive who was about to resign, told *National Mortgage News* that the *New York Times* story was "both right and wrong," but her biggest concern, being the company's "rules person," was that the company had "relaxed its credit guidelines" to stay competitive with companies like Ameriquest, Argent, and New Century, all of which were now out of business or soon would be. She also had something else to say about subprime lending at Countrywide: "It rarely made money for the company. All those years it was losing money because it was spending so much [to expand] into subprime."

"And you know this for sure?" asked reporter Paul Muolo.

"I know this for a fact," she said. "They were spending too much money building it out, opening one subprime center after another."

Countrywide never broke out its profits publicly by subprime versus prime, so it was impossible to tell. For his entire career Mozilo was portrayed by the media as a man whose company put Americans into homes. With loan delinquencies rising and homes falling in value, he and Countrywide were now being portrayed in the media as the poster child of the crisis. "We're besieged," he told *National Mortgage News*. "The press has been very negative and inaccurate."

In early September Mozilo told Muolo that Countrywide would no longer originate subprime loans unless they could be sold to Fannie Mae and Freddie Mac. Roughly 14 months before, Mozilo had forced out his would-be successor, Stan Kurland. A key issue for Mozilo was a huge disagreement he had with Kurland over his "in retirement" role as chairman (only) of the company. Inside Countrywide a top executive described the battle as such: "Angelo basically told him, 'Fuck you. I'm still a player.'" But there was another issue as well: Kurland had been warning about Countrywide's huge foray into subprime—just as Loeb had warned about the company's use of loan brokers. Mozilo had picked the wrong door: He chose Sambol and subprime over Kurland and more conservative loan underwriting.

Certain Wall Street firms—like Merrill Lynch—were still buying subprime loans through their trading desks, but the prices they were offering the originators for any new loans were, at best, par—100 cents on the dollar for a mortgage. Some Street firms were offering only 95, which meant lenders could only originate subprime loans at a loss. Translation: The boom was over. Now it was just a matter of what the aftermath would look like. What had been an $800 billion a year business, one in which Wall Street securitized almost every loan originated, was about to go up in smoke, and there was nothing Mozilo, Stan O'Neal, or Bear's Jimmy Cayne could do about it.

On September 11 Countrywide told its workforce of 60,000 that it was laying off 10,000 to 12,000 over the next few weeks in reaction to declining home loan volumes and declining profits. Bayer, the "rules person" who held the title of vice president of wholesale compliance, resigned before D-day, changing careers and becoming a paralegal at a nearby law firm. She had seen the layoffs coming. In a few weeks the company was set to release third quarter earnings. Stock analysts up and down Wall Street were predicting that the loss could total well over $2 billion, just about wiping out Countrywide's profits for the prior year.

On October 24, two days before the earnings release, rumors began circulating that Mozilo might resign as CEO but remain as chairman.[3] In the morning Muolo from *National Mortgage News* on the East Coast tried the CEO at his Calabasas office. Even though he often was there by 8 A.M. California time, he wasn't there that morning. Muolo sent him an e-mail asking about his resignation. Two minutes later Mozilo called, angry. "What the hell's going on? They're saying I'm resigning? Who? I don't know where this stuff comes from. I'm not resigning." He was at the hospital visiting his mother.

A few days later he decided to give the newspaper an on-the-record interview. Muolo asked him about Wall Street's role in the widening

---

[3] On October 24 Countrywide filed notice with the Securities and Exchange Commission revealing that Henry Cisneros, secretary of the Department of Housing and Urban Development in the Clinton administration, had resigned from its board, saying he wanted to spend more time managing his home building–related company, CityView. A director since 2001, Cisneros had sold $5 million worth of stock from 2004 to 2007. Even though the SEC statement was dated October 24, the resignation was effective October 18. In March two other directors, Kathleen Brown of Goldman Sachs (and sister to former California governor Jerry Brown) and Michael Dougherty, an investment banker from Minnesota, announced their resignations.

subprime crisis—its insatiable appetite for subprime loans that could be securitized into bonds. "It's easy to have hindsight," he said. "No one saw this coming. No one. Look at [Alan] Greenspan. The Fed increased rates 17 consecutive times. Greenspan was testifying on Capitol Hill telling people to take out ARMs. If you want to play the blame game, let's go back and blame the Fed. A federal funds rate of 1 percent? When the Street got into subprime there were virtually no delinquencies. There were no foreclosures and there was equity building in these homes. It was a classic bubble. You don't know when you're in a bubble. You can blame everyone from al-Qaeda to the rating agencies."

Question: Are you sorry you ever got into subprime?

Mozilo: "I can't answer that. We have a stated mission to make a difference in the lives of American families, to get low-income people into housing. You don't know the stuff I've seen. People have sent me photo albums, family albums, how happy they are to have a home." He paused for a moment. "Look," he said. "I have nine grandkids. There is too much division when you have haves and have-nots. You don't have peace in the world. I don't know if I would have done anything different."

The reporter tried the Wall Street question again: Don't they share some of the blame for the growing crisis?

The Countrywide founder didn't hesitate to answer this time. "They were driven by our model [originating and securitizing those same loans]. I didn't realize that they didn't know what they were doing. It got out of control. They were like 'We need more. We need more subprime loans to buy.' Remember back in the 1990s with 125 percent LTV [loan-to-value] loans? We didn't participate in that. But the Street did—they securitized that crap."

The next question was about loan brokers, but Mozilo declined to talk on the record about what he thought of these freelance salespeople that Countrywide had depended on for two-plus decades. His comments, rest assured, weren't exactly charitable. It could have been that he had suddenly remembered the warnings of his late partner, David Loeb, who two decades earlier had cautioned about brokers: "They're crooks."

★   ★   ★

Just about the time Countrywide announced that it was laying off 10,000 to 12,000 workers, it embarked on an internal public relations campaign to boost the moral of its employees, who not only feared losing their jobs but were barraged almost daily by the media about the lender's increasing problems. Even with the $2 billion investment from Bank of America, Countrywide's share price continued to slip, and the Securities and Exchange Commission (SEC) in Washington had opened an informal investigation into Mozilo's insider stock sales over the previous three years, which had brought him $300 million in proceeds. To the few reporters he was still talking to, including CNBC's Maria Bartiromo and Muolo, he continued to defend his actions, noting that every option he had converted into stock and sold had been disclosed and done through a selling program called 10b5-1. However, the SEC also was examining a new program that he had put in place in October 2006 that speeded up the pace of those sales.[4] His explanation boiled down to this: He would be retiring within two years, and all his personal wealth was tied up in stock. "I'm not worried about the SEC probe," he told Muolo. (Mozilo's base salary, though, wasn't exactly paltry. At $23 million—before options and bonus money—it was among the highest in the industry.)

The internal PR campaign was done in conjunction with Burson-Marsteller, a public relations firm that specialized in crisis management at companies whose names were being dragged through the mud. It was aimed at Mozilo's employees and involved dispensing green wristbands that said "Protect Our House." To obtain one, employees had to sign a pledge about their commitment to the company and agree to "unflagging determination" to tell the "real" Countrywide story—the "story about our 40-year mission of helping people. . . ." So went the "commitment" card sent to full-timers by Andrew Gissinger, the lender's chief operating officer.

In one of Countrywide's Long Island branches, a loan officer had this to say about the wristband campaign: "It's a joke. I'm not signing it. I don't know anyone here who has." She tried to cut and paste the e-mail about the pledge and pass it on but was blocked from doing so by Countrywide's computer system. The loan officer said the company was also putting the heat on its salespeople to increase originations at a time when home buying was waning in most markets. "Over the weekend I'm supposed to go out to 10 open houses and get the cards

---

[4] Two weeks before the *Wall Street Journal* broke the news about the informal SEC probe of Mozilo's stock sales, the *Los Angeles Times* first reported that Mozilo had adjusted the timing of his sales multiple times over the previous year.

of Realtors I'm not currently doing business with," she said. "Then I'm supposed to log into our Countrywide server and populate the network. I'm not going to do it. My kid has a game this weekend."

The wristband campaign started just as Betsy Bayer was about to leave the company. "The 'Protect Our House' thing went on for about three weeks," she said. "You had to sign the pledge to get one, but after a while they just gave up and gave the things away."

Another part of Countrywide's campaign to lift the morale of employees was to block their Internet access to a web site called The Mortgage Lender Implode-O-Meter,[5] which had been selling T-shirts lampooning Mozilo, featuring an orange portrait of him (a sly comment on his tan) dressed up like Colonel Sanders. Instead of saying "KFC" (for Kentucky Fried Chicken) the shirts read "CFC" which stood for "CountryFried Financial Corporation." CFC was also Countrywide's stock symbol on the New York Stock Exchange.

Then came earnings day. On Friday, October 26, Mozilo and his senior lieutenants once again marched down the carpet from the corporate suite to the conference room, where they told analysts and the media on a conference call that the company had dropped $1.2 billion in the third quarter—the largest loss in its history. The day before the earnings release, its share price fell to $12, which meant that Ken Lewis' Bank of America was sitting on a paper loss of $600 million on its $2 billion investment. Countrywide hadn't lost money in decades. Even during

---

[5] The Implode-O-Meter was started by a 27-year-old blogger named Aaron Krowne, who considered himself a "citizen journalist." Krowne's web site, which attracted millions of visits in 2007 and 2008, published a running list of failed mortgage companies (and soon-to-be-failed mortgage companies) on the Implode-O-Meter. The web site quickly became a clearinghouse for published news stories from coast to coast as well as a forum for gossip and innuendo as to who might fail next—some of which landed Krowne in legal trouble, which he escaped when one of the ailing lenders suing him for spreading misinformation dropped its lawsuit. Krowne did an impressive job of tracking deceased lenders, but his motives weren't entirely altruistic. He soon began accepting paid advertising on his web site, targeting mortgage firms. He also admitted that from time to time he would short stocks that he was publishing information on. By early 2008 his web site had became profitable enough that he quit his full-time job in software research at Emory University and launched other Implode-O-Meter web sites targeting banks, hedge funds, and home builders. "This is now an online media company," he said. In late 2008 and 2009 he expanded the web site to cover implosions of home-building companies, commercial banks, and even hedge funds.

the recession of 2000–2001 it had managed to earn almost $800 million. The reason for the losses, Mozilo explained, was the subprime "liquidity crisis," adding that Countrywide had been forced to revalue mortgages that it was holding on its books and pay more money to third parties for credit protection, which meant insurance to cover potential losses.

During the Q&A with analysts, Mozilo stayed subdued, letting company president David Sambol, his presumed successor, handle many of the questions. But then he stepped in again, telling the investment banking community that during his 55 years in mortgages he had never witnessed a correction this severe. One analyst took him to task for saying a few months earlier that housing prices might have a "soft landing," but Mozilo said one thing he had learned over the years was that "this business doesn't lend itself to a soft landing. It's way too complex." He clarified that his earlier remarks were meant to be taken as a "normal hard landing." He stopped being subdued, boasting to the analysts that Countrywide would earn money in the fourth quarter and next year.

The analysts seemed to like that, although right after the call some would tell reporters working the story that they couldn't possibly see the company earning money in the fourth quarter. Mozilo boasted that Countrywide's bank, which took deposits from the public, would continue to open new offices. "It's extremely important that we pick up share," he said. There he was again, talking about how Countrywide would grow stronger as others failed. But as part of its earnings release the company also admitted that its loan delinquencies had risen significantly in the quarter. Almost 24 percent of its subprime loans were late, not a good sign. And 3.27 percent of its "A" paper loans were late, too, which on the surface may not seem like a huge number, but Countrywide serviced $1.2 trillion in Fannie/Freddie loans, which meant almost $40 billion in mortgages were in trouble. (Its "A" paper late payments had risen 30 percent in 12 months.)

An analyst asked Mozilo about his nonperforming loans, but he deferred answering the question, saying, "We can't see out six months from now." The conference call had lasted almost two hours. One analyst thanked the Countrywide CEO and his staff for spending so much time with them. "I think this conference call shows the quality of the management team," said the analyst. Even in the face of disaster it appeared as though Mozilo had won over the analysts once again.

The Countrywide CEO seemed happy and quipped, "Well, then write something nice about us in your papers." Most of the investment bankers laughed—but not all of them. Analyst Steve Hanley of Munn Wealth Management in Jacksonville, Florida, jumped in with one last question. "You are asking me, as a money manager, to buy the stock. I've invested other people's money as well as my own. You guys have been giving more detail than normal, but how much money will Countrywide executives spend to support the stock?"

Mozilo seemed somewhat surprised by the question. Over the previous 12 months Countrywide executives, including him, hadn't been buying any of the firm's stock on the open market—they'd been converting options into stock and dumping the shares right away. "It's our job to present the story," he shot back. "It's your job to decide whether to buy or sell." The conference call was over.

Over the next two months the story went something like this: Countrywide's stock would slide a bit, rise, then slide some more. Wall Street firm after firm would announce that they were writing down by billions of dollars the value of subprime CDOs they held on their balance sheets. The numbers were getting huge: Citigroup ($11 billion with potential exposure on CDOs and structured investment vehicles[6] of $45 billion); United Bank of Switzerland (UBS, a major warehouse lender to subprime nonbanks and an investor in CDOs, $10 billion in write-downs); Merrill Lynch ($8.4 billion); Bear Stearns ($1.2 billion). HSBC, the London bank that had bought subprime giant Household Finance earlier in the decade (paying $14 billion), was taking a $3.4 billion loss on subprime loans it held. These were markdowns on their value, not necessarily net losses.[7] The reason they were being marked down: subprime delinquencies. If Countrywide was supposed to be one of the nation's more careful subprime lenders (to hear Mozilo tell

---

[6] A structured investment vehicle (SIV) is an off-balance-sheet investment in subprime bonds or related assets. Typically, a bank sets up an SIV, finds investors, and lends money to those investors. The bank manages the SIV for its investors.

[7] A write-down usually translates into a loss, but if a company has profits elsewhere in the organization the write-down is merely deducted from gross revenues. Few firms reporting billion-dollar write-downs earned enough money elsewhere to offset their subprime problems.

it) and its late payments were 24 percent on A– to D loans, then just imagine what the rate was for the 100 or so subprime lenders that had gone bust since Bill Dallas's Ownit closed its doors a year earlier.

News reports continued to focus on Countrywide's delinquencies and allegations about its lending practices. Several states were now beginning to look at not only how it originated subprime loans and payment option ARMs, but the lender's foreclosure practices. Once again rumors were flooding the market that Countrywide might file for bankruptcy protection. Each time the company shot down the rumors.

★   ★   ★

On the morning of December 3 Mozilo told *National Mortgage News* that "These are unprecedented times for the world. We're the only survivor of the mortgage companies. How come nobody prints that?" He was ranting again about the media coverage of his shop. (Mozilo was under the mistaken impression that Countrywide was still a nonbank, which it wasn't.) In an hour he was set to speak at the second annual housing summit of the Office of Thrift Supervision (OTS) at the National Press Club in Washington, the same forum that Ranieri had spoken at a year earlier, warning how Wall Street was recklessly securitizing subprime loans, and investors in the end bonds had no idea what they were buying. Still angry with the media, Mozilo said he wouldn't be talking to the press afterward, which was true to a degree.

Late in the morning CNBC anchors kept boasting on air how Maria Bartiromo would have an exclusive interview with Mozilo just after the OTS summit concluded in Washington. Just because he wasn't talking to most of the media didn't mean he wouldn't be talking to Maria. (Bartiromo was hosting a speakers' panel at the OTS summit.) She started off with a softball question about Countrywide's efforts to help delinquent borrowers get current again on their loans. In response to a question about the lender's financial strength, Angelo said the company had "adequate capital." He once again mentioned industry consolidation and that as others went under—you got it—Countrywide would gain market share.

Then Bartiromo got tough. She asked him outright about the possibility of Countrywide filing for bankruptcy protection. With a smile, Mozilo said, "The elements are not there for bankruptcy." The CNBC reporter noted that Bank of America's $2 billion investment in his company had now been halved. "Have you talked to them?" she asked.

"Bank of America has been around a long time," he said. "They're a first-class corporation. Their investment in us is a chance for a great company to invest in another great company. It's a terrific relationship." When Mozilo said it there was no doubt that he honestly believed it— even if CNBC viewers might have been thinking: He can't be serious.

Next came the big question: Will Bank of America be investing more in Countrywide?

"No, we're not looking for any more money from them," said the CEO.

Two days later he agreed to another interview with Muolo at *National Mortgage News*, continuing to gripe about the press coverage. (In the weeks before, he had contemplated closing the lender's PR department but was talked out of it by other executives at the company.) He was now angry with the White House for refusing to increase the Fannie Mae/Freddie Mac loan limit, which prohibited the two congressionally chartered mortgage investing giants from buying any loans over $417,000 (the ceiling set by their regulator back in the fall). Mozilo believed that if the White House and Treasury Department allowed for the cap to be increased—at least temporarily—it would help Countrywide, because the two could purchase more mortgages in the secondary market, especially large-balance subprime loans in California. Countrywide could then off-load much of the risk it held on its balance sheet. The trading desks at Wall Street firms like Merrill and Bear had stopped funding most kinds of subprime loans, especially high-balance ones.

"The White House isn't budging," said Muolo, who was based in his newspaper's Washington bureau and had been covering the issue. "They're not going to raise the loan limit unless things get really bad."

"They're ideologues," Mozilo said. "They never sat around their kitchen table with their parents, trying to figure out how to make that month's rent." Then out of nowhere he went into a rant about how the SEC, regulators, and prosecutors were going after Italian-American businessmen. "They went after Quattrone, Nardelli, Grasso," he said, adding a few more names to the list that Muolo didn't recognize.[8]

"You don't really mean that," said the reporter.

Mozilo paused for a moment. Silence. "Yeah, I do." He repeated that he wasn't worried about the SEC probe of his stock sales at all. "Everything was disclosed," he said. "It was because of that *LA Times* article."

★   ★   ★

Besides the constant flow of bankruptcy rumors, its huge third quarter loss, and spiraling subprime delinquencies, Mozilo had one other major problem: payment option ARMs (POAs)—the adjustable-rate loan where the borrower each month was offered four different payment options. One of those options was something called "negative amortization" where the homeowner could keep his or her payments artificially low by adding on to the debt owed. (This was the "I'll worry about it tomorrow" option.) Critics of the loan believed that POAs were dangerous for three reasons: Consumers (1) were building up even more debt by choosing the negative amortization option, (2) were qualified for the mortgage at the low start rates, and (3) were bidding up the prices of homes because they could keep their monthly payments low.

Countrywide did not invent the POA, nor had it invented subprime, but it now found itself the largest originator of POAs in

---

[8] Frank Quattrone was a former investment banker at Credit Suisse First Boston (CSFB) who took dozens of technology companies public during the 1990s tech boom. He was later indicted for obstruction of justice as part of a federal probe into investment banking firms (including CSFB) doling out much-sought-after IPOs to selected clients. The charges against him were later dropped. Robert Nardelli was CEO and chairman of Home Depot (whose board Mozilo sat on for a short time). Nardelli was criticized for receiving a $210 million severance package after being let go when Home Depot's share price and revenue slipped. Nardelli was not the subject of any known government investigations. Richard Grasso was CEO of the New York Stock Exchange. In 2003 it was revealed that he had a deferred pay package of almost $200 million, which had been approved by a compensation committee at the exchange consisting of executives whose companies he regulated. When the SEC complained, Grasso was forced out. A year later New York attorney general Eliot Spitzer sued him, seeking the return of most of the deferred compensation.

the nation.[9] It had reached that pinnacle by funding many of the loans through brokers. Jerry Davis, who brokered loans in the Fresno area, said Countrywide's wholesale account executives began pushing POAs on him in 2006. "Countrywide focused a lot of their business on minorities in the county. World [Savings] did, too." According to Davis, Countrywide wanted POAs so badly that it was offering the broker a three-point fee (3 percent of the loan amount) for bringing in the product. "They rolled the points into the loan amount," he said. "This was the lender's rebate to you." Countrywide would offer brokers training on how to pitch payment option ARMs, he said. "They would say you could do these loans because the property's value would go up 33 percent in a year."

True to form, Countrywide under Mozilo found a product it liked (the POA), carefully entered the market, and then, once comfortable with the product, ramped up and dominated. But Mozilo was by no means stupid. He read the company's monthly reports and by the spring of 2007 grew concerned that so many of Countrywide's POA borrowers were choosing the negative amortization option. In late 2006 Robert Gnaizda of the Greenlining Institute, a public policy and advocacy group based in Berkeley, California, had met with Mozilo to discuss the potential risks of POAs, first and foremost the fact that the loan could lead to a tidal wave of foreclosures. Gnaizda described Mozilo has being dismissive of the issue. If that was the case in 2006, a few months later the Countrywide CEO was being dismissive no more. By mid-2007 Countrywide had begun sending out letters to some of its POA borrowers reminding them that the debt accumulated under the negative amortization option had to be paid back at some point. It was nice that Countrywide had been sending out warning letters to its POA borrowers, but that raised another issue: Didn't the

---

[9] Golden West Financial of Oakland, the publicly traded parent of World Savings, a thrift managed by the husband-and-wife team of Herb and Marion Sandler, had pioneered the POA loan two decades earlier. World Savings executives claimed that their S&L conservatively underwrote the loan and had few problems with it. In 2006 the Sandlers sold Golden West to banking giant Wachovia and retired from the industry. Wachovia, which almost failed in the fall of 2008, was sold to Wells Fargo. Citigroup was also a suitor. Wachovia's biggest financial headache was all the POAs it held on its balance sheet, many of which were originated by World Savings. World funded POAs through both its branches and loan brokers. However, it never disclosed its broker volumes publicly.

customers know that before they had taken out the loan? And what exactly had Countrywide, or the loan broker who funded the loan through Countrywide, disclosed to the customer?

By late 2007 Countrywide held almost $30 billion in POAs on the balance sheet of its thrift—with the negative amortization amount (the "I'll worry about it tomorrow" debt) totaling $1.2 billion. If consumers couldn't repay the $1.2 billion, Countrywide would be on the hook. There was a twist, though. Countrywide had been selling its POAs into securities. "The performance on those securitizations was horrendous," an executive familiar with the company's effort said. "Countrywide was cherry-picking the loans. They were keeping the better ones for themselves, the ones where the FICO scores were 740 or better. They always put the worst-performing ones into the securitizations." David Sambol, said this insider, was "pushing the POA product hard through the call centers."

By now Mozilo was tapping the Federal Home Loan Bank (FHLB) system for advances,[10] which replaced Countrywide's reliance on its commercial paper and warehouse lines. Instead of borrowing from Wall Street and the large money center banks, it had borrowed $47 billion from the FHLB system, a cooperative of 12 banks chartered by the government. The borrowings caught the eye of Democratic Senator Charles Schumer of New York, who headed a Senate committee with oversight over economic issues. The burgeoning mortgage crisis (with Countrywide front and center) fit the bill. Schumer wanted to know why Countrywide was borrowing so much money from the FHLB—and he wanted to know what Mozilo was doing about helping all its troubled borrowers, especially the ones who had POAs or subprime loans.

Every few weeks Schumer would be interviewed on CNBC criticizing Countrywide for not doing more, and singling out Mozilo, which riled the Bronx native no end. (His reaction to Schumer was not printable in a family newspaper.) Even though the senator from Brooklyn was shining the light on Countrywide's lending and workout practices, as chairman of the Joint Economic Committee he had

---

[10] The 12 FHLBs lend money to their members (mostly banks, thrifts, and credit unions) in the form of advances. The advances are loans collateralized by assets held by member institutions. The collateral can include mortgages.

avoided criticizing the financial institutions that had supplied hundreds of billions of dollars in capital to nonbank subprime lenders: Wall Street, whose executives (and companies) had donated handsomely to his campaigns over the years.

By early December Countrywide and several other large lenders—including Bank of America, Citigroup, Chase Mortgage, and Wells Fargo—were part of a government-sponsored alliance of banks called Hope Now, which was trying to help troubled borrowers restructure their subprime and POA loans. The plan—the supposed brainchild of Treasury chief Henry Paulson and his top deputy, Robert Steel—entailed lenders freezing the interest rates on troubled ARMs at or near their low teaser rates. News of the Hope Now alliance began to leak out to the press in late November but with few details reported.

Earlier in the month Mozilo had been in meetings with Paulson and Housing secretary Alphonso Jackson about the plan. As the alliance was being put together, Mozilo claimed that he had been the only CEO from the nation's five largest servicers in the meetings. "Paulson doesn't get it," Mozilo told one reporter about the November meetings. "Who's going to pay for it? Payment option ARMs have resets. The note rate is 2 percent, 3 percent. You can't keep the rate at those levels. The lender will go bankrupt."

As the weeks wore on, so did the Countrywide bankruptcy rumors. Charles Prince—who had cut his teeth in the subprime industry at Commercial Credit of Baltimore—had been forced to resign as chairman and CEO of Citigroup as it continued to write down the value of CDOs held on its balance sheet. First O'Neal at Merrill Lynch, then Prince—the heads of the largest and most powerful investment banking firms in the United States were being fired because of their losses in an industry whose roots could be traced back to repo men like Peter Cugno and Dan Phillips. The biggest difference between the subprime industry of yesteryear and the modern version was that management trainees at Beneficial actually underwrote and collected on the loan, and if the customer was late people like Cugno would visit them at the office, reminding them personally that "You owe me money." Back then subprime firms lent only to borrowers who had a ton of equity in their homes—and they didn't securitize the loans and sell them to overseas banks.

Jimmy Cayne was gone as CEO of Bear Stearns but remained as chairman—but for how long? Bear's stock price was sliding each week as well, as was another huge Wall Street player in subprime, Lehman Brothers. Despite Mozilo's insistence that Countrywide had enough capital, a team of examiners from the Office of Thrift Supervision had decamped to Calabasas, where they were closely analyzing what type of subprime and POA loans Countrywide held on its books and how much the lender should mark down their value. If close to 24 percent of the subprime loans that Countrywide serviced on a monthly basis were delinquent, chances were that billions of dollars' worth of POA and subprime loans (plus several billions more in "A" paper second liens) it held could face markdowns.

On Tuesday morning, January 8, 2008, Countrywide's shares fell to yet another 52-week low: $5.76, which meant the $2 billion stake that Bank of America had in Countrywide was now worth just $660 million. Ken Lewis, Bank of America's chairman and CEO, wasn't looking too good. A company that a year before was worth $25 billion (with a share price of $45) was now veering toward becoming worthless. Over the previous three weeks, almost on a daily basis, newspapers all over the nation were reporting on a new Countrywide-related investigation somewhere. In Pennsylvania and Florida its foreclosure practices were under review—in particular extra fees and charges it heaped on already struggling borrowers. In Illinois the attorney general's office said that as part of a far-reaching probe into the lender's originating practices it was looking at how Countrywide originated both POAs and subprime mortgages through its retail loan officers and brokers. "Payment option ARMs are at the top of our A list," said Debra Hagen, chief of the state's consumer protection division.

In a brief interview with Muolo, Mozilo wrote off the Illinois investigation as old news. "That's been going on since September," he said. He had little else to say that day. "We received those subpoenas several months ago."

On Wednesday, January 9, the company released its monthly origination and servicing numbers for year-end: 7.2 percent of the $1.4 trillion in mortgages it processed monthly were delinquent; this was a blended figure that included both its "A" paper and subprime loans (plus POAs and everything else). Countrywide refused to issue a subprime-only delinquency number—that figure would come in a few weeks when it released fourth quarter earnings, which Mozilo had promised back in October would be in the black.

The company also said that 1.44 percent of those $1.4 trillion in mortgages were in foreclosure—meaning "game over" for homeowners who had borrowed $21 billion from the company. When analysts, institutional investors, and the general public saw the new figures, the selling began. Countrywide was in the worst shape in its almost 40-year history. The day before, its share price sank 28 percent, ending at $5.47. At one point the New York Stock Exchange halted trading in its stock—never a good sign. On Wednesday at the market's open, another 20 percent of value had been lopped off. Ken Lewis' investment in Countrywide was starting to look like a fatal disaster. Mozilo wasn't talking to the press anymore—no more returned telephone calls to Bartiromo, Muolo, or James Hagerty, the Countrywide beat reporter for the *Wall Street Journal*. Amid the rumors about an impending bankruptcy filing were stories that Warren Buffett or Hungarian-born speculator George Soros might be a potential white knight for the company. On Friday, January 11, all the speculation ended: Lewis' Bank of America said it was buying all of Countrywide for just $4 billion (about $7 a share)—twice what it paid for the 16 percent stake in August. No word was given on what might happen to Mozilo.

Over the next few weeks more banks and investment banking firms preannounced or unveiled fourth quarter losses or write-downs tied to their holdings of subprime mortgages, "A" paper second liens that were part of 80/20 loans (a 20 percent second mortgage that served as a down payment and an 80 percent first mortgage), and POAs. As home prices continued to fall, housing values in once hot markets like Florida and Southern California were now down 20 percent. CNBC stock picker Jim Cramer's vision of a financial Armageddon had arrived for both homeowners and bankers. By the time the Bank of America–Countrywide deal was unveiled to the public, Wall Street firms and commercial banks (and a handful of thrifts) had already taken $100 billion in write-downs on their mortgage holdings. All sorts of financial experts and analysts were predicting that eventual write-downs on mortgages, MBSs, and ABSs might cost banks, investment bankers, and thrifts anywhere from $150 billion to $300 billion. One estimate went as high as $1 trillion. To some in the industry it brought back memories of the S&L crisis, when it had become something of a contest for financial analysts and economists—people like independent thrift consultant Bert Ely—to top each other on their predictions of just how costly bailing out the nation's thrifts might be.[11]

As the financial news regarding mortgages and housing values worsened, Countrywide unveiled its fourth quarter earnings in late January. This time there would be no conference call with analysts, no explanation of the numbers, no predictions by Angelo on housing prices and when the market might turn around. What was the point? The way things looked, the entire company—founded in David Loeb's kitchen almost 40 years earlier—would be the property of Ken Lewis' bank by the end of September. A few days after the sale was announced, Lewis broke his silence on Mozilo's future: He would assist in the transition and then retire.

A few days before Countrywide released its fourth quarter earnings, Muolo from *National Mortgage News* called Mozilo at his home early in the morning. The reporter had covered him and Countrywide for 20 years and sometimes interviewed Mozilo early in the morning at his mansion. This time the Countrywide founder had nothing to say. "I'm not talking anymore," he said. His career in mortgages, one that had started as a messenger boy hopping buses and riding the subways of Manhattan, was effectively over.

On January 28, a Monday, his company posted a $422 million loss for the fourth quarter. The profit Mozilo had predicted never materialized. Another quarter like that, and all of Countrywide's profit from the previous year would be wiped out. It held $98 billion in mortgages on its balance sheet under a category called "held for investment," which meant it didn't necessarily have to write them down (like all the Street firms had been doing) unless they went delinquent—but that was the problem. The loans included subprime mortgages, POAs, and second liens that were part of 80/20 structures. Countrywide kept its riskiest loans because, given the events of the previous six months, there was no place to sell them. Wall Street wasn't buying anymore. For $4 billion Bank of America was buying a potential black hole.

---

[11] The S&L bailout cost the government (U.S. taxpayers) $150 billion, excluding interest costs.

Speaking in New York at an investors' conference held by Citigroup where executives from publicly traded financial service firms were asked to give overviews on their prospects, Bank of America's Lewis was asked about Countrywide's loss and whether his bank still planned on buying the ailing lender. "At this point everything is a go for completing this transaction," said Lewis. Week after week he and his public relations staff would be asked the same question over and over again: Is the Countrywide deal still a go? Each time the answer would be yes.

★   ★   ★

On January 17, Congressman Henry Waxman, a Democrat from California who chaired the House Oversight Committee, delivered a document request to Countrywide headquarters in Calabasas, asking for hundreds of pages from Mozilo related to his stock sales, his severance package, and minutes from directors meetings where his pay package had been discussed, among other things. Waxman had scheduled a hearing by his committee a few weeks hence called "CEO Pay and the Mortgage Crisis." Scheduled to testify were Mozilo, Stan O'Neal, and Charles Prince, the recently dismissed chief of Citigroup. The hearing was delayed twice with no reason given, and then rescheduled for Friday, March 7. Some columnists joked that it would be the hearing of the "Three Horsemen of the Mortgage Apocalypse." (In the book of Revelation the Bible tells of the four horsemen of the apocalypse, but when you're talking billions of dollars in losses, what was one less horseman?)

A week before the hearing, a few sources had been telling *National Mortgage News* that yet another Wall Street firm was going to announce a large write-down, but the sources—two of whom once traded mortgages for Wall Street firms—weren't sure which one. The rumor was Bear Stearns, which was about to release its earnings. Lehman was another possibility. Former Bear officials who had lost their mortgage-related jobs at the Wall Street giant speculated that whatever losses were coming had to be tied to the hedge funds that Cioffi had started and Spector oversaw. Not only had Bear created the two hedge funds to invest in subprime assets, but the investment banking company itself held billions of dollars in CDOs, subprime ABSs, and other nonprime mortgage bonds on its balance sheet. But what exactly were those assets worth? Bear, unlike a publicly traded Federal Deposit Insurance Corporation (FDIC)-regulated bank, didn't have to disclose any details about what was on its books or in its trading accounts. As Ranieri had pointed out 15 months earlier, it was the job of the Securities and Exchange Commission to oversee bond disclosures and the firms that played in the market.

The day before Mozilo, O'Neal, and Prince were set to testify before Waxman's committee, the Federal Reserve made an announcement unlike any other in its history: It would provide $200 billion in loans to financial institutions (Wall Street firms being at the top of the list) that needed cash. The Fed, which was now chaired by Alan Greenspan's successor, Ben Bernanke, did so because investment banking firms were having a hard time completing trades on all sorts of assets because of the nervousness surrounding the market. The concerns about subprime assets that started in August with subprime bonds (and the collapse of Bear's hedge funds in late July) had spread to bonds that were considered safe—like "A" paper Fannie Mae/Freddie Mac securities and municipal bonds issued by cities. Exacerbating the situation was the ailing financial condition of the nation's three largest bond insurance agencies: Ambac Financial Group, MBIA Inc., and Financial Guaranty Insurance Company (FGIC). Each was facing huge losses because of insurance claims on about $50 billion worth of subprime bonds they had guaranteed. Four years earlier the three were hardly in the business of insuring subprime assets. Their bread and butter had been the guarantee of municipal (muni) bonds.

On Friday morning, March 7, at 10 a.m., 25 reporters gathered in room 2154 of the House Rayburn Building, a hundred yards south of the Capitol, for Waxman's hearing. About 15 photographers and cameramen were there as well, waiting inside room 2154 and outside in the hallway for Mozilo, O'Neal, and Prince to arrive for the hearing. But instead of facing the press out in the hallway where the reporters might be able to ask questions before the members of Congress got to them, the three men (and directors from their respective compensation committees) entered the room through a back door up on the dais where only elected officials and their staffers were usually allowed. Mozilo entered first, walking down the stairs that descended into the hearing room. As soon as the photographers saw him they began snapping away—click, click, click. Within a few moments he and the others were gathered at the witness table—except for O'Neal, who hadn't yet arrived. The cameramen kept snapping photographs. The picture taking must have gone on for almost five minutes. (For that purpose alone Waxman seemed to be in no rush to start the hearing.) Mozilo avoided looking at the cameramen as well as the reporters sitting 30 feet to his right at the press table. He looked tired and beleaguered, like someone who hadn't slept in days. (His suit: charcoal gray with a red tie.) Then O'Neal came down the stairs and joined them. He and Mozilo shook hands but barely said a word to each other.

The three men and their directors were sworn in, and, as might be predicted, Waxman and his fellow committee members—for the most part—took them to task not only for their huge pay packages but for their retirement and severance agreements: $161 million for O'Neal, $40 million for Prince, and $36 million for Mozilo. In Mozilo's defense, a few days before the hearing he publicly announced that he was giving up his severance money. In his testimony before the committee he criticized the press and "governance experts" who estimated that he might walk away with up to $115 million in severance pay. (The actual figure was $36.4 million.) Mozilo told the committee that he gave up the money because "I did not want this issue to detract from, or in any way to impede, the important task of completing" Countrywide's sale to Bank of America. He still had the $400 million that he received from selling stock the previous four years.

He also noted that in his 55 years in the business, "this is the worst housing market I have ever seen," and defended Countrywide's efforts to help its delinquent borrowers. "In 2007 we helped more than 81,000 families avoid foreclosure," including modifying loan terms. The one thing he didn't mention was that his company's foreclosure practices were under investigation in several states.

During the hearing there were no major fireworks from the panel.[12] It went on as might be expected—Democrats and Republicans raking the three over the coals for making so much money in the face of an

---

[12] The only revelation of much significance was the fact that in late 2006, when Mozilo increased the rate at which he exercised options and sold shares, Countrywide also adopted a stock buyback plan where it spent $2.5 billion of its own money to purchase shares in the open market—a move that would only benefit the share price. Mozilo's response: There was no "relationship" between Countrywide's stock buyback plan and his exercising of options.

economic disaster where three million borrowers might lose their homes over the next year and where nine million had homes (according to research cited by Waxman) that were worth less than their mortgages. Congresswoman Eleanor Holmes Norton of the District of Columbia managed to criticize Mozilo while butchering his name, calling him "Mozlo" over and over again even after being corrected. The lone dissenting Congressman was Representative Tom Davis of Virginia, a Republican who at the start of the hearing called it a "sanctimonious search for scapegoats." Davis, who was set to retire at the end of the year, had no problem with the money the three earned. "We may not like it, but markets at times produce inequities and they correct them," he said. "Government involvement in that process generally makes matters worse, not better." The Republican noted that actors Jennifer Lopez and Ben Affleck "didn't have to pay reparations to moviegoers after *Gigli.*" (The movie, to be kind, was a poorly received romantic comedy that bombed financially.) There were a few chuckles in the hearing room at Davis's remark, but not many.

The fireworks came 10 days later—but they were in New York. The previous week rumors had plagued Bear Stearns that it was having liquidity issues. All week its new CEO, Alan Schwartz, the man with no mortgage experience, denied that anything was wrong. But its share price kept slipping. On Monday, March 10, Bear's stock fell almost $8 to $62, its lowest price since March 2003. Bear issued a statement: "There is absolutely no truth to the rumors of liquidity problems." But the market didn't believe Cayne, Schwartz, or anyone else. The slide continued.

A few days later, on the 14th, a Friday, Bear's stock plunged 27 points, closing at $30—a disaster for the company and its shareholders. Its 52-week high was $159, so shareholders were already unhappy. But if they were depressed at $30, on Monday when the opening bell rang on Wall Street, they would be downright suicidal on the news breaking that morning: Bear, with Schwartz's blessing, had agreed to sell a controlling stake in the 75-year-old company for just $2 a share or $236 million. Just over 84 percent of its value had been wiped out over the weekend, billions lost. One hundred hours earlier the company was worth $3.5 billion; a year before that, $20 billion. Monday was also St. Patrick's Day, a big event in New York with celebrations and a parade down Fifth Avenue. But there was no celebrating at Bear. Its new owner would be JPMorgan Chase, Jamie Dimon's bank. A $2 bill had been taped to a window at the entrance of Bear's headquarters on Madison Avenue. That's what Bear's rank-and-file workers, from traders to secretaries, thought of the deal: two measly dollars.

The next day the *New York Times* reported, "Just like that, some people's stakes of $100 million or more in Bear were ravaged and senior executives like Thomas A. Marano, the head of mortgages, and Bruce Lisman, a co-head of equities, were furious."

The deal had been put together by Schwartz with the assistance of the Federal Reserve and its chairman, Ben Bernanke. As part of the sale to Dimon's bank, the Federal Reserve (which meant the federal government/U.S. taxpayers) would take on the task of managing $30 billion worth of what regulators were calling Bear's "riskiest" assets— the majority of which were CDOs, ABSs, and mortgage derivatives, including credit default swaps. No mention was made of Cioffi's hedge funds, though one former managing director speculated to a reporter, "It has to be the hedge funds that caused this." No one knew for sure. Both Bear and the Fed were light on details.

The key issue with Bear's $30 billion in problem assets was their value. The company had loans against them, and banks that had been lending money to the investment banking giant became nervous that the collateral backing their loans (the CDOs and ABSs) was untradable, hence the rumors of the week before. If Bear needed to sell any of the $30 billion to raise money, there would be no buyers—which meant the $30 billion was, as a technical matter, worthless. By March of 2008 there was no subprime market. Few lenders of note were still making the loans—and Wall Street firms like Bear, Merrill, Morgan Stanley, and just about everyone else with a trading desk had stopped buying subprime bonds. A market had died. Merrill had pulled the plug on First Franklin, Bear on Encore, Morgan Stanley on its affiliate, Saxon Mortgage. It was over.

The only firms buying subprime bonds were private hedge funds, and according to one analyst, they were paying only 10 to 30 cents on the dollar for various tranches of ABS securities. The hedge funds, many of which employed quants who used to work in the mortgage departments of Nomura, Bear, Lehman, and other firms, smelled blood. All of this bad news fed the rumors that Bear was close to bankruptcy. And just as Bear had been margin-calling nonbanks that it had been financing through warehouse lines of credit, Bear's bankers began margin-calling it. Even though the Federal Reserve had promised that $200 billion in loans would be made available to banks and investment banking firms, institutional investors that had been trading and investing with Bear felt it would be too risky to keep doing business with it. They began informing Schwartz of their desire to pull their investments out of Bear. When it became too much, Schwartz went to Bernanke, said investment bankers familiar with the situation. Hoping to avoid an institutional run on other Wall Street firms (more rumors surfaced that Lehman Brothers—which owned an alt-A and subprime lender in Colorado called Aurova Loan Services—was in trouble, too), Federal Reserve officials approached Dimon. Dimon agreed to the deal but told Bernanke that he didn't want anything to do with the $30 billion in CDOs and ABSs. The Fed said fine and outsourced management of the $30 billion to Black Rock Financial, a boutique investment banking firm managed by Larry Fink, a contemporary of Lew Ranieri.[13]

A week later, after the panic about Bear's condition had passed—and after reports that chairman Cayne was preparing a counteroffer to the $2-a-share bid—Dimon increased his buyout price to $10 a share or $1.2 billion. Cayne quickly dropped his idea and sold all of the remaining shares he owned in the company (about 5.6 million), walking away with $60 million. His wife sold all her shares, too, taking home $500,000. Bear was finished. Cayne was now available to play bridge full-time.

---

[13] In the early 1980s, Fink, then the head of First Boston's mortgage department, took Ranieri's MBS structure and improved upon it, coming up with a similar bond called a collateralized mortgage obligation (CMO). CMOs used a trust structure to pay bondholders. The payments were guaranteed, which made investors feel better about buying the instruments. In the modern era many mortgage securities are actually CMOs, although the term *MBS* is still used.

Chapter 12

What the Hell Happened?

Ten Bad Years for Housing in America

The mortgage is an unstable asset.

—Lewie Ranieri

I see the bad moon arising.

—Creedence Clearwater Revival

Jim Rokakis is a serious man, one who looks at housing foreclosure numbers and gets angry. He didn't lose his home, but as treasurer of Cuyahoga County, Ohio, which includes the rust belt city of Cleveland and its surrounding suburbs, he saw almost 51,000 residents fall into foreclosure from 2004 to the end of 2007. In 2008 alone foreclosures swelled to 15,000—a huge number. "The average number of bank-initiated foreclosures in this county averaged 3,300 to 3,500 per year prior to the crisis," he said. Rokakis blamed what he calls a "swarm of speculators, real estate agents, mortgage brokers, and lenders" who focused on the city of Cleveland, in particular a place called Slavic Village, a once-stable neighborhood made up of Polish and Czech immigrants whose demographic had been changing over to other

minorities in recent years. He blamed the speculators and those who
funded them for the death of a 12-year-old girl named Asteve "Cookie"
Thomas, who stumbled into the crossfire of a suspected drug deal. To
some degree, he held them responsible for the death of Joe Krasucki, a
78-year-old resident who had lived in the neighborhood for 40 years.
One night Krasucki heard a loud scraping noise outside his home and
went to investigate. "He caught thugs ripping aluminum siding off his
house," Rokakis later said in an interview. "The price of scrap aluminum
had gone up to $1 a pound." Krasucki was beaten up by the gang of
teenagers who were doing some nighttime prospecting. The senior citizen died 10 days later.

Rokakis blames the destabilization of Slavic Village on the foreclosures, which left at least 800 homes vacant out of 4,500 (at last count).
Once vacant, they became prey to vandals; at least that's how Rokakis,
the county treasurer since 1996, saw it. He blamed the foreclosures on
what he called "weekend tycoons" who had access to easy mortgage
money and began flipping homes in the neighborhood. And he blamed
the easy money on lenders and the Wall Street firms that securitized the
loans, providing liquidity to the market. At the very top of his "lenders to
blame" list was Roland Arnall's Argent Mortgage, the wholesale originator that relied on loan brokers to pitch mortgages to consumers. While
Arnall was presiding over diplomatic affairs in The Hague with his wife
Dawn, the foreclosures continued rolling through Slavic Village. Using
research conducted by Cleveland State University, Rokakis pinpointed
the cause of it all: Between 2003 and 2007, Arnall's company, using loan
brokers, originated just over 11,000 mortgages in the Cleveland area.
By the fall of 2007, loans brought into Argent by its account executives
had negative equity of $230 million, which meant the homes were sup-
posedly overvalued by that much. When *National Mortgage News* began
working on a story about Cleveland State's findings in September of
2007, Arnall's PR man in Orange, Chris Orlando, said he would comment but first he wanted to know how, exactly, Rokakis and university investigators had arrived at their figures, a fair question for sure. The
answer was this: Investigators Thomas Bier and Ivan Maric compared
the loan amount funded by Argent to the county auditor's median market value. (The median is the halfway point between the highest and
lowest value when all the homes in question are lined up end to end.)

When Muolo called Orlando to give him the details for the *National Mortgage News* story, Orlando never returned the phone call. What was the point, really? Argent was now part of Citigroup.

By the fall, 25 percent of mortgages funded by Argent in Cleveland neighborhoods like Slavic Village were in some stage of foreclosure. It can be said of Rokakis that he has dedicated his life to public service. A Democrat, he served 19 years on the Cleveland City Council before he became county treasurer. He can point to the exact year when all the trouble started in Cleveland: 2002, when lobbyists in the state capital in Columbus working for the subprime industry beat back local efforts to eliminate prepayment penalties on loans and mandate credit counseling for borrowers. "They felt they couldn't have local governments—they couldn't tolerate local governments telling them what to do, dictating terms to national lenders," he said. When asked which firm in particular, which lobbyists, he was at a loss to give specifics. "Lobbyists?" he asked. "It's just a sea of faces," though he did single out Bruce McCrodden, the head lobbyist for National City Bank, which had sold Bill Dallas's former subprime shop, First Franklin, to Merrill Lynch. "As we all know, National City and First Franklin were major players in the subprime market and their destructive practices cost us thousands of jobs here when PNC bought out the failing National City."[1]

In early 2006 when Ameriquest agreed to pay $325 million in damages to settle abusive lending charges (without admitting any wrongdoing), Argent wasn't a party to the case. In his lawsuit against Arnall's holding company, Argent chief Wayne Lee highlighted the wholesale unit's "superior performance" (compared to Arnall's retail lender, Ameriquest), noting his division's "legal protocol and financial discipline." In other words, Lee (who wanted the $50 million owed to him under his consulting agreement) felt that even though Ameriquest had some "bad apples" (Adam Bass's words for renegade loan officers who were playing fast and loose), Argent's account executives weren't out there engaged in schemes to qualify borrowers for loan amounts they couldn't afford while charging them higher interest rates and fees.

---

[1] Besides owning First Franklin for several years, National City was a major warehouse lender to nonbank subprime originators.

These were the allegations that Ameriquest's retail loan officers had faced. Lee didn't see Argent in that light at all. But Jim Rokakis did.

Tom Miller, the Iowa attorney general and the lead AG on the states' case against Ameriquest, had been hearing predatory lending allegations for years but decided to go after Arnall's retail arm, leaving Argent out of his sights. His game plan was to attack what he called the company's "culture" where the goal was to "do whatever it takes to make the loan."

The AG said the settlement negotiations with Arnall's attorneys, which included company general counsel Thomas J. Noto, were "hard fought." Despite all the allegations of what Miller called "misrepresentations" by Ameriquest's loan officers, the company was tenacious—just like its loan officers had been. "The big issue was money," Miller told reporter Mathew Padilla. "How much they would pay. They didn't make concessions easily. They would debate points." On occasion Arnall would be involved in the talks with the AGs but usually stayed out of them. By the time Miller got around to going after wholesale lenders and brokers, he had bigger problems on his plate: "Our focus now is on the foreclosure crisis," he said.

In late 2007 the Cuyahoga County treasurer said he wanted to sue someone. He just didn't know where to start. In the fall he wrote an op-ed piece in the *Washington Post,* outlining what he felt had gone wrong in Slavic Village, mentioning the deaths of Cookie Thomas and Joe Krasucki. Financial news stories are usually anathema to television producers (because they're generally about numbers, which means boring pictures), but two homicides and video of hundreds of boarded-up homes led ABC and NBC to send anchors Charles Gibson and Brian Williams, respectively, to Cleveland. Even the foreign press began arriving on Rokakis' doorstep in Cleveland. "Japanese public TV is here today," he said. "On Monday French reporters are coming." The Cuyahoga County treasurer called the mortgage debacle the "perfect crime." He listed the perpetrators: loan brokers, lenders, appraisers, Realtors, and Wall Street.

The only major financial party missing from Rokakis's chain of blame was the rating agencies: Moody's, Standard & Poor's, and Fitch, the three credit watchdogs whose job it was to analyze and then rate subprime mortgage-backed securities (MBSs), all the various tranches[2]

---

[2] A tranche represents a slice of all the different cash flows in a pool of mortgages. One pool of loans can be cut into many smaller pieces, each with a different dollar amount, risk profile, and prepayment rate. As Lewie Ranieri had once noted, "mortgages are about math."

contained within them, as well as collateralized debt obligations (CDOs) built from those very same tranches. In time, he added them to his list. In an interview with *National Mortgage News* he mentioned an analyst from Moody's who had telephoned City Hall "and told me to stop talking so much."

"You'd better stop talking" accusations like that might make Rokakis sound like someone who had gone off the deep end or at least a critic who, perhaps, was carrying things a bit too far. But one thing seemed certain to him: Sharon Dumas, the finance director for the city of Cleveland, told Rokakis that his continued discussions with the media did prompt calls from another rating agency that was concerned what affect all the vacant homes (whose owners were no longer paying real estate taxes) might have on the city's bond ratings. It was yet another slap in the face from Wall Street, said the treasurer. "The same rating agencies that helped prime the pump for the subprime crisis were now threatening the city with a downgrade over the vacant property problem they helped create. Unbelievable, isn't it?" he said.

But "Where were the rating agencies?" was a point Lewie Ranieri had made back in December of 2006 when he noted that these bond market watchdogs had been cast into the role of "quasi regulator" of the nonprime market because so many mortgages—subprime, "A" paper 80/20 loans, stated-income mortgages, and payment option ARMs—were now outside the boundaries of what Fannie Mae and Freddie Mac would buy.

Forget subprime for a minute. In 2006, the second best year ever for the mortgage industry, when lenders originated $3.2 trillion in new loans, $665 billion of the total pie was subprime (A– to D in quality) or about 21 percent, a near record. But another $650 billion or so fell under the rubric of stated-income loans, payment option ARMs, and 80/20 mortgages—loans where the borrowers supposedly had decent credit scores. It appeared that the days of Fannie's and Freddie's dominance in the mortgage market were over. (The two GSEs, however, were supplying backdoor liquidity to the subprime and alt-A business by purchasing some of the end bonds created by Wall Street.) The phrase *private label securities* came into vogue to describe bonds being issued where Fannie/Freddie loans weren't being used as collateral. Wall Street was in charge—lending money to nonbank originators (through warehouse lines), buying and securitizing the loans, designing the loan products, and then eventually owning some of the rank–and–file lenders. Merrill Lynch owned First Franklin and part of Ownit. Bear Stearns laid claim to EMC and Encore Credit. Lehman Brothers owned BNC Mortgage and Aurora Loan Services. The Street, to some degree, had taken over a huge part of the residential mortgage industry, and most Americans who were taking out these loans had no idea that their lender might be a Wall Street firm. Remember: Investment bankers didn't put the names of their firms on their mortgage affiliates. The managing directors from lower Manhattan had borrowed from the Arnall playbook: They were doing their best to "stay under the radar."

In late August of 2007, the McGraw-Hill Companies, the parent of Standard & Poor's, announced that the president of the bond rating agency, Kathleen Corbet, would be stepping down. By then, Bear Stearns' hedge funds were in bankruptcy, Countrywide was struggling with bankruptcy rumors, dozens of subprime nonbanks were closing their doors every week, and New York Attorney General Andrew Cuomo had begun talking to executives at the underwriting outsourcing firms (Clayton Holdings and The Bohan Group) about the loan review work they had been doing for Wall Street over the past four years. Just about every financial firm involved in the mortgage process was now taking some type of heat for rising mortgage delinquencies, the mounting write-downs being taken by overseas banks and investors in subprime CDOs, and the biggie: declining home prices. Now the bond rating agencies were getting the spotlight pointed their way. Wasn't it their job to review the underlying collateral (receiving a fee for their work) and grade the bonds by judging the probability of default? Why hadn't they spotted potential problems with all the subprime ABSs and CDOs being issued during those years? Instead, many of these bonds that began defaulting in the spring of 2007 (and kept right on defaulting) had received investment-grade ratings (BBB or higher) from S&P, Moody's, and Fitch.

When Corbet resigned from S&P, little was said about the reason she was leaving, but a spokesman for the company denied that her departure was tied to all the new criticism being heaped on the agency. In their defense, the rating agencies could argue that whatever the underlying collateral (subprime, 80/20s, stated-income), the bonds had protection because the cash flow on many of these securities was insured by bond insurance giants Ambac Financial Group, MBIA Inc., and Financial Guaranty Insurance Company (FGIC). Richard Wilkes, the mortgage industry veteran who spent most of his career making "A" paper loans (and serving as a consultant to Wall Street), thought otherwise. "Wall Street was into cranking out the volume," he said. "The Street would take out the worst credit pieces and overcollateralize them [with bond insurance]. They could get some of these up to an 'AA' rating. It was like polishing a turd."

Mark Goldhaber, the Genworth mortgage insurance executive who spent his days analyzing legislation, lobbying, and looking at loan level loss data, saw a different problem with the rating agencies. He viewed them as being involved in an inherent conflict-of-interest situation. "If you were a rating agency and wanted the business of a certain sub-prime lender, would you give them a bad grade?" he asked. Then again, his criticism was slightly off. The lenders didn't, as a technical matter, pay the rating agencies. The investment banking firm issuing the bond did. However, anyone who knows how Wall Street works realizes that the idea is to pass on costs. The money Bear or Merrill might pay to S&P to get its bonds rated ultimately will be borne by the lender selling the loans to the Street.

As the criticism of S&P, Fitch, and Moody's continued, executives from the three were called to testify before the Senate Banking Committee. Topic A: Were they asleep at the wheel during the past four years? Vickie Tillman, executive vice president of S&P, in her testimony made a salient point to the committee: "S&P does not rate the underlying mortgage loans made to homeowners or evaluate whether making those loans was a good idea in the first place." She noted that those tasks fell to the actual lender who was dealing with the consumer. It fell upon the company underwriting the loans.

Her agency's job, she continued, was to weigh judgment on "how much cash we believe the underlying loans are likely to generate" toward paying off the bondholders. Then, in her written testimony, she went into a long-drawn-out description of the different software programs and models it had been using, noting that S&P looks at 70 different "inputs" (loan characteristics), including such things as equity in the home, whether the owner lives there, and the extent to which the borrower's income was verified. S&P's job, she said, was to create software models that calculate "probabilities of default and losses realized on default." In other words, it wasn't their fault. Go talk to the lender or the Wall Street firm or Clayton or Bohan, which were supposed to be reviewing the loans prior to securitization.

But an executive at Clayton, who didn't want to be identified, said his company informed the rating agencies of the number of "exceptions" on loan pools as early as 2005. An exception meant the loans being bought by the Street didn't meet all the underwriting guidelines (what the Street would accept on such things as loan-to-value ratios, for example) they had laid out in advance. He said Clayton Holdings took the exception information to the rating agencies. Their reaction? "They said, 'We don't want to see it,'" he told a reporter. "'It doesn't fit our models,' they told us." He said that while grading loans in 2005 the agencies were "basing their results on models from the year 2000."

Then again, Clayton and Bohan—as Carl Chamberlain and other laptop grunts told reporters Muolo and Padilla—were primarily interested in reunderwriting loans as quickly as possible, because that's what the managing directors at Bear, Merrill, and the other Street firms wanted. As Richard Wilkes noted, "Wall Street was into cranking out the volume."

Shortly after S&P's Tillman testified before the Senate, a source began writing Muolo at *National Mortgage News*. He used the pseudonym of "Jon Mayer" and only sent e-mails from his home computer. He claimed to be in upper/middle management at one of the three rating agencies but declined to say which one. His specialty was structured finance and commercial MBS. He said he liked his job but admitted that all the public criticism of the rating agencies was, for the most part, well deserved. In his first correspondence with the newspaper, a well-written three-page letter, he made these five points:[3]

1. We rate deals based upon banker-provided summaries almost exclusively. We perform limited to no independent due diligence. We do, however, disclaimer our ratings against this flaw in our approach. Comical. In a previous work-life, if we ever took banker [Wall Street] numbers at face value we would be fired.
2. We back-fill our files. Under increased scrutiny from regulators, we are in the process of "cleaning up" our files to eliminate incriminating

---

[3] The full letter was edited down for purposes of this book.

evidence. Most of it is likely related to banker [Wall Street] collusion, which is commonplace even today.

3. We have developed highly sophisticated models and then don't use the results to rate the deals. . . . Then after the feedback is provided to the bankers and they tell us our ratings are horrible and that the other two agencies were better and that we will lose business, calls are made and the ratings change.

4. How do the primary contacts with the bankers from within our firm make their case for pay raises? By how much business they brought in.

5. The investor calls we normally receive are a sad commentary on the system. Most (90 percent $+/-$) questions posed us about newly originated deals are so superficial and/or have so little relevance to the real issues of the deals we rate, that it becomes clear very quickly that they have no clue what they are ready to buy.

The man calling himself Jon Mayer didn't want to be interviewed right away. He said in time he might talk but he didn't want his real name used. He wanted to keep his job. Over the next five months Muolo traded correspondence with the source. Eventually, they talked. He still didn't want to go on the record. By January Mayer's tone had softened somewhat but not too much. In one of his last e-mails he wrote, "Better times are ahead eventually and securitizations are here to stay and will help the markets in the long term I believe. I felt I had to end this on a positive note." Over that five-month period all three of the rating agencies—S&P, Fitch, and Moody's—downgraded subprime bonds to which they had given glowing ratings the previous two years.

On January 30 S&P dropped the mother of all downgrades. Early in the morning it issued a press release saying it had placed on its "credit watch" list "with negative implications" 6,389 classes (tranches) of first-lien subprime bonds that it had rated between January 2006 and 2007. The dollar amount of these bonds: $270 billion. But that wasn't all. It also placed on its watch list (with negative implications) 1,973 ratings on 572 CDOs that were comprised of 572 subprime ABSs. And there was one other announcement out of the rating agency. It had reviewed all of the subprime-related structured investment vehicles (SIVs) it had rated as well, noting that nine of 133 had "exposure" to the 6,389 tranches. SIVs were off-balance-sheet investments that were similar to CDOs. The difference was that a bank or Wall Street firm could create (or set up as an investment) SIVs (using borrowed money) and not have to count them as an on-balance-sheet asset. This meant that their regulator in Washington wouldn't know anything about them. By early 2008 the two banks with the largest SIVs outstanding were Citigroup (whose in-house subprime feeders included Associates First Capital, Commercial Credit, and now what was left of the old Argent franchise) and HSBC Holdings, the London-based bank that owned not only a U.S. depository, but the old Household Finance franchise. Each had $49 billion in SIV investments, which they began putting on their books and taking write-downs against. Both anticipated large losses in the months ahead.

By the spring of 2008 the average American trying to understand the nation's mortgage/housing/credit crisis was facing a barrage of numbers to digest. One fact was certain: Housing and mortgages—so essential to the U.S. economy—were (and still are) joined at the hip. They were Siamese twins: One would not exist without the other. When one does well the other follows. Roughly 27 percent of all outstanding subprime mortgages (1.4 million loans totaling $250 billion in loans) were in some form of default. On the "A" paper side, at least 400,000 loans were late. How many of those mortgages would wind up in foreclosure, and how many Americans would be forced into the street, was unclear. It was all guesswork. Mark Zandi, chief economist for Moody's (the bond rating agency), predicted that 3.3 million home loans would go into default, with two-thirds of the homeowners (2.2 million) facing foreclosure. The hardest-hit markets: Florida, Nevada, Arizona, California, with huge problems also in Ohio, Michigan, and Indiana. The last three states were already in a downturn because of high oil prices ($120 a barrel and rising), which in turn had decimated the bread and butter of the U.S. auto industry: sport utility vehicles and trucks.

Throughout the history of the mortgage industry, economists working in its ranks always pointed to one key factor in determining loan delinquencies: employment figures. Even if home prices weren't rising much and the economy was tepid, borrowers wouldn't default as long as they had a job. But over the past year, one sector of the economy had lost more than 120,000 workers: mortgage bankers and brokers. Also, 300,000 construction jobs had vanished. These workers had homes, too. Dan Perl, who closed his small subprime lending company in early 2007 and went into the loan workout business (investing and curing delinquent mortgages through a company called Citadel Servicing), remembers going surfing in the fall and seeing more young men out in the waves off of Laguna Beach than ever before. He struck up a conversation with some of them. "They claimed they used to be in the mortgage business," he said. At least one of Perl's former hires was living in his car. Richard Wilkes recounted how a friend of his had visited a "gentlemen's club" one evening on the outskirts of Houston and bought drinks for two of the dancers. Two months earlier the ladies had lost their jobs working for a mortgage brokerage firm.

As for the lending companies (which had funded the loans) and the investment bankers (the securitizers), how much in additional pain they would suffer was unclear. By the spring the dollar volume of write-downs taken by investment banking firms, banks, and thrifts was at $200 billion. The S&L crisis of the late 1980s and early 1990s cost U.S. taxpayers $150 billion (not including interest payments on the government bonds issued to rescue that industry). Investors in subprime bonds were looking to the bond insurers (Ambac, FGIC, and MBIA) to recover some of their losses, but all three of those firms were facing insolvency because of subprime claims—claims they never really anticipated paying on.

With unemployment rising nationwide (and not just in mortgage and building sectors) and home prices slipping by 10 percent to 20 percent in some metropolitan areas, the Federal Reserve under Ben Bernanke began cutting short-term interest rates in the fall and right on through 2008. By March the short-term overnight rate was 2.25 percent, compared to 5.25 percent the previous September. Even though Bernanke and his fellow Fed governors were alarmed by exploding oil prices and inflation, their greater worry was a wholesale collapse of the U.S. mortgage market and Wall Street, which had securitized more than $1 trillion in subprime loans during the previous 30 months—which is why the central bank assisted in the sale of Bear Stearns to JPMorgan Chase. Not only was the mortgage crisis playing nightly on the network news, but so too were the woes of Wall Street.

A few days after the Fed-assisted sale of Bear Stearns to JPMorgan Chase, protestors organized by the Neighborhood Assistance Corporation of America, a consumer rights lobbying organization (headed by a former loan broker named Bruce Marks), stormed the lobby of Bear's headquarters on Madison Avenue, chanting "Help Main Street, not Wall Street" and carrying signs that read, "Blame the mortgage tsunami on Bear Stearns." The protestors weren't exactly there by invitation from Jimmy Cayne or Alan Schwartz. Thirty minutes later they were escorted out by New York's finest.

As the crisis worsened and became an issue in the 2008 presidential race that pitted Barack Obama against John McCain, a central question continually being asked was one of the most obvious: Where were the regulators—that is, the folks in Washington? What about the Federal Reserve? Hadn't Alan Greenspan seen this coming? Greenspan, who retired from the Fed in early 2006, had made a speech before the National Credit Union Association, the largest credit union trade group in the United States, pontificating that Americans' preference for long-term fixed-rate mortgages meant many were paying more for their homes than if they had taken out an adjustable-rate mortgage (ARM). ARMs typically had lower start rates, and when those rates adjusted they might still be lower than long-term fixed-rate mortgages, or so went the argument. Greenspan also noted that consumers would benefit if only lenders offered more "alternative" loan products. Time and time again the speech would be cited as an example of how Greenspan had basically become a spokesman for all types of alternative (non-Fannie/Freddie) mortgages, including payment option ARMs, and subprime ARMs that adjusted after their two- and three-year start rates expired. The date of speech: February 2004, just before subprime and alt-A originations exploded along with the securitization market.

Blaming Greenspan alone for the subprime crisis might be a stretch, but there's a rich irony that both the general public and media missed. According to activist Bob Gnaizda of the Greenlining Institute in Berkeley, California, Greenspan himself had a fixed-rate loan! The group met with the central banker and his staff semiannually to discuss policy issues such as mortgages and inner city development. In July of 2004, a few months after his ARM speech, Greenlining staffers, including director John Gamboa, sat down with Greenspan. The primary topic was ARMs—in particular payment option ARMs, which were just beginning to catch on in a major way with consumers. The group was worried about potential abuses. Gamboa asked Greenspan whether he had an ARM. According to the Greenlining people, the response from The Maestro was: "No. I have a fixed rate." Had he ever had an ARM? Answer: "No. I like the certainty."

When Bernanke became the new Fed chairman, he and Mozilo spoke before a Greenlining Institute conference in April 2006. The Countrywide CEO was invited both because the company was the nation's largest lender and because, according to Gnaizda, "Mozilo said the right things about minority home ownership rates, and that's a laudable thing to do." (Countrywide was also the largest home lender to minorities, a fact of which Mozilo was extremely proud. Countrywide even issued press releases each year when trade publications like *Inside Mortgage Finance* and *National Mortgage News* published their annual rankings of the largest originators to African-Americans, Hispanics, and other groups. The figures ultimately came from the Federal Reserve.)

When the Greenlining Institute staffers met with Greenspan in 2004, the group tried to push the Fed into making lenders adhere to a voluntary code of conduct in regard to how they dealt with mortgage customers. Gnaizda, general counsel of the group, had been hearing too many stories about loan abuses. The legal settlements on predatory lending allegations regarding Household Finance and Associates First Capital—now the properties of HSBC and Citigroup, respectively— were still somewhat fresh. But Greenspan, according to Gnaizda, just wasn't interested. "He never gave us a good reason, but he didn't want to do it," said the Greenlining attorney.[4]

The biggest problem with being a federal regulator of banks, thrifts, or credit unions is that these agencies don't necessarily regulate depositories on the front end where the loans are made. Federal regulators working out of Washington dictate rules and regulations as to what kind of loans depositories can originate and *hold*. By law, savings and loans (S&Ls) are required to have a majority of their on-balance-sheet holdings in home mortgages. Examiners in the regional offices of both the Office of Thrift Supervision (OTS) and the Federal Deposit

---

[4] Greenspan turned down a request by reporter Matt Padilla to discuss Gnaizda's version of their meeting and other matters.

Insurance Corporation (FDIC) spent their time looking at the quality of assets being held on the books of S&Ls and banks. Alarm bells don't go off until an institution under their control starts reporting losses or write-downs. The predatory/abusive lending case against Arnall's Ameriquest, for example, was brought by 49 state attorneys general. It had nothing at all to do with Washington. Even though Ameriquest received warehouse lines of credit from Wall Street firms and banks, it wasn't an FDIC- or OTS-regulated company.

The Federal Reserve and the Office of the Comptroller of the Currency (OCC), which also regulated banks, had no jurisdiction whatsoever over Arnall's companies. Long ago the future ambassador to the Netherlands had sent a message to Washington by burning his S&L charter and placing its ashes in an urn sitting on a credenza behind his desk. The closest Washington had come to issuing any type of policy statement on how residential loans should be originated was the "Guidance on Non-Traditional Mortgages" working paper that came out in the fall of 2006—long after Ameriquest, Household Finance, Associates First Capital Corporation, and dozens of other subprime lenders found themselves in trouble, accused of taking advantage of homeowners by charging them hidden fees, higher rates, and more points than they realized, and having them take out larger loan amounts than they needed. But again, that working paper had no teeth; it was purely guidance. It could be thrown in the trash and there wasn't much a federal examiner could do—until the late payment notices began to pile up.

Earlier in the decade, accusations of predatory lending were lobbed by consumer groups at certain lenders that specialized in refinancings. In general, a predatory lender is a firm that originates a loan without caring whether the borrower can repay it. Why would a lender do such a thing? Answer: because on a refinancing it can make a ton of money on all the points and fees. If the borrower gets into trouble and can't make the payments, the lender forecloses. But if a company were truly engaged in predatory lending for profit (instead of, say, just being reckless or greedy) such a business model would work only if a house had enough equity that a foreclosure wouldn't harm the profit picture.

The Federal Reserve was in charge of enforcing the Truth in Lending Act legislation, whose lawyerly description is "to protect consumers from unfair or deceptive home mortgage lending and advertising practices." The description is so general that it actually gives the Fed more latitude in dealing with dirtbag lenders. But as Alan Greenspan noted many times, his job as Fed chairman was to fight inflation. Keeping a watchful eye on subprime lenders was not something the central bank did. Alan Greenspan may've been considered one of the greatest Fed chairmen who ever lived, but he wasn't infallible. In the mid-1980s when the nation's top S&L regulator, Edwin Gray, first began to raise questions about Charlie Keating's thrift, Lincoln Savings—eventually accusing the Arizona businessman of speculating on commercial real estate projects with government-insured deposits—Greenspan, then a private economist, wrote to Gray telling him not to worry so much. On Keating's behalf,[5] he wrote a letter to the Federal Home Loan Bank Board,[6] telling Gray that deregulation was working as planned, naming 17 thrifts—including Lincoln—that had reported record profits and were prospering. Four years after Greenspan wrote his letter, 16 of those S&Ls had failed. (By then Greenspan was ensconced as the new Fed chairman.)

In the fall of 2007, while promoting his memoir, *The Age of Turbulence,* he told *60 Minutes* that he was aware that some subprime lenders were making ARMs with low teaser rates that might cause payment shock later on after the rate adjusted, but he didn't realize the harm it might cause. "While I was aware a lot of these practices were going on, I had no notion of how significant they had become until very late," he said. "I didn't get it until very late in 2005 and 2006."

One thing the Fed didn't do, at least until 2006, was to collect subprime loan volumes from lenders. It collected overall loan volumes—including mortgages originated and sold to Fannie Mae and Freddie Mac and insured by the government—but not specific information on subprime mortgages. To be sure, though, the Fed did in fact have subprime data; it just didn't come from the Fed itself. It came from *National Mortgage News,* which besides being a trade newspaper that covered the industry also collected origination figures (both prime and subprime) from some of its 10,000 readers. James Kennedy, one of the

---

[5] As a consultant to Keating, Greenspan had received $40,000 for his work.
[6] The Federal Home Loan Bank Board was the predecessor agency to the Office of Thrift Supervision.

agency's top researchers working on a subprime project for Greenspan, had ordered subprime origination figures for all the nation's top lenders from *National Mortgage News*. According to the newspaper's senior researcher, Deartra Todd, Kennedy in 2002 had ordered a list of the top subprime originators for calendar year 2000, when the business hadn't yet even taken off. A few years later Kennedy had inquired about ordering more data but never followed through. Each year other banks in the Federal Reserve System ordered data from the newspaper, so at least some of them knew just how large the nonprime sector had grown. Whether they shared the subprime rankings with Greenspan is unclear.

If any other banking agencies in Washington were alarmed by the boom that occurred in subprime lending—$2.4 trillion in A– to D mortgages originated from the beginning of 2004 to the end of 2007, or 20 percent of all loans funded in the United States (a record)—they hardly voiced much concern, at least publicly. Perhaps because Wall Street was busy securitizing almost all of the loans being originated, they figured: If it's good enough for the Street it must be okay. But the false sense of security (if there had been such a thing) ended in late February 2007 when Fremont General of Santa Monica, California, an FDIC-insured bank that was also the nation's sixth largest subprime lender, said it would delay both its fourth quarter and full-year earnings releases, which were due shortly. The news sent Fremont General's shares tumbling, down 20 percent alone on the day the news came out, to a new 52-week low, $8.79 (its 52-week high was $24).

When it came to broker-produced loans, Fremont General was also the fifth largest wholesale subprime lender in the nation. A few weeks earlier the lender had cut 8,000 brokers from its approved list of third-party originators, a move that was revealed in a speech by company vice president Mike Koch at an American Securitization Forum trade show in Las Vegas. The reason given: Those brokers were responsible for some of the highest delinquency rates in the nation. When the earnings delay became public, Fitch lowered its ratings on the company, exacerbating its problems. The FDIC took notice. Just after the earnings delay was announced by Fremont, the agency held an emergency meeting in Washington with 28 of its senior executives and another 53 others piped in from regional offices via telephone. "It was like a three-alarm fire and the bells were going off," said one FDIC attorney.

At least four executives from Clayton Holdings were invited to give testimony to the assembled regulators. Why Clayton? The company, which had recently gone public, not only was a due diligence outsourcing contractor to Wall Street, but held itself out as an expert in subprime and alt-A securities, advising clients (buyers and sellers) on such matters as compliance (making sure regulations and laws are adhered to) and surveillance (tracking the performance) of bonds. Clayton had been a paid consultant to the FDIC for about 15 years, noted one company insider. The topic of the meeting: the growing mortgage crisis. According to one executive who attended the meeting (which was never reported on by the press), Fremont was a key topic but "what the regulators wanted to hear from Clayton was color." The executive, who didn't want to be quoted by name, said a Clayton manager told the regulators that the mortgage correction "was going to be painful but that it wouldn't turn out to be an S&L-like crisis." The manager, whose name wasn't revealed, also said there would be "pain" and that it would be "systematic," the chief reason being adjustable-rate mortgages, both subprime and "A" paper loans, $1.5 trillion of which were scheduled to reset at (presumably) higher interest rates over the next 18 months. Not only were consumers going to lose their homes, but if enough loans went bad a couple of hundred banks could go under.

Banks failing could prove problematic for the FDIC, an agency that under former chairman William Seidman had forged a reputation as being a tough and proactive regulator during the S&L and banking crises of the late 1980s and early 1990s. The FDIC insurance fund almost went broke, but Seidman had steered the agency through troubled waters by raising insurance premiums on banks (which brought in much-needed insurance money to help bail out depositors at failing institutions) and not hesitating to close troubled institutions. (Seidman also chaired the S&L bailout agency, the Resolution Trust Corporation.) How tough a regulator was Seidman? Serving in the George H.W. Bush administration, he made the decision to sue one of the president's sons, Neil Bush, for his role in the collapse of a Denver savings and loan called Silverado.[7] But during the first administration of George W. Bush

---

[7] Neil Bush later settled the lawsuit, agreeing to pay damages to the Federal Savings and Loan Insurance Corporation, which insured the deposits of Silverado.

and part of the second, the agency's chairman was Donald Powell, a former Texas banker from Amarillo who also had been a fund-raiser for Bush. In October 2004 Powell made the decision to slash 10 percent of the agency's 5,300-strong workforce through layoffs. Inside the agency some supervisors were concerned that by losing so many workers the FDIC would be left flat-footed in the event of a banking crisis.

Powell left the FDIC in the fall of 2005 after the White House named him federal coordinator of the government's Gulf Coast rebuilding effort, dealing with the aftermath of hurricanes Katrina, Rita, and Wilma. His successor was Sheila Bair, who had done a short stint at the Treasury Department (2001–2002) and while there made her mark by trying to persuade subprime lenders to adopt a best-practices code. This was right before the boom in subprime lending took off. Bair later told the *New York Times* that many subprime firms rejected the idea outright, and those that adopted the code then quickly abandoned it when competition and originations soared. It appeared as though Bair had an idea early on that something wasn't quite right in the subprime industry—at least when it came to firms like Ameriquest, Associates, and Household taking advantage of homeowners who were desperate for money.

A few months after the FDIC's emergency meeting on Fremont General,[8] Bair made a speech in Washington before the New York Bankers Association, making note of rising residential loan delinquencies and an increase in troubled subprime lenders. She blamed the then emerging subprime crisis (before it snowballed into a mortgage/housing crisis and then a worldwide credit contagion) on loan brokers. She said that mortgage lenders that use brokers "need to know" who they are dealing with. During the Q&A, she said brokers "are a big chunk of the problem," but noted that "we don't regulate brokers." No, but the FDIC regulated five of the 20 largest subprime lenders in the nation—all of which used brokers.

Over the next year brokers would be pilloried for helping cause the crisis, but there was one thing the critics were missing: Brokers

---

[8] In April 2008, under pressure from the FDIC, Fremont announced a tentative sale of most of its assets for $90 million to an investment company in Maryland that wanted its 22 branches and $5.6 billion in deposits. Its share price had fallen to just 11 cents from a two-year high of $25.

wouldn't exist without wholesalers, and wholesalers wouldn't be able to fund loans unless Wall Street was buying. It wasn't the loan broker's job to approve the customer's application and check all the financial information; that was the wholesaler's job, or at least it was supposed to be. Brokers didn't design the loans, either. The wholesalers and Wall Street did that. If Wall Street wouldn't buy, then there would be no loan to fund. At the same time, brokers weren't choirboys (and choirgirls), either. Still, a loan where a broker could make several thousand dollars in fees first had to be approved by an underwriter at a wholesale lender like Merrill's First Franklin. The wholesaler had the first opportunity to spot trouble. If the underwriter missed it, there was one last wall to breach: the contract underwriters at Clayton or Bohan, where people like Carl Chamberlain worked.

It can be said of the mortgage/housing crisis of 2007 and 2008 that it was not caused by government deregulation. It wasn't. No major laws were changed to pave the way for what happened. (The Glass-Steagall Act, which banned banks from securities underwriting and prevented Wall Street firms from owning depositories—banks and thrifts—was slowly dismantled during the final years of the Clinton administration. It can be argued that if Citigroup, for instance, weren't allowed to underwrite subprime bonds, its near financial collapse in early 2009 would never have happened.)[9]

But it also can be said that during the Bush years regulators didn't regulate. As Lewie Ranieri noted in his December 2006 speech and then later on in subsequent interviews, the Securities and Exchange Commission (SEC) was more or less absent—when it shouldn't have been. The rating agencies, as Jon Mayer noted, seemed to be rubber-stamping securities with investment-grade ratings just so they could gain business and make additional fee income. In late 2007 and early 2008 when he came to Washington, Ranieri would sometimes visit with regulators at the Office of the Comptroller of the Currency and

[9] Glass-Steagall became law in 1933 in the depths of the Great Depression. One Congressman who was instrumental in dismantling Glass-Steagall working with the Clinton administration was Representative James Leach, Republican of Iowa. Leach maintains that doing away with the 65-year-old law in 1998 had no effect on the mortgage and credit crisis.

the Office of Thrift Supervision, among other agencies. "I think they're starting to get it," he said. "I think I've scared them enough."

Maybe not. On Thursday morning, March 13, 2008, Treasury secretary Henry Paulson called a press conference in Washington to discuss the results of a study done by the President's Working Group on Financial Markets, which consisted of his agency, the Fed, the SEC, and the Commodity Futures Trading Commission. Seven months earlier, Paulson had been pushing the White House's line that the U.S. subprime crisis would not spill over to other parts of the nation's economy or to world economies. Now, finally, the former Goldman Sachs CEO came clean. The report he was discussing that morning before 50 reporters and TV cameramen (most of them live) had concluded: "The turmoil in financial markets clearly was triggered by a dramatic weakening of underwriting standards for U.S. subprime mortgages, beginning in late 2004 and extending into early 2007." The report's diagnosis singled out the credit rating agencies (Fitch, S&P, and Moody's) and "those involved" in securitizing subprime. The diagnosis bullet-point section of the report never once used the phrases *Wall Street* or *investment bankers.*

Paulson told the press that securitization had paved the way for lower-cost mortgages to be made to millions of Americans but also complained about what he called "extreme complexity" of financial instruments (credit default swaps, among other instruments) and a lack of transparency for investors. But he also blamed investors for not knowing what they were buying and cautioned that whatever regulatory changes might lie ahead, the Treasury under his direction would not stifle "financial innovation" in the marketplace, which meant that the creation and trading in such instruments as credit default swaps (used to hedge or speculate, depending on what the customer wanted to do) would continue. The next day Bear Stearns' stock plunged, and by the following Monday the government had arranged its sale to JPMorgan Chase.

As part of his newspaper's coverage on accelerating home foreclosures in Southern California, *Orange County Register* reporter Padilla and another member of the paper, Andrew Galvin, decided to observe a trustee's sale at the steps of the Santa Ana Courthouse, part of a sprawling campus of civic buildings in the heart of Orange County. A trustee's sale is when an agent for a bank (or many banks) auctions homes of delinquent (foreclosed) owners. That day 80 properties were originally set for auction, a total much higher than in previous months. But when the reporters arrived they learned most planned sales were canceled or postponed, often because an owner filed for bankruptcy—a tactic that can delay a foreclosure in California but not prevent it.

It was late 2007. There was a sizable crowd, about 40 people, for the trustee's sale. Crowds tend to be small, because buyers have to show up with the full amount of the home, several hundred thousand dollars, in cashier's checks. Not many folks like carrying around that kind of coin. And homes are auctioned as is, sight unseen. Buyers don't get to peek inside unless they contact the current homeowners and convince them to open up—not a likely scenario.

With a big crowd, Padilla was hoping for some activity. But as Travis Toth, the agent for Fidelity National Title, read off details of homes, the would-be buyers just stood around, still as statues. Almost no one bid, and when someone did make an offer it was a halfhearted lowball bid. No takers for a four-bedroom house in Anaheim, home to the happiest place on Earth (Disneyland), offered for a minimum $684,000 when the buyer owed $778,484. No takers for a two-bedroom condo in coastal Huntington Beach—the bank wanted a little more than the debt of $394,952. And on and on. All 30 properties went straight back to the bank for lack of serious interest. The *Orange County Register* reporters interviewed some folks in the crowd, and found that most were just getting interested in the idea of foreclosure investing. A few serious investors said the properties they wanted had been postponed and also complained it was becoming seriously difficult to make money on foreclosures, since it took time to clean them up and find a buyer, while all that time home prices were sliding to no one knew where.

By the spring of 2008 the two biggest guessing games in economic and finance circles became: (1) How much would the mortgage/housing mess cost companies (and the U.S. economy)? and (2) Just how many Americans would lose their homes? Mark Zandi of Moody's was saying 3.3 million homes. Some consumer groups were saying that by 2009 the number could reach 5 million. On Wall Street and at the large money center banks like Citigroup and Wachovia, the billion-dollar write-downs and losses tied to subprime CDOs kept rolling along. Some firms bolstered their capital by getting overseas investors to buy into their once-vaunted franchises. Citigroup and UBS received sizable investments from Middle Eastern and Singaporean investors.

To make matters worse, the Justice Department was still investigating the collapse of Bear Stearns' two hedge funds, and the FBI had started a new task force to investigate (mostly) subprime companies, with 17 firms on its "must call" list including Countrywide, New Century, and others.[10] In New York, Attorney General Andrew Cuomo had granted immunity to top officials at Clayton Holdings. Cuomo's hope was that Clayton executives would turn on managing directors at Bear, Merrill, and other Wall Street firms that had bought mortgages through their trading desks, securitized them, and then sold them to domestic and foreign investors. Because subprime volumes had cratered, Bear had been firing salespeople and traders on its desk and elsewhere in its mortgage and structured finance departments. As one former company executive told a reporter, "All the people Cuomo should be talking to just walked out the door."

Frank Fillipps, a former mortgage insurance executive who headed Clayton, issued a statement saying his company was cooperating with the AG's office in regard to subprime loans it reviewed that were "exceptions." An exception was a loan characteristic that fell outside the mortgage guidelines a Wall Street firm gave Clayton. Exceptions were supposed to have been flagged by the laptop grunts employed by the firm. But as Carl Chamberlain told reporter Muolo, the guidelines given to the grunts were a joke. "They provided us with one or two copies of the lender's guidelines for a whole job. Sometimes there would be 50 underwriters on-site utilizing these few copies they would give, which were never used by anyone except in a rare instances."

Even though Cuomo's office made a big deal of the cooperation agreement with Clayton, confirming it publicly, one thing his investigators were not doing was talking to the grunts working on the Wall Street underwriting jobs. Several contract underwriters working for both Clayton and Bohan interviewed by reporters Muolo and Padilla said they had never been contacted by the AG or his investigators.

---

[10] According to a report in the *Wall Street Journal,* Countrywide was the subject of a criminal investigation.

But who was at fault, then? Clayton's lead supervisors (who oversaw the grunts) or their contacts at the Wall Street firms? According to Chamberlain, both. "If there was a questionable file, the Clayton lead would consult with Bear, Merrill, whoever was buying. If they felt it was not such a bad issue they would 'make it work.'"

One Clayton official, who did not want to be identified, told Muolo that Cuomo was on a "fishing expedition" with his investigation. (The conversation occurred a few weeks before the company cut its immunity deal.) "Andy is a gorilla. He can be brutal. Some of his own investigators don't like him. They don't know what they're doing." The Clayton executive said the Street didn't really care about loan quality, noting that rejected loans (which received a three rating) were not necessarily turned down by Street loan buyers. "It just meant that the Street firm could use that rating to negotiate a better price [with the lender selling the loan]." The Clayton official wasn't done talking. He blamed the mess on "young Street guys in their 20s," adding, "Due diligence is done only on a small portion of the deals. On the Street it became a case of lemmings. They all followed each other." (In May 2008 Clayton's management issued a statement to reporters Muolo and Padilla in response to several questions. They denied putting any type of quota system on the grunts. "While we do measure productivity and encourage our underwriters to work efficiently, we do not have quotas and we don't fire people or not ask them back for another assignment based on how quickly they work," it said. Clayton added that it was unaware of any instances where leads told underwriters not to use the term *fraud*. It also flatly denied that it was trying to make the loans it reviewed look better than they were, noting that it issued "exception reports" to its Wall Street clients.)

Cuomo wasn't talking with the press about the details of his investigation. A former secretary of the Department of Housing and Urban Development (HUD) during the Clinton administration, he was a lawyer by training who came from a politically well-connected family. His father Mario had been governor of New York, and for a while he was married to a Kennedy. (They later divorced.) In the late 1980s he was involved in a bitter legal battle that pitted him and his business associates against the original management of a Florida S&L called Oceanmark Federal Savings. At the time the younger Cuomo was a

private-sector attorney. The group he represented was allegedly trying to take over control of the thrift from its founders. According to
a report in the *New York Times,* the matter was eventually settled out
of court with Cuomo's group disgorging, at breakeven, the 37 percent
stake in Oceanmark it had accumulated. But before the matter
was settled, Cuomo filed a libel suit against one of his opponents at
Oceanmark, accusing them of attacking him personally to embarrass
the Cuomo family and force him into a settlement. When the headlines got messy (his father was still governor) both parties settled. In
the spring of 2008 Chamberlain was considering calling the AG's office
himself but then decided against it.

Just before Angelo Mozilo stopped talking to Muolo at *National
Mortgage News* he had given a few interviews on various topics. Time
and time again he touched on how best to stem the rising tide of
delinquencies. "You have to stop home prices from sliding," he said.
"You need to get prices going in the other direction." But that wasn't
likely to happen anytime soon. All those payment option ARMs that
his company and countless others had originated—$500 billion worth
in 2006–2007—had given home buyers the ability to buy more house
with less money now. These POAs, which technically weren't even subprime loans, had played a central role in driving up home prices. The
loans also fueled speculators who used these mortgages to keep their
monthly payments low while renting out homes in the hope of flipping them for a quick profit.

During the housing boom so many families in once red-hot markets like Orange County, San Francisco, Boston, Long Island, Las Vegas,
and others turned to POAs because they could keep their monthly
payments low and worry about paying the piper later. What came first:
high housing prices or the POA? It can be argued that prices boomed
artificially in those markets because POA loans created more bidders for
homes. It was a simple case of supply and demand: The more buyers for
a house, the more the price goes up. Take away the POA and no-down-
payment loans and suddenly the pool of buyers is reduced significantly.

---

[11] Andrew Cuomo was a partner in the New York law firm of Blutrich, Falcone and Miller.
The *New York Times* described him as his father's "chief political advisor."

By the spring of 2008 economists at Fannie Mae, Freddie Mac, and other players in the market were forecasting that housing prices wouldn't begin to stabilize until 2009 or 2010. But at the same time so much more was going on in the U.S. economy that was setting the stage for a 10-year potential drought for housing, chief among them: rising unemployment (no job means no money to pay a mortgage); inflation (eventually the Federal Reserve will have to hike rates); rising oil prices (feeding inflation); baby boomers aging (meaning this important demographic would soon be past its peak home-buying years); and failing lenders (meaning fewer companies would be alive to offer mortgages). From December 2006 to the spring of 2008 nearly 300 mortgage lenders either failed or stopped doing business with loan brokers, eliminating this once important way of doing business with the public. Another 10,000 or so loan brokerage firms (out of about 50,000 active companies) had closed, with another 10,000 in danger of failing by the end of 2009.[12] By Mozilo's estimate, almost 40 percent of the lending industry's capacity had been wiped out. Home foreclosures hit a record high, and housing starts (the construction of new homes) reached a 17-year low.

At Countrywide, Mozilo was no longer calling the shots. Executives from Bank of America were running things in Calabasas, consulting with David Sambol, who had been chosen by the bank to head the combined mortgage operation of the two companies and given a hefty salary in the process. However, two months later, Sambol, too, would be out of a job, suddenly announcing his "retirement" when Bank of America has control of Countrywide. Both Bank of America and Sambol would not elaborate. He was 48 years old. Two questions remained: how best to merge Countrywide's huge (but shrinking) mortgage business into Bank of America's and whether the new (combined) mortgage company would still use loan brokers. Bank of America—which was toying with the idea of killing the Countrywide brand name because of all the growing negative publicity surrounding Mozilo and the company he built—had made it clear from day one of the merger announcement that subprime loans would not be offered. The future of the loan brokerage industry looked dim.

---

[12] According to tallies done by both The Mortgage Lender Implode-O-Meter web site and *National Mortgage News*.

Just after the merger had been unveiled, Mozilo was still scheduled to speak at Dick Pratt's midwinter housing conference in Park City, Nevada. Each year for two decades the former Merrill Lynch executive held a three-day seminar on the most important issues affecting the housing and mortgage industries. Attendees got to hear the best of the best voice their opinions, eat fine food, and ski at one of the best resorts in the state. Those who spoke at the meetings were the all-stars of the industry and Wall Street—people like Mozilo, who was scheduled to speak at the 2008 event. Typically, Pratt allowed a few select members of the media to attend and only under the stipulation that all comments were off the record unless the speaker allowed it to be otherwise. Two weeks before the meeting, Mozilo canceled without explanation. Bill Dallas gave the forum's opening speech, entitled "What the Hell Happened? (It Wasn't My Fault. I Just Moved Here.)."

Adam Bass of Ameriquest Capital Corporation, Arnall's holding company (now winding down what was left of its assets after the sale of Argent and Ameriquest's servicing business to Citigroup), was in attendance. The only reporter there was Lew Sichelman, the nationally syndicated housing columnist. A few weeks later Arnall died of cancer in Los Angeles after having resigned his ambassadorship to the Netherlands. He had come back to the United States from Europe to be with a seriously ill son who was also battling cancer. The intensively private man had never let on publicly that he, too, was sick. True to form, he had done his best to live under the radar.

In Calabasas, Mozilo was presumably making retirement plans, but no one knew exactly what his next move might be.[13] If the events of August 2007 had turned out to be merely a correction in the business and not a full-scale decimation of an industry, of the American financial landscape, he would've exited the business something of a hero. Here was a man from the streets of New York who had created a company

---

[13] In the spring of 2008 there were indications that Bank of America's purchase of Countrywide might yet fall apart. A research report issued by Eric Billings' firm, Friedman Billings Ramsey, predicted that Bank of America might have to write down the value of Countrywide's mortgage holdings by up to $30 billion because of defaults and delinquencies. FBR's advice to the bank: walk away from the deal. FBR analyst Paul J. Miller valued Countrywide's shares at $0 to $2 compared to the purchase price of $7.

once worth $45 billion, who built it up against all odds to become number one—and who thirsted to maintain that status in anything having to do with mortgages. He was, more or less, Mr. Mortgage, the public face of an industry, a man who could speak bluntly and honestly about housing and the lenders that financed the clichéd American dream of home ownership.

Those who have known him, friends (and even foes), give him credit for creating a model organization. (Some who had known and competed against him for years were less kind. "Arrogant" was the word used by a former Houston mortgage chief to describe him.) When Mozilo spoke of housing the poorest Americans as well as immigrants (like his grandparents), he was sincere. He had helped millions buy homes, some who never would have had that chance otherwise. He also had become fabulously wealthy doing it. His, like Arnall's, was a rags-to-riches story. If only he hadn't followed Ameriquest into subprime. Mozilo hadn't liked the B&C business in the first place. For most of Countrywide's life, the company had shied away from it.

In one of his last interviews with the Countrywide founder, Muolo again asked him whether he was sorry he had entered that part of the business. Mozilo admitted, "We got caught up in it," and then defensively added, "You had to have an incredible crystal ball to see home values coming down like this." But Mozilo had been in the business for five decades, witnessing boom-and-bust cycles many times before. Should he have known that in this latest cycle (the last of his career) home prices could not keep appreciating at 15 percent to 20 percent a year in some markets, like California?

"I dedicated my life to Countrywide," he said, concluding that day's interview. "I never did spend enough time with my kids. I regret that. My grandkids—I want to go to their games and plays. I told my wife that. It's about the legacy, the name you leave to them."

★   ★   ★

In 1990 the American Dialect Society began picking a "word of the year." At its annual convention, several dozen members would spend a few days locked in a conference room debating which word would receive the distinction. Just because a word got picked as word of the year, though, that didn't necessarily mean it was gaining official entry into the English language. Not at all. It was just something that the group—which dated back to 1889 and whose members included grammarians, linguists, historians, and others (the "rules people," you might say, of language)—did every year to have fun at conventions. In early January 2008 while holding its annual bash in Chicago, the Society (after some debate) chose the word *subprime* to be its word of the year. The other finalists included *Facebook*, *Googleganger*, and *waterboarding*—stiff competition all around.

For at least two decades the term *subprime* had been used in the mortgage industry to refer to consumers whose credit was less than perfect. Now it had entered the American lexicon for two reasons: The country's subprime debacle had sparked a worldwide credit crisis. Overseas banks and investors were now suffering because the subprime collateralized debt obligations (CDOs) they had purchased from Wall Street firms were now defaulting, causing huge losses. A month after Bear Stearns's two hedge funds filed for bankruptcy protection in late July 2007, an Australian hedge fund called Basis Yield Alpha Fund also filed for bankruptcy. Its lenders included the cream of the crop from Wall Street: Citigroup, JPMorgan Chase, Lehman Brothers, and Merrill Lynch. In its bankruptcy filing, Basis Yield Alpha Fund cited mounting losses from subprime mortgage assets—that is, bonds—sold to them by investment bankers in the United States.

And the second reason the word *subprime* had entered the vernacular? American teenagers were now using it as a verb to describe screwing up, doing something bad. As Sherry Muolo, the 15-year-old daughter of co-author Paul Muolo, once put it, "I'd better not subprime that test."

As 2007 rolled into 2008, more tales of foreign banks and financial institutions suffering multibillion-dollar losses because of their investments in subprime CDOs "made in America" began to pile up. In France, Société Générale took a $3 billion loss. In Germany, the government was forced to merge two ailing banks because of their subprime investments. A former investment banker who used to work for Lew Ranieri relayed this story to a reporter: "I just heard the other day about an investor in Abu Dhabi. He said to the Street firm that sold him the CDOs: 'How come I'm losing money? It's triple-A rated.' The Street firm just crapped all over him."

In the summer of 2007, Bush Treasury Secretary Henry Paulson had tried to explain away the nation's subprime crisis and housing collapse as something that was contained to the 50 states—that it wouldn't spread overseas. Paulson's public declarations to that effect had turned out to be horribly wrong. When it came to economic forecasts, the former head of Goldman Sachs wasn't looking too good. The U.S. mortgage mess had sparked an economic worldwide contagion. One little fact that had gone underreported: American bond salespeople were the ones pulling the trigger; they had been peddling subprime CDOs overseas. Did the buyers—both in the United States and in Europe—really understand what they were purchasing?

If you asked Lew Ranieri that question back in 2006, his answer would be an unequivocal "no." Ranieri, when pressed more about the issue, noted, "It's not what you disclosed; it's what you didn't." He said investors didn't necessarily know what the borrower's combined loan to value (CLTV) ratio was (the first and second mortgage combined), whether it was a real appraisal or one pulled off the Internet (automated valuation model), or "whether the guy is a self-employed dishwasher." The way Ranieri saw it, Wall Street, where he had once ruled the roost, was taking CDOs and "selling them to nontraditional mortgage guys. You take these [mortgage] tranches, you put them in CDOs and sell them all around the world." (Even though Ranieri warned against subprime quality and the lack of disclosures on bonds, Franklin Bank, where he was the largest shareholder, ran into financial problems in May 2008. The institution had to mark down the value of what it called "certain uncollectable" second liens. A company investigation also found that management there did not take proper mark-to-market write-downs on some of its assets.)

Arturo Cifuentes, the former Wachovia CDO expert, wasn't so sure about Ranieri's assessment that investors were clueless. "Investors not knowing what they're doing? The disclosures were there," said Cifuentes. "The information was there. That's a lot of bullshit." A reporter asked him another question: Okay, so maybe all the essential information is there. Then how many investors actually read the prospectuses? Cifuentes paused and thought about it: "Some do, and some don't," he said.

In other words, when a bond salesperson from Merrill Lynch calls an Australian hedge fund, the fund manager trusts the person on the other end of the telephone because, after all, the salesperson works at Merrill Lynch. In his book *Liar's Poker*, author Michael Lewis became disgusted with his career as a corporate bond salesman because, in part, he grew to see how the business was all about making the sale and not worrying about what might happen to clients if they were sold a risky corporate bond. It was about making money, or, as Lewis wrote, "In any market, as in any poker game, there is a fool." In the world of subprime CDOs, it was all about transferring risk: from the mortgage lender into an ABS into a CDO. The fool was the last one holding the bond.

Some of these fools were headquartered overseas in faraway lands. Others were foreign banks or investment banking firms that had set up shop in New York City to lend money to nonbank subprime lenders, securitize their mortgages, create tranches, package them into CDOs, and send them across the Atlantic. Some were unlucky enough not to find investors for the CDOs, which meant they held them in their own investment accounts. Germany's Deutsche Bank, Switzerland's UBS Securities, and the Royal Bank of Scotland's Greenwich Capital were all major players in the U.S. subprime market. In April 2008 UBS took a $19 billion write-down on its subprime business, which included securities that had fallen in value and were now worth a fraction of their original worth. UBS's losses were just the beginning of the financial carnage for U.S. investment banks, commercial banks, and thrifts. As home values plummeted by 50 percent in some cities—including the once red-hot market of California—the red ink would total upwards of $1 trillion in collective losses with the possibility of another $1 trillion in financial despair to come by the end of 2010. It looked like there was no end in sight to the bad news and that the nation might even slip into another Great Depression. It would be a rocky ride, to say the least, with all the world affected because of the United States' importance as a buyer of world goods, particularly oil.

Two weeks before UBS unveiled its huge loss, Ameriquest founder Roland Arnall died of cancer and was buried in Griffith Park in Los Angeles. Terry Rouch, who used to work for Arnall as an account executive, was in attendance, as were family, friends, other former employees, and politicians far and wide, including Los Angeles mayor Antonio Villaraigosa, former governor Gray Davis, and current California governor Arnold Schwarzenegger, the retired movie star. During the entire ceremony and procession, Schwarzenegger stood near Rouch, who with his sunglasses and athletic build blended in with the governor's security detail. "Arnold put his hand on my shoulder a few times," remembered Rouch. "He thought I was one of his bodyguards."

Rouch didn't recall anything being said at the funeral about Ameriquest. It was obvious to him that it was neither the time nor the place. The focus, as it should have been, was on Arnall's achievements as a humanitarian, his work with the Simon Wiesenthal Center. "It felt like a political rally with the amount of politicians coming to pay their respects," said Rouch. "It was a touching Jewish ceremony. You could say there wasn't a dry eye in the place—but it wasn't necessarily for the passing of the father of subprime. It was for our own futures."

Chapter 13

TARP, the Great Recession, and the Return of Stan Kurland

Whole kingdoms, sunk into ruin, whose thrones, heavy with gold, instantly scattered.

—HERMAN HESSE

S eptember 2008. The message on the middle-aged woman's red T-shirt boiled down the issue to a political slogan: "Help for Main Street, Not Wall Street." Sitting in a government hearing room, she was a member of the Association of Community Organizations for Reform Now (ACORN), an activist organization that for years had been staging protests outside bank branches in the streets of Washington and elsewhere, arguing that too many of the nation's mortgage lenders had been engaged in predatory lending practices, that is, making home mortgages to consumers who wouldn't be able to repay them. To ACORN and its supporters, the word *predatory* was synonymous with *subprime*, and the way its followers saw it, mortgage bankers would make thousands of dollars in fee income off each borrower and then sell the loan (and the risk) to Wall Street, which in turn securitized that risk and sold it in a bond to some unsuspecting institutional investor, a municipality in Massachusetts for example (which is what Merrill Lynch did on occasion). Over the previous two years the group had taken on a new cause—foreclosures. Foreclosures were the by-product of all those predatory (subprime) mortgages the group had warned about.

The most dire predictions had come true—Americans were losing their personal residences at a rate not seen since the Great Depression. Tent cities were beginning to spring up in cities like Las Vegas, once the hottest housing market in the country, one where homes that hadn't even finished construction were being flipped for 20 percent more than the contract price. But the economic boom was over. Countrywide and Ameriquest were no more. Lenders were no longer originating subprime loans. Every independent subprime lender in the nation had failed—an $800 billion-a-year business evaporating over the course of 18 months.

The housing bust had become a national story being played out on the nightly news seven days a week. Unemployment was rising to multi-year highs. A few weeks earlier gas had been selling for $4 a gallon in California. Even the networks, which hated doing financial news stories because there was no good video to show the viewers, had finally latched onto the story. America's financial meltdown—with the housing and mortgage industry front and center—was suddenly sexy. It was also a political issue in a historic presidential election that pitted the first African American candidate against a Vietnam War hero who had chosen a woman for his running mate. The entire country was now watching. So too was the rest of the world. And the Dow Jones Industrial Average was plummeting like a cannon ball dropped from a skyscraper.

On the morning of September 23, 2008, the woman with the red T-shirt was not alone. She was accompanied by 20 other members of ACORN, some wearing matching T-shirts, others shouting out the slogans printed on their chests. Yet others were there to protest the war in Iraq. The setting wasn't a courthouse but the Dirksen office building, a block from the U.S. Capitol, where all 21 members of the Senate Banking Committee had convened a hearing. It was 9:45. Sitting mostly in the hearing room's back rows, the ACORN protesters, left-leaning for sure, were beginning to get restless.

A few blocks away at the Capitol building and Union Station, tourists were already snapping pictures on a warm fall morning. But outside of the hearing room 30 cameramen, several from foreign news bureaus, had parked their tripods and wide-angle lenses, waiting to hear not just the views of the 21 members of the Senate who made up the Banking Committee but Bush Treasury secretary Henry Paulson and Federal Reserve chairman Ben Bernanke. Along with Paulson and Bernanke, two other men would be testifying to the Senate that morning—Christopher Cox, chairman of the Securities and Exchange Commission (SEC), and James Lockhart, director of the Federal Housing Finance Agency (FHFA), the chief Washington regulator of Fannie Mae and Freddie Mac.

In early July both Paulson and Lockhart had made public pronouncements one after another, trying to assure the nation—and the stock market in particular—that both Fannie and Freddie were adequately capitalized and weren't in danger of failing, despite having posted billions of dollars in losses from delinquent home loans that they owned or guaranteed. But the market hadn't exactly believed them. The share prices of the two had drifted down into the single digits as it became clear to anyone who closely examined their books that together they held $600 billion in subprime and alt-A loans and MBSs. It could be easily reasoned that by the summer of 2008 (with subprime loan delinquencies swelling to 25 percent and alt-A late payments north of 10 percent) that these two government-sponsored enterprises (GSEs) would be experiencing massive losses for several more quarters—which meant investors would shy away from buying their bonds, MBSs, and stock. Fannie—which was linked at the hip with Mozilo's Countrywide—in particular had bought alt-A loans from its seller/servicers (lenders, that is). It now held $307 billion in alt-A mortgages or MBSs. And both Fannie and Freddie were end buyers of subprime and alt-A MBSs and loans from Wall Street—from such Wall Street packagers as Bear Stearns, Lehman Brothers, and Merrill Lynch. Had these two indirectly caused the subprime meltdown by purchasing the end bonds created by Wall Street? They certainly were part of the story, yes. Financial historians and politicians would be arguing over this point for years.

About to testify before the committee, Lockhart and Paulson now had egg on their faces. Two weeks earlier, on September 7, the

FHFA and the Treasury had taken control of Fannie and Freddie, placing them into government conservatorships. Out the door went their CEOs, Dan Mudd of Fannie and Richard Syron of Freddie Mac. The two hadn't technically failed, but they were now under full government control or conservatorship—the U.S. taxpayers owning most of their stock. Lockhart and Paulson had been dead wrong about the two having enough capital to weather the housing meltdown. Without Fannie and Freddie buying mortgages from the nation's banks, its savings and loans (S&Ls), and the dwindling number of nonbank mortgage originators, the entire U.S. mortgage market would have ground to a halt, which meant homes couldn't be bought and sold—that is, unless the buyer was paying all cash.[1]

For the first time in what seemed like decades, all 21 senators on the committee were present for a hearing. They wanted to know what the hell had happened. Most times, 10 or so senators from the Banking Committee might show for a hearing, make a few statements for the C-SPAN cameras, and depart, leaving four or five (sometimes even fewer) committee members to do what was called "the people's work."

Topic A that morning was the government seizure of Fannie and Freddie—a serious issue for sure. But Topic B was an even bigger issue of colossal proportion: With U.S. financial markets on the verge of collapse and banks lending only to businesses and consumers with pristine credit, Treasury Secretary Paulson was now asking the nation's 535 elected officials for an emergency cash infusion of $700 billion to help stabilize Wall Street and the shaky banking industry. The money—which Paulson vowed would eventually be repaid—would be provided through a piece of legislation called the Emergency Economic Stabilization Act (EESA). The bill's chief goal was to implement the Treasury's Troubled Asset Relief Program (TARP). The nation's financial crisis without a doubt had emanated from the housing mess, which was caused by Wall Street backing too many subprime lenders just so they could create bonds from the loans. The subprime juggernaut that had been birthed by Roland Arnall (and many of his former employees who went on to form their own subprime firms) and by Angelo

---

[1] Fannie and Freddie guaranteed (a synonym for insured) or owned $5.4 trillion of the nation's $9.6 trillion in outstanding home mortgages.

Mozilo at Countrywide had come home to roost, thanks to the willingness of Bear Stearns, Greenwich Capital, Lehman Brothers, Merrill Lynch, UBS Securities, and others to securitize any type of home mortgage that wasn't prime. In short, by giving mortgages to literally millions of consumers who should never have received loans in the first place, Ameriquest, Countrywide, and all the Street-owned firms had created an asset bubble (housing) that was collapsing and rippling through the U.S. economy.

And now the bill was due. The public, as might be expected, was hopping mad: $700 billion to bail out banks and Wall Street firms that securitized subprime and alt-A loans? Not only did "Help for Main Street, Not Wall Street" make a good T-shirt slogan, but it fit on a bumper sticker as well. Eight days after Fannie and Freddie were seized by the government, Lehman Brothers, one of the early Wall Street pioneers of subprime securitization and the owner of one of the nation's largest alt-A lenders, Aurora Loan Services of Colorado, would file for bankruptcy protection and eventually be liquidated. At the heart of its collapse: its mortgage business. Exacerbating the crisis was American International Group (AIG) out of New York, the world's largest insurance company. AIG aided the subprime boom by writing insurance contracts called credit default swaps that protected firms that invested in subprime bonds. If subprime MBSs went south—which is exactly what they were doing by the fall of 2008—AIG would be on the hook to pay investors potentially several hundred billions of dollars in claims, which would bankrupt the insurer.

As for the $700 billion in TARP money that Treasury secretary Paulson was asking for (on behalf of the Bush White House), he needed the funds so he could buy what he called "troubled" assets (mostly mortgage bonds) from hundreds of financial institutions, including the very same ones that had securitized subprime loans in the first place. This included Bank of America (which had just inherited Countrywide's subprime holdings), Merrill Lynch, and even Goldman Sachs and Morgan Stanley, which had made some large bets on subprime.

The way Paulson described the situation to the senators was that the capital markets—Wall Street and the nation's banks—had a major clogged artery. The patient (the economy), he reasoned, would have a heart attack if the Treasury didn't have the resources (the $700 billion) to buy troubled mortgages from lenders. Paulson's plan was to give that money to the banks, which would use it to go out and make new loans—to businesses and to homeowners—to unclog that bad artery in the capital markets. He was also asking for permission for the government to buy ownership stakes in some banks. He hoped it wouldn't have to do that, though.

To Senator Jim Bunning, a Republican from Kentucky, the whole idea sounded a bit like a Communist takeover of the U.S. banking system. "It's financial socialism and it's un-American," he told Paulson during the morning hearing, his beet-red face turning darker.

But to hear Paulson tell it, he was trying to avoid a financial Armageddon worse than what had already happened—that is, the takeover of Fannie and Freddie, and the $85 billion in loans it had extended to AIG so it could pay off on its CDS policies. This was the same Paulson who a year earlier had been serving as the White House water boy on the then-emerging subprime crisis, making speeches in the United States and abroad, saying the U.S. subprime mess was contained—that it wouldn't affect what he called the nation's "healthy economy." He had been dead wrong. And now he wanted $700 billion to help fix the problem.

On this morning the senators weren't about to bring up his track record. A few of them had public relations problems of their own. The chairman of the committee, Christopher Dodd, a Democrat from Connecticut, a few years earlier had received a "Friend of Angelo" (FOA) loan from Mozilo's Countrywide, which meant the elected official had received discounted points and fees from the lender. These price breaks were not available to Countrywide's regular customers, only those with personal or business ties to Mozilo or other senior executives at the lender. The FOA story broke in June.[2] The local media back in Dodd's home state and the TV pundits on the national circuit were having a field day with the FOA story. Dodd wasn't

---

[2] The existence of FOA loans was first mentioned in this book, but *Chain of Blame* did not appear in bookstores until July. The book was still at the printer when *Portfolio* magazine and the *Wall Street Journal* broke similar stories in early June.

looking too good, and neither was fellow senator Charles Schumer, Democrat of New York, whose constituents on Wall Street had donated generously to his campaigns over the years. Schumer, ever a homer for the people of New York, had done nothing with his political power to rein in Wall Street's excesses or to shine a light on them. It was lucky for Schumer and Dodd that they weren't up for reelection that year. Neither of them would be too tough on Paulson.[3]

As the hearing got under way, each senator had a chance to grandstand, making a short speech. The political theater was broadcast on C-SPAN for all the voters back home. Most of the senators were indignant about having to spend $700 billion of the public's money for something most Americans didn't understand. Dodd led off the hearing, calling Paulson's Troubled Asset Relief Program (TARP) "stunning for its lack of detail." The former Goldman Sachs chief had started his idea for the bailout legislation by typing out a brief three-page memo a couple of weeks earlier. Dodd wanted to know what the Treasury Department would do if a bailout plan didn't work.

Senator Schumer, looking out for his constituents back home on Wall Street, pontificated that the "lowly mortgage" was at the center of what was now an international banking crisis. But he begrudgingly admitted, "The real danger is if we don't act." Schumer loved being the center of attention at a hearing. It was an often-told joke in Washington that the most dangerous place inside the Beltway was getting between Chuck Schumer and a camera. Meanwhile, the ACORN protestors in the hearing room were getting noisy. Every time a senator expressed the wish that the money be used to help the homeowners who were losing their houses, they'd shout an "Amen" or a loud "Yes!" Dodd, who was running the hearing, wasn't in the mood to hear their protests

---

[3] The two highest-profile elected officials in Washington that received FOA loans were Dodd and Senator Kent Conrad (D–North Dakota). Both were the subject of a Senate Ethics Committee probe regarding the discounts they received through the FOA program. However, in August 2009 the committee cleared the two senators of any official wrongdoing but criticized them for having a lack of curiosity about what it meant to be in the program, saying their behavior suggested the "appearance of impropriety." By the fall of 2009 Dodd's FOA discounts were imperiling his chances of being reelected in 2010, his potential opponents seeking to capitalize on his FOA problem.

and the "Amen" shouts. He banged his gavel. "You settle down or I'll clear this room," he warned. [4]

The senators' opening speeches continued. Robert Menendez of New Jersey cautioned that he wouldn't be "stampeded into rubber-stamping" Paulson's $700 billion TARP plan. Elizabeth Dole, a Republican from North Carolina, who was married to former presidential candidate (and Viagra pitchman) Bob Dole, tried to point the finger of blame for the crisis toward Fannie Mae and Freddie Mac, which many Democrats had gone to bat for over the years. She angrily recalled how she and her fellow Republicans tried to push for stronger oversight of Fannie and Freddie. North Carolina was home to a handful of mortgage insurance companies, including United Guaranty (a subsidiary of AIG) and Genworth, both of which had been charter members of the anti-Fannie/Freddie lobbying group FM Watch. Dole, who didn't finger Wall Street as a culprit in the crisis, was in a close reelection race that fall. (She would eventually lose.)

By the time Paulson finally spoke, 90 minutes had passed. The protestors from ACORN had calmed down. Some had left the room. The Treasury secretary thanked the senators for giving him what he called a "bazooka"—that is, the legislative authority to take control of Fannie and Freddie. He implored them to move forward with the legislation for the $700 billion. "I'm convinced it will cost far less than the alternative," he said.

There was just one problem. The Senate didn't get to vote on the $700 billion bailout first. That was the job of the House of Representatives. On Monday, September 29, less than a week after the Senate hearing, the House voted. Speaker Nancy Pelosi thought she had enough votes, but by the time the final tally came up she was 23 short.

---

[4]ACORN, whose operation and budget was supported by donations and federal grants, found itself under fire in the summer of 2009 when an independent filmmaker video taped some of its employees offering a pimp and his prostitute advice on how to file false tax returns, classify underaged girls working as prostitutes as dependents and to organize an ACORN housing loan for a house to be used as an illegal brothel. Even though the pimp and prostitute were actors, members of Congress voted to prevent the group from obtaining additional federal money. During the Clinton administration the Inspector General of AmeriCorps, the government's volunteer agency, accused the group of "using government resources to promote legislation." ACORN was stripped of its federal grant as a result.

The $700 billion bailout package was nixed 228 to 205. The revolt was led by proud conservatives from the Republican party who said their offices had been inundated by telephone calls from angry citizens back home who didn't want their tax dollars to bail out Wall Street. It was just like the ACORN T-shirts had said: "Help for Main Street, Not Wall Street."

There was only one problem with the Republicans' defiance: They cast their votes while the stock market was still open. By noon that day the vote was complete and the Dow Jones Industrial Average went into a full-scale meltdown, plunging 778 points—a record for a one-day drop. Billions of dollars in shareholder wealth had been wiped out. Now constituents were calling their elected officials in Washington with a new complaint: Their 401(k) and personal investments had been hammered.

The tables had turned—Republicans were now under fire for not passing the bill. The presidential election that pitted Senator Barack Obama against Senator John McCain was less than two months away, with McCain trailing badly in the polls. The public was about to hold the Bush White House (and Republicans in particular, McCain being their candidate) responsible for eight years of hands-off regulation of the financial markets. The Senate decided to take up the vote on Wednesday. By the time it did, the $700 billion legislation had changed: The version the House had turned down was a streamlined bill (just over 120 pages) that dealt mostly with giving the Treasury secretary (Paulson) the power to buy troubled mortgages. This time around it was loaded down with pork legislation, quite a bit of it tied to extending tax breaks for alternative energy and green fuels, but it also threw in a few benefits that Republicans might like, including tax breaks for the construction of race tracks (a nod to NASCAR dads) and the coal industry.

On Wednesday the Senate approved the bill—which had ballooned to 451 pages—by a wide margin. Two days later the House voted and it too passed the bill by a wide margin. Two hours later President Bush signed the bill. The Emergency Economic Stabilization Act (EESA) was now law. The country was about to spend $700 billion to buy troubled mortgage assets.

In order to get the bill passed quickly, Secretary Paulson promised he could get most of the $700 billion back by holding those troubled assets for a few years and then selling them later at a profit or break-even price. But as Senator Dodd had pointed out, the bill was short on details. Even though Bush signed the bill, the stock market continued to suffer: It went down, down, down, experiencing losses not seen since the Great Depression. In the fall of 2008, the Dow was at 8,000 compared to 14,280 a year earlier, a loss of 44 percent.

For a week and a half after Paulson got his money wish, the stock market kept declining in large chunks with an occasional rebound. The Treasury secretary wasn't happy. Some banks had stopped lending to each other and their business customers, exacerbating what was referred to as a credit crisis. Paulson took one more bold step: He unveiled a plan to spend $250 billion of the newly allocated TARP money to instead invest in some of the largest banks in the United States, including his former firm, Goldman Sachs, as well as Bank of America, Citigroup, Merrill Lynch, Wells Fargo, and JPMorgan Chase. The government would own preferred stock in these financial behemoths and show the world that it stood behind its banks, that they were open for business and ready to lend. But not all of these banks were in immediate danger of failing. Paulson, according to the press reports of the day, strong-armed the heads of these banks (Ken Lewis and Jamie Dimon, among others) telling them it was their "patriotic duty" to go along with the idea. He explained that Treasury wasn't taking over these banks—it was becoming a stakeholder.

To the man and the woman on the street watching and reading the news as it unfolded, it all seemed surreal: Nine of the nation's biggest and (somewhat) well-respected banks had been partially nationalized—by order of a Republican president who fiercely believed in free markets. In the months ahead, Treasury would buy preferred shares in dozens of additional banks of varying sizes, shoring up their capital positions. And what about the plan to buy troubled mortgages from financial institutions? Paulson was still promising that it would happen, but few in Washington were holding their breaths.

★ ★ ★

In late June, before the financial markets had collapsed with TARP being a mere idea at the Treasury Department, a senior executive at Countrywide walked down the hall to say good-bye to Angelo Mozilo. On July 1, Ken Lewis's Bank of America was officially taking away the keys. Angelo's career was over for good. His door was open, and the executive later told a friend that "there was Angelo at his desk, crying like a baby." For Mozilo it was the end of the line. The Securities and Exchange Commission (SEC) had stepped up its investigation into his stock sales. He continued to maintain to friends that he had done nothing wrong—that all of his sales had been publicly disclosed and had been done in an ethical manner.

His successor at Countrywide wasn't any of the lieutenants who had served under him there for 20-plus years. Most of those had left of their own accord or had been forced out by Bank of America and offered severance (like David Sambol). The new person in charge of Countrywide's mortgage division, now a unit of Bank of America, was Barbara Desoer, a career bank official who had worked her way up through the ranks of the organization over 30 years. She had moved into Mozilo's office in Calabasas. Previously, she had worked back east at the bank's Charlotte campus in North Carolina. But she wasn't president of Countrywide; she was president of Bank of America Home Loans. With the collapse of the economy—housing and mortgages leading the way—the Countrywide name was poison. Not only were Mozilo and other former senior officers the subject of an SEC probe, but the FBI had opened a criminal investigation of the company. It gave no details on the nature of the probe.[5]

Ms. Desoer was no Angelo Mozilo. A graduate of Mount Holyoke College, a well-regarded women's Ivy League–caliber school in Massachusetts, she had a degree in mathematics and a master's in business administration. She had little in the way of mortgage experience. Her expertise was in technology and operations, a far cry from the sales culture of the old Countrywide crew. Then again, the last thing the bank wanted was another Mozilo. Not only was Countrywide the subject of a criminal probe, but several states were still hitting the company with abusive lending and foreclosure-related lawsuits, legal actions that were now a headache for Ken Lewis and his management team.

By the spring of 2009 Ms. Desoer, who was just north of 50, had been at the helm for several months and began giving press interviews.

---

[5] As this updated edition went to press in the fall of 2009, no criminal charges had been filed against Countrywide insiders regarding the company's operations or lending practices.

By then the world had changed yet again—for Bank of America and for every other major financial institution in the nation. Washington Mutual, the large Seattle-based savings and loan (S&L) that was once a top 10 ranked subprime lender, had failed. It was sold with government assistance to JPMorgan Chase, Jamie Dimon's megabank. Merrill Lynch, the Wall Street poster child for everything that went wrong in subprime, had almost failed. In a deal engineered by Paulson and Bernanke, Bank of America was the new owner.

Bank of America—the largest in the land—not only had rolled the dice by purchasing the nation's largest mortgage and subprime lender (Countrywide) but was now the owner of Merrill Lynch, once one of the largest securitizers of subprime loans. The acquisition deal was actually struck a few days before the Senate TARP hearing but was not finalized for several months. The initial price tag was $50 billion. Lewis even granted an interview to *60 Minutes* bragging about what a great deal it was for the bank because it would give Bank of America the nation's premier retail stock brokerage operation, Merrill Lynch. But what didn't come up during the interview was the fact that Merrill still owned one of the nation's largest servicers of subprime loans, Home Loan Services of Pittsburgh,[6] as well as a sister company called Wilshire Credit of Oregon. Plus, Merrill still had exposure from all the subprime bonds (CDOs, MBSs) it had created but could not sell to institutional investors.

In March 2009 when Desoer sat down with *National Mortgage News* for an interview about Bank of America's plans for its mortgage empire, the bank's common stock was at $5 compared to $33 when the sale was first announced in the previous fall. The bank's shareholders had lost billions on their investment and rumors were starting to surface that Lewis might be on his way out the door.[7] The bank's purchase of Merrill Lynch was starting to look like a boondoggle, despite what Lewis had maintained to *60 Minutes*. The Merrill deal, however,

---

[6] Home Loan Services was the sister company to First Franklin, Bill Dallas's old firm. First Franklin originated mortgages through loan brokers; HLS serviced those loans on a monthly basis.

[7] Under pressure from the bank's board, Lewis finally announced his retirement from the company in September 2009, a few weeks before the compared revealed a $2.2 billion loss in the third quarter.

had not gone over as planned. The more Bank of America's due diligence team poked into Merrill's books, the more it found losses in its mortgage holdings that hadn't been anticipated. The bank had unearthed an additional $15 billion in losses. In late 2008, after EESA/TARP had become law, Lewis had tried to back out of the deal. When Bernanke and Paulson chafed, he asked the government for an additional $20 billion in TARP money (on top of the $25 billion that Bank of America and Merrill had already received). The two men weren't thrilled. According to some press reports, Paulson threatened to have Lewis fired (when you're a stakeholder in a bank you can do things like that) if he backed out of the deal. Lewis caved, but so did Bernanke and Paulson—the government would give Lewis the additional $20 billion to make the deal happen.[8]

Desoer, unlike Mozilo, wasn't much of a talker. When she sat down with Muolo of *National Mortgage News* at the bank's headquarters on Pennsylvania Avenue in Washington (right across the street from the Treasury, its TARP benefactor), her answers to questions were guarded. She carefully chose her words and rarely spoke off script. She wouldn't talk about competitors or spread industry gossip. In other words, she was a banker through and through—sober and serious and by the book. She declined to talk about the bank's plans for Merrill's subprime mortgage unit. (The expectation was that Bank of America would liquidate it, selling its receivables for pennies on the dollar.) She looked tired. The only time she spoke with much passion about anything came when she was asked about Bank of America's efforts in loan modifications.

"Loan mods," as they were called, were the new buzzword in the industry. Loan mods had actually been around for a solid year, but the Obama administration was pushing the nation's 20 largest servicers of these loans (Bank of America, Wells Fargo, Chase, and Citi being at the top of the list) to do more. The concept was this: Take a troubled homeowner who was in danger of losing his house because the rate on his

---

[8] Paulson later testified to Congress that he told Lewis the Federal Reserve could remove management, including Lewis, and the board of directors of Bank of America.

loan had spiked upward or he and/or his wife had lost their jobs, and then rewrite the mortgage, lowering the interest rate (or the loan balance), thus making the monthly payments more affordable. Traditionally, altering the terms of a mortgage (a legal contract) would be unheard of in the industry, but with the economy worsening and the national unemployment rate headed toward 10 percent, mortgage servicers were open to the idea. And there was an incentive offered by the White House: For every loan a company like Bank of America rewrote, the government would pay it $1,000—with more money to come a year later if the consumer was still current on the loan. Bank of America serviced at least 14 million home mortgages, with at least 1.4 million of them delinquent. Multiply that by the $1,000 loan modification incentive fee, and Desoer's unit could earn a nice chunk of change.

Desoer boasted that Bank of America (which, of course, included the entire Countrywide franchise) had modified 74,000 troubled loans during the first two months of 2009. "We modified 230,000 loans last year," she said. "We're committed to 630,000 over two years." When discussing the bank's loan modification efforts with the newspaper, she became somewhat animated. "It's very hard work," she cautioned. "You have to dive deep into the cash flows of each borrower. It can be very painful for some people. You have to establish a relationship with them and win their trust."

"Have you handled any of these loan modifications yourself?" asked the reporter.

Desoer didn't hesitate. "We have 5,000 full-timers working on this. I listen to calls every week—for two hours a week at least. There are so many stories out there—you have a mom or husband who lost their job. It's hard. You have grown men who are crying on the other end of the phone."

★   ★   ★

Desoer's arrival in California coincided with its economy falling off a cliff. Unemployment in the nation's largest state was 7.1 percent and rising quickly. A year earlier just 5 percent of California's residents were jobless. (By the summer of 2009 the rate would be a nerve-racking 11.6 percent.) Foreclosures were averaging a record-busting 80,000 homes a quarter. Job losses contributed to a vicious circle of foreclosures, job losses, and more foreclosures. Similarly, foreclosures dragged down home prices in a vicious circle of falling home prices, increased foreclosures, and even lower home prices. College graduates sat by the phone, waiting for someone—anyone—to call and offer them a job interview.

Things got so bad that one out-of-state lender, Guaranty Bank of Austin, Texas, was forced to take control of a new housing development it had financed. In May 2009, instead of completing the project, Guaranty[9] demolished four luxurious model homes in Victorville, a sparsely populated city some 100 miles north of Los Angeles. During the boom years, developers slapped up homes further and further away from big cities. When the housing bubble popped, newly minted two-story houses sat vacant, symbols of exuberance gone awry. Peter Y. Hong, a reporter with the *Los Angeles Times*, wrote that the developer of the planned 16-unit Victorville project had hoped to sell the houses for more than $300,000 each. Only four homes were finished, and before being turned into rubble, they featured granite countertops and whirlpool bathtubs. Amateur videos of excavators smashing walls and then lifting the debris away became popular items on the YouTube web site, with more than 250,000 views.

A frontier of mortgage experimentation, California became a nexus of job losses and wealth destruction. What was happening there was occurring in almost every state in the nation, to varying degrees. Californians were starting to call it the "Oh-Shit State." The California way of life for up-and-coming mortgage executives who once looked up to Mozilo and Arnall was disappearing. State legislators and Governor Arnold Schwarzenegger came under intense pressure from consumer advocates on the one hand, and bank and housing lobbyists on the other, to stop the bleeding.

A slew of bills circulated through Sacramento, the state capital, all aimed at stopping foreclosures, or at least slowing them down. Don Perata, a Democrat from Oakland and an old hand in the state Senate—he was president pro tem—wanted to force lenders to meet face-to-face with homeowners before taking their houses. The idea was

---

[9] In August 2009 the Federal Deposit Insurance Corporation (FDIC) seized control of Guaranty, declared it insolvent, and sold it to Banco Bilbao Vizcaya Argenteria.

simple: Some people in financial trouble might keep their homes if the lender simply explained their alternatives, such as meeting with a credit counselor or how to get a loan mod.

A tamed version of Perata's bill eventually passed. Lenders had to meet with delinquent borrowers 30 days before filing a notice of default (NOD), a public document that initiates the foreclosure process in California. The loophole: Servicers could get around the requirement by showing they tried to contact a borrower, who declined to talk or ignored all phone calls and letters. And if the borrower did want to talk, then over the phone was fine. Also, the law included only loans made at the tail end of the housing boom, from 2003 to 2007. Of course, none of those caveats stopped Governor Schwarzenegger from praising the bill when he signed it. The former action star said, "Foreclosures not only devastate families, they hurt neighborhoods and depress our economy and our budget."

Governor Schwarzenegger eventually called for a 90-day halt to all foreclosures in California. Such a move would have a monumental impact on the housing market, buying months for homeowners to get their finances in order but forcing banks and servicers to keep eating the carrying costs of dud loans. "The single most powerful action our state can take to shore up its economy is to help Californians stay in their homes," Schwarzenegger said. "Curtailing foreclosures will stop the downward spiral of home prices, free up needed cash for homeowners, help save jobs, and make an immediate positive impact on our economy."

The proposal was greeted with horror in the housing and mortgage industries (including Bank of America), which dispatched their lobbyists to Sacramento. They worked on the state's senators and assemblymen until the final version of the bill, which was enacted in June 2009, said lenders had to stop foreclosures for 90 days unless they could demonstrate that they were busy modifying loans and helping people. Within a week of starting, nearly every major servicer or lender in California had a permanent or temporary exemption from the moratorium.

Politicians could make a show about helping desperate homeowners, but there was another reality they could not gloss over: a gaping hole in the state budget. The housing downturn and steep recession resulted in plummeting tax revenues. During the good go-go years, the mostly Democratic legislature had spent every dime on education, social services, a safety net for citizens, and the prison system. But by 2009, California, the world's eighth largest economy, faced a whopping $26 billion hole in its budget. Many other states had deficits, too, but none as large as that of the Golden State.

Interestingly, the foreclosure crisis created some great job opportunities. Unfortunately, some of the jobs involved conning people out of a few grand. As home-loan delinquencies soared, ads began to populate newspapers, radio, and daytime TV promising to lower a homeowner's payments—loan mods, which were now a growth industry in California. The pitch: Pay us an up-front fee—anywhere from $1,500 to $5,000, or roughly one or two mortgage payments—and we'll get your lender to slash your interest rate, forgive some debt, or stretch out your loan term so that you can afford your mortgage and keep your dream home. Many of these white knights were based in Orange County, the sunny, suburban, and highly entrepreneurial home to the biggest subprime players. One doesn't need a map to read the signs. After subprime imploded, thousands of salespeople needed new jobs. At least some of them, perhaps hundreds, found employment in the now-burgeoning loan mod industry.

Among the most ubiquitous ads on daytime TV were those for the Federal Loan Modification Law Center, whose name made it sound like it was affiliated with the federal government. It wasn't. FedMod, as some called it, was a private company asking consumers to pay $1,000 to $3,000 up front for loan help. In April 2009, the Federal Trade Commission (FTC), which regulates advertising, slapped the company with a complaint, charging that it generally failed to get any kind of loan deal for its clients and that employees repeatedly ignored consumers after they paid the up-front fee. The FTC also alleged that FedMod telemarketers exaggerated the company's success rate and told some homeowners to stop paying their mortgages. Last, the agency charged that in radio and TV ads the company falsely suggested it was affiliated with the federal government—guess the agency didn't like the word "Federal" in the company's name.

When the complaint was revealed, reporter Padilla called Nabile "Bill" Anz, managing attorney for FedMod, to get a statement for the *Orange County Register*. FedMod was based in Orange County central, Irvine, in the ritzy business district near John Wayne Airport. The attorney conceded that his company had been aggressively marketing itself, but said it obeyed the law. He pledged full cooperation with the FTC and said he would even change the company's name, if necessary. In the five or so months FedMod had operated, Anz said his company has taken on about 5,000 clients and achieved loan modifications for 1,000. Granted it can take a couple of months to strike a deal with a loan servicer, but still, the 20 percent success rate was not impressive. Anyone experienced at modifying loans knows before taking on a client whether that person has a shot in hell of getting a deal. Some people are so far underwater they are beyond help. To its critics, FedMod should have been rejecting such people, advising them to save their money to rent an apartment.

Despite being targeted, Anz praised the government's effort to cleanse the mortgage aid business. "There are real criminals, real bad people out there," Anz said. "We do need to get rid of a lot of shady characters." Indeed, by summer 2009 the California Department of Real Estate was investigating 750 cases of potential loan mod scams, up from just 10 a year earlier. The department had already prohibited more than 100 companies and individuals from doing loan mods, either because they were doing so without a real estate license or because they failed to get preapproval from the state. However, the Department of Real Estate has no power over attorneys, who can modify loans without a real estate license. By mid-2009 there was growing concern among government agencies that companies were essentially "renting" lawyers—hiring an attorney to be a front who never actually touched loan files. Renting a lawyer meant avoiding the Department of Real Estate's reach. Driving north from San Diego to Los Angeles, a half dozen or so billboards advertised loan mods, most of them law firms.

After the *Register* ran its story on FedMod and the FTC's crackdown, former employees began calling Padilla, complaining that the company ran a boiler-room call center with all the emphasis on convincing people to give money and none on helping them get a loan mod. Former employees said they never saw an attorney help a client.

Not everyone finding opportunity in the downturn was an alleged scam artist. Some folks once busy making risky loans switched to buying them back cheaply as scratch-and-dent investors, running so-called opportunity or vulture funds. The gig: Call yourself an investor in distressed mortgages, raise millions or even billions of dollars from investors, and offer banks 20 to 70 cents on the dollar for their loans or foreclosed homes.

One of the new vulture investors was Jon Daurio, who used to work for Long Beach Mortgage Corporation, the predecessor of sub-prime king Ameriquest Mortgage. Daurio even set up his new company, Kondaur Capital, in the 16th-floor corner office of a building that was formerly the headquarters of Ameriquest. Also, before becoming a vulture investor he worked for Encore Credit, which was headed by one of the founders of New Century Financial, the golden boy of subprime. In a nutshell, Daurio knew just how poorly underwritten nonprime mortgages had become during the go-go years. He was a subprime industry insider. Daurio gave a detailed interview in March 2009 to the *Orange County Register*'s John Gittelsohn. First question: Was the company's name supposed to sound like "Condor" and really illustrate a vulture company? "No. We see it as soaring to better solutions like a bird," Daurio began. "The name is an amalgamation of my partner, John Kontoulis, and Daurio. Maybe some people see us as vultures because of what we do, but that's not our self-image."

Not pulling punches, the reporter asked Daurio what people should think of a man who used to be a player at a now-defunct subprime sausage machine. "I anticipate a profit, but not like the entities I worked for on my resume. I take pride in helping 200 employees' families support themselves by working here in an economy that is very dismal. I made good money when Encore went public. I was general counsel and not a sales guy. Here, I'm the majority individual shareholder and the CEO of this company. I'm not a sales guy like Angelo Mozilo was at Countrywide or Roland Arnall at Ameriquest, who likely made billions. To me, it's a different mentality. I'm making decisions to keep the company alive for 50 years. It's not like a few years ago when people were making decisions for short-term profits."

And what does Daurio's staff tell folks who can't afford their mortgages? "We try to educate the borrower and say: 'You have too much home. You're underwater. You're sitting on a depreciating asset. The best thing you can do is move.' We'll sometimes offer a died-in-lieu of foreclosure. We'll sometimes give them money to move and a deposit so they can rent an apartment. The benefit to me is I get the property today. The benefit to the borrower is he gets to move on."

Then there was Stan Kurland, the former Countrywide president—and (once) would-be successor to Angelo Mozilo. "When Stan left we just assumed that he wouldn't be going back to work, that he'd be sitting around his pool sipping cocktails while the rest of us slaved away," said Betsy Bayer, the former rules lady at Countrywide. After Mozilo bounced him out of Countrywide, Kurland did take it easy for a while. He could more than afford the bar bill: two days before Countrywide publicly disclosed that the 28-year veteran of Countrywide Financial Corporation was even leaving the company he began unloading all the stock he'd accumulated in it over the years. Over time he had unloaded $130 million worth of stock, at prices that were in the $35-a-share range. He could retire a very rich man.

But as Countrywide—and the mortgage market in general—began to disintegrate, with home prices tumbling and delinquencies rising to record levels, Kurland was watching from the sidelines. Even though Treasury Secretary Paulson had originally promised Congress that he'd use the $700 billion in TARP money to have the government buy toxic mortgages, that idea was now out the window. After the Treasury invested the first $250 billion in the nine megabanks, it went full steam ahead, investing in dozens more. Many members of Congress were outraged that Paulson (with Bernanke guiding him) had pulled what some called a "bait and switch." But Paulson's successor as Treasury secretary in the Obama White House, Timothy Geithner, agreed it was a good idea for the government to prop up banks by buying preferred stock in them, because it got money into the banking system quickly and stopped (at least temporarily) the worldwide panic in the financial markets. But it also meant that plenty of delinquent loans would need to be invested in (at pennies on the dollar) by the private sector (not the government) and serviced by someone. With $1 trillion in loans expected to go bust, the buying and servicing opportunities could be huge.

Kurland began kicking around the idea of getting back into the mortgage business in 2007. "There had been many points where Wall Street firms were reaching out to me on whether I had an interest in participating with them," he told reporter Padilla of the *Orange County Register*. One was Larry Fink, the former First Boston trading desk chief who was now running Black Rock Financial, a midsize investment banking firm in New York. The two men had grown up together in the Valley area north of Los Angeles in suburban Van Nuys. Kurland used some of his own money (how much is still unclear) and teamed up with Fink's Black Rock Financial. With Black Rock's financial muscle they formed the Private National Mortgage Acceptance Corporation—PennyMac for short. The name—whether intended or not—sounded a bit like Freddie Mac and IndyMac, not exactly names that might endear investors to it. Freddie was still operating under a federal conservatorship, and IndyMac (the brainchild of Mozilo and Loeb and then shepherded by Mike Perry) had failed in the summer of 2008 under the weight of billions of dollars in alt-A loans it had funded and securitized through Wall Street.[10] PennyMac was based in Pasadena, the former headquarters of Countrywide. From his office suite Kurland had a panoramic view of the Santa Monica mountains.

Kurland told Padilla that he had created investment funds to buy troubled mortgages at a discount. Investors committed at least $1 billion to the funds, he said. But during its first half-year in operation PennyMac bought hardly anything, leaving some in the industry wondering what its game plan might be. Banks like Wachovia (which almost failed and was now controlled by Wells Fargo) had plenty to sell, as did Bank of America (thanks to Countrywide and Merrill's mortgage holdings). Then again, there was a feeling that many of these "too big to fail" (TBTF) institutions were holding on to their sour loans and asset-backed securities/mortgage-backed securities (ABSs/MBSs), thanks in part to the TARP money the government had invested in them. With the government bolstering their capital positions, why should Bank of America, its Merrill unit, or Wells Fargo sell their toxic assets? There was no urgency to off-load delinquent mortgages, especially at pennies on the dollar. "They all think that the market will return one day and they'll lose less money on this crap," said Dan Perl of loan workout company Citadel Servicing. "They think some of these subprime loans are worth 50, 60 cents on the dollar. I can tell you that they're wrong."

Then in early 2009 PennyMac bought a $558 million portfolio of problem mortgages directly from the FDIC, which had inherited the

---

[10] The delinquency rate on IndyMac's alt-A loans was north of 20 percent at the time of its takeover. Its failure could ultimately wind up costing the FDIC $8 billion, making it one of the most expensive S&L failures in history.

loans when it seized an insolvent bank in Nevada, one of the hard-est-hit housing markets in the nation. No price was disclosed, but later on PennyMac filed a disclosure form with the SEC, revealing it had invested $153 million of investors' money in troubled assets—presumably the FDIC portfolio. But the filing also revealed that those same assets had deteriorated in quality (because of delinquencies) and had been marked down in value by $7 million. PennyMac's goal was to modify the loans, changing the terms to make them more favorable to consumers. Eventually it hoped to resell the mortgages at a profit, while reaping servicing (monthly processing) fees in the process. It also was entitled to that $1,000 loan mod incentive carrot (per loan) offered by the Obama administration.

During the first half of 2009 rumors began to circulate in the mortgage market that PennyMac had (in the words of one troubled asset bidder) "too many chiefs and not enough Indians." Translation: It had hired a large staff (80 people), heavy with executives, and was burning through investors' money. It had rented thousands of square feet of office space with rows upon rows of empty desks. It had planned to hire 250 full-time loan modification experts whose goal was to work on (potentially) billions of dollars in delinquent home mortgages. But by May 2009 it had just 10 loan mod experts manning the phones. "You can have a football game in the space they're renting, lots of room," said one employee who worked there.

PennyMac was starting to garner negative press, and after granting media access to certain news outlets (including the *New York Times*) Kurland pulled a latter-day Mozilo and stopped talking to reporters. He had a good reason: Barely two years old and with no proven track record, PennyMac hoped to sell shares to the public. Its goal was to raise $750 million. There was just one problem: Even though the company talked big in its initial public offering (IPO) filing[11] about all the potential in the troubled loan market, the only portfolio of any size it had bought was the FDIC portfolio. And so far it had lost money

---

[11] Perhaps when PennyMac went public Mozilo was laughing from the sidelines: The new company's ownership structure was that of a REIT where 90 percent of its dividends are paid to shareholders, preventing it from building up a large amount of retained earnings. "REITs? They're like pigs with lipstick," Mozilo once quipped to co-author Muolo.

on the deal, at least on paper. By the time it went public on July 30 investors were willing to buy only $300 million worth of its stock. (It sold 16 million shares instead of a planned offering of 20 million.) Two months after the IPO, PennyMac's shares were thinly traded, never rising higher than its offering price of $20. Despite all the potential in the troubled loan market—a major selling point when Kurland and other company executives went on their IPO road show touting the company to investors—its future looked cloudy; but it continued to bid on delinquent loan pools, including one offered by an affiliate of AIG.

Also looking cloudy was Mozilo's immediate future. Just before PennyMac went public, the SEC formerly charged him with fraud and insider trading in regard to $140 million of stock he had sold during his last three years at the helm of Countrywide. Even though Mozilo had insisted on many occasions that his stock sales were on the up-and-up, that's not how the SEC saw it. Also named as defendants were his anointed successor David Sambol and chief financial officer Eric Sieracki. Investigators at the SEC said that from 2005 to 2007 the men "misled the market by falsely assuring investors that Countrywide was primarily a prime quality mortgage lender that had avoided the excesses of its competitors."

It released private e-mails where supposedly Mozilo had blasted the quality of its nonconforming loans while saying publicly they were fine. The agency said that on June 1, 2006, one day after Mozilo had made a speech publicly praising payment option adjustable-rate mortgages (POAs), he sent an e-mail to Sambol and other executives at the company fearing that too many POAs were originated "based upon stated income and that there was evidence" of borrowers lying about their income on their applications. The SEC charges went on and on—and focused almost entirely on the billions of dollars in "I'll cry tomorrow" loans (the POAs, that is) that Countrywide was funding through both loan brokers and its retail branches. Mozilo had once told *National Mortgage News* that he blamed POA delinquencies on "young people," saying that "they're keeping their credit cards and walking away from their houses. Our generation would never do that."

The new White House was trying to send a message that it was doing something about the financial crisis by holding (alleged) wrongdoers responsible. Robert Khuzami, director of the SEC's enforcement division, said Countrywide investors were left with a "mirage," adding, "The defendants' [Mozilo, Sambol, Sieracki] own words revealed that they saw the warning signs, the trends, the uncertainties and the challenges to their business model and decided not to disclose that information" to Countrywide's shareholders. Appointed earlier in the year, Khuzami had spent 11 years as a federal prosecutor working in the Southern District of New York at Foley Square in lower Manhattan, just north of Wall Street. His specialty was white-collar crime.

Anyone who read the financial and trade press's regular coverage of Mozilo knew that he was not one to gloss over the bad times. The Countrywide conference call to stock analysts on July 24 two years earlier was a perfect example. The mortgage industry was headed for an iceberg that summer and he likened the housing market to the worst since the Great Depression, sparking a major sell-off on Wall Street and igniting, perhaps, the beginning of a worldwide meltdown of financial markets. Still, the way the SEC viewed matters, Mozilo knew Countrywide was taking on increasing risk via POAs and established his stock sale programs and executed them while in "possession of material, nonpublic information." The agency said that the day after Mozilo finalized one of his selling programs in late September 2006, he sent an e-mail to Sambol and Sieracki, telling them that Countrywide was "flying blind on how these loans will perform in a stressed environment of higher unemployment, reduced values, and slowing homes sales."

The three former Countrywide executives quickly lawyered up and issued statements through their attorneys, strongly denying all wrongdoing and accusing the SEC of taking their e-mails and internal comments out of context. A trial—if it came to that—wouldn't occur for well over a year. As the nation's financial crisis, ignited by housing and mortgages, peaked in the summer of 2009, some media outlets were taking a second glance at Mozilo and his role. Articles in both the *New Yorker* and the *Los Angeles Times* focused a bit on his humble beginnings in the Bronx, his immigrant success story (he was second-generation Italian-American), and the fact that Countrywide—despite all the disastrous subprime and POA loans it funded—was still the largest lender to minorities (even if its successor company, Bank of America, was foreclosing on those minorities).

Mozilo's sister, Lori, wrote an essay on the Huffington Post web site called "Villified: What You Don't Know about My Brother, Angelo Mozilo," saying that he always championed equal rights for all: "blacks, gays, women, immigrants." Still, there was talk in some quarters (unconfirmed) that certain family members were even considering changing their last name because of the publicity and attention it garnered. Angelo was lying low. Of course he was, especially in light of the SEC charges. Scott Reckard of the *Los Angeles Times* noted Mozilo was keeping such a low profile that "acquaintances, analysts and members of the public report 'Angelo' sightings like fans spotting a movie star, or informants a fugitive: Mozilo in restaurants in Montecito, Calif., where he owns a compound; Mozilo playing cards, seemingly untroubled by all the accusations."

Afterword

TBTF: A Mortgage Cartel Rises from the Ashes

Before the residential mortgage business blew up—taking down with it the U.S. economy and then the overseas markets— Angelo Mozilo once dreamed of achieving a 30 percent market share in residential lending and servicing for Countrywide. Even in early 2007, as the business began to fray, Mozilo thought the goal of owning three of every 10 mortgage customers was still achievable. Keep in mind that 10 years earlier a company achieving a 4 percent market share was considered the equivalent of scaling Mount Everest. Perhaps Mozilo was in denial. As mortgage companies fell all around him he maintained that as the sick and ailing passed into the grave Countrywide would only grow stronger, picking up all the customers who could no longer be serviced by the dead.

As the bailout of the U.S. economy progressed into 2010, financial regulators the likes of Ben Bernanke, Tim Geithner, and Sheila Bair over at the Federal Deposit Insurance Corporation (FDIC) (arguably the three most powerful banking overseers in the nation) pondered what to do about the concept known as "too big to fail" (TBTF). "Too big to fail" boiled down to an understanding that federal regulators believed that some financial companies (and even automakers) were so large that their bankruptcies would cause such severe damage to the economy that they had to be bailed out by the government (the taxpayers) no matter the expense. As the mortgage industry began to collapse in earnest in early 2008, the insurance conglomerate American International Group (AIG) wasn't even on the radar screen of the Treasury Department and the Federal Reserve until they realized (way too late) that the company had written so many credit default swaps (CDSs) on subprime and other bonds that if it went under it wouldn't be able to pay off on policies written on many of its other (core) businesses, including life insurance and annuities to retirees. And therein lay a major problem.

In the fall of 2008, just after Lehman Brothers collapsed, AIG officials began meeting with Treasury Secretary Paulson and Geithner, who was then president of the Federal Reserve Bank of New York, letting them know that if the government didn't come to its aid, it wasn't just subprime bond investors who would be hurt but millions of innocent Americans. In early 2009 an AIG document labeled "strictly confidential" began floating around Capitol Hill. In it were dire predictions about the financial ramifications if Uncle Sam didn't come to AIG's aid, including one where it wouldn't be able to pay off on $134 billion worth of annuity policies to 6.9 million retirees. These policy holders were earning $50,000 to $60,000 a year. If AIG went away, so too would those annuity payments. But that was just a tease. The document also noted that the company had written 81 million life insurance policies whose face value was a nifty $1.9 trillion. Not only did Paulson and Geithner get the message, but so did Congress.

At its peak AIG's credit default business had a notional value of $450 billion, according to a report in the New York Times. (That figure has since been reduced to under $300 billion.) Notional value was the amount of money AIG would have to pay out if every one of its CDS bets went to zero. The problem was that insurance regulators had no idea of the magnitude of AIG's potential losses on its CDSs. Why? Because the product was totally unregulated. No one at the SEC, Treasury, or Federal Reserve had a clue (until it was too late) that AIG might be on the hook for such gargantuan payouts. AIG was a potential all-consuming black hole in the financial universe, a Death Star so to speak.

Compounding the insurer's exposure was the fact that speculators and investors had bought subprime CDS policies without owning the underlying bonds. Bondholders often purchased CDS policies to protect themselves in the event of default. But a whole new class of CDS buyer had emerged the past five years—one that made bets (by purchasing a CDS) on a class of bonds they didn't even own. AIG was more than happy to write the policies because it earned premiums and it never dreamed that it would have to pay off on them. Over time the government has lent or invested $180 billion in keeping AIG afloat, believing (just like Paulson had said with TARP) that it would get most of its money back—someday. We won't know for years, really. Estimates vary, but AIG's CDS policies could wind up costing taxpayers at least $40 billion.

In this regard AIG's problems exacerbated the already known losses by financial institutions. And after a while, the cost of the financial meltdown became what felt like a never-ending (and surreal) tab totaling in the trillions: $750 billion for TARP; $787 billion for Obama's stimulus plan to help the nation recover; $180 billion for AIG; at least $100 billion to keep Fannie Mae and Freddie Mac solvent; $1.2 trillion in Fannie/Freddie mortgage-backed security (MBS) purchases by the Federal Reserve to keep interest rates low; oh, and the $1 trillion or so already suffered by Wall Street firms, banks, S&Ls, credit unions, and the rest of the known world.

Subprime was the first thread of the financial sweater to unravel in the nation's financial crisis. Subprime loans empowered people who should never have received a mortgage to buy a home. As they defaulted in record numbers, the number of foreclosures since 2007 reached 5 million homes and condos. The ripple in the financial pond went like this: consumers lose their jobs; they can't pay their mortgages; because they've lost jobs and then their houses, they no longer need to buy such household goods as new furniture, couches, or TVs; they can't tap home equity to buy a car, either; businesses that sell these goods suffer, too; sales plummet; businesses shutter and lay off employees, who then can't afford to buy a home; these businesses don't need as much retail space, either—or offices or factories. This hurts construction firms that make such things; it also hurts banks that made those loans; banks fail; they, too, lay off employees. And so on and so on. . . .

Getting back to Mozilo. He is now spending his golden years fending off lawsuits tied to his stock sales (and Countrywide's lending practices). What's left of his company is now the property of Bank of America. Under Barbara Desoer, Bank of America Home Loans is continuing to gain share as weaker companies fold and federal regulators scramble to find merger partners for ailing depository behemoths. It's unclear how much more market share Bank of America can garner, but in terms of lending and servicing it's already at 20 percent in each category and the field is wide open.

Why all this emphasis on market share? As any college business major can tell you, when it comes to running a company it's all about pricing power and economies of scale. When it comes to servicing, the more units you collect on, the lower your cost per loan. When it comes to lending, less competition means you can charge higher fees and rates. It all translates into profits. In the current financial climate the big are getting bigger and the weak are getting weaker. Nonbanks without strong ties to a depository should consider buying one, partnering with one, or getting out.

It's not just Bank of America's 20 percent share the nation should fear—it's the fact that the bank-owned Wells Fargo Home Mortgage also has a 20 percent share (more or less) and together the two are within sight of 50 percent if the grinding wheel of industry consolidation continues unabated. (Maybe Mozilo wasn't so crazy after all.) The term *mortgage cartel* has come up more than once to describe the lock the top four—Bank of America, Wells Fargo, Chase, and Citigroup—have on lending and servicing. But a close look at the numbers (collected by *National Mortgage News*) shows that Chase and CitiMortgage, at least when it comes to lending, are a distant third and fourth.

To some it looks as though Bank of America and Wells Fargo constitute a cartel of two. This is great news if you own stock in those companies or happen to be employed there, but if you work in the mortgage department of a small to midsize competitor it means less of the mortgage pie for you. But most importantly, the cartel-ification of any industry (mortgages, microprocessors, or oil) means fewer choices for consumers. When few control so much, they can charge whatever they like, because there's no competition in the marketplace. The beauty of a cartel—or maybe *monopoly* is the right word—is that less is more.

Wells Fargo and Bank of America both received billions of dollars in TARP money. Someday they plan to pay it all back. Surely, if they run into further financial turbulence Uncle Sam will be there to bail them out because they too are TBTF. The sad reality for the American taxpayer is that as Bair, Bernanke, and Geithner decry TBTF, calling for an end to it, none have presented a workable blueprint on how to get there. No one in Washington is talking about putting real caps on how large a bank or mortgage company can grow in terms of market share or size.

Meanwhile, hundreds of more commercial banks will fail by the end of 2011. None of these will collapse because of subprime residential loans. Most of their woes stem from commercial mortgage lending—that is, funding such real estate projects as housing developments, condos, offices, shopping centers, and the like. There was nothing financially wrong with these projects at their outset, but most were built or started when the U.S. economy was still strong. But with unemployment over 10 percent and U.S. businesses still shedding workers en masse, who needs all that office space or those big box retail stores?

As 2009 turned into 2010, Americans, especially those with little or no down payment money, still needed a mortgage. Many were turning to the government's Federal Housing Administration (FHA) single-family insurance program, which despite high delinquencies (but not as high as subprime) was still profitable—but barely. There is now a fear that too many marginal borrowers are using FHA loans and that in time the program will start losing money and might need government assistance. When subprime boomed from 2003 to 2007 just 3 percent of American borrowers were using FHA insurance. By the beginning of 2010 the ratio was up to 25 percent—a stunning turnaround for a program that seemed as though it were on its last legs. The great irony of the credit crisis is this: It was caused by Wall Street–financed lenders extending too many loans to subprime borrowers. Wall Street never met a subprime borrower it didn't like. Today there are more subprime borrowers than ever before but with no one, except the government, to serve them.

Source and
Interview Notes

T his book is the result of more than 200 interviews conducted by Paul Muolo and Mathew Padilla since July 2007 when the outline for this book was first being put together. Several more interviews date back to early 2006 when the subprime market slowly began to unravel. A few occurred as far back as 1998, around the time of the nation's first subprime crisis, which began in the middle of that year. Many of those we spoke with gave multiple on-the-record interviews, meaning we could identify them by name. Others preferred to speak "on background," which meant we could use their quotes and even say which firm they worked for, but nothing more than that. Some of what was said wound up in news stories appearing in *National Mortgage News* and the *Orange County Register*.

As noted in the text of this book, "Carl Chamberlain," the freelance loan underwriter who worked for PCI (which in turn staffed jobs for Clayton Holdings) requested that his real name not be published in favor of an alias. We granted the same arrangement to "Alex" from

New Century. Both provided valuable insights into what went on at those organizations. We know their real names but have pledged not to disclose them unless they first give us permission. The source calling himself "Jon Mayer," who claimed to work for one of the big three rating agencies, did not provide his real name. As this book went to press, he said he was still employed at a rating agency and wished to remain anonymous.

Several Wall Street managing directors (who are now no longer employed in that capacity) agreed to speak on background. Some of those who provided insight worked at Bear Stearns, Merrill Lynch, and other firms. There are many others who worked on Wall Street who denied our requests for an interview, including former Merrill Lynch CEO Stanley O'Neal. In regard to the collapse of New Century, all four of the lender's co-founders turned down or ignored requests to be interviewed on the record, as did David Einhorn, head of Greenlight Capital, which invested in New Century. Eric Billings of Friedman Billings Ramsey (FBR) also would not talk to us.

During part of the research for this book, Countrywide co-founder Angelo Mozilo provided generous access. Over the years he has granted dozens of on-the-record interviews (on various topics and issues) to co-author Paul Muolo. Mozilo's relationship to *National Mortgage News* goes back two decades. Very little of what he has said over the years was specified by him as off-the-record. His agreement to cooperate with this book began before Countrywide's fortunes started to crumble in earnest in December of 2007. Originally, this book was slated to be less about Mozilo and Countrywide, but all that changed in late 2007 as the lender began to lose money and became the subject of investigations in several states. Mozilo stopped granting interviews in early January 2008.

We attempted to interview all of the people who played significant roles in the mortgage and credit crisis. We tried to reach them by both telephone and e-mail. If this book goes into paperback, we continue to be all ears. Give us a call. Roland Arnall (who died in March 2008), to the best of our knowledge never gave an on-the-record interview regarding any of his mortgage lending ventures. His nephew, Adam Bass, who eventually became vice chairman of Ameriquest Capital Corporation (ACC), occasionally has given press interviews but declined interview requests for this book. ACC spokesman Chris Orlando did, however, answer certain questions via e-mail.

We have made every effort to avoid errors. We reviewed the chapters on many occasions, as did our editors and attorneys at John Wiley & Sons. But because we and our sources are human, it's possible that somewhere in this mass of 100,000-plus words there may reside factual errors. For that we sincerely apologize and would be glad to set the record straight in future editions. Also, some of the subjects in this book may not agree with our central premise that Wall Street's thirst for profits and its near-total disregard for loan quality inflicted massive damage on the U.S. and world economies. For those who see it differently, we strongly encourage you to write your own books.

Also, in 2005, the peak year of the housing boom in the United States, a drumbeat arose decrying the housing market as a dangerous bubble that could threaten the U.S. financial system. But the persistent and often passionate outcries did not always come from the world's largest newspapers or CNBC. The concern about an overheated market came from a new medium that didn't exist 10 years ago: blogs. Among those bloggers who were the earliest to raise questions and sound the alarm were Calculated Risk, Angry Bear, and Housing Panic.

Finally, even though this book is based on original research conducted by the co-authors, there have been other reporters who have done an admirable job covering this crisis as it unfolded and whose work we noticed and credited in this book. We'd like to cite the working journalists at the *Orange County Register* and *National Mortgage News*, but two others as well: E. Scott Reckard of the *Los Angeles Times* and James R. Hagerty of the *Wall Street Journal*. Reckard broke one of the earliest stories about lending abuses at Ameriquest, while Hagerty broke key stories about Countrywide, including the SEC investigation into Mozilo's stock sales and other developments.

Here we list source notes (documents, lawsuits, news stories, web sites) that helped shape the 13 chapters and Afterword. (Most of these are cited in the text, but a few may have slipped past our radar.) We also list two books that provided invaluable historical insight into the S&L crisis and the inner workings of Wall Street.

Newspaper Articles, News Service Reports, Lawsuits, Other Documents

Chapter 1   Angelo Speaks, the Worldwide Contagion Begins

Ken Bruce's "sell" rating and bankruptcy comment on Countrywide: "Liquidity Is the Achilles Heel" by Kenneth Bruce, research analyst, Merrill Lynch, August 15, 2007.

Deposit run on Countrywide Bank: "The Mortgage Meltdown" by E. Scott Reckard and Annette Haddad, *Los Angeles Times*, August 17, 2007.

Angelo Mozilo, personal history and company history: Several interviews conducted by the authors. Also: "The Mortgage Maker vs. the World" by Jeff Bailey, *New York Times*, October 16, 2005; biography and history of Mozilo by the Horatio Alger Association of Distinguished Americans, no date provided; Countrywide corporate history, available through the company's web site at http://about.countrywide.com/History/History.aspx.

Bankruptcy information on HomeBanc: Chapter 11 filing, August 9, 2007, U.S. Bankruptcy Court, District of Delaware.

Chapter 2   The Repo Man Meets the Bald Granny

Associates First Capital Corporation, history: Citigroup web site.

Beneficial Corporation/Beneficial Finance, history and background: Interviews with Peter Cugno, Dan Phillips, and others; *International Directory of Company Histories*, Vol. 8 (St. James Press, 1994).

The Money Store, history and background: "The Money Store: The Rise and Fall of a Subprime Giant," *National Mortgage News* (no author cited), July 10, 2000.

Subprime origination and servicing figures: *Mortgage Industry Directory*, published in several editions by Thomson Financial and then SourceMedia.

Chapter 3   The Death of Bailey Building and Loan, the Rise of Millionaire Loan Brokers and Countrywide

Government sanctions against the Jedinaks: *United States (on behalf of the Office of Thrift Supervision) vs. Russell M. Jedinak*, December 9, 1995, Stipulation and Consent to Issuance of Order of Prohibition and to Cease and Desist for Affirmative Relief; *U.S. vs. Rebecca Manley Jedinak*, December 9, 1995, similar action filed against Mrs. Jedinak. Both actions are in regard to Guardian Savings and Loan of Huntington Beach, California.

Loan broker behavior: "Mortgage Brokers' Sleight of Hand" by Elizabeth Warren, *Boston Globe*, October 2, 2007.

Allegations against Metropolitan Money Store in regard to foreclosure rescue scams: *Melvin J. Proctor, Jr., et al. vs. Metropolitan Money Store Corp., Joy Jenise Jackson, Kurt Fordham, et al.*, filed July 24, 2007, U.S. District Court for the Southern District of Maryland; "Prince George's Fairy Tale Unravels for Woman at Center of Fraud Probe" by Keith L. Alexander and Ovetta Wiggins, *Washington Post*, August 25, 2007; *District of Columbia vs. Metropolitan Money Store, New Century Mortgage Corporation, Joy Jenise Jackson, Kurt Fordham, et al.*, August 29, 2007, Superior Court of the District of Columbia, Civil Division.

Chapter 4   The Beach Boys of B&C

IPO information on Long Beach Financial Corporation: S-1, filed February 19, 1997. Underwriter: Friedman Billings Ramsey & Company.

In Wayne Lee's legal battle with Ameriquest, Roland Arnall is not named as a defendant but is mentioned in the complaint several times. Source: *Wayne A. Lee vs. Ameriquest Capital Corporation*, Docs. 1–20, filed January 26, 2007, in Superior Court of the State of California for the County of Orange— Central Justice Center.

Abusive lending allegations against Ameriquest: "Workers Say Lender Ran 'Boiler Rooms'" by Mike Hudson and E. Scott Reckard, *Los Angeles Times*, February 4, 2005; "Ameriquest Accused of Unfair Practices," *Orange County Register* (no byline), February 5, 2005.

Ameriquest closing retail operations: "Ameriquest Shutters Retail," *National Mortgage News Online* (no byline cited), May 2, 2006; "Ameriquest Shutters Retail, Vows to Carry On" by Paul Muolo, *National Mortgage News*, May 8, 2006.

Origination and servicing figures on Ameriquest: Various sources, including *National Mortgage News, Quarterly Data Report* (SourceMedia), and investor documents prepared by Ameriquest Mortgage Company for a Bear Stearns conference in 2004.

Divorce of Roland and Sally Arnall: "Roland Arnall's Ex-Wife Reopens Settlement Issue," Associated Press, August 23, 2005.

Ameriquest lobbying activities: "Lender Lobbying Blitz Abetted Mortgage Mess" by Glenn R. Simpson, *Wall Street Journal*, December 31, 2007.

Adam Bass's response to predatory lending allegations and his "bad apples" comment: *Baseline* magazine, September 7, 2005.

Information on Dawn L. Arnall: Official State Department biography, Embassy of the United States, The Hague, the Netherlands.

Campaign donation information on the Arnalls: Center for Responsive Politics.

Chapter 5   Angelo Rising

Historical information on Fannie Mae and background on former chairman/
CEO James Johnson: Various interviews conducted by the authors; "A History
of Fannie Mae," company web site; "HMDA Revelation: GSEs Depend on
Few for Bulk of Business," *National Mortgage News*, September 30, 2002;
"A Medici with Your Money" by Matthew Cooper, *Slate*, February 23, 1997.

Background on Countrywide and its history: Biography of Angelo Mozilo by the
Horatio Alger Association of Distinguished Americans (no date provided);
Countrywide corporate history, available through the company's web site at
http://about.countrywide.com/History/History.aspx.

Chapter 6   The Holy Roller of REITs

Background on HomeBanc: Interviews conducted by the authors with various
sources, including Patrick Flood; "Mortgage Woes Take Toll on Lender with
Roots in Faith" by Valerie Bauerlein, *Wall Street Journal*, August 13, 2007;
"Keeping the Faith Wasn't Enough, Collapse Leaves Staff in a Lurch" by Dan
Chapman, *Atlanta-Journal Constitution*, September 2, 2007.

Historical background on Friedman Billings Ramsey and its three co-founders:
International Directory of Company Histories, Vol. 53 (St. James Press, 2003);
Form 8-K filed by FBR with the Securities and Exchange Commission, July
28, 2006; biographies on Eric Billings and Rock Tonkel, published on FBR's
web site, 2007, 2008.

Information on mortgage real estate investment trusts (REITs) taken public by
FBR was supplied by the company to the authors.

Chapter 7   The End of the (New) Century

Income of New Century and its founders as well as their stock sales: Various filings with the Securities and Exchange Commission from 1997 to 2007.

New Century's start-up money allegedly coming from a Ponzi scheme: "As
Bankruptcy Looms for BFA, Questions Arise about Overseers" by Terry
Greene Sterling, *Phoenix New Times*, October 21, 1999.

Baseball bat anecdote in regard to poor underwriting: "Pressure at Mortgage Firm
Led to Mass Approval of Bad Loans" by David Cho, *Washington Post*, May 7,
2007.

Torrence James and Ronald Fontenot's alleged fraud: "Group of Former Inmates,
Others Accused in Colorado Real Estate Scheme" by David Olinger, *Denver
Post*, October 31, 2006.

Mozilo's "aggressor" quote: "Countrywide Counters Trend in Margins" by Jody
Shenn, *American Banker*, April 27, 2005.

Chapter 8   A Conspiracy by Merrill?

Background on Bill Dallas and Ownit Mortgage Solutions: Various interviews and Loan Tool Box biography on Bill Dallas (www.loantoolbox.com); bankruptcy filing by Ownit Mortgage Solutions, January 9, 2007, U.S. Bankruptcy Court, Central District of California, San Fernando Valley Division.

Background on Michael Blum: Various interviews; "Never Has So Much Money Been Flowing into Studio Coffers" by Daniel Gross, *Variety*, January 9, 2006.

Background on Stanley O'Neal: Various interviews; "Merrill Takes $8.4 Billion Credit Hit" by Randall Smith and Jed Horowitz, *Wall Street Journal*, October 25, 2007; "A Risk-Taker's Reign at Merrill Ends with a Swift, Messy Fall" by Landon Thomas Jr. and Jenny Anderson, *New York Times*, October 29, 2007; Merrill Lynch company history at www.ml.com.

Merrill Lynch margin-calling its mortgage banking customers, and loan buyback disputes: "Stung by EPDs, Merrill Margin Calling Its MB Clients" by Paul Muolo, *National Mortgage News*, February 19, 2007; "ResMAE Goes BK, Cites Merrill Dispute," *National Mortgage News Online* (no byline), February 19, 2007.

Merrill Lynch and CDOs: Various interviews; "Wall Street Wizardry Amplified Credit Crisis" by Carrick Mollenkamp and Serena Ng, *Wall Street Journal*, December 27, 2007; testimony of William F. Galvin, Secretary of the Commonwealth of Massachusetts, before the U.S. House of Representatives, Committee on Oversight and Government Reform, March 7, 2008.

Chapter 9   A Warning from Lewie

Background and history on Ranieri: Original interviews with subject and several individuals who worked for him; "A Job Easier Said Than Done for New Savings-Unit Owner" by Sarah Bartlett, *New York Times*, February 20, 1998.

Ranieri's warning on ABS securitizations: "Ranieri: SEC Needs to Step Up on NTMs," *National Mortgage News Online* (no byline), December 11, 2006.

Chapter 10   Deep in the Belly of the Bear

Bear's loan buyback disputes with Encore Credit Corporation and sale of ECC to Bear: "Troubled B&C Lender Sells to Bear Stearns" by Paul Muolo, *National Mortgage News*, October 11, 2006; SEC filing, Bear Stearns 8-K, October 10, 2006.

Warren Spector's departure from Bear: "A Top Official at Bear Stearns Ousted" by Landon Thomas Jr., *New York Times*, August 6, 2007; "How Bear Stearns Mess Cost Executive His Job" by Kate Kelly and Susanne Craig, *Wall Street Journal*, August 6, 2007.

Merrill's seizure of collateral from Bear Stearns in regard to hedge funds: "Merrill Auctions Subprime Assets in Bear Hedge Funds," *National Mortgage News* (no author listed), June 25, 2007.

Ralph Cioffi's and Michael J. Levitt's management of Everquest Financial, which entails BSAM, CDOs, and more: Form S-1 filing with the Securities and Exchange Commission, May 9, 2007, by Everquest Financial Ltd.

Background on Ralph Cioffi: "Cioffi's Hero-to-Villain Hedge Funds Masked Bear Peril in CDOs" by Yalman Onaran and Jody Shenn, *Bloomberg News*, July 3, 2007.

Allegations against Ralph Cioffi of Bear Stearns and Bear Stearns Asset Management (BSAM) regarding management of the firm's two subprime-related hedge funds that filed for bankruptcy in July 2007: *Barclays Bank vs. Bear Stearns Asset Management Inc., Ralph Cioffi, Matthew Tannin, Bear Stearns & Co., et al.*, filed December 19, 2007, U.S. District Court, Southern District of New York; *The Commonwealth of Massachusetts (Securities Division) vs. Bear Stearns Asset Management Inc.*, filed November 14, 2007.

Existence of criminal probe of Bear's two subprime hedge funds: Bear Stearns Form 10-Q, filed with the Securities and Exchange Commission, October 10, 2007 (pg. 66).

Jeff Verschleiser's role in Bear's mortgage trading operations: Various interviews conducted by the authors with industry sources, including Pat Flood.

Chapter 11   Armageddon Times

Allegations against Countrywide on abusive lending: "Inside the Countrywide Lending Spree" by Gretchen Morgenson, *New York Times*, August 26, 2007.

Countrywide's "Protect Our House" wristband campaign: "Countrywide Tells Workers, 'Protect Our House'" by James R. Hagerty and Jonathan Karp, *Wall Street Journal*, October 3, 2007; memo from Andrew Gissinger III, Countrywide president and chief operating officer.

Background on public relations firm Burson-Marsteller: *Corporate Watch*, Issue #2, Winter 1996.

Information on stock sales by Countrywide insiders courtesy of Thomson Financial; trading information available through Yahoo! Finance.

SEC probe of Mozilo's stock sales: "SEC Investigating Stock Sales by Countrywide CEO" by Kara Scannell and James R. Hagerty, *Wall Street Journal*, October 17, 2007.

Countrywide's payment option ARM problems and investigations: "CFC's POA 'Debt' at $1.2 Billion and Growing," *National Mortgage News* (no byline), March 10, 2008; "Illinois Probes Countrywide's Practices," Associated Press, December 13, 2007.

Chapter 12 What the Hell Happened?

Argent's lending practices in the Cleveland area: "Argent Mortgage Company Lending and Foreclosure Activity, Cuyahoga County, Ohio" by Thomas Bier and Ivan Maric, Center for Housing Research and Policy, Maxine Goodman Levin College of Urban Affairs, Cleveland State University, June 3, 2007.

Argent's lending activity in Slavic Village: "The Shadow of Debt," op-ed piece by Jim Rokakis, *Washington Post*, September 30, 2007.

Iowa Attorney General Tom Miller targeting loan brokers and wholesale lenders: "Iowa AG Warns on LO Culpability," *National Mortgage News* (no byline), April 3, 2006.

Standard & Poor's downgrades on 8,342 ratings: S&P press release, January 30, 2008.

Standard & Poor's response and defense of its rating practices: Testimony of Vickie A. Tillman, executive vice president of S&P's credit market services before the Committee on Banking, Housing, and Urban Affairs, U.S. Senate, September 26, 2007.

Treasury Secretary Henry Paulson and the roots of the credit crisis: "Policy Statement on Financial Market Developments" by the President's Working Group on Financial Markets, March 13, 2008.

S&L-related lawsuits involving Andrew Cuomo: "Florida Suit Names Andrew Cuomo," December 23, 1987, Associated Press (no byline); "Suit Involving Cuomo's Son over Savings-Loan Is Settled" by Jeffrey Schmalz, *New York Times*, April 19, 1988.

Foreclosures in Orange County: "Bidders See Bargain Homes at Anaheim Auction" by Andrew Galvin, *Orange County Register*, February 3, 2008.

Chapter 13 TARP, the Great Recession, and the Return of Stan Kurland

TARP and Stan Kurland material: original reporting and interviews by the authors; "PennyMac Sitting on Unrealized Loss of $7 Million," by Paul Muolo, *Mortgage Servicing News*, August 2009.

SEC charges against Mozilo et al.: *Securities and Exchanges Commission vs. Angelo Mozilo, David Sambol, and Eric Sieracki*. Cased filed June 14, 2008, in U.S. District Court for the Central District of California. Case #: CV09-03994. No trial date had been set as this edition of *Chain of Blame* went to press.

Afterword TBTF: A Mortgage Cartel Rises from the Ashes

Market share numbers for Bank of America, Wells Fargo, and other courtesy of the *Quarterly Data Report*, a *National Mortgage News*/SourceMedia Publication.

Books

Inside Job: The Looting of America's Savings and Loans by Stephen Pizzo, Mary Fricker, and Paul Muolo (New York: HarperCollins, 1989, 1991).

Liar's Poker: Rising Through the Wreckage on Wall Street by Michael Lewis (New York: W.W. Norton, 1989).

The $700 Billion Bailout: What It Means for You, Your Money, Your Mortgage, and Your Taxes by Paul Muolo (Hoboken, NJ: John Wiley & Sons, 2008).

Glossary

Note: In the world of mortgage lending, definitions can vary from company to company and from professional to professional—which may be why there is sometimes so much confusion surrounding the mortgage process. What follow are definitions of loan types, products, origination channels, company types, and other phrases that make up the alphabet soup of residential mortgage banking.

"A" credit quality loan   A mortgage where the borrower has the best credit rating possible—usually north of 700. Fannie Mae and Freddie Mac—which have government charters—tend to buy these loans, although they also purchase some subprime and alt-A credits. By purchasing mortgages, Fannie and Freddie provide liquidity to the residential market. Also known as a prime or conventional loan.

ABX index   An index or instrument created by a handful of Wall Street firms, including Deutsche Bank, that represents the value of a basket (sample) of asset-backed securities collateralized by subprime loans. Investors can go either long or short the index.

account executive (AE)   A professional whose job it is to work with loan brokers. Brokers sell or facilitate mortgages to the public but do not use their own money to originate the loan at the closing table. An account executive works for a wholesale lender who "table funds" (brings a check) to the closing, where the house is actually sold and the title changes over to the new owner(s).

alt-A mortgage (loan)   A nonconforming mortgage where the borrower has a higher than subprime credit score. Alt-A is short for alternative A. Typically, these loans may not be immediately eligible for purchase by Fannie Mae or Freddie Mac because they have underwriting anomalies that might include higher than normal debt-to-income ratios, or irregular income. However, Fannie and Freddie have bought billions of dollars' worth of bonds backed by some alt-A loans.

asset-backed security (ABS)   A bond backed by subprime, alt-A, or other types of nonconforming loans. The term *ABS* is used to distinguish these securities from bonds backed by Fannie Mae/Freddie Mac quality loans.

automated valuation model (AVM)   An electronic appraisal based on property information gathered on the ground in a neighborhood and then disseminated over the Internet.

collateralized debt obligation (CDO)   A bond created from tranches of other bonds. A tranche represents cash flow from a pool of different mortgages. In an attempt to diversify risk, a CDO might contain many different tranches from different asset-backed securities. (CDOs not only buy tranches of other securities, but they issue their own tranches, layering and complicating the risk inherent in the security.)

collateralized mortgage obligation (CMO)   A type of mortgage-backed security (MBS) where the cash flows from the underlying loans are paid into a trust that guarantees payments to the end investor. CMOs consist of various tranches that have different cash flows and maturities.

correspondent channel (lender)   Under a correspondent loan transaction, a mortgage company purchases an already originated loan from another lender. Usually, the purchase happens right away or shortly after the loan is funded in the primary market.

credit default swap   An instrument used to hedge against losses, or to speculate on the value of bonds (mortgages or otherwise). Credit default swaps act as an insurance policy of sorts where one party must pay another one in the event the bonds lose value. The total credit default bets against a bond can actually outweigh the size of the bond being bet against.

credit score/FICO score A grade given to a consumer based on his/her credit history. A credit score involves a statistical analysis of a borrower's ability to pay. Credit scores were first developed by the Fair Isaac Corporation of Minneapolis. (In general, a subprime borrower is someone whose score is 620 or under. "A" paper borrowers have scores north of 700. A borrower whose credit is in between those two numbers might be considered an alt-A or some other type of credit.)

early payment default (EPD) A loan that goes delinquent within 60 to 90 days of being originated. Wall Street firms require lenders (the sellers of the loans) to buy back EPDs or compensate them for the potential loss.

80/10/10 loan A loan transaction where a borrower buys a home with a down payment of 10 percent, borrows another 10 percent using a second lien, and then takes out a first mortgage for 80 percent of the purchase price.

80/20 loan A loan transaction where the borrower takes out two mortgages simultaneously: a first lien representing 80 percent of a home's purchase price and second lien that serves as a down payment. By doing so a borrower can avoid paying private mortgage insurance (PMI), because the first lien represents 80 percent of the loan amount. (Mortgage insurance is required on Fannie Mae/Freddie Mac–eligible loans if the down payment is less than 20 percent.)

FHA/VA loan A mortgage insured by one of two government agencies, either the Federal Housing Administration (FHA) or the Department of Veterans Affairs (VA). These loans often are packaged into bonds issued by the Government National Mortgage Association (GNMA, Ginnie Mae). The FHA and GNMA programs are administered by the Department of Housing and Urban Development, whose secretary is appointed by the president.

first lien (mortgage) The first deed of trust recorded against a house. Some consumers have two loans taken out against their house (or even three or four). The lien that is recorded first has priority over all other liens, which means in the event of foreclosure if any money is recovered on the sale of the house the first lien holder gets paid before other debtors.

gain-on-sale (GOS) accounting   After a company securitizes sub-prime loans into a bond, accounting rules allow that institution to book all the future income (based on the bond's expected cash flows) immediately. For the lender issuing the bond, the goal is to conservatively estimate what those cash flows might be, taking into account loan prepayments and delinquencies.

government-sponsored enterprise (GSE)   An investment company chartered by the federal government to buy residential mortgages from banks, savings and loans (S&Ls), nondepository mortgage bankers, and others as a way to add liquidity to the market. Fannie Mae and Freddie Mac are the two largest GSEs serving the residential mortgage market. Even though they have government charters, the federal government does not, as a technical matter, insure their bonds, debt, or stock (though investors believe that in the event of defaults, the federal government would in fact guarantee payments). Fannie and Freddie also guarantee the bonds they issue.

home equity loan   A second deed of trust (or lien) that is taken out by a consumer on his/her home. There are two types of seconds: a closed-end loan for a fixed (set) amount and an open-end loan that has a cap but can be borrowed against in different increments.

jumbo mortgage   A loan whose dollar amount is above the Fannie Mae/Freddie Mac loan limit, which was $417,000 up until early 2008, when the ceiling was temporarily increased to $730,000.

league table   A ranking of mortgage companies. This can apply to investment banking firms that securitize loans, lenders, servicers, or some other type of data point.

loan broker   A mortgage professional who offers different loan products to the consumer. The loan or mortgage broker does not use his/her own money to originate the loan. The money comes from a wholesale lender (a firm like Wells Fargo, Countrywide, etc.). The broker receives a fee from the wholesale lender once the transaction closes. The wholesale lender funds and then owns the loan.

loan buyback agreement   A contractual obligation between the originator of a loan (the lender) and the investor that buys the mortgage in the secondary market whereby the lender agrees to repurchase the note if it goes bad. The buyback period usually covers loans that go delinquent within 60 to 90 days of being originated. Some buyback clauses might cover 30-day delinquencies.

loan officer (LO)   A professional who sells and facilitates mortgages to a consumer. A loan officer usually works for a retail lender, though sometimes loan brokers or account executives are referred to as loan officers.

loan production (loan funding)   Activity that entails the origination of a mortgage to a consumer. The phrases *loan production, loan funding*, and *loan origination* are synonymous.

loan-to-value (LTV) ratio   When a mortgage is originated, the LTV is a calculation that shows how much cash or equity the home buyer is putting into the house. If a homeowner makes a $10,000 down payment on a $100,000 house and takes out a mortgage of $90,000, the LTV would be 90 percent.

loan trader   A professional who buys and sells (trades) loans for a living. The loans are sold to the trader by a mortgage lending company such as a bank, S&L, or nonbank lender. A loan trader might work at a Wall Street firm or a large lender like Wells Fargo.

mortgage-backed security (MBS)   A bond backed (collateralized) by residential loans. The term *MBS* usually refers to "A" paper bonds that are guaranteed by Fannie Mae or Freddie Mac, but not always. MBSs can range in size from several hundred million dollars into the billions.

mortgage banker   A company that originates loans to borrowers using its own money. This might be a bank, savings and loan, credit union, or nonbank lender. The nonbank lender would need to borrow from a warehouse provider to obtain the money to make mortgages.

mortgage broker   See *loan broker*.

mortgage conduit   A legal structure (legal company) through which a Wall Street firm or mortgage banker buys already funded mortgages from another firm. Conduits are registered with the Securities and Exchange Commission to facilitate bond offerings.

mortgage insurance   A policy issued by one of the nation's seven mortgage insurance firms that generally covers up to 20 percent of a lender's loss on a delinquent loan. (Not all types of loans are eligible for mortgage insurance.)

nonbank lender (or nondepository)   A mortgage lender that finances its residential originations by borrowing money from a Wall Street firm or commercial bank. Nonbanks do not offer deposit accounts to the public and are not regulated by a federal bank or S&L regulator.

payment option ARM (POA)   An adjustable-rate mortgage loan where the consumer is offered four different payment plans each month, including a negative amortization choice where a low monthly payment (if this option is used) will actually increase the debt owed to the holder of the loan.

primary market   A term used to describe the actual origination of a loan, where the loan process begins. After a loan is originated and funded, it might be sold. When it is sold, that is considered a secondary market transaction.

real estate investment trust (REIT)   An ownership structure where a company pays out 90 percent of its earnings from real estate in the form of dividends to its shareholders. REITs were created to lessen the federal corporate tax rate a company must pay.

retail origination   A mortgage made directly from a lending institution to a consumer with no intermediary (broker) being involved in the transaction. A retail origination can be done through a branch or over the Internet or through some other direct-to-consumer channel.

secondary market   After a loan has been originated to a consumer (in the primary market), it may then be sold to another company; this is considered a secondary market transaction. A loan, like a bond, can change hands more than once.

second lien (second mortgage) This often is a home equity loan that is taken out after a first mortgage has already been recorded. On a new home purchase, sometimes both a first and second mortgage (lien) are recorded at the same time, but the first always has priority (must be paid off first).

securitize To issue a bond backed by a pool (group) of mortgages.

servicing Entails the monthly processing of a loan, including collecting the payment from the consumer and passing on the principal, interest, taxes, and other charges to the proper parties. For doing this each month the company (the servicer) receives a fee. Servicing is a separate business from lending, although the two businesses are related.

stated–income loan (liar loan) A mortgage where the consumer states his/her income without the lender asking for documentation of the salary stated. The lender accepts the income stated as is if the borrower has a FICO score north of 700, which is considered "A" paper or prime quality. There are variations on this loan, including "low-doc" (maybe a bank statement with no W-2) and "no-doc" (no income or asset documentation or verification).

structured investment vehicle (SIV) An off-balance-sheet investment in subprime bonds or related assets. Typically, a bank sets up an SIV, finds investors, lends money to them, and then manages the investment. A bank may be an investor in its own SIV. Investors in SIVs generally use short-term loans (commercial paper) to buy into long-term assets (bonds backed by subprime mortgages/ABSs). Borrowing short-term to invest long-term can be a dangerous financial wager if interest rates move rapidly up or down.

subprime mortgage (loan) A loan originated by a lender that is A– to D in quality. Consumers who have the best credit ratings with the highest FICO scores are considered "A" credit quality. Subprime borrowers usually have several blemishes on their credit histories, including missed payments on mortgages and other types of installment debt such as credit cards.

warehouse line of credit A loan extended from a large bank or Wall Street firm to a nonbank, which uses that money (line of credit) to originate mortgages directly to the public or through loan brokers. Nonbank mortgage lenders use warehouse lines because, unlike government-insured depositories (banks, S&Ls, credit unions), they do not have any other source of funds. (S&Ls and banks use the deposits they hold to originate loans.)

wholesale lender   A mortgage company that uses loan brokers to find customers for it. A wholesaler does not employ loan brokers but instead pays the broker a fee once the mortgage actually closes. The wholesaler supplies a check at the closing table to fund the mortgage being made to the consumer.

yield spread premium (YSP)   This represents a fee payment from the wholesale lender to its loan broker for bringing in a mortgage at an interest rate higher than prevailing rates. It is a reward for the higher-yielding loan. The YSP must be disclosed on the loan closing documents. Consumers might accept a higher rate on their loan because the points being charged are lower. However, they also might be unaware that they are not getting the best possible interest rate.

Acknowledgments

This book was a year in making, longer if you count the early reporting we did before *subprime* became a household word. There are more people who deserve our gratitude than space allows.

First among them are our families: Paul's wife Ann, daughters Sherry and Katherine, and his parents Louis and Norma; Mathew's wife Lucia, daughter Anna, and mother Geri. Without their support the long nights of fact checking and reinterviewing sources would not have been possible.

High also on our list is our agent, Denise Marcil, and her colleague, Michael Congdon, as well as John Wiley & Sons editors Emilie Herman and Debra Englander, who believed in this project early on, encouraging us to move forward.

Specials thanks to Tim Murphy, publisher of *National Mortgage News,* and especially the senior editorial staff—Mark Fogarty, Bonnie Sinnock, Brian Collins, Glenn McCullom, and Bradley Finkelstein—who patiently excused Paul's absences from the Washington office when news was breaking all around (especially Brian). And special thanks to

Andras Malatinszky, who five years ago talked Paul into writing a Web column that resulted in numerous leads and new sources.

Matt would like to thank current and former *Orange County Register* editors Julie Gallego, Diana McCabe, and Glenn Hall, now editor of TheStreet.com, for their patience and understanding while working on this book, as well as for their strong mentoring. He would also like to acknowledge the fine reporting on the subprime meltdown by current and former *Register* colleagues John Gittelsohn, Ronald Campbell, Jeff Collins, Andrew Galvin, and Mary Ann Milbourn. Matt would also like to thank *Orange County Business Journal* editor Michael Lyster for turning him on to the subprime industry and editor Rick Reiff for his early teachings.

A special hats off to the late Stan Strachan, who taught Paul everything he knows about reporting. And finally, our gratitude to the many whom we could not name in this book: the contract underwriters who worked for Clayton Holdings and the Bohan Group, the mortgage executives who sold loans to Wall Street, and some of the managing directors on the other side of the table. All spoke to us at the risk of their careers.

About the Authors

Paul Muolo is co-author of *Inside Job: The Looting of America's Savings and Loans*, a *New York Times* best seller. He also is executive editor of *National Mortgage News*, the leading independent trade publication/web site for the residential finance industry. Over the years his articles have appeared in *Barron's*, the *Sunday New York Times*, the *Washington Post*, *EuroMoney*, *Playboy*, and other publications. He has appeared as a guest on mortgage, real estate, and banking issues on ABC, CNN, CNBC, and Fox Business Network. *Inside Job* won several journalism awards, including the Investigative Reporters and Editors best book of the year and the Adult Editors Book Award. It was nominated for a Pulitzer Prize. Muolo lives in Maryland with his wife and two daughters.

Mathew Padilla is a financial author and journalist. He led the *Orange County Register* newspaper's coverage of the subprime implosion of 2007 and his work was recognized for excellence by the Society of American Business Editors and Writers. He lives in Southern California with his wife and daughter.

Index